MW01252932

Doing Good and Ridding Evil in Ming China: The Political Career of Wang Yangming

Sinica Leidensia

Edited by

Barend J. ter Haar
Maghiel van Crevel

In co-operation with

P.K. Bol, D.R. Knechtges, E.S. Rawski,
W.L. Idema, H.T. Zurndorfer

VOLUME 116

Doing Good and Ridding Evil in Ming China: The Political Career of Wang Yangming

By

George L. Israel

BRILL

LEIDEN | BOSTON GUELPH HUMBER LIBRARY
205 Humber College Blvd
Toronto, ON   M9W 5L7

Cover illustration: The cover image comes from Zou Shouyi's *Illustrated Biography of Master Wang Yangming*, and shows two native headmen surrendering to Wang Yangming at his headquarters in Nanning, Guangxi. Wang's predecessor had sought approval from the Ming court for mobilizing armies to suppress their rebellion by force, but was relieved of duty. When Wang replaced him as supreme commander, he was able to achieve a peaceful resolution to the conflict. The headmen willingly bound themselves and came before him in early 1528.

Library of Congress Cataloging-in-Publication Data

Israel, George Lawrence, 1966-
  Doing good and ridding evil in Ming China : the political career of Wang Yangming / by George L. Israel.
    pages cm. -- (Sinica Leidensia, ISSN 0169-9563 ; volume 116)
  Includes bibliographical references and index.
  ISBN 978-90-04-28008-3 (hardback : alk. paper) -- ISBN 978-90-04-28010-6 (e-book) 1. Wang, Yangming, 1472-1529. 2. Neo-Confucianism. I. Title.

B128.W364I87 2014
181'.112--dc23

                        2014021608

This publication has been typeset in the multilingual 'Brill' typeface. With over 5,100 characters covering Latin, IPA, Greek, and Cyrillic, this typeface is especially suitable for use in the humanities.
For more information, please see brill.com/brill-typeface.

ISSN 0169-9563
ISBN 978-90-04-28008-3 (hardback)
ISBN 978-90-04-28010-6 (e-book)

Copyright 2014 by Koninklijke Brill NV, Leiden, The Netherlands.
Koninklijke Brill NV incorporates the imprints Brill, Brill Nijhoff, Global Oriental and Hotei Publishing.
All rights reserved. No part of this publication may be reproduced, translated, stored in
a retrieval system, or transmitted in any form or by any means, electronic, mechanical,
photocopying, recording or otherwise, without prior written permission from the publisher.
Authorization to photocopy items for internal or personal use is granted by Koninklijke Brill NV
provided that the appropriate fees are paid directly to The Copyright Clearance Center,
222 Rosewood Drive, Suite 910, Danvers, MA 01923, USA.
Fees are subject to change.

This book is printed on acid-free paper.

MIX
Paper from
responsible sources
FSC
FSC® C109576
www.fsc.org

Printed by Printforce, the Netherlands

Contents

Acknowledgments

This book began as a dissertation project completed at the University of Illinois, Urbana-Champaign, in 2008. Earlier versions of two chapters appeared in "To Accommodate or Subjugate: Wang Yangming's Settlement of Conflict in Guangxi in Light of Ming Political and Strategic Culture," *Ming Studies* 60 (2009): 4–44; and in "The Prince and the Sage: Concerning Wang Yangming's 'Effortless' Suppression of the Ning Princely Establishment Rebellion," *Late Imperial China*, vol. 29, no. 2 (2008): 68–128.

I am grateful for all of the support and assistance I received while completing the dissertation at the University of Illinois. Without the insightful advice and unflagging support of my advisor, Professor Kai-wing Chow, this book would not have come to fruition. As well, a doctoral fellowship from the Chiang Ching-Kuo Foundation provided critical support in the final stages. I would also like to express thanks to my colleagues at Middle Georgia State College, especially Stephen Taylor. The flexibility he gave me in terms of my teaching schedule allowed me to find the time to take the dissertation through many revisions and to transform it into a monograph. As well, many thanks go to Anna Mancilla for being so helpful in locating the resources I needed to complete my research.

I would also like to thank Dr. John Dardess for reading and commenting on the manuscript; his thoughtful input and encouragement have been invaluable. Also, the conscientious reading by the reviewers at Brill helped me identify careless errors and weak arguments. I also deeply appreciate the help I received from Heddi Goodrich, who conscientiously combed through the book in the final stages of editing and helped me tighten up the writing, fix careless errors, and clarify terminology.

Finally, I am indebted to my wife Thi-Ha Hoang and my children Brandon and Julia for their support and encouragement while I spent so much time writing the manuscript and preparing it for publication.

List of Maps

Abbreviations

MS	Zhang Tingyu 張廷玉, ed. *Ming shi* 明史 [Ming history]. 1739. Reprint, Beijing: Zhonghua shuju, 1974.
MSJSBM	Gu Yingtai 谷應泰. *Ming shi ji shi ben mo* 明史紀事本末 [Record of Events in the Ming History from Beginning to End]. c. 1650. Reprint, Taipei: Sanmin shuju, 1963.
MSLWZSL	*Ming shi lu Wuzong shi lu* 明實錄武宗實錄 [Ming Veritable Records for the Reign of Wuzong]. In *Ming shi lu fu jiao kan ji* 明實錄附校勘記 [Veritable Records of the Ming Dynasty with Appended Record of Collation]. Nangang: Zhongyang yanjiuyuan lishi yuyan yanjiusuo, 1965.
MSLSZSL	*Ming shi lu Shizong shi lu* 明實錄世宗實錄 [Ming Veritable Records for the Reign of Shizong]. In *Ming shi lu fu jiao kan ji* 明實錄附校勘記 [Veritable Records of the Ming Dynasty with Appended Record of Collation]. Nangang: Zhongyang yanjiuyuan lishi yuyan yanjiusuo, 1965.
MTJ	Xia Xie 夏燮. *Wenbai duizhao quan yi Ming tong jian* 文白對照全譯明通鑒 [Comprehensive Mirror of the Ming, Bilingual Classical to Modern Chinese Complete Translation]. Edited by Shen Zhihua. Beijing: Gaige chubanshe, 1994.
WYMQJ	Wang Yangming 王陽明. *Wang Yangming quan ji* 王陽明全集 [The Complete Works of Wang Yangming]. 2 vols. Shanghai: Shanghai guji chubanshe, 1992.
NP	Qian Dehong 錢德洪 and Wang Ruzhong 王汝中, eds. "Nianpu 年譜 [Chronological Biography]." In *WYMQJ*, vol. 2, *juan* 33–35.

Introduction

Today we have already reached Longnan, and tomorrow we will enter the
lairs. At a specified time, armies will simultaneously advance from all
directions. The bandits are confronting strategic conditions that will definitely result in their defeat. Formerly, when I was [campaigning] in
Hengshui, I sent a letter to [Yang] Shide stating, "Defeating the bandits in
the mountains is easy, but defeating the bandits of the mind difficult—
what is so great about my eradicating petty thieves?" Should you, my honorable friends, totally eradicate the bandits in your hearts and bellies, so
as to achieve the great deed of wiping out and pacifying, this truly is the
rare and outstanding achievement of a great man. I am confident that
over the last few days I have formulated a victorious strategy, and shall
soon be memorializing victory. What happier occasion than this could
there be?[1]

The eminent Ming dynasty (1368–1644) philosopher Wang Yangming 王陽明
(1472–1529) wrote this letter to a student early in 1518 just prior to sending
troops into settlements located in northern Guangdong Province.[2] The cause,
as he saw it, of the armed disturbances led by people living in these "lairs," was
that they had been operating largely outside the reach of the state and had
consequently become habituated to a lifestyle of banditry, repeatedly preying
on law-abiding subjects. Accustomed to outlawry as they were, Wang had no
choice but to use military force to bring them under control, so that he could
then implement long-term measures to govern the region. After two months of
campaigning, he reported to the Ming court that thirty-eight settlements had
been successfully occupied, sixty-seven ringleaders and their some two thousand followers had been killed or captured, and nearly nine hundred dependants had been taken captive.[3] Having cleared out these "nests" of "bandits," as
he referred to them and their communities, he was then able to establish a new

---

1 Qian Dehong 錢德洪 and Wang Ruzhong 王汝中, eds., "Nianpu 年譜 [Chronological
   Biography]," in Wang Yangming 王陽明, *Wang Yangming quanji* 王陽明全集 [The Complete
   Works of Wang Yangming] (Shanghai: Shanghai guji chubanshe, 1992), vol. 2, 35:1248. Hereafter,
   NP.
2 Wang Yangming's given name is Shouren 守仁, and his courtesy name was Boan 伯安.
   Yangming was a sobriquet adopted for use by his friends, and will also be used throughout the
   book.
3 Wang Yangming 王陽明, *Wang Yangming quanji* 王陽明全集 [The Complete Works of Wang
   Yangming] (Shanghai: Shanghai guji chubanshe, 1992), vol. 1, 11:382. Hereafter, *WYMQJ*.

county in this once weakly governed land. For him, that is how the Ming state and its governing scholar-official class could bring a civilizing influence to this troubled local society, and indeed the region was largely stabilized.

But this was just one of many successful military operations that this revered Confucian scholar and official led, and the new county was just one of many measures he would devise to restore and maintain order in the aftermath of the campaigns. Wang Yangming had already, in 1517, supervised a series of campaigns in Fujian Province that resulted in the occupation of perhaps fifty settlements and the capture or killing of twenty-seven hundred people, as well as several offensives in southern Jiangxi, for which he could report eighty settlements occupied and nearly fifty-five hundred "bandit" ringleaders, followers, and dependants killed or captured.[4] And just two years later, in 1519, he rapidly suppressed an alarming rebellion by a Ming prince and his thousands of followers. Finally, towards the end of his life, in 1528, Wang led a campaign against peoples living in the hinterlands of Guangxi Province, whom he referred to as "incorrigible Yao bandits." His victory over these non-Chinese natives, who had long troubled the region, meant nearly five thousand of them captured or dead.[5] Nevertheless, the number of casualties beguiles Wang Yangming's reluctance to use force unless it was absolutely unavoidable, and his compassion and leniency towards those culpable, due in part to his powerful intuition into what motivated both the rebels and his own men. In the aftermath of each of these military actions, he implemented a host of measures aimed at strengthening local governing institutions and instilling order in communities.

Though clearly a brilliant strategist, what was truly close to Wang Yangming's heart were his teachings. As the letter to his student also suggests, while serving as a Ming official, Wang was also explaining to students and other officials how his military campaigns and political measures were to be understood in light of his thought. Overcoming self-centered desires ("bandits of the mind") is analogous to repressing social unrest ("bandits in the mountains"), though far more difficult.[6] Similarly, after quelling the princely uprising, he

---

4   For the campaigns in Fujian, see *WYMQJ*, vol. 1, 11:303–306; for southern Jiangxi, *idem*, 11:365.

5   Ibid., vol. 1, 15:506.

6   By "bandits of the mind," I take Wang Yangming to be referring to *si yu* 私慾 (selfish desires) or *ren yu* 人欲 (human desires or passions). In his philosophical discourse, he frequently pairs these terms with *tianli* 天理 (principle of Heaven or Heavenly principles), and proposes a clear distinction between the two, between a moral law grounded in a moral order that transcends the individual and self-centered desires that arise when the individual fails to perceive and act upon that moral law. For a discussion of terms and translation, see Julia Ching, *To Acquire Wisdom: The Way of Wang Yang-ming* (New York: Columbia University Press, 1976),

underlined to students that his handling of this seemingly traumatic course of events amounted to nothing more than following the guidance of a natural and spontaneous moral knowing he called "innate knowledge of the good (*liangzhi* 良知)."[7] That is how, he explained, he was able to remain untroubled throughout the campaign. And while implementing measures to restore order among Chinese and non-Chinese populations in Guangxi, he explained to subordinate officials why genuine love and compassion (*cheng ai ce da* 誠愛惻怛) must be the foundation for the kind of civilizing relationships he envisioned developing between the governing class and subjects, including those of different ethnicities.[8] All individuals, he believed, were capable of such love and compassion, of such humanity, because they all possess an innate knowledge of the good and a human nature (*xing* 性), and it was these virtues which needed to be fostered in order to bring about social order. Clearly, for Wang Yangming, theory and practice did not happen in isolation from one another: his ideas had political implications and his political actions tell us something about the ramifications of his thought. That is what makes a study of his political career so interesting.

Wang Yangming lived during the middle of the Ming dynasty and is widely recognized for having changed the course of the Confucian tradition, a topic that has received much attention.[9] But what is equally significant about him is that he was recognized both in his own time and thereafter, both in China and Japan, not only for being an important philosopher and teacher, but also for his successful record as a civil official, military commander, and military strategist. Also quite unique is how his philosophy evolved in the context of harrowing challenges thrust upon him by a despotic Ming political environment, a con-

---

268–70; and David W. Tien, "Metaphysics and the Basis of Morality in the Philosophy of Wang Yangming," in *Dao Companion to Neo-Confucian Philosophy*, ed. John Makeham (New York: Springer, 2010), 52.

7   For a discussion, see Chapter Three.

8   For a discussion, see Chapter Six.

9   It is not my intention to provide a bibliography for the study of Wang Yangming and the many schools his followers initiated. The reader may consult the works cited in the References for more extensive lists. For more recent studies with bibliographies, see Chen Lai 陳來, *You wu zhi jing: Wang Yangming zhexue de jingshen* 有無之境: 王陽明哲學的精神 [Amidst the Realm of Being and Nonbeing: the Spirit of Wang Yangming's Philosophy] (Beijing: Renmin chubanshe, 1991); Tien, "Metaphysics and the Basis of Morality;" Philip J. Ivanhoe, *Ethics in the Confucian Tradition: The Thought of Mengzi and Wang Yangming* (Indianapolis: Hackett Publishing Company, 2002); and Qian Ming 錢明, *Yangming xue de xingcheng yu fazhan* 陽明學的形成與發展 [The Formation and Development of Yangming's Learning] (Nanjing: Jiangsu guji chubanshe, 2002).

nection he did not hesitate to draw for colleagues. That he conducted himself so impeccably and adroitly under such difficult circumstances while promoting his ideas in various pedagogical venues and simultaneously serving as an official and carrying out military campaigns has endeared him to many in East Asia, where he is seen as a person who embodied the Confucian ideal of "sageliness within and kingliness without (*nei sheng wai wang* 內聖外王)," and who practiced what he preached.[10] This is another reason why his record as an official invites closer study.

In fact, Wang Yangming often espoused a theory that echoed this very ideal: the unity of knowledge and action (*zhi xing he yi* 知行合一). For him, knowledge of right and wrong was not merely something to be learned in the abstract and then applied at a later time. It was rather something that, in any social setting, should be immediately evident to the mind in a personally meaningful way, so much so that the appropriate response would necessarily follow right from it.[11] Moral principles were first and foremost constituted in the mind through a kind of natural and spontaneous moral intuition that provided a guiding light in any circumstance.[12] Sometimes Wang would speak of this moral knowledge as Heavenly principle (*tianli* 天理) arising in the mind (*fa jian* 發見), and at others as the innate knowledge of the good. But he also pointed out to students and colleagues that various obstacles often obscured this good knowledge, causing people to fail to perceive and act on it.

He also offered various solutions. Earlier in his teaching career, Wang Yangming often told his students that an effective method for illuminating and purifying this moral knowing—so that the goodness of human nature and natural moral principles would become transparent to their minds and actualized in their conduct—was to preserve Heavenly principles and expel human desires (*cun tianli qu ren yu* 存天理去人欲).[13] That is, he urged them to hold in mind what they knew to be right by virtue of their moral intuition and to act on that, while on the other hand rejecting self-centered impulses and motivations.

---

10   For the history of this concept as it pertains to the study of Wang Yangming, see Sun Degao 孫德高, *Wang Yangming shigong yu xin xue yanjiu* 王陽明事功与心學研究 [Research on Wang Yangming's Worldly Achievements and Learning of the Mind-heart] (Chengdu: Xinan jiaotong daxue chubanshe, 2008), 5–14.

11   For the natural capacity of the mind to know moral principles, see Wang Yangming, *Instructions for Practical Living and Other Neo-Confucian Writings by Wang Yangming*, trans. and ed. Wing-tsit Chan (New York: Columbia University Press, 1963), 15; for the unity of knowledge and action, idem, 12–15. For a discussion of this theory, see Chen, *You wu zhi jing*, 93–117.

12   For further discussion, see the opening to Chapter Three.

13   Cf. Wang, *Instructions for Practical Living*, 15–17.

Later in life, he spoke of extending the innate knowledge of the good (*zhi liang zhi* 致良知). He explained that as people go about their lives and encounter real-life situations, they predictably experience a host of intentions, thoughts, and desires in response. Some of these might be good, while some were not, but because the ability to distinguish right and wrong is something all are endowed with by nature, people can choose to act on what is right and reject what is wrong. That is not only how things in life will be made right, but also how one's capacity to know what is right will become ever more refined. To quote directly from Wang's philosophical discourse: "If as we come into contact with the thing to which the will is directed, we really do the good and get rid of the evil to the utmost which is known by the innate faculty [innate knowledge of the good], then everything will be investigated and what is known by our innate faculty will not be deficient or obscured but will be extended to the utmost."[14] By "investigate" Wang means "rectify," and the ability of the individual to tap into moral knowledge allows him or her "to rectify that which is unjust so it can return to its original justness." And that, in his view, is how the world is transformed and brought in line with moral principle, for "to rectify that which is not just is to get rid of evil, and to return to justness is to do good."[15] Doing good and eradicating evil is the crux of Wang Yangming's practical solution to unifying knowledge and action.

That is a brief and simple synopsis of some of the teachings Wang conveyed to his many followers throughout the course of his long teaching career. He believed that all people possess a human nature; by this nature all are capable of moral goodness; this moral goodness can appear to the mind as self-evident moral principles; those principles provide the impetus to right conduct; and, by acting upon them, both the mind and the world will become more closely aligned with a higher moral order. Equally as important, all of this gives people common cause, the will to community, and higher levels of social organization. Wang also believed that at heart people are able to perceive that all things are one. He called this unity "the one substance of humanity" (*yi ti zhi ren* 一體之仁), and saw that the many virtues comprising the ethics he espoused, including most importantly the capacity to be humane, ultimately derived from that deeper reality.[16] The oneness of all things was the most basic moral

---

14   Wang Yangming, "Inquiry on the *Great Learning*," in Wang, *Instructions for Practical Living*, 279.

15   Ibid.

16   One of his clearest statements on the relation between morality and unity is his "Inquiry on the *Great Learning*." See *WYMQJ*, vol. 2, 26:968. For a study of his philosophy of the "one substance of humanity," see Chen Lisheng 陳立勝, *Wang Yangming wan wu yi ti lun: cong*

intuition and the foundation of that natural moral goodness that brings people together into groupings, from the family to the community to the state.

All of these notions—of human nature, good and evil, theory and practice, and the oneness of all things—not only represent important elements of Wang Yangming's much-studied philosophy, but also had important—and serious— implications for his less fully studied political career. Wang provides an excellent case study of an important Confucian philosopher who not only elaborated upon these theories, but who also had the opportunity to act on them in his career. That is because he was appointed to high official posts requiring him to restore order throughout areas of South China, populated by an array of more or less marginal social groups, at a time when the Ming state was establishing control over those regions. Through a chronologically organized study of Wang Yangming's political career, I hope to revise our understanding not only of what he did in his capacity as a Ming official, but also of the implications of that for our understanding of his philosophy and ethics. Faced as he was, for example, with social unrest and armed disturbances, how did Wang Yangming determine if there might be just cause for behavior that was threatening to the Ming state? Why did he sometimes find it necessary to resort to violence, and to exterminate peoples that his ideas should have predisposed him to see as capable of goodness? Just what was it in real-life situations that counted as good and evil, and what implications did these judgments have not only for the rebellious populations or intractable non-Chinese ethnic groups he was charged to govern but also for our understanding of his ethics? It was one thing to teach students about their innate moral capacities, the oneness of all things, and how they should practice doing good and eliminating evil in their daily lives, but quite another for a Ming official to decide what all that really meant in terms of managing resistant or restive populations or devising measures and institutions to help local populations recognize their own potential for moral goodness, as well as juggling how all of that was to fit in with their local societies and the broader goals of the Ming state. Practicing what he taught was truly a complex and daunting task.

To be sure, much ink has been spilled on the study of Wang Yangming. A recent search under his name in Worldcat.org for books in any language yielded 797 results. Articles abound, and in both China and Japan there are

---

shen yiti de lichang kan 王陽明萬物一體論：從身一體的立場看 [Wang Yangming's Discourse on the One Substance of the Ten Thousand Things Examined from the Standpoint of the One Body] (Taipei: Taida chuban zhongxin, 2005).

journals specifically devoted to "Yangming Studies."[17] Adding to this list might therefore seem unwarranted. However, if we take into consideration monographs in the English-language literature, there are no full biographies of Wang Yangming and only a 1939 study of his political career.[18] And although biographies abound in the Chinese- and Japanese-language literature, only a few include detailed studies of his political career, and even fewer carefully study it in light of his Neo-Confucian philosophy.[19] Notable recent examples of the latter include Okada Takehiko's landmark five-volume *Ō Yōmei taiden* (*Comprehensive Biography of Wang Yangming*) and Dong Ping's *Wang Yangming de shenghuo shijie* (*The World in which Wang Yangming Lived*).[20]

These studies have added immeasurably to our understanding of what Wang Yangming achieved in his role as a Ming official, and that is significant because prior to the twenty-first century most work on this subject was largely idealistic and hagiographical or heavily conditioned by Marxist theory. As a revered Neo-Confucian philosopher of traditional China, Wang Yangming's career served either to validate Confucian ideas or to prove that these were merely the ideology of governing scholar-official elites and thus largely in the service of power. As Leo Shin has so presciently noted, because his service as a high official had major ramifications for the peoples he was assigned to govern, Wang Yangming has become something of a case in point for driving home

---

17 An example for Japan is the journal *Yomeigaku* 陽明學 (Tokyo: Yōmei Gakkai); for China, *Yangming xue kan* 陽明學刊 (Guizhou: Guizhou renmin chubanshe).

18 Chang, Yu-chuan, *Wang Shou-jen as a Statesmen* (Beijing: Chinese and Political Science Association, 1946).

19 The definition of this term has been much debated. John Makeham states that Neo-Confucianism "is a category employed to describe a set of 'family resemblances' discerned across clusters of philosophical ideas, technical terms, arguments, and writings associated with particular figures from the Song to Qing (1644–1911) periods—in other words, concepts, ideas, and discourse rather than schools." (John Makeham, "Introduction," in *Dao Companion to Neo-Confucian Philosophy*, ed. John Makeham [London: Springer, 2010], xii.) He affirms William Theodore de Bary's assertion that Neo-Confucianism is an identifiable tradition inclusive of what in the Chinese sources is spoken of as "the learning of the Way," "the learning of the sages," "the learning of principle," and "the learning of the mind-heart." He also cites Peter K. Bol's conclusion that it is a cumulative and self-referential tradition. For Bol's views, see *Neo-Confucianism in History* (Cambridge, MA: Harvard University Asia Center, 2010), 78–83.

20 Okada Takehiko 岡田武彦, *Ō Yōmei taiden* 王陽明大伝 [Comprehensive Biography of Wang Yangming], 5 vols. (Tokyo: Meitoku, 2002–2005); Dong Ping 董平, *Wang Yangming de shenghuo shijie* 王陽明的生活世界 [The World in Which Wang Yangming Lived] (Beijing: Zhongguo renmin daxue, 2009).

these different perspectives.[21] What then seems to get lost in these narratives is a detailed studied of what he actually did, and one that uses a much greater range of contemporary accounts.

A few examples will suffice to illustrate this point. In his *Comprehensive History of Chinese Thought*, Hou Wailu states that "Wang Yangming's political activities, as well as his policies, are of course related to his system of philosophical idealism."[22] He thus insists that Wang's ideas and achievements must be analyzed together. Employing a somewhat rigid analysis conditioned by the Maoist environment of 1950's China, he and his co-authors found little of value in Wang's political philosophy. Borrowing from the letter cited at the outset to this introduction, Hou explains that Wang Yangming's achievements can be summarized as "defeating the bandits of the mind" and "defeating the bandits in the mountains." Whereas the latter refers to the suppression of peasant or minority non-Chinese resistance by the forces of feudal autocracy, the former refers to the desires or interests of the oppressed. For Hou, Wang's philosophizing was nothing more than "a spiritual whip in the hands of the feudal landlord class—feudalistic moral law."[23] Hence, he concludes that "looking at Wang Yangming's so-called 'meritorious achievements' as a whole shows that while he was extremely faithful to the ruling feudal classes, he was nevertheless very cruel in his suppression of and rule over the masses."[24]

While this Marxist analysis might seem easily dismissed as a product of its time, historicist readings of his philosophy, according to which it is an ideological construct that served the interests of power, have persisted in coloring perceptions of his political career. In his chapter on Wang Yangming in the *History of Chinese Political Thought*, Chen Hanming observes that his dream of "awakening" people's "innate knowledge of the good (*liangzhi* 良知)" had potent implications for his political practice. That is because he allegedly tended to read political and social conflict as moral problems best solved through methods for bringing the political order in line with the ethical norms he espoused. These included requiring people to develop character through "self-overcoming (*ke ji* 克己)" and "preserving Heavenly principle and ridding self-centered desires (*cun tianli qu ren yu* 存天理去人欲)." "In this way," Chen explains, "people will not have 'bandit-like' thoughts appear, and will naturally

---

21   Leo Shin, "The Last Campaigns of Wang Yangming," *T'oung Pao* 92:1–3 (2006): 101–102.

22   Hou Wailu 侯外廬, *Zhongguo sixiang tong shi* 中國思想通史 [Comprehensive Intellectual History of China] vol. 4, *Song, Yuan, Ming* 宋元明 (Beijing: Renmin chubanshe, 1957–1963), 875.

23   Ibid., 905.

24   Ibid., 882.

be able—through the virtues of gentleness, kindness, respectfulness, and yielding—to enter into the dead end that is autocratic despotism, becoming either modest and self-disciplined hypocritical gentleman under the system of sagely rule or tame and good obedient people under the system of autocratic rule."[25]

Chen further explains how Wang's belief in the importance of "polishing and tempering oneself through active involvement in affairs" betrayed his will to enforce moral principles and norms that buttressed a conservative, autocratic feudal order. Thus, his suppression of rebellions by farming populations and ethnic minority groups, formation of militias, enactment of household registration systems, and implementation of community compacts served that end. As for Wang's lifelong teaching that "knowledge and action must be unified," "this implied the requirement that people should at all times and places self-consciously abide by the moral norms of the feudal social order, thereby forming good social ethics and an orderly society."[26] For Chen, Wang's virtue ethics can only be read in a historicist light. Far from pointing to anything transcendent, they are in reality ciphers for various forms of oppression.

As opposed to an ideological reading of Wang Yangming, other scholars more clearly sympathetic to or inspired by his philosophy and life, as well as by the tradition of Confucianism, lean towards viewing his political career as an extension of both his virtue and the soundness of his ideas. To some degree, these accounts follow the pattern of the earliest accounts of Wang Yangming penned by his admirers, such as his student Qian Dehong's 錢德洪 (1496–1574) *Chronological Biography* and his colleague and one-time student Huang Wan's 黃綰 (1480–1554) *Record of Conduct*. A goal shared by both was to show how Wang's life and career demonstrated his sageliness and the validity of his teachings. Naturally, this entailed shaping those events to fit a kind of traditional Confucian narrative.[27] A good example of a modern study of his philosophy that similarly idealizes his political service is the work of Cai Renhou, who writes that "in the diction of his memorials [communications to the court], there is not one part that does not speak of the hardships of the people, not one part that does not speak of bringing stability to the people. This is all

---

25 Chen Hanming 陳寒鳴, "Wang Yangming xin xue ji qi houxue de zhengzhi sixiang 王陽明心學及其後學的政治思想 [Wang Yangming's Learning of the Mind-heart and the Political Thought of His Students]," in *Zhongguo zhengzhi sixiangshi* 中國政治思想史 [A History of Chinese Political Thought], ed. Liu Zehua 劉澤華 (Hangzhou: Zhejiang renmin chubanshe), 1996.

26 Ibid., 538.

27 For the *Chronological Biography,* see *NP*; for the *Record of Conduct,* see Huang Wan 黃綰, "Shi de ji 世德記 [Record of Conduct]," in *WYMQJ*, vol. 2, 39:1406–1430.

founded upon his concern for the welfare of the people, that genuine and sincere compassion whereby one 'looks upon the people like a wound upon one's
own person, and therefore cannot help but cry out.'"[28]
    Along similar lines, in her study of Wang Yangming, Julia Ching draws con-
nections between his philosophy and his political ideas and practice. Referring
to a set of what might be considered Wang's key statements on political philosophy, Ching notes that "out of these texts emerges a unified picture, rich
with meaning, of Yangming's understanding of sagehood as culminating in an
experience of oneness with Heaven and Earth and all things, an experience
which permeates the sage's thinking and being and acting, which becomes
identified with *xin* 心 [mind-heart] or *liangzhi* 良知 [innate knowledge of the
good] or *benti* 本體 [original substance], overflowing into a concrete awareness of his social and political responsibilities."[29] She also highlights how, in
the history of Confucian political discourse, this ideal combination of self-cultivation (virtue) and political practice was referred to as "sageliness within and
kingliness without."[30] Although more will be said later about this ideal, for the
moment suffice it to note that, for scholars sympathetic to Wang Yangming's
philosophy and impressed by his person, Bao Shibin's judgment would hold
true: "The way of sageliness within and kingliness without has been the dream
diligently pursued by Confucians, and Wang Yangming successfully realized
this unification of [the two]."[31]
    Yet what is noteworthy about the scholarship holding these differing per-
spectives on him is the fact that such assertions are largely unaccompanied by
a critical biography or an effort to fully reconstruct the historical setting for
Wang's political actions and arguments, and this obvious gap in the scholarship is where my study steps in. By reconstructing his political career, valuable
insight into the practical meaning and implications of Wang Yangming's principle philosophical ideas might be acquired, which is why I will view them
through this lens, leaving aside the traditional systematic account of his philosophical development. My goal here is to sketch out how his philosophical language was implicated in the events that comprised his official career, as well as
to demonstrate how a background horizon of cultural assumptions, historical

---

28   Cai Renhou 蔡仁厚, *Wang Yangming zhexue* 王陽明哲學 [The Philosophy of Wang
       Yangming] (Taipei: Sanmin shuju, 1974), 145.

29   Ching, *To Acquire Wisdom*, 126.

30   Julia Ching, *Mysticism and Kingship in China: the Heart of Chinese Wisdom* (Cambridge:
       Cambridge University Press, 1997), 106.

31   Bao Shibin 鮑世斌, *Mingdai Wang xue yanjiu* 明代王學研究 [Research on Wang's
       Learning during the Ming Dynasty] (Chengdu: Bashu shushe, 2004), 16.

circumstances, and social imaginary—to borrow the terminology of Charles Taylor—not only conditioned how Wang Yangming viewed the problems he was confronting and formulated plans for solving them but also tell us a great deal about the full import of his ethical philosophy. Such an analysis reveals that overly voluntarist and direct causal connections between Wang's knowledge and his actions must be problematized according to the vicissitudes of historical circumstance, and also suggest that the nature of that knowledge itself might be further defined through exploring the dense web of meanings in which it was embedded.[32]

In the present study, Chapter One begins with a survey of Wang Yangming's early life and political career. It was only later, in 1516, when he was forty-four years old, that he was commissioned with his first truly significant appointment, at least as measured by the level of his responsibilities and the documentary output—the grand coordinator of Southern Gan. Up to that time, most of the posts he received were only briefly held or of the nature of sinecures. However, these earlier experiences helped shape not only they way he would deal with the problems faced in later, more complex, assignments, but also the ideas he would later teach to his students and colleagues. Thus, for Chapter One, the goal is not only to describe his early political career, but also to sketch out his political thought.

The remaining five chapters, Chapters Two through Six, take up sequentially the series of important appointments Wang Yangming received between 1516 and 1528. At first, the settings for these appointments were varying levels of chronic social disorder, outlawry, and armed resistance by a variety of mostly marginal Chinese and non-Chinese populations in weakly administered regions of South and Southwest China. After subduing these restive peoples through a combination of armed suppression and negotiation and then implementing longer-term policies, Wang felt compelled to address other emerging threats to the stability of either the Ming state as a whole or the respective region in which he was stationed. Having spent nearly two years, from 1517 to 1518, campaigning around the border regions of three provinces surrounding southern Jiangxi, as well as designing measures to achieve long-term stability, Wang Yangming then faced, in 1519, what would turn out to be the second most significant princely rebellion in the history of the Ming dynasty. Uniquely qualified, prepared, and stationed for the task, he rallied a largely volunteer army around him and moved confidently to confront the Prince of Ning, Zhu

32   For a discussion, see Roger Chartier, *Cultural History: Between Practices and Representa-tions*, trans. Lydia V. Cochrane (Ithaca, NY: Cornell University Press, 1988), 19–48. For Charles Taylor's notion of social imaginary, see my discussion in Chapter Five.

Chenhao, in and around Nanchang, the provincial capital. While Chapter Two covers the course of events in southern Jiangxi, Chapters Three and Four cover the princely rebellion and the aftermath, during which time Wang remained stationed in Jiangxi Province as grand coordinator. The remaining two chapters begin with his last assignment in 1527, when he was dispatched to quell an uprising by native headmen in the southwestern province of Guangxi, something he managed to pull off without resorting to violence. However, once again, having completed that task, Wang Yangming then on his own initiative proceeded to go after what he perceived to have been a long-entrenched scourge on the region perpetrated by "Yao bandits."

At all of these posts, Wang was caught up in a web of demands. Firstly, he was positioned between the interests of the Ming court, provincial and local officials, as well as the societies those officials were charged to govern. And each of these had their own dynamic: factionalism at the top, differing opinions and levels of competence and corruption among subordinate officials, and complicated relations between the many social groups that comprised the local scenes. Thus, his first responsibility was to interpret the demands of the court and navigate any politics behind those—and there was much intrigue there that would greatly test Wang's famous imperturbability—and then communicate in such as a way that the court would find his solutions acceptable and approve them. Secondly, he had to read the climate of opinion among provincial and local officials and then find ways to compel or convince these subordinates to work with him in achieving his policy goals. Thirdly, he had to identify the causes of strife in the areas he was assigned to govern, and that meant figuring out who was involved and who was at fault. He was very skilled indeed at inquiring amongst the local officials and commoners, sometimes to the point of unveiling complex, deeper-seated economic and social tensions, which he would later endeavor to resolve. As I have explained, even though his first response in each case usually entailed a measured degree of force, in the aftermath he turned to a combination of administrative and educational institutions that would most directly impact the people living in those regions. In terms of restoring order over the long term, it was these institutions for which he held out the most hope, for Wang Yangming believed that the state had a vital role to play in guiding people towards seeing their natural capacity for moral goodness.

Left aside in this study is a critically important element of Wang Yangming's political life. While serving as a Ming official and developing his doctrines, Wang also managed to foster an educational movement—with political ramifications principally among the educated scholar-official class—by attracting disciples and teaching in academies, schools, and informally. Just how he went about this will make for another fascinating study, but what makes a study of his career just as interesting is that because Wang Yangming was serving as a representative of a Ming state in the process of extending control into rough and tumble internal frontiers, over a variety of marginal social and ethnic groups, his actions—both military and institutional—touch on matters of empire, ethnicity, and violence. His ideas can as well be viewed in this historical light without necessarily denying their universal significance. Besides, since Wang Yangming is one of the most admired individuals and influential philosophers in China's history, a closer look at how he conducted himself "as a statesman"—to borrow from the title of Chang Yu-chuan's 1939 study—would seem to be justified on its own merits. Wang's reputation seems fully justified, not only because his handling of what turned out to be one dreadful set of problems after another provides more nuanced insight into the world of his ideas, but also because he repeatedly proved himself to be a remarkable human being.

Early Career

If an account of Wang Yangming's political career were to begin with his first truly significant appointment—at least as measured by both the level of his responsibilities and what the documentary trail allows—then the starting point would be 1516. That was when he received the commission of grand coordinator, charged to manage uprisings in southern Jiangxi and neighboring regions. Chapter Two of this book begins with that assignment. But in terms of understanding the intellectual sources Wang brought to bear on the problems he would confront in South China, I begin with an overview of elements of his early life and career that shaped his political views.

Wang Yangming, whose given name was Shouren 守仁, was born in 1472 to a gentry family of Yuyao County 余姚縣 in the province of Zhejiang 浙江省, during the reign of the Chenghua 成化 emperor Zhu Jianshen 朱見深, who came to the throne in 1464 and reigned from 1465 to 1487. When Wang was fifteen, this emperor was succeeded by his eldest son, the Hongzhi 弘治 emperor Zhu Youtang 朱祐樘, who held the throne from the death of his father until 1505.

Insofar as his forefathers provided models for his own evolving identity as a child and teen, the young Shouren would have been expected either to pursue a career of examination success and service to the emperor or to forgo this most honorable of paths and rather devote himself solely to a life of scholarship. Shouren's sixth-generation ancestor, Wang Gang 王綱, after passing through the transition from the Mongol Yuan to the native Ming Dynasty, chose the first path, serving the Ming founder Zhu Yuanzhang in mostly mid-level positions, including one that entailed campaigning against Miao populations in South China. Over time, he earned a reputation for talent in both the civil and military arts.[1] When Wang Yangming visited a temple established in his ancestor's honor in Zengcheng 增城, Guangdong right after his last assignment and just prior to passing away, he would likely have felt this was the ancestor whose career most resembled his own.[2]

Shouren's fifth-generation ancestor, Wang Yanda 王彥達, however, perhaps out of grief over his father's death, chose to remain at home and lead a life with

---

1 Zhang Yimin 張壹民, "Wang Xingchang xiansheng zhuan 王性常先生傳 [Biography of Sir Wang Xingchang]," in *WYMQJ*, vol. 2, 38:1380–81.

2 *NP*, 35:1323.

a touch of eremitism, plowing his fields and caring for his mother, donning only simple garb and eating plain food.³ Shouren's great-great grandfather, Wang Yuzhun 王與准, also chose not to serve. He did earn a reputation not only for avoiding public service by hiding out in the mountains but also for being quite learned, writing as he did a commentary on a revered classical text, the *Classic of Change*.⁴ Such traditions of scholarship in Shouren's family would continue right down to his own time; his great grandfather Wang Jie 王傑 not only received a licentiate and entered the National Academy in Nanjing, but was also an accomplished classicist who composed studies of the *Classic of Change*, *Spring and Autumn Annals*, and the *Rituals of Zhou*.⁵ Likewise, Shouren's grandfather, Wang Lun 王倫, was well versed in classical traditions, although he did not translate his accomplishments into examination success and an official career, choosing instead to lead a somewhat reclusive life in his hometown.⁶

If any family member set the highest expectations for Shouren and provided the best conditions for success in an official career, it was his father, Wang Hua 王華 (1446–1522). Passing the highest-level examination in 1481, Wang Hua also finished in first place as optimus. This ensured he would serve as a compiler in the prestigious Hanlin Academy, which in turn vaulted him into a successful career at the courts of both the Chenghua and Hongzhi emperors.⁷ Indeed, having been appointed to the academy, Hua left for the capital with the eleven-year-old Shouren, likely just one year after he had relocated the family to Yue City 越城, the county seat of Shanyin 山陰, Zhejiang. Thus, while studying in a private family school in Beijing, Wang Yangming spent most of his teen years among Ming China's national elites.

In his account of Wang's life, Deng Aimin usefully proposes that 1499 marks a turning point. That year, Wang Yangming obtained the highest examination degree, becoming a presented scholar and consequently receiving his first assignment from the Ming court. Deng also points out that by this time he was largely finished with study of the military arts and literary composition, intellectual pursuits he would later come to view as trifling. Henceforth, he would

---

3   *WYMQJ*, vol. 2, 35:1381.

4   Hu Yan 胡儼, "Dunshi xiansheng zhuan 遁石先生傳 [Biography of Sir Dunshi]," in *WYMQJ*, vol. 2, 38:1381–82.

5   Qi Lan 戚瀾, "Huaili xiansheng zhuan 槐里先生傳 [Biography of Sir Huaili]," in *WYMQJ*, vol. 2, 38:1383–84.

6   Wei Han 魏瀚, "Zhuxuan xiansheng zhuan 竹軒先生傳 [Biography of Sir Zhuxuan]," in *WYMQJ*, vol. 2, 38:1384–85.

7   For a full account, see Lu Shen 陸深, "Hairi xiansheng xingzhuang 海日先生行狀 [Record of Conduct for Sir Hairi]," in *WYMQJ*, vol. 2, 38:1391–1400.

engage in more extensive study and practice of Buddhism and Daoism while continuing to wrestle with Cheng-Zhu Neo-Confucianism.[8]

Cheng-Zhu Neo-Confucianism, also known as "the learning of principle (*lixue* 理學)," refers to the reordering of the Confucian tradition by Song Dynasty philosophers, most particularly Cheng Yi 程頤 (1033–1107), Cheng Hao 程顥 (1032–1085), and Zhu Xi 朱熹 (1130–1200). Zhu Xi synthesized the work of his two important Song predecessors, among others, in part by including their work in his extensive commentaries on classical texts, commentaries which would become part of the standardized curriculum for the examination system in late imperial China during the Yuan and Ming dynasties. Cheng-Zhu Neo-Confucianism was also the main component of a broader intellectual movement referred to as the "learning of the sages (*sheng xue* 聖學)" and "the learning of the Way (*daoxue* 道學)." Although mastery of this learning was essential for examination preparation and therefore entry into the scholar-official class, its avowed purpose was to foster virtuous men, men of wisdom, of good character and conduct, the key prerequisite for effective service and leadership. Of course, the models for virtue were the great sages of antiquity, whose wisdom was available through the records of their words and deeds.

Stories from Wang's early life indicate that, prior to passing the highest-level exam in 1499, he had grappled with both the institutional and philosophical dimensions of the "the learning of the sages." Even at age eleven, while attending a private family school, he contradicted his teacher's assertion that examination preparation was the most important matter, rather insisting that it is secondary to "reading books to learn to become a sage and worthy."[9] As he would often state the case to students later in life, although obtaining degrees is indeed important for entering officialdom, examination preparation is ultimately in the service of a higher calling, that is, the call to sagehood and the path of virtue. His model here was Zhu Xi, someone he viewed as almost godlike. Yet accounts of this period of time highlight his increasingly conscientious study of but frustration with the great Song master's philosophical ideas. For example, Wang met the important Ming Confucian Lou Liang 婁諒 (1422–1491), who confidently affirmed for him that achieving sagehood was a real possibility and introduced him to his understanding of Zhu's ideas. Such experiences encouraged him to apply those ideas in practice, something he did per-

8   Deng Aimin 鄧艾民, *Zhu Xi Wang Shouren zhexue yanjiu*朱熹王守仁哲學研究 [Research on the Philosophy of Zhu Xi and Wang Shouren] (Shanghai: Huadong shifan daxue chubanshe, 1989), 80.

9   *NP*, 33:1221.

haps too literally in the 1490s, while in his twenties.[10] Wang attempted to "investigate things (*ge wu* 格物)" fully and obtain insight into principles by gazing on bamboo in meditation or pursuing studies in a more focused and orderly way, only to end up frustrated and even ill.[11]

Most likely, Wang Yangming's practice of Cheng-Zhu Neo-Confucianism, as he understood it, failed to yield the kind of personally meaningful knowledge or liberating insight he was seeking, and sagehood therefore seemed out of reach. On top of that, study of the standard commentaries failed to yield examination success at the highest level, at least until 1499: he failed the metropolitan examination twice, in 1493 and 1496.[12] His disappointment over these related endeavors is generally considered to be the impetus for his taking up other wide-ranging pursuits, most notably in the areas of literature, the military arts, and the Daoist pursuit of longevity. Although he dabbled in these subjects while residing periodically in the capital and in Zhejiang, he later rejected them all as either frivolous or secondary to the Confucian ideal of sagehood he sought.

Nevertheless, these subjects would prove to be anything but inconsequential for his official career. His background in literature, along with his father's status, enabled Wang Yangming to move among literary circles both in his hometown and the capital. Most notably, the year he finally received the metropolitan degree, he spent some time with the leading lights of the Seven Early Masters, a group of up-and-coming young officials at the capital who championed principles for a literary movement. And although Wang would later assert that a person should seek to become a Yan Hui 顏回—a renowned disciple of Confucius, as opposed to a Li Bai 李白, a celebrated Tang dynasty poet—he wrote much highly regarded poetry throughout his life. Many of his letters and official communications were likewise carefully crafted, literary masterpieces in their own right.[13]

Perhaps even more valuable for his later political career was the time he spent on the military arts. It was not unusual for literati to take an interest in studying texts on military strategy, and Wang was no exception.[14] When

10   Ibid., 33:1223.
11   Ibid., 33:1223–24.
12   Ibid.
13   For a discussion, see Tu, *Neo-Confucian Thought in Action*, 40; Deng, *Zhu Xi Wang Shouren zhexue yanjiu*, 79–80.
14   Frederick Mote, *Imperial China: 900–1800* (Cambridge, MA: Harvard University Press, 1999), 555; Kathleen Ryor, "*Wen* and *wu* in Elite Cultural Practices during the Late Ming," in *Military Culture in Imperial China*, ed. Nicola Di Cosmo (Cambridge, MA: Harvard University Press, 2009), 219–25.

Minister of War Wang Qiong 王瓊 (1459–1532) appointed him grand coordinator of Southern Gan in 1516 for the purpose of quelling disturbances in that region, Wang Yangming's reputation for being knowledgeable about military theory was one of the reasons. By 1498, at age twenty-seven, he had already won a degree of notoriety for submitting an impressive, forceful memorial addressing matters of security along the northern border.[15] The insight he displayed when proposing solutions to the ongoing threat of these mounted steppe warriors undoubtedly derived from his keen and intensive study of the military classics, as well as from his personal experiences. At age fourteen, while accompanying his father to Beijing, he had traveled to the northern frontier, just north of Juyong Pass 居庸關, where he spent time with tribesmen riding horses and practicing archery, "aspiring to administer the border affairs of all the empire."[16] Wang identified with Ma Yuan 馬援, a famous Eastern Han Dynasty scholar-general learned in both classical studies and the military arts who battled "barbarians" on the western frontier. Tu Weiming believes that Ma "was to play a significant role in shaping his self-image later when he was charged by the court with leading military campaigns in south Jiangxi and Guangxi."[17] These life-long interests were still alive when he submitted the memorial. According to the entry in the *Chronological Biography* for the tenth year of the reign of the Hongzhi emperor (1497):

> During this year our teacher studied the military arts. At the time reports from the border were quite urgent. The court recommended talented generals, and there were none whom were not alarmed. Master Wang believed the military examinations only succeeded in obtaining officers skilled at horseback riding, archery, and fighting, but were unable to produce [individuals] skilled at strategy and leadership. Therefore, he turned his attention to the study of the military arts, and there were no military classics he did not study in depth. Whenever he was in attendance at a banquet, he would for his pleasure gather together seeds and lay them out in battle formation.[18]

That Wang studied the military classics in depth is indisputable, given his annotations to and brief commentary on the *Seven Military Classics*, a standard

---

15   Entitled "Statement Concerning Military Affairs along the [Northern] Border," this memorial is yet extant. See *WYMQJ*, vol. 1, 9:285.

16   *NP*, 33:1222.

17   Tu, *Neo-Confucian Thought in Action*, 37.

18   *NP*, 33:1224.

compilation of the most important military works from ancient China, assembled during the Song Dynasty.[19] He was so familiar with them that throughout all his campaigns, when explaining his battle plans to subordinates, he would routinely cite familiar terminology from these texts, especially *Sunzi's Art of War* and *Wu Qi*.

Once he had passed the metropolitan exam, between 1499 and 1516 Wang Yangming entered a new phase in his life, during which time he alternated between a series of mostly minor mid-level assignments and periods out of office. In the fall of 1499, he was assigned to construct a tomb for Wang Yue 王越 (1425–1497), who had received the noble title Count of Weining 威寧伯 for his military service. Having only just completed his study of the military classics in 1497, he put his knowledge to good use when he organized the laborers into military formations to complete the task. For this honorable service, Wang Yangming received a treasured sword from the count's family and, having finished this assignment, was then placed in the Ministry of Works for the purpose of observing its internal workings.[20]

In 1500, Wang was appointed secretary in the Yunnan Bureau of the Ministry of Punishments, where he would have been expected to play a role in supervising the administration of justice and management of prisons and convicts for a particular territory.[21] Although this posting did not entail leaving the capital, in 1501 he was sent to review cases in the Southern Metropolitan Area, after which time he spent nearly a year traveling Mount Jiuhua 九華山 visiting Daoist and Buddhist establishments. While we know very little about his accomplishments while serving at the ministry, what information we have suggests he was concerned to make things right. According to one account, the ministry's two highest officials were raising pigs with prisoners' food rations, something Wang put an end to when he slaughtered the animals and shared

---

19   The entire text is not included in Wang Yangming's *Collected Works*. For the full annotated commentary, see Wang Yangming 王陽明, *Wu jing qi shu ping* 武經七書評 [Commentary on the Seven Military Classics] (Taipei: Taiwan chubanshe, 1978). The Seven Military Classics include *Sunzi's Art of War*, *Three Strategies of Huang Shigong*, *Wu Qi's Art of War*, *Wei Liaozi*, *The Methods of the Sima*, and *Questions and Replies between Tang Taizong and Li Weigong*. This collection was assembled during the Song dynasty. For a discussion, see Xie Xianghao 謝祥皓, *Zhongguo bingxue: Song Ming Qing juan* 中國兵學: 宋明清卷 [Chinese Military Studies: Song, Ming, and Qing Volume] (Jinan: Shandong renmin chubanshe, 1998), 32–39; Ralph Sawyer, *The Seven Military Classics of Ancient China*, trans. Ralph D. Sawyer and Mei-Chun Sawyer (Boulder, CO: Westview Press), 1993.
20   *NP*, 33:1225.
21   Charles Hucker, *A Dictionary of Official Titles in Imperial China* (Stanford: Stanford University Press, 1985), 74.

them amongst the guards and prisoners. He is also said to have redressed many mishandled cases.[22]

By early summer 1502, Wang Yangming had returned to the capital from his assignment and travels, but his stay was brief; having fallen ill, he requested leave to return to his family in Zhejiang, where he remained until mid-1504, when he returned to the Ministry of Punishments.[23] By 1492 chronic illness (likely a type of pulmonary tuberculosis) had become a pressing theme in Wang's life. It would remain so until the very end, providing some of the impetus behind his early pursuits of Daoist techniques of longevity, as well as his later repeated requests to leave office after periods of service.[24] As Tu Weiming has pointed out, he was not only ill at this time but also possibly dissatisfied with his official career and what he came to regard as the superficial literary pursuits of his colleagues in the capital. This explains why he took leave, spent more time in Buddhist temples and scenic spots with Daoist associations, and then withdrew to a grotto in Mount Siming 四明山, Zhejiang Province, where he practiced breathing techniques.[25]

As was the case for many scholars during the Ming, a cycle of service and withdrawal from the public sphere was a major theme throughout Wang Yangming's life.[26] At this point, however, this pattern did not carry the meaning it would for him later. From 1505, because of his growing reputation as a Confucian thinker, he began to accrue a following, and during his time out of office he taught his philosophy in various venues. Eventually, he would teach his students that liberation, or true freedom, need not entail renouncing public life or social relations, as it might for Buddhists and Daoists. Rather, he emphasized that the spiritual realms to which they were aiming are better understood and apprehended merely by conforming to principle in all that one does, principles that naturally derive from human nature. Wang's first insight in this regard came to him when he was most intensively pursuing longevity through exercising detachment from the "dusty world," as practiced in Daoism and Buddhism. At the very moment that he felt a strong urge to flee his worldly commitments, he realized that his father and grandmother remained powerfully in his thoughts, and concluded that to ignore them would be to extinguish his true

---

22   Fu Weilin 傅維麟, *Ming shu lie zhuan* 明書列傳 [Book of Ming Biographies], in *Mingdai zhuanji congkan* 明代傳記叢刊, ed. Zhou Junfu, vol. 7 (Ming wen shuju, 1991), 87:358.

23   *WYMQJ*, vol. 1, 9:299.

24   Wang, *Instructions for Practical Living*, 249.

25   Tu, *Neo-Confucian Thought in Action*, 57–59.

26   For a discussion of eremitism more generally, see Frederick W. Mote, "Confucian Eremitism in the Yuan Period," in *The Confucian Persuasion*, ed. Arthur F. Wright (Stanford: Stanford University Press, 1960), 206–212.

nature. This is when he relocated to the beautiful West Lake in Hangzhou in preparation for returning to office.[27] This is also a likely turning point in his spiritual pursuits, as he moved back in the direction of the learning of the sages.[28]

During the summer of 1504, at age thirty-two, Wang Yangming returned to the Ministry of Punishments, but he was soon transferred to a mid-level position at the Bureau of Military Appointments in the Ministry of War, where promotions, demotions, and retirement for military officers were processed.[29] While this appointment itself was of little significance, his service as a provincial examiner in Shandong Province that fall proved to be of greater consequence. A regional inspector of that province had invited him to serve in this role, as a court official delegated to preside over a triennial provincial examination for candidates for the civil service. As part of his duties, he provided examples of model essays for the questions posed in the examination, and although scholars disagree on the extent to which these responses came directly from his hand, they all agree that they reflect Wang Yangming's statecraft thought, despite conforming to this formal setting, and thus coming off as stuffily orthodox and preachy.[30]

Judging from his preface to these essays, Wang was very serious about this solemn duty, a solemnity enhanced by the setting of the examination: a province that was home to China's most revered Confucian sages, Confucius and Mencius.[31] His task was to find local men of ability who might match up to the worthies of ancient times. Should he fail, he may very well be the one to blame. Thus, his model essays presumably reflect the kind of basic knowledge of the nature of politics and service that he expected such men to have. And even though the themes would have seemed largely conventional, several of his ideas in these essays would have a major impact on his political career; in fact, he would continue to speak of their importance throughout his philosophical discourse, even if worded in different terms.

---

27   *NP*, 33:1225–26.
28   Okada, *Ō Yōmei taiden*, 1:287.
29   *WYMQJ*, vol. 1, 9:299. For this position in general see Hucker, *Dictionary of Official Titles*, 570.
30   The *Chronological Biography* states that Wang Yangming composed these essays (*NP*, 33:1227). Both Qian Ming (*Yangming xue de xingcheng yu fazhan*, 31) and Dong Ping (*Wang Yangming de shenghuo shijie*, 17) state that some sections were composed by Wang, while others consist of outstanding responses or model essays he selected. Okada Takehiko follows the *Chronological Biography* (*Ō Yōmei taiden*, 1:292).
31   *WYMQJ*, vol. 1, 22:839.

A topic Wang chose for one of the essays testing knowledge of the Four Books was a passage from the *Analects*: "The term 'great minister' refers to those who serve their lord according to the Way and who, when this is no longer possible, relinquish office." [32] The model essay explains that a worthy official serves not because he seeks prestige or higher status, but rather because he wishes to serve the ruler with the Way or, in other words, to serve a higher justice, or timeless moral principles. These principles were exemplified and passed on by the ancient sage-kings Yao and Shun. By following them, the worthy official awakens the ruler's goodness, including his sense of social responsibility and concern for the welfare of the people. He does so by always speaking of humanity and righteousness, while also pointing out for the ruler the error of his ways and refusing to cater to his whims or bend to his will, should his wishes be immoral. If he is unable to serve the ruler with the Way, the worthy official should retire.[33]

This essay has several important things to say about the source of moral authority and the nature of the monarchy. Firstly, the Way is a body of moral knowledge that can reliably guide a ruler's conduct. At one time, in what was something like China's golden age, sage-kings embodied this morality in their rule. At some point, however, this knowledge became the preserve of worthy officials, who now had the authority to interpret it for sovereigns that hailed from dynastic houses. The story behind this shift is alluded to in other essays, which presented a version of history that would have been wholly familiar to students of Neo-Confucian thought.[34] According to this view, in ancient times politics and morality were indeed one and the same, and the first sage-kings, Yao and Shun, in fact selected their heirs based on merit. Even during the ensuing Three Dynasties (Xia 夏, Shang 商, Zhou 周), hereditary rulers generally adhered to principles when governing. It was only towards the end of that time, during the later Zhou, that hegemons appeared who governed based on self-interest. Fortunately, as monarchical rule became increasingly unprincipled and tyrannical, a series of sagely philosophers, beginning with Confucius,

---

32   Confucius, *The Analects*, trans. by D.C. Lau (Penguin, 1979), 109. The passage is from *Analects* 11:24. The Four Books include the *Analects, Mencius, Great Learning*, and *Doctrine of the Mean*. Zhu Xi selected these from the classical corpus because he believed that combined they provided a complete introduction to the learning of the sages. During the Ming dynasty, these texts were the core of examination testing and preparation. For a discussion, see Mote, *Imperial China: 900–1800*, 340–46.

33   *WYMQJ*, vol. 1, 22:862.

34   For a discussion of this philosophy of history and its significance for the identity of Neo-Confucians during the late imperial period, see Bol, *Neo-Confucianism in History*, 129–33.

were taking steps to preserve the Way in their teachings.[35] The last in this line prior to the imperial era was Mencius. Thereafter, this teaching was lost until the Song Dynasty, when Zhou Dunyi (1017–1073), Cheng Hao, and Cheng Yi recovered it. That is the body of knowledge that Zhu Xi had organized and made available in the Four Books and his accompanying commentaries. In brief, Wang saw himself as belonging to an educated, governing elite that was the repository of moral knowledge and had the role of speaking truth to those in power. No doubt, he knew that some took this role seriously while most saw the moral knowledge constituting the Way as mere platitudes to be mastered for examination purposes. As we shall see, though, Wang himself would pay a hefty price on several occasions for staunchly adhering to Confucius's principle that a worthy official must "serve their lord according to the Way," even if that meant being dangerously outspoken.

Corollaries to this principle are explained in his model essays on topics chosen from other classics. In these, the critical role of the virtuous minister is repeatedly emphasized. The great official, we learn, compels a worthy ruler to distance himself from mean persons—the flattering and artfully tongued. Instead, the sovereign must employ noble men, for his choice of servants determines whether order or anarchy shall prevail in the realm. These men are able, through transmitting and teaching the Way, to help the sovereign identify sprouts of goodness in his own heart and thereby renew his virtue daily. By so doing, the ruler sets an example of impartiality, justice, and goodness and is thus able to retain the confidence of the masses and curtail their selfish desires and evil propensities.[36] In short, the ruler's legitimacy depends upon his ability to correctly influence his subjects and to win their approval, but his ability to succeed at this will depend upon how carefully he listens to those who understand what virtue is and how it is to be acquired.

Perhaps at this time, during the reign of the Hongzhi emperor, who showed a willingness to hear out his Confucian advisors and embody these ideas in his rule, Wang may have believed this feasible. But as luck would have it, he would spend most of his career in the service of two of the most notorious rulers in Ming history, the Zhengde 正德 (r. 1506–1521) and Jiajing 嘉靖 (r. 1522–1566) emperors. This largely explains why he would channel all his efforts into

---

35   These ideas are implicit in the essays comprising the examination record. In one essay, he
      does discuss the role of Mencius in this "Succession to the Way (*daotong* 道統)." That is
      the term Neo-Confucians used to describe the line of transmission of the Way, and Wang
      explains that those who teach this were essential to the ruler's success (*jundao* 君道, the
      way of the ruler). (*WYMQJ*, vol. 1, 22: 846–47).

36   Ibid., 22:846–47.

teaching outside the court and serving people with the Way in his capacity as a local or higher-level territorial official.[37] While doing so, he placed the ortho-dox sovereign-centered political model in the background, and instead called upon the people to identify the sprouts of goodness in their own minds and hearts as the basis for ethical practice in local settings. He would also devise institutions designed both to encourage people to do so and to monitor the outcome. This does not mean, however, that he gave up on the ideal that the sovereign serves as the exemplar providing the transformative influence nec-essary to awaken people and consequently to restore the utopian conditions of the golden age of times past.

Another idea that comes out of these essays is that by according with prin-ciple in all that he does, the great man also accords with the Way of Heaven, the transcendent cosmic-moral order: "Only sages are pure in moral principle and without self-centered desire, their ritual etiquette is the body of Heaven and Earth, their mind and heart is the mind and heart of Heaven and Earth, and therefore all that they do is nothing other than what Heaven and Earth do; therefore, it is said 'accord with principle and become one with Heaven.'"[38] This means that those who preserve the Way and convey it to their sovereigns are in effect bringing the social and political order in line with a transcendent one and thus directing it towards its telos. Throughout his life, Wang would maintain the essential correctness of this idea, although he would later articu-late it in different terms, calling it "according with principle by accumulating righteousness" (ji yi 集義), and explaining that this entails acting upon a natu-rally and innately given moral conscience and intuition, or what he calls "the innate knowledge of the good" (zhi liang zhi 致良知).[39] This self-transcending method of cultivation was, he would state explicitly, the reason why a Ming princely rebellion was so naturally and effortlessly suppressed, among other virtuous political acts. More generally, it applies across the board as a powerful legitimating principle for political action because it suggests that a deeper moral order reveals itself to the wise, to those who have the clarity of mind to perceive it.

It is this higher moral law that the emperor is to bear witness to in his con-duct, so that his subjects will more easily perceive it for themselves. An essay on a phrase from the Classic of Rites clarifies how this works: "Just as the body will feel at ease in what the mind-heart likes and loves, so will the people desire

---

37   For a brief, insightful synopsis of the reigns of these respective emperors, see John Dard-ess, Ming China, 1368–1644 (Lanham: Rowman and Littlefield, 2012), 43–52.

38   WYMQJ, vol. 1, 22:844–45.

39   For further discussion, see pp. 199-204.

what the sovereign likes and loves."[40] Here is a principle that is at the heart of an order of virtue tied to an autocratic political order through the notion of stimulus and response (*ganying* 感應), the idea that influences emanating from the superior/interior elicit a like response from the inferior/external. In a sense, the state reifies the hierarchy in human moral development, ideally modeling the refinement and wisdom that comes with growing moral awareness. The government civilizes because the most civilized govern. More simply, we learn, the ruler is to the people as the mind-heart is to the body. Therefore, if the ruler loves humaneness and righteousness, so will his subjects. But if he loves violence, then disorder will ensue, and he may very well unseat himself. Again, this is why having good men around the sovereign is critical.[41] Later, however, in light of the poor quality of rulers in place during much of his lifetime, Wang would decenter this vision *to a degree*, increasingly placing the political order in the hands of each individual's singular ability to act upon his own innate moral goodness, even if that knowledge yet remained characterized in part by sentiments suited to this *ganying* model and the metaphor of bodily unity undergirding it.

There is much more in these essays, especially as reflected in the five policy questions, that suggest not only that by 1504 Wang Yangming was more fully committed to and oriented by the political ideology widely accepted by Confucian scholar-official elites, but also that he was taking that discourse in directions that would later bear fruit in his philosophical development and official career. Indeed, he had begun to highlight what he saw as a failure to clarify the Way of Confucius, which is at the root of why, for instance, people mistakenly veer towards such heterodox traditions as Buddhism and Daoism, which he too had pursued.[42] Following the Way requires study of the ancient sages and learning to will what they willed. By so doing, the scholar learns to exhaustively examine principles, accord with the mean, overcome himself, and return to such fundamental moral principles as humanity. In the end, self-centered desires will be extinguished and the principles of Heaven will flow.[43] Finally, in order to address the pressing problems of the time, Wang insists that "there is no greater task today than shaking up the lines of the net," for only by so doing does it become possible to govern the realm.[44] In this context, he is referring to

---

40   *WYMQJ*, vol. 1, 22:853.

41   Ibid., 22:853–54.

42   Ibid., 22:861.

43   Ibid., 22:865.

44   Wang Yangming's call for "shaking the lines of the net" and this translation are further discussed in Chapter Five.

the enforcement of legal norms so that the moral fabric of society will be re-
generated. The principal culprits here are incompetent officials who, though
remiss in their duties, still manage to stay in their positions of power. Thus,
institutions for selecting and promoting the best candidates for office and removing the mediocre must be reinvigorated. In short, the emperor and the
Ming court should assert their moral authority.[45]

After administering the examination in Shandong, Wang Yangming returned to his post at the Bureau of Appointments at the Ministry of War in
Beijing. The year 1505 was yet another turning point, for it was during this year
that he furthered his commitment to the "learning of the Way" by accepting
students and holding sessions of philosophical inquiry with them in the capital.[46] This commitment was only strengthened when he befriended Zhan
Ruoshui 湛若水 (1466–1560), at the time a compiler at the prestigious Hanlin
Academy who was achieving some recognition for having studied under renowned Ming philosopher Chen Xianzhang 陳獻章 (1428–1500). Both Zhan
and Wang shared a certain disdain for what they considered to be the prestige-
seeking literary pursuits of scholars in the capital, as well as worry over what
they saw as a widespread failure among the scholarly elites to internalize Confucian learning in a personally or spiritually relevant way. That is why they
vowed to advocate for a better understanding of this learning, by calling upon
those around them to attend to virtue and become resolved to pursue sagehood. In an epitaph, Zhan asserted that by this time his close friend had clearly returned to the orthodox fold of the "learning of the sages and worthies"—that
is, after having experimented for years with the military arts, literature, Daoism, and Buddhism.[47] Zhan also notes that they were both inspired by renowned Song Dynasty philosopher Cheng Hao's principle that "the humane
person is united as one body with all things."[48] This principle would not only
deepen in significance in the context of Wang's philosophical development,
but also in the context of his political career. The aspiration to and perception
of unity was not only powerful impetus to empathetic consideration for others, it was also an ideal that might lead an official to privilege the welfare of the
governed over the interests of the Ming court.

---

45   *WYMQJ*, vol. 1, 22:868.

46   *NP*, 33:1226.

47   Zhan Ruoshui 湛若水, "Yangming xiansheng muzhiming 陽明先生墓誌銘 [Epitaph for
      Sir Yangming]," in *WYMQJ*, vol. 2, 38:1401.

48   For a discussion of Cheng Hao's doctrine of unity and *ren* (humanity) see Zhang Dainian,
      Key Concepts in Chinese Philosophy (New Haven, CT: Yale University Press, 2002), 304–305.

Broader political developments would soon radically change the course of Wang Yangming's mundane political career, for in 1505 the Hongzhi emperor became ill and passed away, leaving the throne to his eldest son, Zhu Houzhao 朱厚照. If Wang Yangming hoped the new emperor would assert his moral authority, distancing the fawning and incompetent and promoting the best-qualified men across the realm so that they might cooperate in improving customs and mores, he was soon sorely disappointed. Upon taking power, the fourteen-year-old emperor immediately revealed an inclination to disregard the advice of his father's revered advisors in the grand secretariat. Instead, he allowed his decision-making power to fall into the hands of eunuch favorites who had raised him from a young age in the East Palace and retained his affection by encouraging profligate and irresponsible behavior. A crisis then erupted as the most powerful high officials of the Ming court engaged in a power struggle with these grand eunuchs, who managed to gain control over not only the process for issuing edicts but also the workings of the emperor's security and intelligence-gathering apparatus.[49] Now the political world that had taken shape around the emperor was the grotesque opposite of the ideal Wang had outlined in the Shandong examination essays.

Protest over the Eight Tigers, as these eunuchs were known, mounted throughout the summer and fall, coming to a head in the fall of 1506, when Grand Secretaries Liu Jian and Xie Qian, with a good deal of support in and outside the court, moved to curtail their power and finally convinced the emperor to take some action against them.[50] But because the grand secretaries were insisting on capital punishment, the chief eunuch, Liu Jin 劉瑾, pleaded for mercy before the sovereign, insisting that his high officials were usurping too many of the ruler's prerogatives. The young and sympathetic emperor thus requested that Liu merely be sent off to the southern capital of Nanjing; however, the grand secretaries refused. Frustrated with their unwillingness, the emperor sided with the Eight Tigers, pardoning them of all accusations and further ensconcing them in power. Liu and Xie were coerced into leaving office, while many of those supporting them were arrested.[51]

---

49   For brief accounts, see James Geiss, "The Cheng-te Reign, 1506–1521," in *The Cambridge History of China*, vol. 7: *The Ming Dynasty, 1368–1644*, ed. Frederick Mote and Denis Twitchett (Cambridge: Cambridge University Press, 1988), 403–408; and Dardess, *Ming China, 1368–1644*, 45–48.

50   Tan Qian 談遷, *Guo que* 國榷 [Deliberations on the Reigning Dynasty] (Beijing: Zhonghua guji chubanshe, 1958), 46:2872.

51   Yu Huaiyan 余懷彥, *Wang Yangming yu Guizhou wenhua* 王陽明與貴州文化 [Wang Yangming and the Culture of Guizhou] (Guiyang: Guizhou jiaoyu chubanshe, 1997), 11.

Now beholding the shift in power at the Ming court, officialdom was even further outraged; an investigative censor and Nanjing secretary of scrutiny, both of whom had the duty to remonstrate, jointly submitted a memorial calling for the treacherous to be removed from power and able advisors to be recalled. Liu Jin countered with a falsified edict ordering the arrest of the two officials, and thus it was that guards from the Embroidered Uniform Guard were dispatched to detain them and bring them in a cart to the capital, where they would be imprisoned and beaten.[52]

In view of these stunning developments, Wang Yangming was moved to take action by "serving the sovereign with the Way" and hence, in his view, speaking truth to power. In a memorial submitted on December 6, 1506, having duly noted that he was, in his capacity as a secretary at the Ministry of War, speaking out of line and therefore placing his life at risk, he called upon the emperor to rescind these orders and promote a climate of trust and confidence. Drawing upon the metaphor of bodily unity, he pointed out that officials are to the emperor as ears, eyes, hands, and feet are to the head. Should these be obstructed in any way, the head will surely suffer as a result. It had been these officials' duty to speak forthrightly. If their advice has any merit, he explained, it should be heeded; if not, it can be quietly disregarded. In this way, channels for communicating loyal advice will remain open, and matters of utmost urgency to the country will come to the emperor's attention. But should officials come to fear suffering the same consequences as those men of integrity who had acted solely out of devotion to their country and sovereign, the consequences would be dire. When the sovereign is benevolent, officials are righteous; he should therefore demonstrate his impartial and selfless benevolence, as well as a courageous willingness to rectify mistakes by rescinding the orders. Then the sagely virtue of the sovereign, Wang concluded, will be manifest near and far, the people greatly pleased, and the realm at peace.[53]

This clearly brave political act did indeed place Wang's life at risk, for although the tone of the memorial shows that he was confident in the strength of his argument, the advice fell on deaf ears, only incurring the enmity of Liu Jin, who ordered the Embroidered Uniform Guard to detain him as well. He subsequently suffered as many as forty lashings in front of a gate to the imperial palace, imprisonment for about a month, and then exiled to a remote postal station in southwest China.[54] Thus it was that Wang Yangming got a true taste of the power of Ming despotism. According to Yu Yingshi, having likely

---

52   Tan, *Quo que*, 46:2876–77.

53   *WYMQJ*, vol. 1, 9:291–92.

54   *NP*, 13:1227.

had his clothing removed and lost consciousness for a time, Wang underwent this extremely painful and humiliating experience—a punishment for officials that was largely a Ming invention—which was surely so psychologically traumatic that it played a direct role in the liberating insights he had while in exile.[55]

Yet even in the immediate aftermath, while imprisoned, Wang found some measure of comfort in being crowded into a cell with other scholar-officials who had suffered a fate similar to his and discussing the Way with them; as well, poems composed while in prison and shortly after being released express his unwavering determination—"my mind is even more immovable than a boulder."[56] This is a stance he would have no choice but to take till the very end of the emperor's reign, for his initial conviction—that the events of 1506 were the outcome of a potentially sagely but youthful ruler misled by wicked eunuchs—turned out to be naïve idealism. As a matter of fact, in early 1507, at the very moment Wang Yangming was being blacklisted as part of a traitorous political faction in an edict promulgated by Liu Jin, as well as being pursued by Liu's agents while en route to his hometown, the Zhengde emperor was having his Leopard Quarters constructed in the northwest corner of the capital.[57] At this secondary palace, where he would reside for much of his reign, he could escape the stifling routines at the imperial palace expected of him by the regular civil service administration. Instead, he surrounded himself with eunuchs and border commanders who were more than willing to provide their sovereign with the kinds of entertaining diversions he preferred. As for Wang, to evade Liu's assassins, he staged a suicide by throwing some of his clothing into the Qiantang River, after which he traveled around Mount Wuyi 武夷山 in Fujian, apparently on the cusp of renouncing the world. But when a Daoist monk suggested to him that failure to proceed to his assignment—in actuality, his exile—might place his family at risk, he departed for this most humble of official posts, noting in a poem that "hardship and ease have never impeded my mind, how do they differ from clouds passing across the sky?"[58]

Longchang Postal Station 龍場驛, to which he was assigned, was located in Guizhou Province, about forty kilometers to the northwest of Guiyang 貴陽, the province's capital, in a remote mountainous backwater with a damp tropi-

---

55   Yu Yingshi 余英時, *Song Ming lixue yu zhengzhi wenhua* 宋明理學與政治文化 [The Learning of Principle and Political Culture during the Song and Ming Dynasties] (Taipei: Yunnong wenhua, 2004), 263.

56   *WYMQJ*, vol. 1, 19:674.

57   *MSLWZSL*, Zhengde 1507/3/28 正德二年三月辛未 entry.

58   *NP*, 33:1227–28.

cal environment and a number of non-Chinese native ethnic groups living in comparatively undeveloped conditions.[59] It is hard to imagine an assignment that would be viewed with more disdain by Ming scholar-officials. Nevertheless, the two years Wang spent here, after traveling nearly fifteen hundred kilometers west and arriving in the spring of 1508, signaled a turning point in his life. Here, under such challenging circumstances, he experienced what Yu Yingshi calls "the most renowned, one-time sudden enlightenment" in the history of Confucian learning; as a result, he also began to teach a number of doctrines that would remain fundamental to his philosophy for the rest of his life, doctrines that were significant challenges to prevailing orthodoxy and which therefore drew much scrutiny.[60]

Upon arriving, Wang Yangming not only found that he lacked a place to stay and was surrounded mostly by natives, with whom he could not communicate, but he also faced the possibility that Liu Jin's agents might yet kill him. Four years later, he would repeatedly explain to colleagues that he looked upon these challenges as material for steeling his resolve and tempering his character, and sublimated them into spiritual insight and further refinement of his philosophical ideas.[61] With the help of a few Han Chinese living in the area that could communicate with the natives, and no doubt his decidedly positive attitude and friendly approach towards them, he soon overcame their suspicion of outsiders and obtained assistance in building a simple thatched hut. It was here at first, and later in a nearby mountain grotto, that Wang Yangming began to engage in a form of meditation, hoping to overcome his fear for his life and achieve a measure of calm and clarity in order to accept whatever fate was in store for him. At some point, Wang awakened one night to an epiphany that left him convinced he had obtained the insight necessary to carry on without fear and even to rectify the troubles of his time.[62] This is what is referred to in the Wang Yangming literature as the "Longchang enlightenment," although the precise content and broader significance of it have been much discussed and debated.

At the very least, this experience influenced how Wang conceived of the sources of moral authority and the basis for practical action. It also provided a different interpretation of the much-debated meaning of certain key terms used in classical texts and Cheng-Zhu commentaries that were a central component of the examination system. His unpleasant encounters with Ming

59   Dong, *Wang Yangming de shenghuo shijie*, 27.

60   Yu, *Song Ming lixue*, 277.

61   Cf. *WYMQJ*, vol. 1, 4:154.

62   *NP*, 33:1228.

politics and disenchantment with the status-oriented pursuits of the educated elites had led him to believe that moral regeneration was essential. Very much in line with tradition, he placed the onus of achieving this goal on pedagogy, which in its present state was in dire need of change. Wang had come to believe that the call to and practice of virtue, as the lifeblood of a tradition going back to Confucius and to the even more distant sagely rulers, had been drained away by trifling scholasticism, superficial dogmatism, or other meaningless endeavors, whereby the pursuit of knowledge had become tied to power and cultural capital. In light of this, he drew attention to the poignant reality that individuals are fundamentally self-sufficient, autonomous moral agents for whom principles are given by nature, as well as highlighting the need to demonstrate this truth by taking action, action implicit in the very process by which knowledge is constituted in the moral subject.[63] While Chen Lai insists that Wang Yangming's statement at this time that "mind-heart is principle (*xin ji li* 心即理)" is the fundamental conclusion of the Longchang enlightenment,"[64] Qian Ming believes that it was largely about redefining the meaning of "investigating things (*ge wu* 格物) and exhausting principle."[65] As for this latter point, Wang had indeed come to believe that the imperial examination and standard pedagogy focused excessively on the commentary for this terminology in the *Great Learning* supplied by the awe-inspiring Song Dynasty philosopher Zhu Xi, leading thus to such an emphasis on broadly learned inquiry as to obscure the fundamental truth that the moral subject is independently and naturally knowing. And without that reality, the call to action had also been lost. For this reason, "investigating things" should rather be interpreted as rectifying matters based on principles that grow directly out of introspection.

No doubt, as many have pointed out, Wang Yangming had now provided an encouraging philosophical justification for the staunchly independent stance he adopted vis-à-vis a eunuch-dominated Ming court, with all the consequences that entailed. Insofar as the self is by nature a moral compass, and a person follows the direction provided by that compass, a certain measure of transcendent steady-handedness and calm will accompany him through the most trying of times, and under any circumstances. This is a stance he would retain

---

63   I am providing a brief interpretation of the meaning of "my nature is self-sufficient (*wu xing zi zu* 吾性自足)," as the *Chronological Biography* describes Wang Yangming's insight at this time, as well as his early teaching during the subsequent period of time spent in Guizhou, that "mind is principle (*xin ji li* 心即理)" and that there is "unity of knowledge and action (*zhi xing he yi* 知行合一)." See *NP*, 33:1227–28.

64   Chen, *You wu zhi jing*, 24.

65   Qian, *Yangming xue de xingcheng yu fazhan*, 154.

throughout the rest of his life, including during the period of time he spent in "exile," where he maintained such a positive outlook and proactive approach.

At one point, the most powerful official in the region, Grand Coordinator and Censor-in-Chief Wang Zhi 王質, perhaps to curry favor with the eunuch-dominated Ming court, dispatched an underling to harass and further defame the demoted Wang Yangming; however, the local natives, now on friendly terms with Wang, assaulted the man. Assistance Surveillance Commissioner Mao Ke 毛科, friend to Wang Yangming and a native of Yuyao County, dispatched a letter in which he strongly urged him to apologize in person to Wang Zhi, explaining why it would be in his best interest to do so and warning of the dangers should he refuse. Unapologetic and unyielding, Wang cleverly replied that the humiliated underling was not doing the bidding of Wang Zhi. He also observed that, because he had not instructed the natives to defend him, there was nothing to apologize for. More generally, redefining the meaning of calamity and fortune for his friend, Wang stated:

> The gentleman views loyalty and trustworthiness as in his best interest, and ritual etiquette and righteousness as a great fortune; should these fail to be upheld, even should your salary be ten thousand *zhong* 鍾, and your title of nobility as prestigious as that of a marquis or prince, the gentleman will conclude these are calamities and harmful. But as for where loyalty, trustworthiness, etiquette, and righteousness direct him, even should his heart be sliced open or head smashed, the gentleman sees it as in his best interest and acts upon it, taking this as a great fortune.[66]

He might as well have been sending a memorial directly to the Ming court.

Over the course of 1508, having befriended enough locals, Wang got their help in building a crude academy consisting of simple wooden structures so that he could teach his evolving ideas and insights. This attracted the attention of not only scholars in the region, many of whom ventured there to hear what he had to say, but also provincial authorities stationed in Guiyang. In 1509, at the repeated request of Assistant Education Intendant Xi Shu 席書 (1461–1527), Wang Yangming traveled to that provincial seat, where he spent a period of time lecturing at and writing up programs of study at the recently renovated Wenming Academy 文明書院. Since this was the only academy in the provincial capital, Wenming thus had the honor of becoming the first place where Wang Yangming taught his "unity of knowledge and action."[67]

---

66   *WYMQJ*, vol. 1, 21:801–802.
67   *NP*, 33:1228–29.

Tu Weiming explains that the context for Wang's proposing this doctrine was his dissatisfaction with the way students placed success in the examinations—and therefore political success—over moral self-transformation. Grasping this moral code was indeed demanded of them by the classical texts and their commentaries, but students would merely memorize it mindlessly, reciting and writing about it by rote. Learning had lost its meaning as pedagogy became about the utilitarian pursuit of status. Indeed, moral knowledge had become "all talk" and "no action," bookish and scholastic, divorced from the most fundamental of ethical concerns: How is one to act? The fact that scholars discuss matters of morality all day and never act shows they don't grasp the import of what they have learned.[68] Thus, this doctrine was to serve as medicine for a disease. As Tu explains, to know is "to manifest what one has truly understood in concrete action."[69] In other words, to borrow from Antonio Cua, genuine moral knowledge includes not only recognition of a duty but also actuating import as a guide to moral conduct.[70] But while the sage, "who acts spontaneously according to his moral convictions,"[71] easily follows this transition from knowing to acting, others of lesser capacity must make a commitment to continually engage the self-transcending moral capacity of the mind and the nascent moral sense it provides in any setting.

Wang Yangming's effort to construct a modest academy near the postal station, and his more extensive work at Wenming Academy—where perhaps upwards of two hundred students may have been brought by provincial officials or come of their own accord to seek his instruction—belong more properly to his political life, as broadly defined. It was through these actions that he was pressing forward with his plan to rectify the many problems he saw about him and reinvigorate the ethos of the literati by initiating an educational reform movement. At least since 1505, he had been not only defining the physical location for this movement as schools and academies or other informal settings, but also defining the spheres for social action as those pertaining to "the Way of the teacher and friend."[72] In other words, he had come to believe that the place to make a difference might lie outside the halls of power, in a local setting, where enlightened instructors of the Confucian Way had meaningful

---

68   Wang, *Instructions for Practical Living*, 11.

69   Tu, *Neo-Confucian Thought in Action*, 151.

70   Antonia S. Cua, *Unity of Knowledge and Action: A Study in Wang Yang-ming's Moral Psychology* (Honolulu: University of Hawaii Press, 1982), 15.

71   Ching, *To Acquire Wisdom*, 68.

72   The *Chronological Biography* mentions this under the 1505 entry (*NP*, 33:1226), and Wang Yangming would highlight its importance in the years to come.

personal contact with students, and friends could encourage each other in their pursuit of sageliness.

Wang Yangming's experience with natives in the area only threw into sharper relief the deficits of character among Han Chinese that had troubled him for so long, forcing him to further redefine the nature of vulgar and refined, uncultured and cultured. True enough, he was well aware that his colleagues had not expected he would be able to bear living in this area, among uncivilized and illiterate natives who lived in primitive conditions and knew little of the ways of the Chinese, including the hallowed traditions of ceremony and etiquette, and the revered laws and institutions handed down from ancient times. And yet, in a record commemorating the construction of one of the buildings that would become part of the Longgang complex, Wang notes that even with all this refinement on display, so many Chinese remain two-faced, devious, and vicious, among other vices that stand in sharp contrast to that natives' simple candidness and honesty. To be sure, these natives are a bit superstitious, have minimal etiquette, and are too unreserved in their expression of sentiment, but like unhewn jade or wood of good quality, with the proper effort they might be shaped into refined and civilized people.[73] Although Wang denied at this time that he was up to the task of influencing the natives in this way, he certainly provided a prospectus for his actions when he was ordered to southwest China for far different reasons later in life.

During the period from 1510 to 1515, Wang Yangming would steadily rise through a series of relatively minor offices that required little work. He thus spent much of his time developing his philosophy and promoting his ideas in various pedagogical venues, thereby accruing a growing following of students and interested visitors and correspondents.[74] Indeed, with only a few notable exceptions after 1506, when he submitted a memorial implicitly indicting Liu Jin, until 1515, when he twice attempted to take leave of office on grounds of illness, we have no memorials to the court or official communications to subordinates that might give us a glimpse of his work in this succession of posts.

The one exception is his period of service as a magistrate of Luling County 盧陵縣 in Jiangxi Province, a post to which he was appointed in 1509.[75] After arriving on March 18, 1510, Wang Yangming would spend about seven months shouldering the typical responsibilities of a magistrate, including matters of local law and order, taxation, managing yamen personnel, public works, and education. However, his proclamations to the people and communications to

---

73   *WYMQJ*, vol. 1, 23:890–91.

74   Dong, *Wang Yangming de shenghuo shijie*, 47.

75   *WYMQJ*, vol. 2, 28:1027.

provincial authorities reveal that he was troubled by a few things. For one, de-spite having produced great literary traditions indicative of a most civilized population, the peoples of Luling were exceedingly litigious, as evidenced by the excessive number of lawsuits that had piled up at the magistrate's ya-men.[76] On the other hand, Wang was particularly disturbed when about one thousand county residents came crowding into his yamen voicing their anger over onerous levies on local products that Luling didn't even produce. These levies were exacted by a grand defender, a powerful eunuch agent of the Ming court specifically dispatched for this purpose (and, on other occasions, to over-see military operations). Also, yamen underlings were taking advantage of their authority to engage in extortion.

To rein in yamen functionaries abusing their power, Wang Yangming simply issued proclamations calling upon locals to bring them to his attention, a mea-sure that was likely of limited impact given the temporary nature of his ap-pointment.[77] Managing provincial authorities who were pressing him to meet the grand defender's demands was harder, but the way he did so would become a pattern in his political life. He decided he would meet legitimate demands of the masses as much as he could: always a minimalist in matters of taxation, he promised to take up the issue and rectify it, so the crowd gradually dispersed. He would convincingly plead for relief for the people by enumerating to the court in the most vivid terms their multiple hardships, including the heavy tax burden. He would mention the potential for widespread flight and banditry. Finally, he would take the blame for mishandling the whole matter and failing to meet the superior's demands: "Cashier and return me to the fields, as a warn-ing to those who don't perform their duties well."[78]

The compilers of Wang Yangming's *Chronological Biography* characterized his approach to managing the population as such: "He did not rely on intimida-tion and punishment but rather established as his fundamental principle in-fluencing people's minds and hearts with positive and sensible guidance."[79] To do so, he turned to those in the community who were recognized local author-ity figures and therefore held more personal and direct influence over people in the villages and towns under his jurisdiction. In fact, he was able to quickly clear out the accumulated litigation by reviewing the cases and turning much of the work of mediation over to village officials (tithing captains) and respect-ed elders. He also had them regularly admonish the people of their respective

76   Ibid., 28:1031.
77   Ibid., 28:1028.
78   Ibid., 28:1032.
79   *NP*, 33:1230.

locales—in public—for frivolity, wiliness, and allowing their anger to get the better of them, even at risk of bringing destruction upon their families. These respected villagers would further exhort them to abide by the virtues of forbearance and tolerance.[80] The idea here was to give priority to "explanation and instruction" from persons of authority who understood and could guide people towards their own better judgment, as opposed to relying on formal institutions and resorting to punitive measures. In this way, harmony in the community might be built from the ground up, by appealing to people's natural goodness.

Despite this general approach, Wang did at one point limit all complaints to matters of life and death only, even limiting those to two lines. He occasionally sighed at how difficult it was to instruct people and eventually announced that he would no longer hear cases, because any matters of importance should come to him only through his own inquiries or via respected elders. He states in one document that "it is not the case that I don't have severe punishments with which to penalize you for your depravity, but my days of governing here are short, you don't yet trust me, and my benevolence has not yet touched you; thus, although it is the norm, in my heart I yet feel uncomfortable with governing you uniformly in accordance with the law."[81] Even at this early stage, the tension between the apparent simple goodness innate to all people and the harsher social reality around him was causing some measure of frustration for the magistrate.

In the fall of 1510, after serving for seven months in Luling, Wang Yangming returned to Beijing for reassignment, and towards the end of the year was appointed secretary in the Sichuan Bureau of the Nanjing Ministry of Justice. But with some assistance from friends in the capital, in early 1511 he was transferred back to Beijing in the post of secretary in the Bureau of Honors at the Ministry of Personnel, one of four responsible for processing enfeoffments, honorific titles, and the inheritance of official status. After serving as a metropolitan examiner, that summer he received a promotion at the ministry, to the position of vice director of the Bureau of Appointments, one of four that managed appointments, rankings, promotions, demotions, and transfers. His last appointment in Beijing came in the spring of 1512, when he was promoted to director of the Bureau of Evaluations at the same ministry, where personnel records were maintained pending promotion, demotion, retention, or dismissal.[82]

---

80   Ibid.

81   *WYMQJ*, vol. 2, 28:1028.

82   *NP*, 33:1231–32. Descriptions of responsibilities for these posts come from Hucker, *Dictionary of Official Titles in Imperial China*.

In December, after nine months at the bureau, Wang was promoted to vice minister of the Nanjing Court of the Imperial Stud, an office that would take him once again outside the capital. This was a second-tier agency responsible for executing policies of the Ministry of War for managing state horse pasturages and related military equipment, and in actual fact it required his presence just northwest of the southern capital (Nanjing), in Chuzhou 滁州. He departed Beijing late in 1512 and, after spending a period of time in his home province of Zhejiang, he proceeded to Chuzhou, arriving there on November 18, 1513.

The offices Wang held during these two years were not particularly significant, but in terms of his evolving political thought, the ideas he was talking over during this time were indeed of great import. His thoughts about "what was wrong with the world, what the causes of this mess were, and who can do what to clean it up"[83] can be pieced together from letters he wrote during this time as well as records of his conversations with his first student, Xu Ai 徐愛 (1488–1518). Xu had also been assigned to a new post in 1512, and because they were both Yuyao men, they decided to travel together down the Grand Canal on their way home for a visit. It was on that occasion, going into the spring of 1513, that Xu held philosophical conversations with his teacher, colleague, and friend. These would later become the first set in the first volume of the *Instructions for Practical Living*.[84]

Although his theories applied across the board to all people, the object of Wang's teachings at this time was primarily the literati class and thus, by extension, those whose duty it was to govern the rest. In terms of what was wrong with the world, he explained, the most pressing problem was nearly everyone's failure to perceive and act upon their natural moral goodness. Everyone has a mind (*xin* 心), and that is what governs the body. This mind also contains a nature (*xing* 性) bestowed by Heaven, from which all goodness originates, which is what Mencius was referring to when he stated that human nature is

---

83   Thomas Metzger, *A Cloud Across the Pacific: Essays on the Clash between Chinese and Western Political Theories Today* (Hong Kong: The Chinese University Press, 2005), 4. That is how he sums up what is at the heart of a political theory.

84   The conversations were conveyed to Wang's student Xue Kan 薛侃 (1486–1545), who then compiled them together with other records and printed them as the first volume of the *Instructions for Practical Living* in 1518. For a discussion of the history of this text, see Okada, *Ō Yōmei taiden*, 3:12; Wing-tsit Chan 陳榮捷, *Wang Yangming chuan xi lu xiang zhu ji ping* 王陽明傳習錄詳註集評 [Wang Yangming's Instructions for Practical Living with Detailed Annotations and Compiled Commentary] (Taipei: Taiwan xuesheng shuju, 1983), 7.

good.[85] Everyone is capable of perceiving this goodness as the fundamental
quality of awareness. That is because, as conditions require, Heavenly principles emerge from nature within the mind-heart, thereby defining a natural
course of action. "The mind is naturally able to know what is moral," Wang
says, "because moral knowing is the essence of mind (*zhi shi xin zhi benti* 知是
心之本體)."[86] For example, when a son is with his father, insofar as his "mind
is pure in Heavenly principle (*chun hu tianli zhi xin* 純乎天理之心)," his "mind
of sincere filiality (*cheng xiao de xin* 誠孝的心)" will arise, and he will therefore know how to appropriately serve his father.[87] That is why knowledge and
action are originally unified, and it isn't necessary to study prescriptions for
conduct in advance. Wang also refers to this arising of the moral mind as the
manifestation in awareness of Heavenly principle (*li zhi fa jian* 理之發見).[88]
He describes how similar moral knowledge arises in the context of other intersubjective relations, such as between ruler and minister, between friends, or
between all members of humanity. The moral principles appropriate to each of
these relations are virtues, and he identifies humaneness and compassion as
the most fundamental.[89] Humaneness and compassion define the fundamental quality of moral knowing as well as what it means to be human, and to love
these virtues and desire to make them more completely a part of conscious life
is the natural moral endowment of human beings.[90] People are by nature good
and humane, filial to their parents, loyal to their sovereign, and conscientious
with their friends, and appropriate social action necessarily flows from that
reality.

　　However, the problem is that most people are unaware or only partly aware
of the innate moral goodness of human nature, and therefore fail either to perceive it or act on it. That is because the natural operation of the mind has been
obscured by self-centered desires, and people have therefore permitted themselves to find satisfaction in things other than what they should. Unaware that
what they really seek is virtue, people instead hanker after recognition, status,
and wealth. On several occasions, Wang states that people are literally drown-

---

85　*WYMQJ*, vol. 1, 4:155. The translation here is from Julia Ching, *The Philosophical Letters of*
　　Wang Yang-ming (Columbia, SC: University of South Carolina Press, 1973), 29–30. Some-
　　times *xin* is translated as 'mind-heart' so as to suggest both the cognitive and affective
　　dimensions of the self that the character indicates.

86　*WYMQJ*, vol. 1, 1:6.

87　Ibid., 1:2.

88　Ibid., 1:6–7.

89　For humaneness (*ren* 仁), see *WYMQJ*, vol. 1, 21:811; for compassion (*ceyin* 惻隱), see 1:6.

90　Ibid., 4:160.

ing in unhealthy conventions and customs.[91] Their minds are like polluted water, whose natural clarity must be restored.[92] More specifically regarding the
literati, he bemoans their hair-splitting scholasticism, emphasis on irrelevant
knowledge, and how they have allowed themselves to be deterred by the pursuit of glory and fame.[93] Unlike the ancients, who would never have followed
someone that was morally corrupt, people today won't follow someone who is
morally correct. They find it easier to be corrupt then risk the ridicule, jealousy,
and envy that being righteous always seems to incur. More generally, he notes
in a dire assessment, "The world today is morally degenerate. It does not differ
from a sick man approaching death."[94]

The causes of this mess are directly tied to what can be done to clean it up.
Only those who understand human nature and who therefore are virtuous and
wise can provide the necessary leadership and correctly teach the Way to others. But that is no easy task: "The nature of true learning has not been made
clear for even so much as a day," he told one colleague, and "those with determination are few."[95] We have already seen how, in the model essays for the
provincial examination in Shandong, Wang subscribed to the more general
Neo-Confucian proposition that this learning had been handed down through
a long line of sages going back to the sage-kings of antiquity. He repeated that
theme in a preface he composed for his friend Zhan Ganquan when Zhan was
preparing to depart the capital: Mencius, he noted, was the last to understand
this thread in ancient times, and it was only 2,000 years later that Zhou Dunyi
and the Cheng brothers recovered it.[96] As for conditions in his time, he explained to another friend, "Few are those who realize their potential for virtue
and capitalize on their abilities."[97]

But these few are the key to the restoration of a better world, of the kind that
once existed in the golden age. In a letter to his colleague Chu Chaixu 儲柴墟,
Wang states, "Nothing under Heaven is greater than the Way, and nothing more
honored than virtue." The most essential virtue is humanity, which is what
makes a person a person as well as what should be taught to others. Friends
should encourage each other to pursue the virtue of humanity and teachers
should discuss it with their disciples. Considerations of status (nobility and

---

91   Ibid.
92   Ibid., 7:233.
93   Ibid., 7:230–31.
94   Ibid., 21:815. For this translation, see Ching, *Philosophical Letters*, 823.
95   Ibid., 4:160.
96   Ibid., 7:230.
97   Ibid., 4:158.

lowliness), rank, and age (seniority) are of secondary importance. Wang notes that the sage Yi Yin 伊尹 once said, "Heaven, in giving life to the people, causes those who are first enlightened to enlighten those who are later enlightened. . . . I am [one of] the first enlightened of Heaven's people. If I do not awaken others, who will do so?" And that, for Wang Yangming, is the same pressing question everyone must ask today. His answer was:

> My idea is that when one already has a little portion of wisdom, one ought to wish at once to share this little portion of wisdom with others, and when one already has a little bit of enlightenment, one ought to wish at once to share this little bit of enlightenment with others. The more people there are who possess a little wisdom and a little enlightenment, the easier it will be to have them share with one another their wisdom and enlightenment. And then, after this, we might look forward to great wisdom and great enlightenment.[98]

Wang humbly denied that he was one of those with the ability to spread around wisdom, despite the unspoken suggestion that he was doing just that. But regardless of what he really thought about his own achievements, the broader point here is that the standard for leadership is established by a transcendent order and by those awakened to it. Moral exemplars who understand the goodness of which all are capable by virtue of their natural endowment must provide the leadership necessary to get them to see just what that endowment is. By so doing, they are bringing a social world corrupted by self-centered desires in line with one that is in accord with human nature. That is why Wang Yangming will consistently solicit the input and assistance of those he deemed virtuous, including respected, prominent members of communities who had established cooperative relations with local officials.

After serving as vice minister of the Nanjing Court of the Imperial Stud, Wang Yangming was then promoted to the position of chief minister of the Nanjing Court of State Ceremonial, an agency supervised by the Ministry of Rites and charged with conducting such important ceremonies as receiving foreign embassies and state funerals.[99] Although these last two assignments were more of the nature of sinecures, they were nevertheless prestigious posts, being as they were two of the eminent eighteen lesser and greater ministers (*qing* 卿) with a middle-upper level rank of four. They might well be viewed as

---

98   Ibid., 21:8111–13. For the translation of these quotations, see Ching, *Philosophical Letters*, 21–22. Yi Yin was a (possibly legendary) minister during the early Shang Dynasty.

99   *NP*, 33:1235–36.

stepping stones to more significant assignments, which is indeed what was to
come. After arriving on May 18, 1514, Wang Yangming spent nearly two and a
half years in Nanjing, before receiving a communication from the Ministry of
Personnel elevating him to a far more complex assignment—that of grand coordinator of Southern Gan.

Aside from memorials related to the details of taking up this assignment,
the only primary record we have pertaining to official matters dating to his
time in Nanjing is a memorial Wang penned in 1515. It is significant because
Wang proffers advice to the Zhengde emperor regarding a sovereign's duties,
and in doing so reveals his own thinking about the role of the monarchy. He
composed it when the emperor decided to send a large embassy led by his eunuch directors to the "Western lands" for the purpose of bringing back a "living
Buddha" said to have the ability to know a person's past incarnations.[100] Skilled
in the arts of persuasion, Wang affirms the emperor's laudable intentions,
while nevertheless noting that what he seeks from the teachings of the Buddha
can be found in a far superior form, and one uniquely suited to bringing peace
and order to China—the teaching of the sages. He draws the ruler's attention
to the fact that his opinion differs from all those remonstrating officials who
had already spoken up against the emperor engaging in such unorthodox pursuits:

> The humble opinion of your servitor is singularly different from this, but
> I am only concerned that the emperor's love for the Buddha is not being
> correctly interpreted. Should it indeed truly be the case that the emper-
> or's love for the Buddha is earnest and sincere, and not merely a case of
> loving appearances but rather genuinely desiring to seek out the truth,
> then the sageliness of Yao and Shun can be attained, and the vigor of the
> Three Dynasties can be recovered. How could this not be a great blessing
> to all under Heaven and a great happiness for the country? Your servitor
> wishes therefore to speak of the true meaning of love for the Buddha.[101]

Wang explained that in fact this showed the emperor's aspiration to become a
sage, while his wish to obtain the Buddha's teachings reflected sprouting wisdom. Reinterpreting this wish according to Mencian discourse, he suggested
these were "sprouts of goodness," and his "initial will to do what is good." But

---

100 Xia Xie 夏燮, *Wenbai duizhao quan yi Ming tong jian* 文白對照全譯明通鑒 [Compre-
     hensive Mirror of the Ming, bilingual classical to modern Chinese complete translation],
     ed. Shen Zhihua (Beijing: Gaige chubanshe, 1994), 46:419. Hereafter, *MTJ*.
101 Ibid., 9:293–96.

because Confucian advisors had failed to convey the teaching of the sage-kings Yao and Shun, the emperor felt compelled to seek elsewhere in order to interpret these aspirations. Fortunately, performing a comparison could demonstrate that the merit-worthy elements of the Buddha's teaching were conveyed in a superior way by China's ancient sages. So just what was the emperor seeking?

> You thought of the teachings of Buddhas far away in the western lands, believing that their way is able to cause people to be pure in heart and cut off desire; to fulfill their natures and destinies in order to transcend the rounds of birth and death; to be able, in friendliness and compassion, to love all [suffering] beings; to save and set across [the ocean of suffering] all beings; to remove those causal mental afflictions [leading to the fruit] of suffering; and thereby to [assist them] in mounting happiness.[102]

Given the extreme hardship caused by relentless natural disasters, flourishing banditry, and growing poverty, Wang assured the emperor that his desire to relieve his subjects' suffering was indeed correct, but that should he really expect to achieve these ends, he must first embrace the way of the sages of China and reject the way of barbarian sages residing in distant lands.

Nevertheless, Wang also affirmed that the way of the Buddha might be suited to barbarians because, even if the methods are inferior, the aims are roughly similar: "As for the Buddhas, these are the sages of the barbarians; as for the sages, these are the Buddhas of the Middle Country. In principle, for outsiders, the Buddha's teachings can be employed for the purpose of transforming and guiding the ignorant and obstinate. But in our country, it is correct to employ the way of the sages in order to participate in the natural cultivation and completion of all things."[103] He also affirmed Sakyamuni's compassion and indifference to his own welfare when it came to saving others from danger and hardship. That is why the Gautama Buddha's great compassion reached all beings. However, he was only able to achieve a modicum of success by practicing asceticism in the mountains and traveling around. China's great sages had, on the other hand, achieved a just order quite effortlessly. By merely sitting upright within their palaces, with arms folded and doing nothing, everything under Heaven found its rightful place: the nine clans were harmonious, the ten thousand states mutually cooperative, the people at peace. He added:

---

102   *WYMQJ*, vol. 1, 9:294.
103   Ibid., 9:295.

The Buddha is able to employ expedient means when speaking of the Dharma, to awaken the masses from ignorance, to forbid people from drinking, to stop people from killing, and to release them from anger. His penetrating divinity and wondrous functioning can also truly be called great. Yet, on the other hand, he must teach [the people] face to face, constantly pouring instructions and advice into their ears. Only then does he succeed. But as for Yao and Shun, their brilliance covers all under Heaven, reaching above and below. As for the operation of their highest sincerity, [they] are naturally trusted without speaking a word, bring about change without moving, and complete [all things] effortlessly.[104]

With much hyperbole, this is how Wang Yangming explained the superiority of the Confucian Way to the emperor. He also insisted that throughout the land it is possible to locate great scholars who are able to transmit this way to their ruler, and that the emperor should begin by seeking among his high officials. By so doing, the emperor would indeed find the correct interpretation of his sincere intention to love the Buddha, as well as learn about the superior methods for ruling the country passed down by the sage-rulers of ancient times.

This memorial, however, was never submitted. Wang Yangming had already passed through a severe trial after submitting the one concerning Liu Jin, and he was likely choosing to be prudent, fearing his advice might be viewed as sarcastic and even mocking of an emperor that had never displayed anything other than disdain for stifling lectures or sitting upright with arms folded deep inside the Forbidden City. But the context for this piece does not compromise the fact that for Wang the goals of the Ming state were ultimately of a soteriological nature, to assist subjects in recovering a lost natural condition, something that would be greatly facilitated by having in place wise, learned men and a sagely sovereign modeling for the masses the goodness of human nature.

Now, in stating this, I am revising an interpretation of Wang Yangming that emphasizes his focus on the individual and on local social action. Frederick Mote, for example, states:

Beyond reaffirming Mencian altruism, however, and as a quietly understated adjunct to his political thought, Wang Yangming encouraged a reorientation of the political focus away from emperor, state, and government. He turned that focus to the people who led and who made up the small community. He turned away from the traditional leadership role of the high elite in central government offices to the local context of social

---

104   Ibid.

life in which elite and commoners shared in the responsibility for themselves and to one another. He had come to see this as the most hopeful
arena of Confucian social action.[105]

The philosophical corollary to this local turn would be Wang's emphasis on the
moral autonomy of the subject and the innate capacity of all, as bearers of a
Heavenly-mandated human nature and mind-heart, to become sages.

To be sure, Mote's analysis takes into account the record from Wang Yangming's entire political career, and the "reorientation" away from the central
state is most relevant to the policies Wang would pursue during the remainder
of it. Yet I believe this argument should not be overstated, for three reasons.
Firstly, if we look ahead in his career, it is clear that Wang would never have the
chance to serve the emperor directly as part of the Ming court, as he would
instead be commissioned to restore order in marginal lands or border zones. It
was therefore quite natural that, distant as he was from the capital, Wang had
to come up with local solutions to pressing social problems, although most of
these solutions did involve some degree of government management or oversight. Secondly, as David Nivison suggests, although Wang rejected the idea
that moral knowledge could be mastered in advance through learned study,
and rather emphasized a kind of innate moral sense naturally responsive to
any situation, he insisted that "in a particular problem-situation, any morally
perfected person would 'hear' the voice of inner knowing in essentially the
same way" as other morally upright people.[106] This analysis helps us to understand why, when assigned to manage populations that he deemed unwilling or
incapable of hearing this voice, Wang Yangming might feel justified in using
military force to exterminate them or in implementing civilizing measures
that might enable them to do so. That is, where necessary, the state could legitimately speak for this voice. Thirdly, his thinking about the political was always firmly grounded in the Way of the sages and the broader aims outlined in
the Shandong examination essays. In the final analysis, his understanding of
human nature and individual identity always remained closely tied to sagely
rule and government by men of virtue, as well as to the ethnic consciousness
of the community of which he was a part.[107] It would be no exaggeration to say

105   Mote, *Imperial China: 900–1800*, 682.
106   David Nivison, "The Philosophy of Wang Yangming," in *The Ways of Confucianism: Investigations in Chinese Philosophy*, ed. Brian W. Van Norden (Chicago: Open Court, 1996), 224–
25.
107   The sage-king ideal is one of the major issues William Theodore de Bary addresses in his
exploration of the problems with the Confucian tradition. See his *The Trouble with Confucianism* (Cambridge, MA: Harvard University Press, 1991), 1–3.

that the state remained for him in a very powerful sense the carrier or vehicle of the Way. This is at least one way we can make sense of the determination with which he so effectively wielded the power of the state to restore order in the areas he was assigned to govern.

It was during the next year, in 1516, that Wang Yangming received the commission of grand coordinator of Southern Gan, his first truly significant appointment, at least as measured by his responsibilities and the documentary output. We have no other primary records for the work Wang Yangming did in the many offices he held from 1511 to 1516, but much more in the way of letters, poems, and records of conversations from these years, which is why so much has been written about his evolving teaching during this period of time. For while at or between these leisurely assignments—first in Beijing, then in his home province of Zhejiang, followed by Chuzhou, and lastly Nanjing—he was largely preoccupied with holding sessions of philosophical inquiry and carrying on correspondence with a growing circle of scholar friends, colleagues, and students committed to, or curious about, his views on the learning of the sages and on leading a life of virtue in service to the Way. The relevance of some of these teachings to his first major assignment, as well as what he would do in this capacity, are the topics of the next chapter.

CHAPTER 2

Pacifying Southern Gan

Wang Yangming, it was said, "should receive sacrifices for a hundred generations."[1] These words, commemorating the renovation of a Heping County (Guangdong) memorial hall built in Wang's honor, were recorded by Qing scholar Shao Tingcai (1648–1711). Shao believed that among those four Ming scholars receiving sacrifices together with Confucius in the Confucian temple-schools, it was the "Marquis of Xinjian Master Wang Wencheng who truly brought to completion the accomplishments of the many scholars following after Confucius and Mencius."[2] But for the purpose of this record, Shao could take this outstanding contribution to the Learning of the Way (*daoxue* 道學) for granted. What was important for this inscription was to celebrate Wang's achievements as an official, for this memorial hall was built in honor of his having pacified banditry and set in motion the measures necessary to establish a county seat at the center of a region long shaken by social disorder.

Summarizing his achievements, Shao explained that those occasions when "Master Wang resorted to the military instrument to suppress disturbances and restore law and order in the lands of the South are known as the pacification of Gan, the capture of [Prince Zhu Chen]hao, the campaigns in Si[en] and Tian[zhou], and the punitive expedition in Chopped Rattan [Gorge]."[3] Indeed, this concisely sums up Wang Yangming's career as an official during the last twelve years of his life. But for the purposes of this inscription, what mattered most to Shao was Wang's first series of (three) campaigns and the counties he established in the aftermath: Pinghe in Zhang[zhou Prefecture], Chongyi in [Shao]zhou Prefecture, and Heping in Hui[zhou] Prefecture."[4] Among these three, Shao believed Heping was the most important for reason of its location: in addition to being situated amidst four counties and at the juncture of three provinces, it was the largest in scale. So significant was the administrative change to the region that "although Master Wang receives sacrifices in Confucian temple-schools because of his contribution to the

---

1 Shao Tingcai 邵廷采, "Heping xian chongxiu Wang Wencheng gong ci bei ji 和平縣重修王文成公祠碑記 [Stele Record for the Renovation by Heping County of a Memorial Hall for Sir Wang Wencheng]," in *WYMQJ*, 40:1532.
2 Ibid.
3 Ibid.
4 Ibid. Chongyi County is, in actual fact, located in Nan'an Prefecture.

Learning of the Way, the people of Heping County sacrifice to Master Wang because of his meritorious deeds and the favor he showed."[5] Shao explained in brief the background behind this blessing:

> For over twenty years, ever since Chi Zhongrong occupied Hedong and Sanli, usurping the title of king and illegally appointing officials, Jiang[xi], Guang[dong], and Min [Fujian] had not been at peace. Master Wang quickly drew up his master strategy, detained Zhongrong in his military headquarters, and oversaw the march of armies from all directions, fighting with the beast and pulling up the weeds. [He established] boundaries and fields, [built] walls and moats, gathered those in flight, settling notable families, building schools, exercising restraint over fiscal and labor demands on the population, discarding levies and relaxing bans, causing [an area] accustomed to running about like wolves and rushing about like boars [on violent rampages] to change altogether into a highly cultured village.[6]

It was Wang's good will for the region that, according to Shao, moved the people of this once bandit-infested territory to erect a memorial hall and offer sacrifices to him in memory of his having "loved the people as if they were his own children."[7]

Shao's representation of Wang Yangming's efforts to elevate the customs of the people he was charged to govern echoes Wang's own understanding of what he was trying to do in South China. Today, his efforts might rather be viewed as a civilizing project, a result of his determination to impose order on a violent region of the country populated by Han Chinese and non-Han locals and migrants alike, among which were a number of people engaging in banditry. For him, the critical issue was what was required for "a territory of savage bandits to be transformed into a land of respectful good etiquette and ceremony, [Han] caps and gowns."[8] So when he deployed militias to quell endemic violence, and followed up with measures to maintain long-term security and improve local practices, his ultimate goal was to create a better life for the subjects he was appointed to govern, in accordance with his ideals.

---

5 Ibid.
6 Ibid.
7 Ibid.
8 *WYMQJ*, vol. 1, 10:352.

Wang Yangming had been given the commission, in October 1516, at the age of forty-four, of grand coordinator (*xun fu* 巡撫) of Southern Gan 南贛.[9] In Ming documents, although Southern Gan might occasionally refer to two prefectures in the southern part of Jiangxi Province—Nan'an 南安 and Ganzhou 贛州—it usually refers to the territory that fell under the jurisdiction of this grand coordinator. This included the bordering regions of Jiangxi, Fujian, Guangdong, and Huguang. The appointment was the result of his acquaintance with Minister of War Wang Qiong, who recommended that he be commissioned to handle the troubled region. Although they likely never met, having served for years in the capital in various capacities and now at this time as the powerful minister of war, Wang Qiong may have had some knowledge of Wang Yangming's reputation as an official and skill in the military arts.[10]

In the greater context of the development of Ming political institutions, Wang's appointment was the outcome of the first Ming emperor's decision to decentralize and separate powers at the provincial level so that he could centralize and concentrate power in his own hands.[11] The three provincial commissions—administrative, surveillance, and regional military—were responsible respectively for civil, judicial, and military affairs in each of China's

---

9   In addition, as was common practice by that time for grand coordinators and supreme commanders, he was also given the nominal concurrent appointment of left assistant censor-in-chief. For this practice, see Hucker, *Dictionary of Official Titles*, 546. According to Okada Takehiko's analysis in *Ō Yōmei taiden*, he was appointed left censor-in-chief (4:174).

10   In his "Record of Conduct," Wang Yangming's student Huang Wan states that the two were personally acquainted, and that Wang Qiong specifically recommended Wang based on his estimate of his ability (*WYMQJ*, vol. 1, 40:1534).

11   For a discussion of the institution of grand coordinator and supreme commander, see Fan Yuchun, "Ming dai dufu de zhiquan ji qi xingzhi 明代督府的治權即其性質 [The Administrative Authority and Character of the Office of the Supreme Commander during the Ming Dynasty]," 49–55; and Hucker, *Dictionary of Official Titles*, 75–76. The post of Southern Gan Grand Coordinator was first established in Hongzhi 6 (1494), although the exact jurisdiction changed over time. By 1513, the following prefectures and counties were included: Nan'an and Ganzhou Prefectures in Jiangxi; Tingzhou and Zhangzhou Prefectures in Fujian; Binzhou Subprefecture in Huguang; and, in Guangdong, Shaozhou Prefecture, Nanxiong Prefecture, the counties of Pingyuan, Chengxiang in Chaozhou Prefecture, and the counties of Heping, Longchuan, and Xingning in Huizhou. For the relevant sources and a discussion, see Jin Runcheng 靳潤成, *Ming chao zongdu xunfu xiaqu yanjiu* 明朝總督巡撫轄區研究 [Research on the Territorial Jurisdiction of Supreme Commanders and Grand Coordinators during the Ming Dynasty] (Tianjin: Tianjin guji chubanshe, 1996). It should be noted, however, that Heping County was established by Wang Yangming. .

thirteen provinces. But they did not have authority over one another. Thus, when pressing problems arose within provinces, a lack of clear chains of command invariably caused paralysis or permitted officials to elide responsibility. Serious armed disturbances were particularly troubling, for when these disturbances spread over more than one province, it became glaringly obvious that there were problems coordinating military campaigns that drew on the armies and provisions of each. To facilitate intra-provincial coordination, throughout the fifteenth century the court began to dispatch court dignitaries "to pacify and soothe (*anfu* 安撫)" and "tour and inspect (*xunshi* 巡視)." Over time, these "touring pacifiers (*xunfu* 巡撫)" began to appear as resident coordinators from the central government in the provinces as well as in special frontier zones and other strategic areas."[12] Eventually, some of these duty assignments became indefinite tenures, and those delegated high officials typically holding other substantive court titles would normally be given the concurrent title of censor-in-chief so as to increase their esteem and influence. As censors, they could impeach and had direct access to the throne.

Similarly, to address the problem of inter-provincial coordination in military affairs, at the same time the court also began to delegate supreme commanders (*zongdu* 總督), an office that evolved out of the grand coordinator system. They too were special-purpose representatives of the central government sent out to expedite the work of regular provincial authorities, including grand coordinators.[13]

As grand coordinator, Wang Yangming was one of the few having both intra- and inter-provincial authority. His orders, promptly circulated to subordinate officials in early 1517 when he arrived at his headquarters in Ganzhou, clearly stated the nature of his duties. The court recognized that outlaws had been roving at will in this region for years, and that one of the reasons was a lack of centralized authority. That is why he was specially delegated "as grand coordinator of Jiangxi's Nan'an and Ganzhou Prefectures, Fujian's Tingzhou and Zhangzhou Prefectures, Guangdong's Nanxiong, Shaozhou, Huizhou, and Chaozhou Prefectures, and Huguang's Binzhou Prefecture to pacify and soothe the soldiers and people, to construct walls and moats, and to put an end to treachery and corruption."[14] Wang was thus granted the authority to coordinate civilian and military provincial and local officials serving in nine prefectures spread over four bordering provinces where armed disturbances were common, state presence weak, and lines of authority confused. In this same communication,

---

12   Hucker, *Dictionary of Official Titles*, 75.

13   Ibid.

14   *WYMQJ*, vol. 1, 9:525.

he characterized conditions as he saw them, carefully noting for his subordinates that he understood the magnitude of the problems for which he would
hold them accountable: "The mountains and streams are steep and perilous.
The forests are vast and dense. The bandits hide in their midst and regularly
come out to plunder and maraud. When they are pursued in the east they flee
to the west. When they are captured in the south they flee to the north." As a
result, he noted, local security personnel and officials had largely ignored the
problem or shirked responsibility. They had failed to unite, capture, and attack
and therefore allowed the problem to fester.[15]

Although he had tried to decline the assignment,[16] a story recorded by his
followers concerning his demeanor just prior to his departure from Hangzhou,
Zhejiang, suggest he was not terribly disturbed by the prospect of leaving the
peaceful West Lake to confront what were by then a number of infamous bandit bosses with criminal networks spread throughout poorly governed territory. During a conversation between two of Wang's students, Wang Siyu 王思輿
and Ji Ben 季本 (1485–1563), Siyu stated, "During this journey Yangming will
serve meritoriously." When Ji Ben asked him how he could be so certain, Siyu
replied, "When I came across him he wasn't the least bit phased (*bu dong xin*
不動心)."[17] "Unperturbed" might be another translation for this term.

Indeed, Wang Siyu was invoking the Mencian concept of the unperturbed
mind in an effort to capture Wang's state of mind and connect it to his potential for success.[18] Likely, the compilers of Wang's *Chronological Biography*
added this incident to illustrate how their revered master was coming to exemplify a paradigm for sagehood. According to this paradigm, individuals who
embody virtue and understand human nature are the ones capable of moving
a society towards its ideal, normative state.[19] A corollary to this is the steady-
handedness and measured response that comes with such understanding. In
an effort to promote their master, throughout his campaigns and in the aftermath, Wang's followers would praise not only his success in battle but also how

---

15   Ibid.

16   Ibid., 9:297.

17   *NP*, 33:1238.

18   For "the unperturbed mind" see Mencius 2:A:2 in *A Source Book in Chinese Philosophy*,
        trans. and ed. Wing Tsit-chan (Princeton: Princeton University Press, 1963), 62.

19   Cf. Rodney L. Taylor, *The Religious Dimensions of Confucianism* (New York: State Univer-
        sity of New York Press, 1990), 43–47. He discusses the Neo-Confucian quest for sagehood,
        and notes that descriptions of it usually consist of personality traits, as opposed to the
        phenomenology of the "realized state of sagehood." He states, "It is not the state of sage-
        hood that seems to be of concern, but rather the life of the sage, and it is this life that is
        the telling comment upon realization of the goal." (46)

his behavior lived up to the image of sagehood that Wang was then articulating in his teachings. His indifference to his own personal wellbeing, his decisiveness, and his effectiveness in quelling disorder illustrated a rare ability to harmonize inner sageliness (possessing virtue) with outer kingliness (being commanding and governing). Wang Yangming was well aware of the difficulty of achieving both. Once, just before marching his troops into bandit lairs, he explained to his student Yang Shide 楊仕德, "While defeating the bandits in the mountains is simple, defeating the bandits of the mind is difficult—what is so great about my eradicating petty thieves?"[20]

Although the identity of these "thieves" is sometimes difficult to discern, the issue is not unimportant. The fact that Wang's victory memorials provide lists of literally hundreds of successfully defeated and occupied communities (village settlements) in southern Jiangxi, northern Guangdong, and southwestern Fujian clearly suggests that these were not mere outlaws. In fact, persistent use of the term "bandit" (zei 賊) was a rhetorical strategy aimed at covering up more complex social problems. Descriptions from official reports sent to the grand coordinator paint a picture of marginal lands with shifting populations of locals and migrants, Han Chinese and non-Han ethnic groups, all fighting over land and other resources. Huang Zhifan's analysis of southern Jiangxi illustrates a problem common to the entire region; here, increasing migration from middle Jiangxi, Fujian, and Guangdong to an area touted as being "spacious land with few people" only exacerbated conflict. In fact, for Huang, the accelerating violence was the result of population growth and economic integration. As more and more people moved into the highlands in search of resources to exploit and land to develop, they came into conflict with the existing, mostly registered populations of the developed lowlands.[21] A verse from a poem Wang inscribed on a cliff in Nan'an upon completing a campaign verifies this analysis for southern Jiangxi, while also showing his bias towards the settled populations: "Everywhere the fields in the mountains have been completely penetrated by She 畲; half the pitiable common people find themselves without a home."[22]

As the story unfolds, I will address the issues raised by Wang Yangming's use of ethnic labels like "She." In general, the type of ethnic discourse he would later routinely employ while dealing with non-Han ethnic groups in Guangxi is

---

20   NP, 33:1248. Not surprisingly, this letter is cited in the *Chronological Biography*.

21   Huang Zhifan 黃志繁, *"Zei" "min" zhi jian: 12–18 shiji Gan nan diyu shehui* " 賊" "民" 之間: 12–18 世紀贛南地域社會 [Between "Bandits" and "Commoners": Southern Gan Regional Society from the 12th to the 18th Centuries] (Beijing: San lian shudian, 2006), 108–110.

22   *WYMQJ*, vol. 1, 20:747.

notably absent from Wang's communications during this time. Rather, he more frequently resorted to the pejorative "bandits" and then determined which had to be eradicated and which could be resettled. He would frequently inform his subordinates that for "bandits who have long persisted in evil and remained unrepentant to the end," extermination is called for. But for "those innocents coerced into following" who might yet "have a change of heart and be receptive to the civilizing influence [of the state]," offers of amnesty and a policy of appeasement are acceptable.[23]

David Robinson, in his study of a rebellion and widespread banditry occurring just a few years prior, notes that "through an ever-shifting mix of physical coercion, education, moral suasion, negotiation, and co-option, it was held that even the most recalcitrant elements could be transformed into useful members of the wider community."[24] This is also an apt description of Wang Yangming's approach and repertoire of measures, although in the ensuing events physical coercion first entailed campaigns of eradication in order "to daily cut back and monthly whittle away, causing [banditry] to totally disappear."[25]

That will be the topic of the rest of this chapter: the process by which Wang eradicated those who could not be reformed but implemented measures with the goal of civilizing the region, so that a "territory of savage thieves and bandits shall change into a land of propriety, justice, [Han] caps and gowns."[26] The first three sections cover three major campaigns, while the fourth addresses measures he took in the aftermath to ensure a long-term peace. In concluding, I will also show how Wang's military action and civilizing discourse relate to aspects of his thought. His mix of moral suasion and force may well have been just one variation of the tools officials commonly resorted to when facing armed disturbances, but as one of the great Ming Confucians, Wang also provides us with a rare opportunity to read his political actions and rhetoric in light of his moral philosophy.[27]

---

23   Ibid., 9:308.

24   David Robinson, *Bandits, Eunuchs, and the Son of Heaven: Rebellion and the Economy of Violence in Mid-Ming China* (Honolulu: University of Hawaii Press, 2001), 13.

25   *WYMQJ*, vol. 1, 9:315.

26   Ibid., 10:352.

27   Rebellion and outlawry were widespread throughout the country during the mid-Ming, especially in southeast China. For general discussions with bibliographies related to this topic, see Dardess, *Ming China, 1368–1644*, 116–23; and James W. Tong, *Disorder under Heaven: Collective Violence in the Ming Dynasty* (Stanford: Stanford University Press, 1991). For a discussion of debates over subjugation versus appeasement in the matter of south-

Pulling the Weeds at the Margins of Fujian and Guangdong

After departing Hangzhou on December 25, 1516, Wang Yangming first passed through Nanchang, Jiangxi, where he boarded a vessel. He then proceeded to sail along the Gan River directly to the prefectural seat of Ganzhou, arriving there on February 6, 1517. Along the way, Wang was already receiving reports of banditry raging in the weakly administered mountainous region straddling southwestern Fujian and northeastern Guangdong. In a victory memorial submitted to the Ming court in the aftermath, he justified his interventions by explaining that the bandit ringleaders Zhan Shifu and Wen Huoshao had with their "gang of evildoers" gathered a following of over ten thousand and, relying on places of difficult access, "engaged in treachery for almost ten years."[28] Because "the rats and the foxes have been permitted to rampage about uncontrolled, [and] the snakes and swine gradually granted total license," he explained to the court, they have "looted and plundered, burning [down homes] and driving [residents] out, plunging several prefectures into an abyss of misery."[29]

This was not the first time "rats and foxes" had rampaged in this region. According to the *Comprehensive History of Fujian*, "ever since the Southern Song, Fujian's southwest was continuously turbulent."[30] In 1448, an uprising particularly alarming to the Ming court was kicked off in this region by a certain Deng Maoqi. It eventually grew into a rebellion that spread like a wildfire throughout much of the province, drawing in hundreds of thousands of supporters and requiring the mobilization of capital regiments. Although this rebellion was eventually suppressed, between this time and Wang's campaigns, provincial officials were repeatedly mobilizing troops to suppress armed disturbances growing out of village settlements located throughout this region.[31]

These rebellious populations that were of such concern to Wang Yangming were by no means insignificant in the number of members. According to his victory memorial, approximately fifty settlements ("lairs") were occupied and twenty-seven hundred people captured or killed. Several thousand homes

---

ern Jiangxi as well as how people became categorized as bandits, see Huang Zhifan's thorough study (*"Zei" "min" zhi jian*).

28   *WYMQJ*, vol. 1, 9:306.

29   Ibid.

30   Xu Xiaowang 徐曉望, ed., *Fujian tong shi* 福建通史 [Comprehensive History of Fujian], vol. 4, *Ming Qing* 明清 [Ming and Qing Dynasties] (Fuzhou: Fujian renmin chubanshe, 2006), 87. For the role of taxation and tenant-landlord relations, see Tong, *Disorder Under Heaven*, 184–87.

31   Ibid., 85.

MAP 1   *Principal locations for Wang Yangming's campaigns while he served as grand*
           coordinator of Southern Gan, 1517–1518.

were burned down. All of these settlements were located at the border of Nanjing County 南靖縣, Fujian, and Raoping County 饒平縣, Guangdong. When
Wang petitioned to have a county created from part of Nanjing and the territory of neighboring counties, as well as to make Hetou 河頭 the county seat,
he was following the advice of locals who had already petitioned the prefect of
Zhangzhou with this proposal.[32] These men included "righteous commoners,"
elders, and a Confucian licentiate—what were clearly prominent residents of
Nanjing. They claimed that although the mountainous territory surrounding
Hetou was on paper a part of Nanjing's subcounty administrative system, in
reality it was largely beyond the reach of the state. Those residing there would
have to travel five days to reach a county seat, and what filled the void was
lawlessness. For years, they noted, people living up in these mountains had
been plundering neighboring villages and causing much suffering. That may
be why Wang's victory memorial includes reports of a large quantity of recovered stolen goods, including oxen, horses, silver, copper, and cloth.[33]

These communications, however, offer no other clues as to the origins of the
social strife, and no ethnonyms are used to distinguish the captured and killed.
However, the 1513 gazetteer for Zhangzhou Prefecture states that She 畲 settlements could be found in the densely forested, mountainous lands of southern
Nanjing. It also states that at one time Miao 苗 had practiced slash-and-burn
agriculture in the area, but that they had already migrated elsewhere; now only
outlaws hide out there.[34] If the bandits' ethnicity is blurry, the origins of their
behavior is even more so. One factor was likely conflict with residents of the
community who had established good relations with the local authorities. Furthermore, the *Comprehensive History* shows that intertwined issues provided
ample grounds for social tensions in the region: official corruption, onerous
taxes and levies, landlord-tenant tensions, poverty and hardship, and migration.[35]

Regardless, Wang's judgment regarding these disturbances throughout the
four-province region as a whole was that they resulted from three linked prop-
ositions. "The reason banditry daily blazes," he stated, "is indiscriminate and
excessive offers of amnesty; the reason offers of amnesty are indiscriminate
and excessive is insufficient military strength; the reason military power is

32   *WYMQJ*, vol. 1, 9:318–21.

33   Ibid., 9:306.

34   Chen Hongmo 陳洪謨 and Zhou Ying 周瑛, eds., *Da Ming Zhangzhou fu zhi* 大明漳州府
      志 [Prefectural Gazetteer for the Great Ming's Zhangzhou Prefecture], 1513 ed. (Beijing:
      Zhonghua shuju, 2012), 7:152.

35   Xu, *Fujian tong shi*, 58–67.

insufficient is a failure to clearly delineate rewards and punishments."[36] Following this logic, the grand coordinator was determined to establish a disciplined military presence in the region, but he was not to rely on the regular military hierarchy of guards and battalions that fell under the authority of provincial military commissions. As David Robinson has pointed out, "By no later than the mid-fifteenth century, they played only a minimal role in maintaining local order;" and that is why security forces organized by local governments, such as local militias and police stations, were critical.[37] Wang Yangming would engage in a similar organizational effort.

Upon arriving in Ganzhou, Wang quickly implemented policies for the purposes of forming local armies and, more generally, militarizing the region from the ground up. But in order to form an effective militia, the grand coordinator also had to put an end to other problems undermining officials' ability to act effectively. This included collusion between sub-official functionaries and, on the one hand, registered subjects and, on the other, bandits, a partnership that always gave the latter a strategic advantage. In order to bring an end to sympathy and collaboration between bandits and registered subjects, as well as to get at the deeper problem of population movements beneath the sight of the state, Wang introduced a mutual surveillance and responsibility system.

Local Militia and the Mutual Surveillance System

The initial orders that Wang Yangming dispatched to officials of the military defense and branch provincial surveillance commission circuits of the territories under his jurisdiction called for enlisting and training local militias and the implementation of a ten-household registration system. As things were, he explained, because the local guards and battalions of the regular military hierarchy had mostly been deserted, sending remaining "worn out soldiers" to fight powerful bandits would be akin to "driving a flock of sheep to attack a fierce tiger."[38] This explained why officials had repeatedly resorted to mobilizing native armies from neighboring provinces, an ineffective policy for reason of their invariably slow arrival: "By the time the troops have assembled and deployed, the creatures have already gone into hiding, leaving no bandits behind to exterminate; after waiting for a time for the armies to withdraw, the rats and foxes again band together into gangs, becoming a lawless mob."[39]

---

36   *WYMQJ*, vol. 1, 10:334.

37   Robinson, *Bandits, Eunuchs, and the Son of Heaven*, 41.

38   Ibid., vol. 1, 8:527.

39   Ibid. Native armies refers to armies composed primarily of non-Chinese and commanded by native chieftains. In this case, these usually were drawn from Zhuang populations and chieftains in neighboring Guangxi.

Frederick Mote has asked why China's civilian farming society was able, in times of crisis requiring militarization, to generate individuals with the skills to organize forces and use them effectively.[40] He points to elite traditions of scholarly study of the military classics that played a role in scholar-official elites being able to serve as commanders when times demanded it. With regard to non-elites, he points both to the transmission of martial arts in connection with secret doctrines and to the teaching of combat skills by professional teachers, likely retired soldiers.[41] Although Mote suggests that this still does not completely explain how "so many men of humble backgrounds" could become great commanders, or how thousands more could serve as competent staff and field officers,[42] in any case Wang Yangming had no trouble finding excellent commanders and soldiers amongst the local population. He wrote, "In ancient times those who excelled at deploying the military instrument commanded townsmen and took them to battle and borrowed soldiers from villages to raise an army, so how could a subprefecture and eight prefectures be lacking in people bravely willing to work up their courage and fight?"[43]

Wang's plans included having military defense circuit officials order each county under their jurisdiction to conscript anywhere from four to six hundred soldiers, train them, and place them under the command of any military officers or civilians with a reputation for valiance and strategic acumen. This included selecting the strongest and bravest *nushou* 弩手 (crossbowmen), *dashou* 打手 (men skilled at hand-to-hand combat), and *jikuai* 機快.[44] These men were members of local militias; local security personnel skilled in the military arts stationed at local police stations or official yamens; or simply "local stalwarts" from the regular population with a reputation for being fierce, brave, and strong.

Apparently the surveillance commissioner for Jiangxi's southernmost military defense circuit had already assembled a militia to guard passes and towns in his circuit. But Wang felt these were insufficient "to attack [the bandits' lairs] and penetrate deeply [into the mountains], to annihilate enemy forces and overrun their positions."[45] Rather, he believed that, of the forces he was assembling, one-third could be allocated to towns and passes for security and defense, while the rest could be placed under competent officials, trained to

---

40   Mote, *Imperial China: 900–1800*, 555.

41   Ibid.

42   Ibid.

43   *WYMQJ*, vol. 1, 16:527.

44   For a discussion of these terms see Robinson, *Bandit, Eunuchs, and the Son of Heaven*, 41.

45   *WYMQJ*, vol. 1, 16:527.

await his orders and ready to deploy at a moment's notice. Therefore, all maneuvering would proceed directly from him.[46] "In this way," Wang explained to his subordinates:

> The soldiers garrisoning each county will be sufficient for protecting, defending, guarding, and intercepting, while the officers recruited by the defense circuits will be capable of catching the enemy by surprise when responding to emergencies. The thieves and bandits will gradually become aware that there is that which they should fear and look deeply into their hearts, while the law-abiding subjects will have that upon which they can rely and live without fear. Thereafter, righteous denunciation of their crimes can resound afar, and humane aid and comfort can be implemented. This is the essence of the method for quelling banditry.[47]

Once the armies were assembled, Wang expected frequent drilling in order to verify "the timeliness with which they advance and retreat to the sounding of gongs and beating of drums." He also intended to send out orders for practice deployments, in order to see how effectively they marched and retreated along the relevant routes.[48]

When Wang Yangming was traveling through areas under his jurisdiction, he noted with dismay that suspect individuals of uncertain origins were residing in both soldier and civilian households. In addition, he believed registered subjects were also harboring and communicating with individuals engaging in banditry. "That banditry has not been quelled," he informed officials, "owes to this."[49] To exercise control over such social disorder and misguided sympathies, Wang opted for a system of mutual surveillance, which was effective largely as a deterrent. He thus ordered circuit officials to implement a ten-household unit placard registration system (*shi jia pai fa* 十家牌法). The logistics were fairly simple: officials were to compile "single-hearth families" into ten-family units and place the name, native place, occupation, and other information about each member on a placard. This placard was to rotate daily among these ten families, each of which was to check every household in the unit to ensure no unfamiliar faces were present and to determine the whereabouts of any absent members. Any suspicious activity or individuals

---

46   Ibid.
47   Ibid.
48   Ibid.
49   Ibid., 16:531.

were to be reported to officials, failure to do so possibly bringing collective punishment upon the entire unit.[50]

Wang's system was a variation on the *baojia* 保甲 (watch and tithing) system first established by Wang Anshi 王安石 (1021–1086) in 1076 but later experimented with in various forms by Ming officials prior to Wang's time. The overall goal was to create mutual surety and a village defense system in areas troubled by piracy (as along the southeast coast) or banditry. Although it was never put into effect on a nationwide scale, after Wang's time, regulations were issued to officials who chose to implement it, and by the end of the Ming the system had spread to half of China.[51]

The logic behind the system as Wang understood it was explained to officials at a later date, when he held the appointment of grand coordinator of Jiangxi and then supreme commander of Guangxi and Guangdong. While he was campaigning against "Yao bandits" in the Rattan Gorge of Guangxi in 1528, he received a report from officials in Guangdong proposing that local militias be kept behind to guard cities. Concerned with problems caused by standing armies, Wang reprimanded these officials for getting themselves into the predicament where they had to continuously rely on the military to maintain order. He blamed this on their failure to implement his mutual surveillance system: "Should local officials truly have been able to conscientiously implement [the ten-household unit placard registration system], then everywhere would be soldiers, every household soldiers, everyone soldiers, and preparation for defending and guarding would be thorough, and the soldiers needed to pursue and detain would be gradually reduced, thereby reducing the financial burden on the people, and relieving them of service."[52]

Likewise, in 1520, while residing in Nanchang as grand coordinator of Jiangxi, Wang dispatched a communication to local officials expressing his frustration with their failure to implement this program. He spelled out in detail just how it deterred crime:

> Should each tithing be given responsibility for supervising and watching over itself, then members of the tithing will not shelter bandits. When tithings to the right are like this, and tithings to the left also like this, then within the towns and villages there will be none that are not like this. When it reaches the point where this county is like this, and the next

---

50 Ibid., 16:528–32.

51 For a discussion, see Timothy Brook, *The Chinese State in Ming Society* (London and New York: RoutledgeCurzon, 2005), 36–38.

52 *WYMQJ*, vol. 1, 18:635.

county is also like this, then among the subprefectures and counties near and far there are none that won't be like this. Such being the case, how could banditry possibly arise? When the people of one tithing supervise and watch over the ten families within their unit, it is very easily effective. But should one tithing permit one bandit, then ten will permit ten bandits, a hundred one hundred bandits, and a thousand one thousand bandits. When the number of bandits massed together reaches thousands, even should the soldiers of a county be mobilized to eradicate them, it will naturally already be extremely difficult to act effectively. Today local officials invariably fail strictly to implement the ten-household system, and when [the area] becomes full of bandits, they then raise armies and mobilize a crowd, desiring in such and such a place to station soldiers, and in such and such a place to intercept and capture, not administering through fundamentals, but rather through the ancillary, not doing what is easy, but rather what is difficult. This is all the result of, in normal times, being remiss in one's duties and sticking to old ways.[53]

However, when he ordered the implementation of this system, Wang Yangming did not intend that its effectiveness would solely lie with its deterrent effect—the threat of collective supervision and punishment. Rather, he envisioned that it would also provide a platform for "changing and guiding" the people, instilling virtue, fostering social order, and letting people know that the state was nearby and concerned with their welfare. When he first implemented the system as grand coordinator, he composed a proclamation to the men of each prefecture in which he duly acknowledged the hardships they faced in this war-torn region, while also calling for moral rectification. Wang believed social disorder was to a substantial degree the result of misguided conduct and even willful wrongdoing. Thus, aside from listing out the virtues requisite to each individual's social station, Wang called for all to be observant of the law, submit their taxes, practice frugality, show forbearance, avoid resorting to litigation, encourage others to act virtuously, and confront those who would engage in evildoing. "Fathers, elders, and sons," Wang queried in a proclamation, "have you ever known a friendly and yielding, humble and respectful person that isn't loved and respected? Have you ever known someone

---

53   Ibid. Banditry in Southern Gan had, however, already reached a level where this system of collective responsibility could no longer work. Wang therefore pursued a two-pronged policy for ending banditry: implementing fundamental deterrent measures to build security from the ground up and, out of necessity, using the ancillary to control festering violence.

who is vicious, greedy, and violent, and who acts out of self-interest and domi-neers over others, and yet is not despised?"[54] "It shall be your duty to bring about an atmosphere of courteousness," he instructed his subjects, "in order to foster habits of honesty and sincerity."[55] To ensure the proclamation's effec-tiveness, it was to be inscribed on the back of each tithing's registration plac-ard, and read out loud regularly.

As for the role of local officials, anyone reported for engaging in banditry was to be arrested, sent to the local yamen, and punished. Those whose "errors and wickedness were not beyond redemption" and who might yet benefit from instruction were to be reported to officials, kept on a list, ordered to "change and reform" themselves, and called upon to ensure they were indeed doing so. Wang also encouraged officials to oversee and accompany those households under their jurisdiction in rotation.[56] As for particularly "recalcitrant and re-sistant" locales, they were to visit them in person, "inquiring of people's hard-ships, in order to connect with their subjects."[57] Should they be unable to make such a journey, they were to select respected elders in these communi-ties, treat them with due deference, and ask them to travel to the troublesome and remote areas to "in every possible way offering transformative guidance."[58] If successful, these elders were to be rewarded generously. Through these methods, Wang hoped, "reformative education will bloom, and customs and mores will improve."[59]

Overall, Wang's goal was to foster confidence that the state was looking after subjects' wellbeing so that institutions instrumental to good governance could be established, and key to achieving this were such paternalistic pedagogical techniques that had the power to stir up grassroots sentiment. Citing Men-cius's notion that "in the matter of winning over the people, good rule is not as important as good teaching," Wang chided local officials for not even manag-ing to achieve good rule: "If you were truly to look upon the people as you do your own children, how could you tolerate your failure to educate and exhort, and then go about applying beatings and floggings?"[60]

By the time Wang sent out orders for implementation of the placard regis-tration system and mobilization of local militias (in early February, 1517), he

---

54   *WYMQJ*, vol. 1, 16:532.
55   Ibid., 16:529.
56   *WYMQJ*, vol. 2, 31:1153.
57   Ibid.
58   Ibid.
59   Ibid.
60   Ibid.

had already dispatched communications to officials in Fujian and Guangdong, ordering them to take action in the violent, bandit-infested periphery shared by the two provinces. Here, he had decided, were incorrigible individuals now unreachable by other more ideal pedagogical techniques, making it incumbent upon him to "administer with the ancillary," and take military action.

The First Campaign

The plan Wang Yangming dispatched to officials responsible for the Zhangnan Military Defense Circuit in southwestern Fujian and the Lingdong Circuit in eastern Guangdong is mentioned only in passing in his first victory memorial.[61] He states that, while passing through Nanchang on January 24, 1517, he came to understand that dates for deployment were poorly coordinated, prompting him to send out this initial plan.[62] But by the time the documentary trail picks up again, the grand coordinator was already reprimanding officials for suffering defeats during a series of battles and for attempting to delay further action until the fall.

According to the report from Fujian's Surveillance Commissioner Hu Lian, on February 8, 1517, regional civilian and military officials marched five thousand troops to Changfu village in the prefecture of Zhangzhou 漳州, thereafter pursuing the "bandits" to neighboring settlements. As the commissioner described the scene, "the bandits were numerous and the terrain perilous, lairs and haunts many and, in addition, along every route ambushes were set up, such that conditions were extremely violent."[63] Although the officers reported capturing or killing 432 "bandits," including key ringleaders, and burning over a hundred homes, the remaining bandits had fled to Zhangzhou's Xianghu Mountain 象湖山 near the border of Guangdong, linked up with others, and fortified themselves within impregnable locations.[64] Forces pursued these remnants to the foot of the mountain, where they camped out, ready for

---

61   During the Ming, provinces were divided up into multi-prefecture circuits. Military defense circuits (*bing bei dao* 兵備道) were multi-prefecture jurisdictions under the special military supervision of a vice commissioner or assistant commissioner of the provincial surveillance commission. Both the provincial surveillance commission and provincial administration commission also maintained branch offices in, respectively, general surveillance circuits and general administration circuits. These circuits were also each headed by a commissioner detached from his home commission but with full authority to represent it in supervising the circuit. It was primarily these officials that Wang Yangming was working with throughout this time.

62   *WYMQJ*, vol. 1, 9:306.

63   Ibid., 9:301.

64   Ibid., 9:303.

further confrontations. However, "fearing that the bandits were many and our troops few," commanders requested reinforcements. "Because Xianghu Mountain is towering and precipitous," they reported, "to date our troops have been unable to attack it. At this time the bandits' strategic power grows daily, and should we not add reinforcements of native troops, wait until fall and winter to combine our forces, mobilize, and attack, [I] fear further catastrophes may follow."[65]

When he received these first battle reports, Wang Yangming was still stationed at his headquarters in Ganzhou, Jiangxi, hundreds of kilometers away, and he was not pleased by these developments. In sum, he accused his commanders of "clearly failing to obey lines of command, and deliberately violating the battle plan."[66] Suspicious that some of them had "out of fear recoiled from and retreated from engaging the enemy,"[67] Wang ordered circuit officials to carry out a full investigation, although this wasn't to interfere with his original plans. "At a time when there is an urgent need for men, we can for the time being [only] make a record of their crimes, investigate, and supervise campaigns of extermination," he explained.[68] In fact, the grand coordinator expected that upon receiving his new battle plan, these commanders would "atone for their crimes by serving meritoriously."

Wang's response was to order his commanders to merely *pretend* to do the very thing they wanted to do anyway: cease campaigning and await reinforcements before taking further action during the fall. This was the first of many occasions when Wang employed subterfuge to gain strategic military advantage. Perhaps even more significantly, he based his decision on an assessment of the men's state of mind, in the belief that "those who excel at deploying the military instrument according to the disposition of forces," as he informed his commanders, "borrow victory from the enemy."[69] In this case, he perceived that commanders in Fujian were "in high spirits and up for a fight," and "looking forward to achieving meritorious victory." However, he warned them that they had waited too long to act and lost their momentum, allowing the bandit gangs to band together, build obstacles, pits, and weapons. That is why he proposed that, "it is correct to give the appearance of slowing [mobilization] and letting down our guard, awaiting the opportune moment to advance." Any precipitous action, he warned, would only further cement the will of the bandits,

---

65   Ibid.
66   Ibid., 9:306.
67   Ibid., 16:536.
68   Ibid.
69   Ibid., 16:534.

who would then grasp "what is called knowing our soldiers are able to strike, while not realizing the enemy cannot be struck."[70]

Wang sensed that the mood was different altogether in Guangdong, where the enemy bandits had rightly surmised that commanders had planned to await the arrival of native troops before taking further action. But for this reason, Wang believed, they will have let down their guard. That is why the commanders had to drop their prudent plans to await reinforcements and "turn weakness into strength." He knew that although "my soldiers are not ready to attack," this is only because they did not realize "that the enemy can be attacked."[71] To achieve this goal, Wang had an official communication circulated ordering a (feigned) withdrawal at the very moment that he was sending confidential communications to his commanders ordering them to prepare for deployment. Officers and soldiers were to be notified:

> The weather is warming, and your farming responsibilities will soon come around. In addition, the mountain routes are rugged and perilous, forests dense and shaded. Should rain showers come repeatedly, and a miasmatic fog suddenly appear, this truly will not be conducive to penetration by soldiers and horses. It is therefore advisable to retain militia in strategically critical locations, and drill them for defense. The remaining soldiers and horses may be gradually demobilized, waiting until after the fall harvest, when the weather has cooled, to assemble forces from three provinces, unify them, and advance.[72]

To be even more convincing, commanders were to feast the troops and give out rewards.

While thus encouraging the bandits to let down their guard, Wang ordered commanders to continue scouting out their movements and to maintain a crack force ready for surprise attacks. When the opportunity arrived, these forces were to rapidly and quietly advance at night. Wang envisioned this smaller force employing the "unorthodox (qi 奇)" by pouncing on an unwitting adversary. Taking lesser-traveled routes, these soldiers were to move rapidly into strategic position and stun the bandits by suddenly beating drums and yelling. They could then charge, annihilating their front lines and overrunning their positions.

---

70   Ibid.
71   Ibid.
72   *WYMQJ*, 16:532–33.

This next phase of attack on Xianghu Mountain began on March 11, with Wang Yangming personally overseeing it. As he later explained to the court, "Your servitor immediately departed Ganzhou, personally leading several armies to and stationing in the vicinity of Changting 長汀 and Shanghang 上杭.... I oversaw and commanded each official secretly in accordance with the battle plan to advance with the speed of a spreading fire and subjugate [the bandits], atoning for their crimes with laudable service. Anyone daring to be evasive or shirk responsibility was to be punished according to military regulations."[73] Over the next few weeks, several contingents from both Guangdong and Fujian mounted a series of attacks on settlements spread throughout the mountainous region. Dozens of lairs were cleaned out and 114 key ringleaders and thousands of followers and their dependents were killed or captured.[74]

Although Wang Yangming does not appear to have been at the front lines during the initial attacks, he was likely present at the ensuing battles at the mountain fortresses at Ketang Grotto 可塘峒, where some bandits were still holding out. "Although the bandit ringleaders have mostly been captured, many cunning remnants have yet fled; should we fail to jump on this opportunity rapidly to strike and annihilate them, the root of the weeds shall remain and, I fear, again sprout and spread."[75] Wang stated he was preparing to depart the prefectural seat of Zhangzhou to review the regiments, oversee these final battles, and then travel the area with officials for the purpose of coming up with a long-term strategy to contain violence and ensure stability.[76] From there he would travel west to the border of Fujian and Guangdong, where the campaigns came to an end early in April 1517.

Although he ordered extermination, the grand coordinator also urged officials to exercise restraint. Orders evidence his regret over the use of force, fear that it would be excessive, and also the difficulty he had stomaching the inevitably bloody results. En route to Changting, the prefectural seat of Tingzhou 汀州, he composed a poem expressing his sentiments:

Throughout my life, strategic military deployment has not been my forte;
Yet I am commanding armies entering Ting and Zhang;
The sun setting beyond so many mountain peaks, banners and flags afar;
In unison, a spring breeze, the sound of drums and flutes rising;
Not depending upon General Er Shi when going out to the borders;

---

73   Ibid.
74   Ibid., 9:305.
75   Ibid., 16:537.
76   Ibid., 16:538.

Knowing full well the excellent way Zhao Chongguo pacified the Jiang;
Devastation everywhere, yet unable to provide the slightest relief;
Instead thinking of my old thatched cottage in Zhongshan.[77]

Here Wang contrasts the incompetence of Li Guangli 李廣利 (General Er Shi)
who, during the Han Dynasty, wasted many lives and much in the way of resources during four years of campaigning, with the success of a Han general,
Zhao Chongguo 趙充國, who became renowned for pacifying Western Jiang
with minimal losses. Like Zhao, he also wished to leave it all behind.

Anecdotal evidence also shows that, while campaigning, Wang was taking
steps to prevent sympathy for the restive populations and simmering resentment among other groups from evolving into a major uprising. Believing that,
if threatened with extermination, some would be more open to negotiating
and returning to their livelihoods, he ordered officials to distribute proclamations to parties they believed would be receptive to a peaceful settlement. According to a report from one prefect, after his forces destroyed some thirty
"lairs," captured and killed fourteen hundred, and burned down two thousand
dwellings, he sent out proclamations and ordered county officials to offer amnesty to those "coerced" into banditry. He claimed that 1,235 men came forward
with 2,828 family dependents and were then resettled and returned to their
livelihoods.[78]

Also, according to the *Tingzhou Prefectural Gazetteer*, Wang Yangming believed that among the followers of bandits who were lording it over the locale
of Yanquan there were many who unwittingly got caught up in the fray. In an
effort to avoid a slaughter, he composed a proclamation and had one thousand
copies printed, dispatching respected elders to carry these along with cloth
and silk to the respective troublesome areas. They were to "instruct [the ban-
dits] in calamities and felicities and permit them to reform themselves."[79] The
ringleaders were said to have come forward and surrendered, while their
"gangs" dispersed.

One proclamation Wang Yangming dispatched is yet extant, and succinctly
captures the subtle manner by which he appealed to the populations under his
jurisdiction:

77   Ibid., 20:744.
78   Ibid., 9:305.
79   He Yun 何雲, Wu Yan 伍晏, and Shao Youdao 邵有道, eds. *Jiajing Tingzhou fu zhi* 嘉靖汀
      州府志 [Tingzhou Prefectural Gazetteer of the Jiajing Reign] (Shanghai: Shanghai shu-
      dian, 1990), 643.

There has never been an instance of someone who does what is good and does not receive good fortune, nor has there ever been a case where someone engages in wickedness and does not suffer calamity. Do not tyrannize the few with the many. Do not bully the weak because you have the power to do so. You must apply yourself to bringing about a flourishing practice of propriety and righteousness, forever becoming good and honest people. Among the younger people and lower classes (*qunxiao* 群小), should there be someone who doesn't respect instruction and goes out to stir up trouble and engage in wrongdoing, elders and headmen should detain and escort them to the official yamen for punishment in accordance with the law. [By so doing, you will], first of all, clearly demonstrate your sincere intention to do what is good and remove what is evil (*wei shan qu e zhi cheng* 為善去惡之誠) and, secondly, weed out the henbane and bristle grass, preventing them from spreading and leaving behind trouble for such good and honest people as yourselves. Having recently received orders to tour and pacify this region, I only wish that you common people should live in security and be content with your livelihoods, together enjoying great peace. I only regret that my abilities and knowledge are shallow and limited, that although I hold in my breast love for the people, I have not been able to govern in a way that demonstrates love for the people. Recently, because I supervised the campaigns in the many bandit lairs around Xianghu and Ketang, all bandits from which have been captured, killed, and eradicated, the army has been stationed here. At this time when spring plowing should begin, I deeply desire to come in person to the countryside where you reside and inquire of your hardships, but because those accompanying me are many, I fear I will bring undue hardship upon you. Thus, I have dispatched officials and respected elders for the express purpose of making known [my will] by proclamation, as well as rewarding fathers, elders, headmen, and others with cloth, so that you shall see my sincere desire to comfort and provide relief. You are many and I cannot reach all of you. Please grasp my intentions.[80]

In the aftermath of the campaign, Wang would also introduce a number of other measures, such as building a county seat and police stations, all of which amounted to increasing the presence of the state in southwestern Fujian, something he would also do after his next two campaigns.

---

80   *WYMQJ*, vol. 1, 16:538–39.

Once Zhan Shifu's mountain stronghold in Ketang had been cleaned out, Wang felt confident he had adequately restored order to the restless mountainous territory at the border of Fujian and Guangdong. As he memorialized to the emperor, "Your servitor and other officials received orders to exterminate, and within three months defeated and annihilated the ringleaders, cleaning out their lairs and haunts."[81] For this reason, he believed that "the people have been relieved of their terrible predicament, and the many prefectures have won an enduring peace conducive to renaissance."[82] Wang's approach appeared to have worked: pressing officials to act or face serious consequences and personally supervising his commanders on location had rid them of what he perceived as equivocation—"recoiling in fear," "shirking responsibility," of "dilatory conduct"—in the face of the threat posed by thousands of resistant mountain dwellers clearly skilled at fending off their adversaries.

However, the reprieve in violence in this region was not being matched by success to the west, in the border regions of southern Jiangxi, northern Guangdong, and southeastern Huguang. They were rocked by what seemed like endless armed disturbances in spite of the fact that Wang Yangming had already ordered mobilization of local militias. For this reason, in late May, he returned to Ganzhou, and began preparing for further military deployments.

The "She Bandits" of Hengshui and Tonggang

While Wang Yangming was stationed in Fujian, he was receiving reports from officials in southern Jiangxi and northern Guangdong that must have greatly displeased him. That is why, on April 4, 1517, he dispatched a memorial with the results of his investigation into official negligence. In light of earlier reports of endemic banditry throughout the region, he had already ordered officials in these areas to mobilize armed forces and confront these "mobs," set up ambushes, cut off return routes, and occupy undefended lairs. In this way, he had expected that "when advancing, the brigands will have nothing to gain, and when retreating no place to go—in no more than a short time, you can catch all of them."[83]

Yet based on what he was hearing now from Commissioner Yang Zhang, the militia commanders had failed to competently deal with the violence and had even negotiated with the bandits. This, of course, had only encouraged

---

81   Ibid., 9:306.
82   Ibid.
83   Ibid., 9:301.

festering violence. Reports were coming in of encounters between outlaw gangs in several counties in Ganzhou Prefecture and militias led by local civilian and military officials. One stated that on the first of March some six hundred bandits appeared at the county seat of Xinfeng 信豐. Another six hundred squatted in a location in the same county, and when a local official led a militia to confront them, a reported two thousand more appeared to counter them.[84] Behind this "seriously violent situation," it was believed, was the guiding hand of the most renowned ringleaders in the region, whom Wang would soon face.[85]

Even Commissioner Yang was guilty of such failures, and his report offers a vivid sense as to just what they were dealing with:

> This official supervised and commanded a local contingent of militiamen, rallying our courage and engaging them in battle, killing over twenty bandits. But unexpectedly a mass of bandits surged over our front lines. Warrior Chen Lifang, Hundreds Commander Zhong Desheng, and others, seeing that they were outmatched, all failed to maintain discipline, and dispersed in advance. Nankang County's Requiting with Service Righteous Scholar Yang Xiju and others nevertheless still fought to the death with these bandits without retreating, all suffering injuries and dying. When Registrar Wang Zuo's horse stumbled, he was also seized and taken. The bandits' strategic advantage was bringing them victories, and they were going to attack the county seat so we, along with Xiao Cheng, Lin Jie, and others, assembled a large number of soldiers and withdrew to Nanying Mountain to intercept them. When the circuit commissioner arrived at the county in person to oversee the extermination, the bandits gained knowledge of this and withdrew to Niuzhou, somewhat distant from the city. On the twelfth [March 4, 1517], these bandits dispatched someone to request amnesty. On the thirteenth, we received orders to dispatch Xiao Cheng to go [to the bandits] and negotiate a truce. Registrar Wang Zuo was released, and the bandits returned to their lairs.[86]

Unhappy with this outcome, Wang Yangming composed a memorial indicting these and other officials on several counts: Xinfeng County's magistrate and two battalion commanders, for example, "only seemed to know how to fortify themselves within the confines of the county seat's walls, and were unwilling

---

84   Ibid., 9:300.
85   Ibid.
86   Ibid., 9:300–301.

to deploy forces to provide reinforcement." Other military and civilian officials, at critical strategic positions where they should have cut off the bandits, "just looked indifferently upon the maneuvering of these bandits, making not the slightest effort to deploy troops to intercept and ambush the enemy."[87]

Although Wang Yangming also petitioned for rewards to be given to other officials who had dealt capably with similar armed disturbances throughout the region, the endemic violence and such incompetence were sufficient for him to conclude he needed to spell out for the Ming court why order was not being restored to the region. In doing so, he hoped to obtain the authority he believed he needed to effectively deploy armies and motivate and discipline his subordinates. He informed the emperor that although all of these officials should be punished, given such urgent conditions they could for the time being receive reprimands, atoning for their crimes by putting forth a concerted effort to do noteworthy deeds at a later date.[88] It is to his further analysis of conditions in the region and the powers he was requesting that I now turn.

On the Origins of and the Quelling of Banditry

On May 27, 1517, and again on June 16, Wang Yangming memorialized the court requesting full discretionary power to act as conditions required without interference from other authorities, and greater authority to dispense rewards and punishments during campaigns. He pointed out that the Ministry of War had already granted previous grand coordinators the authority to move decisively against "outlaws of the marsh." Indeed, upon first arriving at his headquarters in Ganzhou, he had such orders copied onto a thousand sheets and distributed to all his subordinates. As a result, he informed the emperor, he was able to report some successful campaigns.[89]

But conditions throughout southern Jiangxi remained dire. The summary report Commissioner Yang submitted to Wang Yangming described several particularly troublesome areas inflamed by a long list of well-known ringleaders, who appeared to be allying with each other and planning to lead a potentially serious uprising.[90] So serious were conditions throughout the region that the supreme commander of Huguang had already memorialized and received permission to begin mobilization for a massive coordinated campaign involv-

---

87   Ibid., 9:301–302.
88   Ibid., 9:302.
89   Ibid., 9:317.
90   Ibid., 9:313.

ing forces from Guangdong, Huguang, and Jiangxi.[91] Wang would soon argue
for a series of campaigns on a smaller scale directed at what he believed to be
three distinguishable hot spots, each of which could be dealt with separately,
strategically speaking.

The grand coordinator's first campaign, initiated in November 1517, was directed against strongholds of what are routinely referred to as "She bandits
(*She zei* 畲賊)" located primarily in Shangyou County 上猶縣, Nan'an Prefecture. Wang's communications list dozens of settlements located in three critical areas that he deemed legitimate targets of attack that he would eventually
occupy and destroy. These areas, all located in mountain ranges in the western
half of the prefecture, were Tonggang 桶岡, Hengshui 橫水, and Zuoxi 左溪,
the latter two referring to tributaries of the Gan River. In concluding a later victory memorial, Wang reported that eighty-four settlements ("lairs") were destroyed and over six thousand people killed or captured.

These numbers obviously suggest something more going on here than brigandry. In a petition requesting establishment of a county, local elites claimed
that these "She bandits" were originally migrants from Guangdong who had
been given permission by a previous grand coordinator to settle in these areas
of the prefecture. Initially, they chopped down trees in the mountains and
planted crops, settling into their livelihoods and growing in number. Over
time, they came into increasing conflict with local residents, and began to
plunder villages throughout the region, followed by county and prefectural
town seats. As these elites saw it, part of the reason the population grew to—in
their estimate—ten thousand, was that others were continually joining these
migrants. Some were vagrants from other counties in the province fleeing taxation and labor service; others were craftsmen wishing to ply their trades. So
unbridled had these She peoples become, the petition stated, "they appointed
regional commanders and usurped the title of king."[92]

The petitioners believed creating a new county in this area would prevent
this problem from recurring, for by that time the grand coordinator had, as
they saw it, "captured the principal evildoers, and eliminated the evil ether."[93]
But it would take time to eliminate this mixed bag of migrants and marginal
mountain dwellers that had apparently coalesced into a coherent group with a

---

91   These communications, which primarily concern ongoing conflict with "Yao" and other
      ethnic groups throughout Huguang, may be found in Qin Jin 秦金, *An chu lu* 安楚录
      [Record of the Pacification of Chu], in *Zhongguo yeshi jicheng xubian* 中國野史集成續
      編, vol. 16 (Chengdu: Bashu shushe, 2000), 10:773–881.

92   *WYMQJ*, vol. 1, 10:350.

93   Ibid.

degree of solidarity vis-à-vis the local registered populations. Upon returning from Fujian in late May, Wang Yangming could already report some early successes in the campaigns led by Commissioner Yang and other local officials. According to the commissioner, after Wang assumed office in early 1517 and ordered the formation of militias, the She bandits sent their dependents and possessions to fortresses located deep in the densely forested mountains, only permitting stalwarts to emerge during daylight hours in order to tend to the fields. Thereafter, during the spring, bands of She numbering in the hundreds repeatedly appeared in the area and plundered the stockaded villages of local residents.[94] In addition, reports by local officials indicated that a key leader by the name of Xie Zhishan had not only assumed the title of "King Pacifying the South," but also appeared to be planning to link up with a Yao chieftain who had been plundering northern Guangdong. They were, it was suspected, manufacturing weapons and planning to attack the county seat of Nankang 南康. Afterwards—the report claimed—they planned to enter Guangdong and, with government forces away fighting recalcitrant ethnic groups off to the west, maraud over a much larger territory.[95]

Even by this time, Wang Yangming had already given Yang Zhang and his commanders the go-ahead to clean out and pacify the area, making sure "not to leave a soul behind."[96] He too was becoming convinced that, as he told the court, a "treacherous plot" was astir. The brazenness with which these outlaws were illegally bestowing phony titles upon themselves and the turmoil they were causing was only further evidence.[97] That is why he was pleased to report that on July 8, 1517, several contingents set out to strike numerous settlements in Nan'an Prefecture, some of which contained only a few dozen bandits who had remained behind to guard them. When charged at, they were alarmed and routed, some fatally wounded by arrows and poison crossbows, others falling off cliffs. Other settlements to which these men and their dependents had retreated were located in even more inaccessible mountainous areas. These were surrounded and burned to the ground. At daybreak, commanders reported, all that remained were charred remains and indistinguishable seared faces, making counting heads a difficult task.[98]

Diehards Xie Zhishan and Lan Tianfeng were among those remaining main culprits whose heads were not yet on display as a warning to those who would

---

94   Ibid., 10:329.
95   Ibid.
96   Ibid., 10:331.
97   Ibid., 10:330.
98   Ibid., 10:329.

persist in evildoing.[99] When the grand coordinator memorialized on September 13 with his plan for a coordinated attack on what he perceived to be one of the "roots" of banditry in the region, he cited Commissioner Yang's report that, even after these initial campaigns, Xie twice led bands numbering nearly two thousand to attack the prefectural seat of Nan'an:

> [The aforementioned ringleaders] are ignorant, violent, and poisonous, rely on places of difficult access to do evil, usurp the title of king, appoint phony commanders, gather mobs with the likes of themselves numbering in the thousands, and wantonly spread their poison over three provinces. [They have] attacked and laid siege to Nan'an Prefecture and Nankang County's walls and moats, killing a guard commander, assistant magistrate, and other officials. [They] roamed around and plundered Guiyang and Yizhang in Huguang Province, as well as such counties of Longchuan, Wan'an, Taihe, and Yongxin in Ji'an Prefecture. The children of law-abiding subjects were enslaved and slaughtered by them, and their residences and granaries were burned down. The area of those roads and fields lying in fallow because obstructed or occupied by them amount to seventy thousand *qing*.[100] ... The powerful outlaw leaders Xie Zhishan and Lan Tianfeng refer to themselves as the grandchildren of Pan Huang. They have in their possession a precious seal with a portrait on it supposed to have been passed down to them, deceiving masses of bandits, who come under their influence.[101]

When Wang Yangming provided the rationale legitimating his call for military campaigns, he relied on damning reports like these, confidently informing the emperor that the men listed as killed or captured had for over ten years up to the present "occupied over one thousand *li* and wreaked utter havoc over several prefectures, usurping the title of king, plotting rebellion, laying the foundation for a catastrophe, and planting the seeds of wickedness, their fiercely burning torturous blaze already for years afflicting the area with great suffering."[102]

The unidentifiable charred remains of those considered "She bandits" are perhaps a fitting symbol for just how difficult it is to describe She identity. It is

---

99   Ibid., 10:331. These were Wang Yangming's specific instructions to Yang Zhang regarding how to dispose of captured bandit leaders.

100   One *qing* is roughly equivalent to 6.66 hectares, or 16.47 acres.

101   *WYMQJ*, vol. 1, 10:342.

102   Ibid., 10:349.

also difficult to determine the extent to which the label "She 畲" was of ethnic import at this time, as opposed to merely indicating unregistered or unruly peoples of the hills made up of migrants and vagrant Han outsiders. Wing-Hoi Chan believes distinct ethnic differentiation was primarily a late- or post-Ming political development based on a small percentage of She who maintained surname endogamy and common descent myths. Noting that weak state presence and large numbers of vagrants are a common feature of reports of "She bandits" up to the Ming, Chan believes that throughout the Ming the term "She" was not used as an ethnic category but rather "locally or popularly to refer to vagrants of Jiangxi or Tingzhou [Fujian]."[103] For him, these were primarily migrant populations later joined by marginal elements. Indeed, we do find in Wang's official communications repeated reference to tax evaders, vagabonds, unregistered men and their families, and others seeking to practice their trades entering the She settlements so as to pursue their livelihoods, what Wang described as "joining the She and becoming a thief."[104]

Chan also believes the reason Wang Yangming had nothing to say about cultural difference was because there was none, that any ethno-cultural distinctiveness is in fact absent from descriptions in other contemporary sources as well.[105] Such a conclusion does, however, leave unaddressed the question as to just why these resettled migrants from Guangdong, as records in the *Nan'an Prefectural Gazetteer* state, repeatedly referred to themselves as "She" and claimed descent from Panhu.[106] To explain their shared Panhu symbolism and obvious group solidarity, Chan proposes a combination of political opportunism and socio-economic tensions between registered local populations and migrant and marginal populations living on the fringes.[107] Modern She, who sometimes refer to themselves as "sojourners of the mountains," consist of a small number of intermarrying surnames sharing myths of common ancestry going back to Panhu. According to legend, this founding ancestor and his descendents were, for service to the emperor, granted exemption from taxation and free occupation of a mountainous region. This myth was found among both She and other ethnic groups—especially Yao—inhabiting the region,

103   Wing-hoi Chan, "Ethnic Labels in a Mountainous Region: the Case of the She Bandits," in *Empire at the Margins: Culture, Ethnicity, and Frontier in Early Modern China*, ed. Pamela Kyle Crossley, Helen Siu, and Donald S. Sutton (Berkeley: University of California Press, 2006), 267.

104   *WYMQJ*, vol. 1, 16:548.

105   Chan, "Ethnic Labels," 269.

106   Liu Jie 劉節, ed. *Jiajing Nan'an fu zhi* 嘉靖南安府志 [Jiajing Period Nan'an Prefectural Gazetteer] (Shanghai: Shanghai shudian, 1990), 510 (12:10), 536 (12:21).

107   Chan, "Ethnic Labels," 257–58.

and could serve not only as a basis for forging ties locally but also for negotiating relations with the Ming state.[108]

Although Chan believes this myth and associated descent claims might be traceable to certain populations—indigenous or otherwise—located in the larger region Wang was assigned to govern, he reads the evidence for She ethnicity in Nan'an Prefecture altogether situationally. That is, it may have been nothing more than the adoption of Panhu symbolism by migrants and vagrants who were in conflict with local populations and seeking ties or political alliances with populations recognized as "Yao" in neighboring Huguang and Guangdong. Indeed, numerous references to cooperation and sympathies between populations in southern Jiangxi and Yao chieftains in these areas can be found in Wang Yangming's and Supreme Commander Qin Jin's communications.[109] That was why it was necessary to mobilize forces in all of the provinces and to plan a concerted attack on what Wang Yangming on occasional refers to as thousands of "Yao" spread across the three provinces.

Chan too underlines that for the most part Wang Yangming's communications lack the language that might have suggested he saw many ethnic differences in these people. This was not the case during later campaigns when he was dealing with ethnic groups in Guangxi. What seems more likely was that when he used ethnic appellations to identify sub-ethnic or marginal elements of the Han population, he was implying that they were savages simply for reason of their unacceptable conduct. Their behavior suggested they were the "other," the uncivilized, throwing them into the broader category of "barbarians" that existed in neighboring territories in similarly marginal areas. Certainly, this way of thinking was characteristic of Ming officials. In particular, what Wang saw as wicked and therefore "savage" were certain forms of behavior especially offensive to representatives of the state: conflict with law-abiding populations, attacks on the state and anything symbolizing such, and attempts to turn the world upside down by usurping imperial and official titles.

Such undermining of the state's authority in fact suggests that these "savages" felt they had a rightful claim to the promise of justice held out by the powers that be. This failure on the part of the state could become a rallying point for the kind of fearsome resistance state representatives interpreted as recalcitrance and savagery. That there were social tensions between locals and migrants is clear, and it does not take much imagination to suspect a great deal of inflammatory injustice and accept the conclusion reached by Chan: "The marginal place these peoples occupied may have freed them from registration and

---

108   Ibid., 255.
109   *WYMQJ*, vol. 1, 16:545.

corvée labor, but it also created a situation in which they were forced to become rebels."[110] Social historians have studied migration patterns in this region
during the Ming, as well as how conflicts erupted between migrants, local registered subjects, non-Han ethnic groups, and the state over land, loans, leases,
taxes, and rent.[111] The overall conclusion reached by James Tong—that banditry flourished in areas of weak state control—applied first and foremost to
this region.[112]

Although Wang Yangming informed the court that his investigations proved
these "bandits were utterly brimming over with wickedness," and could be likened to ulcers which, should they fail to be aggressively treated, would destroy
other internal organs,[113] it is true that in other cases he understood that among
them were otherwise decent people who, finding themselves in circumstances
outside their control, were forced into a life of crime. Where such was the case,
it was incumbent upon the state to take compassionate action designed to
ameliorate these factors. In his instructions for a community covenant, a kind
of blueprint for grassroots local organization aimed at reducing social tensions
in and integrating communities, Wang insisted that the reason some engage in
criminal activity is that "the government did not govern them properly or teach
them in the right way." In addition, parents had failed to teach and discipline
their children, and fellow villagers had failed to positively influence each other.
As a result, he notes, minor conflicts often lead some to join bandits to exact
revenge, and even outlaws who have been resettled are often treated badly, and
thus return to their old ways.[114]

He also pointed out that government corruption and class tensions sparked
unrest. Should there be anyone abusing the power they have through political
connections by, for instance, descending on communities to demand gifts,
elected covenant officers were to petition to have them investigated. These
might be government clerks, local military officers, honored commoners, village elders, or tithing heads. Likewise, Wang noted in a letter to the Minister of
War Wang Qiong that should he raise taxes in the region it would only lead
commoners to flee to the bandits. Finally, Wang underlined how the predatory
lending practices of local powerful families forced poor farmers to sell off their

110   Chan, "Ethnic Labels," 269.
111   Ibid., 269–71.
112   Tong, *Disorder under Heaven*, 6–7.
113   *WYMQJ*, vol. 1, 9:315.
114   Ibid., 17:599–600.

land "to the point that the poor people have no place to take their grievances, depart, and become thieves."[115]

Nonetheless, in the case of the so-called She bandits of Nan'an, Wang apparently believed he had exhausted all options and had no reason to view them as victims gone astray; he could therefore with a clean conscience employ the military instrument and eradicate them. In an official communication to Supreme Commander Qin Jin 秦金, in fact, he proposed having officials survey the settlements under their jurisdiction and draw up a map differentiating "lairs" and law-abiding villages. He also ordered subordinates to obtain written pledges from local village leaders stating they would not harbor bandits or collaborate in any way, at risk of collective prosecution.[116] Under the principle of "avoiding burning both pearl and stone as the root and trunk of banditry are uprooted,"[117] the grand coordinator also ordered other measures to encourage outlaws to surrender.

Wang's overall approach is documented in an analysis of conditions he sent to the emperor in the spring. Based on consultations with officials and village elders, he could only conclude that the reason banditry had increased was that too often authorities were giving in to bandits' demands. Connecting this with his request for greater military authority, Wang linked such excessive appeasement measures to a weak military presence in the region, and the weak military presence to an ineffectively applied reward and punishment system for both officers and the rank and file.[118] Nothing more clearly suggests Wang had adopted the essentially hard-line approach to problems in the region first formulated by Jiangxi's surveillance commissioner, Yang Zhang, who concluded that bringing order to the region required formally elaborating the statutes for military administration of the Ming legal code and backing them up with real action.

Wang begins with his claim that while appeasement works when dealing with mostly coerced innocents capable of reform, such an approach only further emboldens hardened criminals. That is what had taken place in southern Jiangxi where, owing to officials' hands-off policy, law-abiding subjects found themselves without recourse, and therefore had no choice but to cooperate with the bandits: "In the beginning they were merely trying to avoid calamity, but in the end they joined and positively benefited them."[119] Wang presented

---

115   Ibid., 17:601.
116   Ibid., 10:349.
117   Ibid., 16:548.
118   Ibid., 9:308.
119   Ibid., 9:309.

what amounts to a picture of a lawless frontier controlled in large measure by gangs of bandits holding local populations hostage, which is why he wanted armies "sufficient to eradicate the rebel leaders and clean out their lairs and haunts, so the people's anger will be avenged and the danger to the area removed."[120]

How had appeasement practically become the norm? Wang asserted that officials were complicit in this snowballing lawlessness, sacrificing the local population to avoid tarnishing their reputations, because they were powerless to confront the powerful bandit leaders. He pointed out to the court that it was far easier to appease and sit on the sidelines than to deploy force. Should they fail in doing so, political adversaries would smear and impeach them, and they would be forced "to atone for their crimes by killing bandits."[121] In other words, officials had every reason to avoid involvement: "They would rather afflict the people with great suffering than dare to dispatch just one soldier to fight against a spreading enemy. They would rather allow the orphaned and widowed to cry out, those in distress and suffering hardship to have no place to turn to, than risk offending appeased bandits by raising one division."[122]

Why was the military presence in the region insufficient, leaving officials with no choice but to tolerate the intolerable? For Wang Yangming, the problem was a failure of leadership. Those with the authority to reward and punish must wield it to revive military institutions. For him, success in war was largely a matter of timing and discipline, and neither was in good order in the region. The bandits always had the upper hand because, whenever officials mobilized forces, this invariably transpired so slowly that they had ample time to make themselves invisible. Yet even more significant was the issue of motivation among the troops stationed in southern Jiangxi. Wang quoted the ancient military strategist Wu Qi for his court audience stating, "'If laws and orders are not clear, rewards and punishments not trusted, then even if you had one million men, of what use would they be?' As for the soldiers' state of mind, should they fear me they won't fear the enemy, but should they fear the enemy they won't fear me."[123]

It was just such misplaced fear that was at the root of the problem: "The troops of Nan'an and Ganzhou are yet sufficient to number in the thousands, so how could it possibly be the case that they are of no use for deployment? Yet

---

120 Ibid.
121 Ibid.
122 Ibid.
123 Ibid., 9:310. Wang is citing Chapter Three of the *Wuzi* 吴子. For this translation see Sawyer, *Seven Military Classics of Ancient China*, 214.

when the *gong* is struck they don't stop, and when the drums are beat they don't advance; even before they see the enemy they are defeated, and before they engage in battle they run away."[124] That was why the grand coordinator wanted greater discretionary power to reward and punish: "To advance and serve with one's life without being motivated by the promise of rank and reward and to withdraw and flee without threat of execution is to be assured of death should one advance but possibly receive the great fortune of surviving should one draw back—why should they bring upon themselves the calamity of a sure death?"[125]

On October 1, 1517, in response to his two petitions, Wang was granted the additional title of military superintendent (*tidu junwu* 提督軍務), greater discretionary power (*bianyi xingshi* 便宜行事), as well as the banner and card (*qi pai* 旗牌). This signified what amounted to virtually unlimited power to act on his own authority without outside interference. According to Okada Takehiko, his request for broad powers under such circumstances was unprecedented and politically risky, and it was only with the support of the Minister of War Wang Qiong that concerns at court were overcome.[126] In fact, throughout the year, Wang had been dispatching letters to the minister, explaining how "multiple lines of command" were the principal causes of the ineffective response to disorder in the region. He emphasized that "in the matter of military campaigns, what is to be treasured is concentration of authority as well as avoiding insofar as possible control from a distance;" otherwise, regional officials would not understand that they must follow orders and discipline will fail to be instilled.[127] In short, as he would also explain to the emperor, "Through the handles of rewards and punishments, the spiritedness of the Three Armies will be bolstered; with the clout of the card and banner, soldiers near and far will be summoned; with the authority of the superintendent of military affairs, the officials of eight prefectures and one subprefecture will be controlled."[128] Thus, having received these orders, Wang immediately circulated the emperor's accompanying imperial command-edict to all of his subordinates, in preparation for the next series of campaigns.

---

124 *WYMQJ*, vol. 1, 9:310.

125 Ibid.

126 Okada, *Ō Yōmei taiden*, 3:232. For a discussion of the additional powers such titles gave to grand coordinators, see Fan, "Mingdai dufu de zhiquan ji qi xingzhi," 51–52; and Zhang Zhelang 張哲郎, *Mingdai xunfu yanjiu* 明代巡撫研究 [Research on Ming Dynasty Grand Coordinators] (Taipei: Wen shi zhe chubanshe, 1995), 193.

127 *WYMQJ*, vol. 1, 11:376.

128 *WYMQJ*, vol. 2, 27:1004.

Organizing the Armies

The now further empowered grand coordinator gave tactical orders for "clearing away the mass of evildoers"[129] to ten contingents composed of commanders and soldiers drawn from the population of civilian and military officials and commoners under his jurisdiction. He envisioned that these forces would be highly organized, disciplined, and united. These contingents, divided up according to prefecture or county of origin, each consisted of roughly one thousand men drawn from local security personnel, "stalwarts," resettled outlaws, soldiers from local units of the regular military hierarchy, and simply those skilled in archery, crossbows, hand-to-hand combat, guns (*chong* 銃), and other weaponry. They were to be led by the long list of named civilian and military officials we find in those official communications conveying Wang's battle plans: prefects, magistrates, vice-magistrates, county jailors, a regional military commissioner, and guard and battalion commander.[130]

Aside from the composition of his armies, Wang Yangming was also deeply concerned with organization and discipline. Under the principle that "in the practice of warfare nothing is more critical than the ranks, and for the method of regulating the group, nothing comes before division into units,"[131] the military superintendent spelled out for his commanders just how armies of two thousand four hundred soldiers were to be amalgamated from squads of twenty-five. Between these would be platoons, companies, brigades, and divisions, and all would be commanded by men with specific titles, each of whom was responsible for the discipline and punishment of those immediately beneath him. To control deployments, these units were to manufacture two identical tallies with characters naming the unit, one to remain with the unit and one to go to Wang's headquarters. In a communication, Wang explained the goal of this organization to his commanders: "The officers and soldiers must support each other, the large and small mutually assist each other, like the body moving the arm and the arm moving the finger—[in this way] deployments shall naturally occur in unison, large groups will be regulated as if they are small, and perhaps [we] will have a well-ordered army."[132]

To motivate these soldiers beyond what they might expect from the spoils of war or removing troublemakers from their region, and drawing on his "high authority to reward and punish" as military superintendent, Wang Yangming provided lists for his commanders of violations for which officers or rank and

---

129   *WYMQJ*, vol. 1, 16:550.
130   Ibid., 16:548–55.
131   Ibid., 16:542.
132   Ibid.

file were to be executed. For example, for drawing back from the battlefront; violating commands and orders; causing any turmoil for residents when passing through communities; while in the barracks, speaking in private of strategy or speaking recklessly about calamities and felicities, good and ill luck.[133] Other orders addressed units: "Whenever at the front lines confronting the enemy, should a platoon suffer a defeat because they deviated from orders, the squads shall all be executed; should the neighboring platoon fail to come to their assistance, all shall be executed."[134]

These are just some of the many specific orders Wang Yangming handed down to his commanding officers, for the purpose of instilling in the ranks fear of the consequences of disobeying orders. But at the very time he was putting in place these measures necessary to create a disciplined and organized fighting force composed of skilled troops, he was also evaluating strategic conditions and formulating an overall plan, one for the region as a whole and one more specifically for the first of what would amount to a series of three campaigns.

Wang Yangming's strategy can be sketched out in brief. In light of the repeated armed disturbances throughout the region, Supreme Commander of Guangdong and Guangxi Qin Jin had already in the spring proposed raising a massive three-province army for a concerted campaign. Commander Qin subsequently received orders from the Ming court to proceed.[135] However, Wang echoed Commissioner Yang's claim that while a large campaign might be the ideal, it was not feasible given current conditions, and therefore he laid out his plan for a series of more focused strikes.[136]

The grand coordinator was weighing two factors when deciding how the campaigns should be carried out. Firstly, the enemy was spread out over a large area and could be broken down into three different, identifiable groups with different leaders and interests, all separated from each other by some distance: the "She bandits" of Nan'an Prefecture in Jiangxi, the bandits centered in Lechang 樂昌 in northern Guangdong, and the bandits in Litou 浰頭, a place located in Huizhou Prefecture, Guangdong. As Wang estimated it, due to the distances between them and the fact that they consisted of "many kinds of people," alliances between these groups were fragile and fleeting; therefore, he was confident he could control them through stratagem.[137]

---

133   Ibid., 16:550–51.
134   Ibid., 16:551.
135   *NP*, 33:1251. These orders are cited in Qin, *An chu lu*, 10:780–82.
136   *WYMQJ*, vol. 1, 10:333.
137   Ibid.

This was a key factor, as Wang also had to take into account the availability of his armies: for example, forces in Guangdong could not be assembled and trained as quickly as those in Huguang and Jiangxi. He therefore proposed first attacking the many bandit lairs in Nan'an Prefecture, Jiangxi, while controlling the other areas of strategic concern (Lechang, Litou) with proclamations offering amnesty. In general, he estimated that the leaders of each trouble spot would prefer to avoid major confrontations with large forces and therefore not come to each other's assistance should they not see an immediate threat. Psychologically speaking, they would be open to such deception, and Wang therefore embraced this principle when formulating the plans he would circulate to officials. His Huguang and Jiangxi forces could, while separating out other hot spots with amnesties, campaign in Nan'an. Having defeated these bandits, those in Lechang would be isolated and easily defeated by a concerted attack involving armies in the provinces of Guangdong and Huguang. Lastly, the bandits to the east, in Litou, believing troops in Jiangxi were yet far off and withdrawing, could easily be taken by the combined Guangdong and Jiangxi forces. Such a plan would fall under the following principles: "Warfare is without a predetermined strategic balance of power, what is to be valued is timing;" "attacking where they are unprepared;" and "according to the configuration of the terrain, determining which ordering of coordinated attacks is advantageous."[138]

The Campaign in Nan'an

Preserving the element of surprise in order to throw the enemy off guard, was also central to Wang Yangming's strategizing for the first of these campaigns. Discussions with local officials (and now commanders) during the fall of 1517 centered upon what were viewed as three strategically critical She bandit strongholds located in Nan'an Prefecture that dozens of enemy settlements depended on: the mountainous and heavily forested areas of Hengshui, Zuoxi, and Tonggang. By that time, Supreme Commander Qin Jin was already planning, in a campaign coordinated with armies arriving from Guangdong and Jiangxi, to attack Tonggang on November 15, 1517. The general consensus among officials seemed to be that this should be the first target.[139]

However, the grand coordinator's opinion was otherwise, and when he dispatched orders with detailed plans for just how commanders of each of the ten contingents were to deploy, departing from which locations at what time, passing through which lairs and meeting up at what destinations, he explained why they must first go after what he called the "belly and heart" of the bandits,

---

138   Ibid.
139   Ibid., 10:342.

"causing the root and trunk to be totally uprooted, leaving not a soul behind."[140] These were the "lairs" in and around Hengshui and Zuoxi. But although Tong-gang was a crucial route for bandit movements, it served merely as a "wing" for the belly and heart. Attacking it first would place forces between the enemy and cause them to lose the strategic advantage. Secondly, interrogations of captured She bandits had revealed that their leaders believed this to be the first target.[141] In Wang's opinion, those of Hengshui and Zuoxi, on the other hand, scorned the military and believed a campaign against them was still far off in the future, and had therefore let down their guard. What better time to "attack when they least expect it"? "Having destroyed Hengshui and Zuoxi," he informed his commanders, troops can then march to Tonggang, "riding on bamboo-splitting power, carrying all before us, advancing victoriously."[142]

Wang Yangming departed Ganzhou on October 21 with his contingent at the very moment others were setting out from their respective locations in sur-rounding counties, first passing through Nan'an's Nankang County and then encamping at a settlement named Zhipeng. Stories about his conduct through-out this time highlight his efforts to maintain the utmost secrecy and gather as much intelligence as possible. While residing at his headquarters in Ganzhou, for instance, Wang Yangming's routine was to exit from the side gate of his headquarters, enter the archery grounds, and hold discussions and practice archery with students, only taking leave in the evening. The day prior to his departure, Wang was said to have stuck to his routine, even staying up so late that students politely suggested he might return to his yamen for a rest. When they returned the next morning to pay respects to their master, a guard at the gate turned them away, explaining that the grand coordinator had departed with troops early in the morning, but that he was unsure as to which direction they had traveled.[143]

---

140   Ibid., 16:553.
141   Ibid., 16:548–49.
142   Ibid., 16:343–44.
143   This anecdote is recounted in Feng Menglong 馮夢龍, "Huang Ming da ru Wang Yang-ming xiansheng chu shen jing luan lu 皇明大儒王陽明靖亂錄 [Record of the Pacifica-tion of Disorder by the Great Ming Confucian Wang Yangming]," in *Feng Menglong quan ji* 馮夢龍全集 [Complete Collected Works of Feng Menglong], vol. 30 (Shanghai: Shang-hai guji chubanshe, 1993), 69–70. I do reference Feng Menglong's account of Wang Yang-ming's career in subsequent chapters when his narrative aligns with earlier sources. For a study of the origins of Feng's information, Zhang Zhaowei's annotated edition is useful. See Feng Menglong 馮夢龍, *Huang ming da ru Wang Yangming* 皇明大儒王陽明 [The Great Ming Confucian Great Wang Yangming], ed. Zhang Zhaowei 張昭煒 (Beijing: Jiu-zhou Press, 2014).

When Wang Yangming arrived in Nankang on October 23, he detained two officials suspected of fraternizing with bandits. On threat of execution, they volunteered as much information as they could about the layout of the bandit lairs and, more importantly, brought forth a certain craftsmen by the name of Zhang Bao, who was said to have detailed knowledge of the terrain because he had often helped the bandits build their fortresses. Although he had been forewarned that this region had remained out of reach to government forces due to its precipitous mountains, deep ravines, and dense forests, the grand coordinator was not surprised when the maps he had Zhang draw up pinpointing the bandit fortresses showed paths for advancing and withdrawing, ways of ascending and descending the mountains, and other details about accessing this uninviting terrain.[144] He had already received many reports about bandits in these areas tunneling into mountains, fortifying themselves at critical defiles, and constructing "flying ladders" to ascend the jutting faces of mountains, whose peaks would once more become unreachable once the ladders were destroyed.[145]

After strikes begun on October 26 had come to a close on December 15, 1517, Wang Yangming was able to report to the emperor that 80 settlements had been occupied, 86 leaders and 3,160 followers captured and executed, and 2,336 dependents taken prisoner. These were the same folks who were scattered about eking out a living in such forbidding terrain, fighting with and preying upon local registered populations, in some kind of alliance with Yao populations of neighboring provinces, and who acted so in accordance with their self-proclaimed king and descendant of the revered progenitor Panhu 盤瓠, ironically the very one who—as legend had it—had been such a noble and loyal supporter to the emperor.

On October 25, when Wang Yangming and his contingent arrived at a location some thirty *li* from "bandit lairs," they discovered that despite having been taken by surprise, the enemy had managed not only to fortify themselves quickly within gorges but also to prepare logs and boulders to shower down upon his forces. In response, Wang ordered his armies to pretend they were standing down and encamping, by cutting down trees and building shacks, digging trenches and building up mounds. At the same time, he ordered two aides to lead undetected four hundred men skilled at mountain climbing, ascend the surrounding peaks, and spread out in and around the bandit settlements. Among these settlements was Hengshui, where the key leader Xie Zhishan and his accomplices were located, believing it "was located right in

---

144   Feng, "Huang Ming da ru Wang Yangming," 71–72.
145   *WYMQJ*, vol. 1, 16:548–49.

the middle of perilous terrain, and could therefore be relied upon as an impregnable location."[146]

The purpose behind this tactic was to gain the strategic advantage over the
bandits. Once spread out over and above enemy positions, these soldiers were
to time their attack with soldiers down below and then to unfurl their flags,
light fires from "thousands of stoves" filled with grass, and fire off the firearms
and cannon they had carried along with them. According to his report to the
court, that is indeed what happened when his troops approached one of the
key passes:

> At the very moment when the bandits were relying on their advanta-
> geous terrain to confront us, they suddenly heard explosions like thunder
> on mountain peaks near and far and [saw] smoke and flames rising
> everywhere. Our troops, while yelling out, pressed ahead with determina-
> tion, simultaneously shooting arrows and firing their guns. All of the ban-
> dits were alarmed and routed, at a loss as to how to proceed and, believing
> our troops had already entered and destroyed their lairs and haunts, they
> abandoned their defiles and withdrew.[147]

What followed after the initial attack was a series of battles extending over
thirteen days as the contingents made their way through the area and attacked,
occupied, and burned out dozens of settlements, met up in Hengshui and
Zuoxi, and then spent a period of time pursuing those in flight. The pursuit was
arduous. Wang later presented to the court a picture of soldiers making their
way along routes barely passable with their dense brush, deep ravines, and
steep cliffs full of pits, fallen trees, and other traps such as sharpened bamboo
branches set up by the enemy. "When they came upon insurmountable barri-
ers," he stated, "[the soldiers would] hang ropes from trees on the cliffs, ascending in single file and descending swiftly like monkeys, repeatedly losing footing
and falling into deep ravines."[148]

Following his initial battle plan, Wang hoped to build on the momentum
from these victories and achieve a quick victory over remaining strongholds in
and around Tonggang, yet more impenetrable territory. Wang described it as
an area of about one hundred square *li* surrounded on all sides by green cliffs
soaring to an immeasurable height; so dense was the forest that not even the
sun or moon could be seen. Only five paths could be used to climb the

---

146   Ibid., 10:345.
147   Ibid., 10:344.
148   Ibid., 10:345.

mountains, but all required planked paths or ladders for scaling the cliffs and ravines, and whenever the bandits were being pursued, just a few men would be able to prevent penetration simply by dropping boulders on their heads from the peaks.[149] For this reason, Wang informed the court, previous campaigns had invariably failed and concluded with measures for appeasement.

Under such conditions, Wang Yangming again opted for stratagem, envisioning that "should we move forces and encamp in nearby terrain, rest the soldiers and allow the crack troops to recuperate, make a display of our might and, in advance, dispatch an envoy to instruct [the bandits] in misfortune and fortune they will surely become afraid and request to surrender. But should there be some that don't follow, we shall take advantage of their indecision, and spring an attack on them."[150] While three officials were ascending the cliffs around Tonggang to meet up with the settlement leaders on November 11, Wang was deploying contingents at each of the five known paths in preparation for a concerted assault. According to what he later gathered, the envoys' peace offer did indeed cause a degree of conflict and hesitation among the leadership, thereby causing them to temporarily let down their guard. This left them unprepared for an assault launched amidst heavy downpours just three days later on the fourteenth, at which time contingents began ascending the cliffs of Tonggang and pursuing the bandits all over the territory within.[151] Although campaigns to clean out remnants in flight lasted until mid-December, Wang could report that on November 26 "the bandits of Tonggang were mostly eradicated": the bulk of the lairs had been cleaned out, large numbers killed and captured, and "an undetermined number in the deep ravines and gullies starved to death, died of illness, or fell to their deaths."[152]

Wang Yangming remained directly involved in the campaign at Tonggang, leading those under his command to Chaliao 茶寮. This was at the center of routes coming from several directions, right in the middle of Tonggang, as well as a critical bandit defile. While there, he noted to the court, "having some spare time, I personally surveyed the configuration of the terrain and the disposition of troops, [having them] occupy advantageous terrain and critical defiles, and having several hundred soldiers chop wood and build planked pathways along the cliffs, cut into the mountains, and build roads."[153] Most important among these initial projects was establishing a battalion at Chaliao

149   Ibid., 16:557.
150   Ibid., 10:346.
151   Ibid., 10:349.
152   Ibid., 10:348.
153   Ibid.

Pass, and to this end soldiers were designated to begin construction of a foundation and earthen wall.[154]

It was also at Chaliao that Wang Yangming would leave a record of these campaigns in the form of a commemorative stone tablet, which remains even today. The inscription begins by pointing to the great turmoil the "Yao" of three provinces created for subjects throughout the region, and follows up with a brief description of the mission with which the court entrusted him, the course of the series of battles that ensued, numbers killed and captured, and some of the measures taken to make the area secure and accessible. Nonetheless, Wang's conclusion was hardly celebratory:

> On *jiaxu* [November 15, 1517], [our troops] again battled, and the bandits were utterly routed. On *dinghai* [November 28, 1517], [we] totally annihilated them. All told eighty-four lairs were destroyed, three thousand captured and killed, and over thirty-six hundred taken prisoner.... On *xinchou* [December 12, 1517], the armies were withdrawn. Oh my! Arms are instruments of ill omen, only to be used when there is no other option. This stone at Chaliao is being inscribed not to glorify victory, but rather because of the seriousness of a rebellion. Composed by Military Superintendant and Censor in Chief Wang.[155]

Why the gloom? Wang was citing wisdom from the *Classic of the Way and Power*, according to which, "arms are instruments of ill omen, not the instruments of gentlemen. When one is compelled to use them, it is best to do so without relish. There is no glory in victory, and to glorify it despite this is to exult in the killing of men. One who exults in the killing of men will never have his way in the empire."[156] Indeed, throughout this time Wang Yangming repeatedly expressed his fear that, as a poem he inscribed nearby the stele put it, "complete eradication may mean some [innocents] suffer coercion; [I] yet fear that the sharp blade of the military was applied in excess."[157] Should this be the case, he well knew, many would simply turn to the very mode of livelihood that was bringing chaos to the region.

While Wang's concern for innocent people is evident enough, what of those incorrigible individuals who forced him to apply instruments of ill omen and whom he repeatedly condemned? After the bandit chieftain and self-pro-

---

154   Ibid., 16:558.
155   Ibid., 25:947.
156   Lao-Tzu [pseud.], *Tao Te Ching*, trans. D.C. Lau (New York: Penguin, 1963), 89.
157   *WYMQJ*, vol. 1, 20:747.

claimed king Xie Zhishan was captured at Tonggang, he was brought before Wang Yangming. Wang's *Chronological Biography* records the following exchange:

> Wang: "How did you amass such a large gang as you did?"
> Xie: "This also was not easy."
> Wang: "What do you mean?"
> Xie: "In this world, whenever I crossed paths with a true man I would absolutely not allow him easily to pass me by. I would employ every means possible to win them over, sometimes setting out much wine, sometimes assisting them should they have an emergency. [I would] treat them with the virtue of a minister and speak frankly with them, and there were none whom did not respond."[158]

This must have struck him because later, when speaking with a student, Wang is said to have asked, "During this lifetime of ours, when scholars like ourselves seek the benefits of friendship, how does it differ from this?"[159]

Is it possible that Wang Yangming's sense of regret throughout this time was the result of the contradiction between the supposedly incorrigible conduct of the "Yao savages" and moments like these? According to one account, Wang had ordered Xie's head put on display by the outer gate of a government yamen, and this conversation took place just prior to his decapitation.[160]

Records from the *Nan'an Prefectural Gazetteer* largely confirm what the *Chronological Biography* claims transpired upon Wang Yangming's return with troops during the last month of 1517: "When the troops arrived in Nankang, people lined up along the streets to burn incense, greet them, and pay their respects, and every subprefecture, county, pass, and battalion they traversed erected a memorial hall."[161] According to the record for the memorial hall next to the Confucian temple-school, when people lined up along the routes bowing and shouting, "We will live, the one who has brought peace to us is Master [Wang]," he replied, "Truly it was Heaven that has caused the people of this place to live, what had I to do with it?"[162] In the end, it appears, a higher justice was served.

---

158 *NP*, 33:1247.

159 Ibid.

160 Feng, "Huang Ming da ru Wang Yangming," 84.

161 *NP*, 33:1247. Records for other halls in honor of living officials constructed at this time in Nan'an Prefecture, Nankang County, and Shangyou County may be found in Liu Jie, ed., *Jiajing Nan'an fu zhi*, 511 (12:10), 535 (12:21), 548 (12:36).

162 Ibid., 511 (12:10).

Eradicating the Bandits of Northern Guangdong

The story of the crimes and fate of the Chi brothers and their accomplices epitomizes what should by now seem like a familiar drama of events unfolding in the region under Wang's charge. In his report to the grand coordinator, Commissioner Yang Zhang cited a litany of crimes perpetrated by the "big thumb" and root of the troublesome populations in the region: "The Litou bandit ringleaders Chi Zhongrong, Chi Zhongning, Chi Zhong'an, Gao Yunxian, Li Quan and others squatted on [this] territory over a period of years, arrogated the title of king to themselves, illegally appointed phony officials, repeatedly attacking and laying siege to [neighboring counties], killing government troops, burning stockaded villages, capturing and killing men and women, for years without one day of rest."[163]

Judging from reports cited in Wang Yangming's communications, the commissioner does not appear to have been exaggerating. His report was based in part upon what he was gathering from local elites and county officials residing in northern Guangdong near the Sanli 三浰 River in the Jiulian 九連 mountain range. A petition requesting establishment of a county seat records the recollections of local elders, according to whom the territory included in Longchuan County was formerly a prefecture with two counties populated by registered law-abiding subjects. But at some point during the first Ming emperor's reign, bandits marauded over the area, killing or chasing them off. Since that time, "lairs have increased and registered subjects decreased," and "authority and education have failed to reach there." Consequently, all that remained was one county under the jurisdiction of Huizhou Prefecture and a great deal of territory in the hands of bandits.[164] The local elders also reported that over the previous twenty years, some one hundred bandit chieftains led by the likes of Chi Zhongrong 池仲容, along with their gangs of several thousand, had occupied fields belonging to commoners in areas of Longchuan County, attacked nearby prefectural and county seats, and provided refuge and leadership for fugitives from surrounding provinces.[165]

In the aftermath of his last major campaign in the region, Wang Yangming did come to believe the request was justified and thus memorialized the court for permission to establish a county seat at Heping 和平, Guangdong.[166] More recent troubles largely centered round this level settlement located conve-

---

163   *WYMQJ*, vol. 1, 11:358.
164   Ibid., 11:367.
165   Ibid.
166   Ibid., 11:355–70.

niently amidst four counties and at the juncture of three provinces. The Chi
kinsmen likely hailed from a powerful lineage residing there, but because they
repeatedly attempted to occupy the fields of neighboring residents, they invariably wound up in feuds with other well-known lineages. According to one
account, "the wealthy would be forced to let him [Chi Zhongrong] borrow silver and rice, and should anyone resist him in the slightest he would burn them
down, leaving no one behind."[167] Eventually, the Chi kinsmen fell afoul of authorities and forced over half the estimated two thousand families in Heping
to flee to a nearby town for protection. When officials responded by sending in
troops, the Chi forged alliances with other "bandits" in the region but also drew
in fugitives and what Wang would later recognize as being a large number of
migrants. Eventually, Heping and its surrounding territory, all amidst mountains and rivers that largely cut the area off from the nearest government seats,
became—as Wang characterized it—an area infested with hundreds of bandit
lairs. He described the territory as "the hideouts of petty thieves," "the gathering point of those in flight," where bandits moved about freely from one place
to another, as well as a place where "plots for rebellion" brewed in secret.[168] He
claimed that when officials mobilized large armies composed of non-Chinese
native troops from neighboring provinces to clean them out, they simply dispersed before the troops arrived, only to return when the coast was clear. In the
end, officials were mired in fruitless cycles of appeasement of and attacks
upon leaders who merely in appearance offered to surrender but in reality carried on with their evildoing.[169]

Of all the outlaws Wang Yangming had dealt with up to this point, the opinion he held of these was the lowest. In the aftermath of campaigns that began
on February 16, 1518 and concluded on April 17 with the destruction of a total of
thirty-eight lairs and the capture and killing of some two thousand, the grand
coordinator composed a powerful indictment for the emperor, in which he
thoroughly demonized an enemy that brazenly flouted all standards and blatantly manipulated appeasement to further their criminal activities:

> The bandits' principal ringleaders Chi Zhongrong and others have for
> years wreaked havoc among the people, harassed three provinces, and
> plotted rebellion in secret. They have appointed officials and usurped
> titles, their wicked crimes overflowing to the heavens. Compared to the
> bandits of Shangyou, they are far more ferocious, unruly, and difficult to

---

167 Feng, "Huang Ming da ru Wang Yangming," 81.
168 *WYMQJ*, vol. 1, 11:368.
169 Ibid., 11:365–68.

control.... Although they also have the characteristic of plundering and kidnapping, they in fact harbor the intention to usurp official titles and set up a separatist regime. Thus, they summon the rootless from all directions and conceal the evil and wicked from near and far. They plot and plan day and night, gradually putting together a treacherous plot. In addition, the bandit principals Chi Zhongrong, Chi Zhong'an and others all have the strength to fight with fierce tigers and defeat powerful macaques. They have for long had a reputation for savage ferocity, and bandit gangs in all directions submit to them. Thus, they rely on impregnable locations and their obstinate persistence, and the more they are attacked the greater their blaze becomes.[170]

In light of such depravity, the grand coordinator moved decisively against the Chi kinsmen and their allied "gangs," "within two months destroying the unruly treacherous, removing the danger that had spread over three provinces for several decades."[171]

So who was Wang Yangming demonizing? The locals stated that the purpose of their petition for a county seat was to "control Yao settlements 瑤洞" and "change customs and mores."[172] At other points in Wang's communications, the principals are referred to as chieftains (*qiuzhang* 酋長). When one adds to this the number of settlements involved (a reported thirty-six), the size of the territory, and the occasional statement by Wang that neighboring areas needed to be appeased so as to prevent them from getting involved, it is distinctly possible that ethnic tensions played a role—in both fostering solidarity among so many people over such a large area, as well as feeding social tensions that could potentially erupt as uprisings.

Once again, however, labels suggesting ethnic difference or a Han/non-Han distinction are notably absent in Wang Yangming's communications concerning these peoples. One possibility is that what appear to be migrants who came into conflict with locals were in fact peoples ancestral to the Hakkas (*kejia* 客家). S.T. Leong believes that many of those populations that were later (during the Qing) recognized as Hakka resided in these areas of the upper reaches of the East River or had migrated from them during the Ming dynasty. Much of the conflict was clearly internal to the region, and involved a number of recognized leaders hailing from what appear to be several different feuding lineages. Should that be the case, the strife, according to Leong, was likely an early stage

---

170   Ibid., 11:365.
171   Ibid., 11:366.
172   Ibid., 11:367.

of the creation of a Hakka ethnicity during the Qing: "Migration was the particular context in which ethnic consciousness and conflict merged, in terms of
a conflict between 'natives' and 'newcomers.'"[173] Nevertheless, for Wang Yangming the criminal behavior of these outlaws was simply brazen wickedness,
willfully misguided actions of those who had chosen this path. It is indeed difficult to move beyond this perception to ferret out other reasons why these
peoples were constantly clashing with other locals and the authorities, and
seemed driven to draw in others like themselves to set up a polity of their own,
if that is what they were really up to.

The Master of Deception

Of all the campaigns Wang Yangming directed, we have the most detailed information concerning his tactics for negotiating with, manipulating, coercing,
deceiving, enticing, and maneuvering among the parties involved in his suppression of the bandits of Litou. Accounts suggest that, behind the scenes and
prior to his campaigns, the grand coordinator was extraordinarily adept at slip-
ping himself into local conflicts and tensions (and politics) to gain the upper
hand, as well as using ploys to deceive his enemies. It was probably for this
reason, among others, that he was able within three months to rein in this festering problem officials had failed to control for years.

Wang Yangming's effort "to defeat the enemy in advance" began long before
troops marched into Upper, Middle, and Lower Litou on February 16, 1518. Even
prior to taking on the armed disturbances in Nan'an Prefecture during the fall
of 1517, he had sent out an offer of amnesty to the powerful lineages ensconced
in northern Guangdong, in a deliberate move to prevent further attacks. The
goal, as he told the court, was to "check and drive a wedge between [the adherents of] his [Chi Zhongrong's] gang."[174] The powerfully worded proclamation
he addressed to them stated in no uncertain terms just why he had good reason
to annihilate them and why others throughout the region likewise had good
reason to harbor enmity towards them. It explained that he nonetheless fully
understood that there might be mitigating circumstances leading them to behave as they had, as well as spelling those out so as to make them feel understood. Lastly, it concluded with a demonstration of largesse, by letting them
know how deeply troubled he was by the thought of having to annihilate them
and offering them the chance to come forward and reform.[175]

173   Sow-Theung, Leong, *Migration and Ethnicity in Chinese History: Hakkas, Pengmin, and
        their Neighbors*, ed. Tim Wright (Stanford: Stanford University Press, 1997), 20.
174   *WYMQJ*, vol. 1, 11:359.
175   Ibid., 16:560–62.

The proclamation, sent out shortly before his campaign against the She bandits, achieved its intended effect. After Wang Yangming dispatched a licentiate and an honorary commoner from his yamen in Ganzhou to carry the offer along with gifts of silver and cloth, they journeyed south to the fortified settlements around Litou, and indeed succeeded in bringing back a number of headmen.[176] The grand coordinator treated these men with great honor, pardoned them of all crimes, and took advantage of their offer to requite with the service of killing bandits. In no time, the headman Huang Jinchao and five hundred men accompanying him were assembled into a contingent, and would serve in armies that campaigned in Hengshui.[177]

The Chi men, however, were not won over by the proclamation, and refused to come in. Wang imagined they would have reasoned in private conversation: "It has not been for merely a year that we have engaged in banditry, and there has been more than one occasion when officials have come to offer amnesty, so how could we believe this?"[178] For this reason, Wang surmised, they chose to remain in Litou and observe how other local leaders were being received and treated. Noting how they served under him during the Hengshui campaigns, and alarmed by the rapidity with which the She bandits were eradicated, Chi Zhongrong, in consultation with other leaders, chose to send his younger brother Chi Zhong'an 池仲安 with a small contingent of men to surrender and offer service to the military superintendent.

By this time, however, Wang Yangming had already made up his mind that the Chi kinsmen were, as others had been telling him, "crafty, cunning, savage, and ferocious." He thus viewed the arrival of a Chi brother as nothing more than subterfuge, an attempt on the part of these ringleaders to spy on his movements and serve as infiltrators.[179] "To guard against any trouble from them," he explained to the Ming court, "while maintaining vigilance in preparation for defensive action, I put on the appearance of offering generous treatment, to put their minds at ease."[180] Chi Zhong'an and his men were also allowed to serve in the battle at Tonggang, but deployed in such a way as to prevent them from returning quickly to their settlements.

After that campaign concluded and Wang had returned to Nankang on December 27, 1517, his strategizing continued apace, especially because Chi Zhongrong and his supporters in Litou had continued to prepare themselves

176   Ibid., 11:360.
177   Ibid.
178   Ibid., 11:359.
179   Ibid., 11:360.
180   Ibid.

against an attack. A key element of Wang's strategy was to build connections with local enemies of the Chi lineage and their allies. Prior to the campaign in Tonggang, the grand coordinator had already dispatched a summons to people living in neighboring counties who claimed to have suffered harm from these men. He asked them to come to his military headquarters and strategize with him. Several dozen arrived, and their advice to Wang was that he should call up a large army of native troops from outside the area, in preparation for a massive assault. But as before, Wang rejected this plan, for the lesson he had learned from previous campaigns of a similar nature was that the bandits knew how to melt away as the slow, cumbersome armies assembled and deployed. After formulating an initial battle plan that would rely heavily on the element of surprise and local support, he asked these men to return home, assemble militias, and at such time as armies were to advance, occupy all passes and intercept the bandits.[181]

Of more immediate significance would be the assistance Wang received from two powerful leaders of local families from Longchuan County. The headmen Lu Ke, Zheng Zhigao, and others were said to be "resettled outlaws" who had earlier accepted an offer of amnesty from Wang Yangming.[182] These local leaders of some three thousand people had been engaged in feuding with the Chi for some time, and Wang intended to exploit this to his advantage, by feigning to support the Chi lineage against them.

The success at Tonggang gave the leaders at Litou more cause for concern, something Wang Yangming suspected when he dispatched someone to bring them bulls and wine, offer reassurances, and spy on their movements. The Litou bandits justified their ongoing defensive preparations by saying they feared reprisals from the Lu and Zheng clans (who, they claimed, were raising armies). Wang pretended to believe their explanation, even dispatching a military communication to regional officials ordering a complete investigation of the latter. Ever the actor, he also sent a message to Chi Zhongrong to tell him to prepare to a clear a path for his troops to pass through should he need to lead a punitive campaign against those rival clans.[183]

On December 27, Lu Ke and Zheng Zhigao called on Wang Yangming at his military headquarters in Nankang, presenting a written complaint listing the crimes committed by Chi Zhongrong and his accomplices, including virtually everything Wang had already heard from regional officials.[184] Wang explained the ensuing series of events to the court:

---

181   Ibid.
182   Ibid., 11:357–61.
183   Ibid., 11:360.
184   Ibid.

I had already gathered intelligence concerning this matter, and when Ke and others arrived, I pretended to be very angry, accusing them of raising an army on their own authority and killing for revenge individuals whom had planned to or already surrendered. For their crimes [I informed them] they should be executed. Now they are manufacturing baseless accusations and taking advantage of the situation to frame [their adversaries]. Furthermore, Chi Zhongrong has just sent his younger brother to lead troops and requite with service, sincerely to submit and change, so how could this be? I then bound up Ke and the others and prepared to execute them. At the time Chi Zhong'an and those under him were present at my headquarters, and seeing Ke enter and inform against them, became alarmed and afraid. But after [seeing how I acted], they were pleased, lining up and calling out, competing with each other to denounce Ke and the others for their wicked crimes. In response I ordered them to compose a written complaint, and stated I would detain [Ke's] dependents and slaughter them.[185]

While all of this transpired, Wang Yangming secretly let Lu Ke and the other headmen know this was all an act, including the light thirty lashings they would receive as well as their temporary imprisonment. His younger brother was secretly sent back to Longchuan to continue assembling a force in preparation for the impending campaign.[186]

While staging this show in Nankang, Wang continued the offensive in Litou. He dispatched two men to bribe Chi Zhongrong's confidantes and have them convince him to come to his headquarters and levy charges against Lu Ke and Zheng Zhigao. On January 1, the grand coordinator returned to the censorate seat at Ganzhou with the now imprisoned enemies of the Chi kinsmen. While his envoys were bringing gifts to and warning Chi Zhongrong that failure to come forward and put the final nail in the coffin of their local adversaries might lead the grand coordinator to suspect there may be some merit to their case, Wang Yangming staged another show at the prefectural seat. To celebrate recent victories in Nan'an and prepare for the New Year, after issuing proclamations announcing victory and the restoration of order, he ordered troops feasted and dispersed, lanterns hung throughout the city, music, and other festivities. And should the Chi brothers have harbored residual doubts, the younger brother Zhong'an was ordered to return to assist his brother in

---

185   Ibid., 11:362.
186   Ibid.

defensive preparations, something they should not relax at a time when factions of the now imprisoned Lu Ke and Zheng Zhigao might seek revenge.[187]

Wang Yangming successfully used many such measures born of the "way of deception" throughout all of his campaigns, and this stratagem was no exception. Once again, his ploy achieved its goal: "On February 3, 1518, Chi Zhongrong and [forty] others arrived in Ganzhou, and seeing that the regiments of troops had dispersed and returned home, and that all around the streets and marketplaces lanterns were hung and plays were being staged for a celebration, they believed troops would not be called up again."[188] Apparently, Chi Zhongrong even bribed a prison guard to allow them to see if Lu Ke was shackled and imprisoned. Seeing that this was indeed the case, he became so excited he dispatched someone home with the message "only now are our plans fully assured."[189] Little did he know that that night Wang freed Lu and the others, as they were to return home in preparation for the impending assault.

Once the headmen had departed their settlements in Litou, Wang began secret preparations for a campaign that was to commence on February 16. Needing to buy further time for mobilization, Wang feasted his unwitting adversaries and convinced them to stay over at a local temple and enjoy the New Year's festivities.[190] But just what exactly transpired during the next few days is difficult to say. On the one hand, based on what Wang Yangming recounted in his victory memorial, it would seem that his perpetuation of the hoax was purely a strategy to gain time: as soon as the armies were ready for deployment, the Chi brothers would be executed.[191]

Nonetheless, the *Chronological Biography* suggests something more than pure cunning was at stake here for Wang Yangming. After settling "Zhongrong and his gang of ninety-three" in Xiangfu Temple, the grand coordinator ordered several in his company to supervise them, give them *qingyi* and greased boots (common Han clothing), and teach them ritual etiquette. The goal here was "to observe their intentions."[192] For this he received a barrage of criticism from local scholars and commoners, some of whom were telling him, "This is nothing more than to cultivate bandits and leave behind a calamity in the making."[193] Wang apparently agreed: "Observing their covetousness and

---

187   Ibid., 11:360.
188   Ibid., 11:362.
189   Ibid.
190   Ibid.
191   Ibid.
192   *NP*, 33:1250.
193   Ibid.

savagery and that in the end they could not possibly be changed," states the *Biography*, "master again determined that the bandit chieftains must be annihilated."[194] Therefore, as his victory memorial narrates the events, "On the third [of the first month], surmising Lu [Ke and the others] had returned home and soldiers had assembled in large numbers in their respective counties and prepared for deployment, I set up a feast in my hall, and concealed armed officers in preparation for an ambush. Zhongrong was invited in with his gang, and all were captured. I produced the written complaint originally composed by Lu [Ke], interrogated them, bound them, and placed them in prison.[195] On that day, Chi Zhongrong and his accomplices were all slaughtered in what must have been something of a bloodbath, and apparently much to Wang's disappointment: "Master [Wang] believed it a great shame he was unable in the end to reform them; it was already after three in the afternoon, he had not yet eaten, became dizzy, and vomited."[196]

The Campaign

No sooner had he been notified that Chi Zhongrong and his men were on their way to his headquarters, then Wang Yangming "dispatched messengers with orders for each county to deploy contingents along the routes," among which was Battalion Commander Meng Jun. He was to proceed to Longchuan County with orders for Lu Ke and Zheng Zhigao.[197] Meng actually brought two different orders, one to be produced for the "bandits" when passing through Litou en route to the location of their adversary's territory, and the real one with specific details concerning the time and route for deployment. Apparently, the remaining Chi kinsmen fell for this. As Wang explained to the court, "When the bandits heard Jun was to arrive, they came out and blocked the road, greeting him and inquiring as to the reason for his passing through. When Jun took out the orders and showed it to them they all bowed, fighting amongst each other for the chance to help guide him through the territory. It was only after arriving in Longchuan that Jun first produced the orders for deployment of Lu Ke and the others troops.[198]

No one in Litou appears to have been suspicious of the orders for the arrest of Lu's gang, for there had been positive reports from leaders at Ganzhou who had witnessed firsthand the imprisoned Lu Ke and Zheng Zhigao as well as the

---

194   Ibid.
195   *WYMQJ*, vol. 1, 11:362.
196   *NP*, 33:1250. Cf. Feng, "Huang Ming da ru Wang Yangming," 90–102.
197   *WYMQJ*, vol. 1, 11:362.
198   Ibid.

grand coordinator's flawlessly convincing demeanor as he feasted the "reformed subjects" and saw to it that they were amply entertained by the New
Year's festivities. All of the deception, in Wang Yangming's view, had gone without a hitch and achieved its desired effect: the enemy's guard was down, defenses relaxed.[199]

Campaigns began on February 16, 1518 with nine contingents setting out
from Longnan 龍南 and Xinfeng County in Jiangxi and Longchuan County 龍
川縣 in Guangdong. Wang's dry recounting in the victory memorial—of the
list of civilian and military officials commanding each contingent, the numbers and types of soldiers composing them, the settlements struck during a
series of campaigns extending over two months as they maneuvered in the
mountainous territory around the Li River, and the numbers killed and captured—conceals a regional social dynamic that we can only now catch glimpses of. "Resettled outlaws (*xin min* 新民)" constituted a significant component
of these locally raised armies, among which could be found the army raised by
Meng Jun after he arrived at Lu's settlement in Longchuan. This battalion commander led the eighth contingent, which included honorary officials and reformed commoners such as Lu Ke. Beginning on the seventh day of the first
month, they descended upon settlements in Upper, Middle, and Lower Li, attacking and occupying them, killing some two hundred reported leaders and
followers, and burning down a reported 173 homes.[200]

When Wang Yangming first arrived in Ganzhou, he initiated a military dynamic different from what his officials were accustomed to. He repeatedly rejected proposals for assembling large armies composed primarily of "native
troops," and instead raised militias by fully wielding his authority and also entered into local social dynamics. Through a combination of rewards and punishment, impassioned appeal and subtle coercion, sympathy and deception,
he formed connections and alliances beneficial to his goals. It is at least notable that, as a result of the campaigns carried out by just this contingent, not
only were the men involved able to cement the support of authorities, but they
also seized a large amount of property, including bulls, horses, and silver.

Wang Yangming's own contingent was also among those that set out on the
sixteenth and converged on Litou. He marched his soldiers from the prefectural seat of Ganzhou through Longnan County, directly striking a large settlement in Lower Li. As he described the scene:

---

199   Ibid.
200   Ibid.

Suddenly discovering that soldiers were advancing from all directions, they all became panic-stricken and at a loss for what to do. They then divided up and came out to fend us off. All of their crack soldiers, numbering over a thousand, occupied defiles and set up ambushes, combining their power and confronting us at Longzi Peak. Our soldiers assembled into three charges, mounting a pincer attack. . . . The bandits were totally routed and fled. Screams shook the mountains and valleys. Our soldiers, riding on the victory, pursued them to the north, occupying Upper, Middle, and Lower Li.[201]

However, after he occupied Litou and campaigned in nearby settlements, those in flight were still able to mount substantial resistance from the mountain peaks in the Jiulian Mountains. Wang estimated some eight hundred capable men had managed to fortify themselves on peaks so sheer that troops had no way to enter. He believed that if soldiers attempted to pass through the narrow gorge below the cliffs, the bandits would simply "roll boulders and logs, so that not even one among one hundred soldiers would survive."[202]

To overcome this seemingly unbeatable strategic advantage, the grand coordinator selected seven hundred crack troops and ordered them to wear the clothing of captured enemy. They were to pretend to be amongst the bandits in retreat, and at dusk cross over the ravine beneath the precipices occupied by the bandits. According to Wang's report, the stratagem was successful, for the bandits mistook these men as being some of their own in flight and even called out to them. When his troops feigned a response, the bandits hesitated to attack, giving the soldiers time to estimate their strategic positions and cut off the enemy's routes of retreat. As Wang explained, "It was only the next day that the bandits first realized it was my troops, and they joined their forces together and charged us. But our troops had already occupied strategically advantageous positions, attacking from above and below. The bandits could not maintain their positions, so they retreated in defeat."[203]

Based on reports in early April from local guides and scouts, who informed him that "all savage and cunning bandits with a long history of evildoing" had been killed or captured, Wang Yangming believed his campaigns could be brought to a conclusion.[204] All that remained was to extend amnesty to other

---

201   Ibid., 11:363.
202   Ibid.
203   Ibid., 11:364.
204   Ibid.

regional villages that had been "coerced by the bandits, [and] that had not engaged in evildoing for very long."[205]

When Wang Yangming sent his victory memorial to the court, he stated that the reason his small force was able so quickly and at so little expense to achieve an unprecedented victory was the awe-inspiring power and virtue of the court and its foresightedness in granting him the authority necessary to unify lines of command: "How could this [victory] possibly be attributed to my and other officials' superior virtue and ability?"[206] Still, we also have good reason to suspect a great deal of self-confidence on his part. In a letter sent to his student Xue Kan 薛侃 (1486–1545) just prior to initiating this last campaign, he was willing to take some of the credit for the victory:

> Today we have already reached Longnan, and tomorrow we will enter the lairs. At a specified time, armies will simultaneously advance from all directions. The bandits are confronting strategic conditions that will definitely result in their defeat. Formerly, when I was [campaigning] in Hengshui, I sent a letter to [Yang] Shide stating, "defeating the bandits in the mountains is easy, but defeating the bandits of the mind difficult—what is so great about my eradicating petty thieves?" Should my honorable friends completely eradicate the bandits in your hearts and bellies, so as to achieve the great deed of wiping out and pacifying, this truly is the rare and outstanding achievement of a great man. In recent days I believe I have already formulated a victorious strategy, and shall soon be memorializing victory. What happier occasion than this could there be?[207]

On May 28, 1518, after withdrawing his forces in April and returning to Ganzhou, Wang indeed reported this success to the court. Nevertheless, in early June he was forced to return to northern Guangdong for several weeks to clean up remaining resistance, only to return to Ganzhou mid-July. Perhaps it was at this point that he became convinced of the true success of his initial plan—firstly to judge the seriousness of each lair's crimes and on that basis determine whether appeasement or extermination was called for, and secondly "daily to cut back and monthly to whittle away, causing them to totally vanish and be annihilated."[208] While lingering for a while at the beautiful Longnan Jade Stone

---

205   Ibid.
206   Ibid., 11:349.
207   *NP*, 33:1248.
208   *WYMQJ*, vol. 1, 9:315.

Cliff located in the Jiulian mountain range, Wang carved a poem into the rock stating in part, "The evil ether of one hundred *li* cleaned out in one campaign, thunder and rain over ten thousand peaks cleanses the returning troops."[209] As for those who escaped "the net of extermination," the grand coordinator ordered officials to remain vigilant in their efforts to search out and capture, "pulling up the roots and sprouts," and never forgetting "it cannot be said a chopped down tree won't sprout nor that ashes might not yet burn."[210]

Recuperation

Wang Yangming's period of service as grand coordinator of Southern Gan left a permanent mark on the region, but not so much for reason of his campaigns as for the three county seats he ordered the establishment of thereafter, counties that remain on the map today: Pinghe 平和 in southwestern Fujian, Chongyi 崇義 in southern Jiangxi, and Heping 和平 in northern Guangdong. Within a few years, each of these counties, with their government yamens, Confucian schools and city-god temples, local officials and clerks, police stations, and local military establishments, reached a scale sufficient to carry out such standard duties as maintaining security, registering the local population, collecting taxes, and handling litigation. Already, within a matter of years, a record for each county could be found in the form of *juan* (chapters) in the gazetteers for those prefectures and provinces holding jurisdiction over them.[211] No doubt, the explanation the compilers of the chapter on Pinghe County in the *Zhangzhou Prefectural Gazetteer* gave for choosing that county's name would have made sense to the compilers of the others: it meant "changing chaos into order."[212]

Changing chaos into order is just one of the many ways the local elites petitioning for these counties, local officials supporting them, and Wang Yangming himself spoke of civilizing the areas of concern. Sometimes this process would be described as changing an area of banditry into an area of ritual etiquette and standard Han clothing (*guan shang* 冠裳). More often, descriptions of these marginal areas focused simply on how far they still had to go: "Govern-

---

209   Ibid., 20:750.

210   Ibid., 16:559–60.

211   For Pinghe County, see Luo Qingxiao 羅青霄, ed., *Zhangzhou fu zhi* 漳州府志 Gazetteer of Zhangzhou Prefecture, 1572 ed. (Zhangzhou: Guan kan ben), microfilm, *juan* 28. For Chongyi County, see Liu Jie, ed., *Jiajing Nan'an fu zhi*, 820.

212   Luo, *Zhangzhou fu zhi*, 579 (28:1).

ment institutions and education have failed to reach [these areas], and the mean people do not know of laws and measures."[213]

Wang believed that the state had failed to correct these territories' enduring problems of brigandry and strife once and for all and achieve a lasting peace. After repeated campaigns in each of the three territories, previous officials had never followed up by putting in place measures to assure that "authority and education" reached these remote areas, invariably allowing those bandits that had escaped the "net of extermination" simply to return and foment the same cycle of conflict and violence. When petitioning for a county seat in Pinghe, Fujian, Wang wrote:

> At this time, although the many lairs of Xianghu, Ketang, Dasan, and Jian-guan have been occupied and cleaned out, is it not possible that some remnant evildoers and vestiges of their gangs have fled to the mountains and valleys? In the past, because county seats were not established after campaigns of subjugation, [the bandits] gradually returned to and occu-pied their old lairs. The origin of ongoing disorder is to be found here. Today, should [we] actually establish a county seat on this land, this is what is known as slapping the back and clutching the throat: the bandits will without being removed eventually disperse on their own, and more-over be changed into law-abiding subjects.[214]

Instituting such measures was, for Wang Yangming, analogous to curing illness. When making the case for a county in northern Guangdong, he warned the court that although the lairs and haunts had been cleaned out, should further action not be taken immediately to establish long-term control, banditry would surely return. That is because it is like a chronic disease:

> The malady of banditry is akin to a person taking ill. Raising forces for a campaign of subjugation is analogous to prescribing acupuncture and medication for aggressive treatment; building a county and resettling is the way of recuperating with drink and food. Relying only on aggressive treatment with acupuncture and medication, without building up health with good nourishment means that not only would the illness return in the spin of a heel, but also vital energies will be extinguished and symp-

---

213   *WYMQJ*, vol. 1, 9:319.
214   Ibid., 9:320.

toms will worsen. Thereafter, even should one be a Bian Que or Cang Gong,[215] there will be no room left to apply one's expertise.[216]

To this end, aside from implementation of all those policies necessary to establish and operate county seats, Wang Yangming also instituted other measures to strengthen the health of the region in the aftermath of the campaigns. Most of what he was trying to achieve would have fallen under the category of "changing [people] through education (*jiaohua* 教化)" and "bringing about a change in prevailing customs and habits (*yi feng yi su zhi shi* 移風易俗之事)," language so common in Ming sources that he could simply reference these "matters" in general terms when sending communications to local officials.[217] But in terms of his moral philosophy, the implications were profound, for what this meant to him was finding ways to encourage the recovery of people's natural moral goodness. He therefore encouraged the growth of grassroots organizations to complement the security emphasis of the ten-household placard registration system, which was designed for mutual aid and moral reform.

What this meant in more concrete terms was the establishment of community schools for children, a community covenant for subcounty level society, and orders for officials to print out proclamations to the people in large numbers and ensure that families composing the "hundreds" and "tithings" units throughout Nan'an and Ganzhou each received a copy.[218] These documents share a similar set of concerns, ideas, and policies. In the background is Wang Yangming's optimistic teaching that the mind is principle, that all that the mind gives forth in terms of thinking, willing, and sentiment, can and should be naturally and spontaneously derived from a wellspring of goodness—of universal moral principles—as long as the self was not wrapped up in self-centeredness and clouded by accumulated bad habits and practices. To recover this original condition, individuals must make a daily, honest, and earnest effort to build upon those easily recognizable traits of the originally good mind. The role of the community is to provide excellent venues for fostering this growth in virtue, but also to provide appropriate sanctions for errant individuals. Therefore, these various institutions simply provide a platform for people of different stations to come together in a structured setting and assist each

---

215 Bian Que was a renowned ancient medical scientist believed to have founded pulse diagnosis. Cang Gong was also renowned as a medical scientist, and lived during the Western Han.

216 *WYMQJ*, vol. 1, 11:370.

217 Ibid., 16:566.

218 Ibid.

other in recognizing lapses in moral judgment and conduct and, if there is a sense of regret, undertake reform.

To be sure, Wang's detailed prescriptions for how children's schools or sub-county level communal institutions were to meet and monitor the good or bad conduct of members, to establish protocols for encouraging the former and discouraging the latter, and to preserve the values of unity and harmony, might on the surface seem overbearingly conformist. Building on his doctrine that the purpose of education is fundamentally ethics, Wang's school regulations stipulate that at the beginning of each day teachers must ask each student "whether at home they have been negligent and lacked earnestness in their desire to love their parents and to respect their elders, whether they have over-looked or failed to carry out any details in caring for their parents in summer or winter, whether in walking along the streets their movements and etiquette have been disorderly or careless, and whether in all their words, acts, and thoughts they have been deceitful or depraved, and not loyal, faithful, sincere, and respectful."[219] Naturally, pupils are to be honest, and correct any mistakes.

However, what is perhaps refreshing about Wang's approach to educating the youth is the stress he places on mitigating what he saw as the ill effects of a sternly disciplinarian approach. He notes that students look upon schools as prisons and teachers as enemies because they are often beaten as well as dragged through a dry curriculum of rote memorization and recitation; as a result, they learn to pretend, deceive, and cheat. Having thus placed a substantial share of the blame on parents and teachers, Wang outlines a curriculum aimed at creating a positive and cheerful environment in which students will want to learn. Thus, he stresses singing, practicing good etiquette, and reading.[220]

More notably, Wang's community covenant for Southern Gan 南贛鄉約 calls for local communities to come together and, in a notably egalitarian fashion, select about twenty "elderly and virtuous" persons to organize local society for monthly meetings at a local temple. The principal purpose of these meetings was to exhort good conduct and to address the needs of members of the community, to monitor and keep a record of their conduct, as well as to provide a public setting in which good behavior would be appropriately commended and bad behavior punished. At the beginning of each meeting, in a formal setting, a covenant officer was to read the covenant and have members take a series of vows together, such as: "From now on, all of us covenant members will reverently obey warnings and instructions. We will unite as one mind

---

219   Wang, *Instructions for Practical Living*, 184.
220   Ibid., 183.

and join together in virtue, and will arrive at goodness together. If anyone should be of two minds, outwardly doing good but secretly doing evil, let the gods and spirits destroy him."[221]

After this, a covenant officer was to call forward anyone recognized for good deeds not only by covenant officers but also by anyone in the audience. After that individual's name and deeds were made note of in a record book, the covenant leader was to state, "So-and-so has done such and such good deed and so-and-so has been able to correct such and such mistake. This means that they can cultivate their personal lives. So-and-so has enabled his fellow clansmen to do such and such good deed or correct such and such mistake. This means they can keep their families in order. If everyone does this, how can our customs not be sound? All of us in this compact should take them as models." The doer of good deeds was then to be toasted, at which time they were to decline the honor in a most humble way.[222]

As for doers of evil deeds, covenant officers were to call forward anyone about whom they had knowledge of misbehavior, state what they had heard, and solicit further information from the members, in order to verify. What followed embodied ritually the very kind of culture of benevolent paternalism that characterizes much of Wang Yangming's approach to social and political life:

> When the covenant recorder finishes recording, the covenant chief shall say to the guilty, "However, we are not interested in punishment but in early reform." The guilty shall kneel down and plead, "How dare I not reform quickly but instead cause my elders to worry for me again?" The covenant chief, assistant chiefs, and covenant recorder shall all say, "We have not been able to advise and instruct you in time so that you have fallen into this trouble. How can we be free from guilt?" They shall now all drink to punish themselves. The guilty one shall kneel and again plead, "As I already know my own guilt and as you, venerable sirs, take this to be you own guilt, how dare I not submit to the most severe punishment right

221   Wang Yangming, "The Community Compact for Southern Kan-chou," in *Instructions for Practical Living*, ed. Wing-tsit Chan, 299. For a study of the compact, see Kandice Hauf, "The Community Covenant in Sixteenth Century Ji'an Prefecture, Jiangxi," in *Late Imperial China* 17, no. 2 (1996): 7–11. I here follow Chan's translation, except for his translation of *yue* as "compact", here translated as "covenant." The covenant itself can be found in *WYMQJ*, vol. 1, 17:599–604.

222   Wang, "The Community Compact," 304.

away? If you permit to reform, please do not drink and that would be my good fortune."[223]

At that point, the accused was to withdraw and drink more, while the officers were to acknowledge his willingness to accept punishment and change, and demonstrate their sense of release from responsibility by setting down their wine cups. Thereafter, after further ritualistic formalities and a meal, covenant officers were to close with a kind of exhortation to virtue, explaining the importance of embracing humility and renouncing pride while repenting and changing one's ways.

Much like the ten-household placard registration system, the community covenants also served the purpose of extending the reach of the state into local society, as another kind of subcounty level organization.[224] The household registration system achieved this through a system of collective responsibility and reporting. The covenants played this role through contacts between the elected officers and the local magistrate. Those who failed to reform and persisted in evildoing were to be reported to the local government so that they could be arrested and punished. On the other hand, the officers were also to protect the covenant members from predation by corrupt elements within the government, such as yamen clerks or garrison captains who might demand gifts or engage in extortion.[225] Wang seemed to envision that if a county had the right magistrate and his subcounty organizations selected out the right men, they could work together to weed out such negative influences from society and from the government.

As for what Wang Yangming himself was doing to implement these measures while in Ganzhou for the rest of 1518, the *Chronological Biography* records:

Wang Yangming circulated proclamations, sending them to fathers, elders, and sons of the counties falling under the jurisdiction of Nan'an and Ganzhou Prefecture, [calling on them] mutually to admonish and encourage, build community schools, invite teachers to teach their children, sing poetry, and practice ritual etiquette. When coming and going on the streets and avenues, and approached by officials or seniors, they would all cup their hands together and stand upright in greeting. Master [Wang] would praise, instruct, and guide them. After a time, city

223 Ibid., 305.
224 Brook, *Chinese State in Ming Society*, 38–40.
225 Wang, "The Community Compact," 300–302.

residents came to know of capping and mourning, and morning and evening the sound of singing reached out-of-the-way alleys. Eventually, in a
harmonious way there gradually arose a cultured atmosphere of good etiquette.[226]

Civility, respectful good etiquette, and sensibly frugal ceremony, all fostered
through pedagogy, poetry, and simple example. Should this also have begun to
take hold in other recently pacified territories of the broader region under his
jurisdiction, Wang Yangming's goal of changing "a territory of savage bandits
into a land of respectful good etiquette and ceremony, caps and clothing," was
truly beginning to be realized.[227]

Conclusion

Is it possible to pass judgment on Wang Yangming's campaigns and the measures he took in the aftermath of each? Earlier generations of scholars who
studied him from a Marxist point of view may have believed so. They find a
great deal of irony in the fact that Wang Yangming, at the very time he was
campaigning, viewed the eradication of banditry as analogous to purifying the
mind of errant desire and self-centeredness. For these scholars, the peoples
Wang Yangming suppressed—typically referred to as peasants or minority ethnic groups—are victims, while Wang Yangming is the representative of a re-
pressive autocracy in service to a feudal landlord class and its self-righteous
ethics and imperial ideology.[228] As such, his list of virtues and vices and discourse on principle and desire only served to reestablish hierarchical class relations, while also forcing his social perceptions onto the masses in such a way
that mere resistance would be seen as a crime.

Wang Yangming did in fact employ rhetorical strategies common to governing elites in order to solve complex political and social problems, and at some
level he could not help but interpret these through the lens of his virtue ethics.
In fact, on a more personal level, he notes that the hardships he faced while
serving during this time only served further to verify his evolving thinking
about the best practices for perfecting virtue. This included, for example,
"steeling oneself in the affairs of life (*shi shang mo lian* 事上磨煉)," as opposed

---

226 *NP*, 33:1252.

227 *WYMQJ*, vol. 1, 10:352.

228 Cf. Hou, *Zhongguo sixiang tongshi*, vol. 4, *Song, Yuan, Ming*, 875–904.

to sitting passively in meditation.[229] Prior to taking office in southern Jiangxi in 1517, he had spent nearly two years in Nanjing, where he found himself with a growing following of students. Even back then, he noted with dismay that his having advocated quiet-sitting as one way to calm the mind, purify it of selfish desires, and find an inner balance, had spawned certain bad practices. These included a preference for quiescence and an inability to carry that stillness, and balance, into action. His students, it seems, were too easily disturbed by worldly affairs, and that prevented them from responding in a morally correct and virtuous way to the challenges they were facing, and therefore from achieving harmony while still engaged in life.

As a result, Wang began to stress various spiritual practices to be carried out by his students while they engaged in whatever matters, official business or otherwise. These included most notably "preserving Heavenly principles and expelling self-centeredness (*cun tianli qu renyu* 存天理去人欲)" by becoming truly determined (*li zhi* 立志), being sincere in all that one wills (*cheng yi* 誠意), "doing what is good and ridding evil (*wei shan qu e* 為善去惡)," and disciplined self-examination, attentive observation, and self-overcoming (*xing cha ke ji* 省察克己).[230] In more positive terms, practitioners were to be firm in their determination to allow their natural goodness further growth: "When a good thought is preserved, this is Heavenly principle.... This thought is like the root bud of a tree, becoming truly determined being nothing more than standing for long upon this good thought."[231] To preserve good thoughts is to be sincere in one's intentions and, as Okada Takehiko has pointed out, "being sincere in one's willing" is the crux of Wang's teaching from the time he was in Nanjing through to the end of the campaigns. This teaching was only later complemented by his more important teaching of "extension of the innate knowledge of the good (*zhi liangzhi* 致良知)," a topic to which I return in Chapter Two.[232]

The documents in which these doctrines are espoused were the first philosophical writings Wang Yangming allowed to be printed. While residing in Ganzhou, he continued, as time permitted, to promote his evolving philosophical doctrines by teaching his growing numbers of students. Some of this ever-increasing following consisted of former students or colleagues who joined

---

229   See, for example, Wang Yangming's letter to his student Xue Kan (*WYMQJ*, vol. 1, 4:171), where he discusses how his recent military campaigns had led him to realize that up to this time he had never once truly applied effort.

230   See, for example, Chen Lai, *You wu zhi jing*, 326–28.

231   *WYMQJ*, vol. 1, 1:19.

232   Okada, *Ō Yōmei taiden*, 2:124-136.

him during this time, while others were men living in the region who were interested in his ideas and sought him out for instruction. Most held minor degrees or minor office or were at least in the process of pursuing these and moving up.

Therefore, while actively carrying out his duties as an official, Wang also remained actively engaged with philosophical issues pertinent to the governing scholar-official elite or those posed to become a part of it. To that end, he allowed his close disciples to print not only a record of his conversations with them but also his preface to and commentary on a key classical text, as well as an analysis of how the great Song philosopher Zhu Xi had realized late in life that he had been wrong regarding certain philosophical matters but had failed to integrate those insights into his commentary on classical texts. These were, respectively, the first volume of *Instructions for Practical Living*, "Preface to the Ancient Edition of the Great Learning," *Commentary to the Ancient Edition of the Great Learning*, and *Zhu Xi's Final Conclusions Arrived at Late in Life*.[233] These are the works that provided the classical locus and theoretical justification for the precepts Wang Yangming had been teaching. As a substantial assault on ideological orthodoxy, these are crucial for understanding his broader efforts to change politics and political culture by changing the curriculum in virtue ethics.

Not surprisingly, encouraging individuals to reform themselves through preserving moral goodness and cultivating sincere intentions was also the crux of his institutional program in Southern Gan. Whether it be the ten-family placard registration system, public proclamations, community schools, or a community covenant, Wang urged everyone to help everybody else involved to move forward with that "single thought to do good," and therefore to "be filial to your parents and respectful to your elders, teach your children, live in harmony with your fellow villagers, help one another when there is death in the family and assist one another in a time of difficulty, encourage one another to do good and warn one another not to do evil, stop litigations and rivalry, cultivate faithfulness and promote harmony, and be sure to be good subjects so that

---

233   With the exception of the *Commentary to the Ancient Edition of the Great Learning*, these works are all included in the *Collected Works of Wang Yangming* (WYMQJ). For *Instructions for Practical Living*, see WYMQJ, vol. 1, *juan* 1–3; *Zhu Xi's Final Conclusions Arrived at Late in Life* (*Zhuzi wan nian ding lun* 朱子晚年定論) is appended to the last *juan* of *Instructions for Practical Living* (WYMQJ, 3:127); for "Preface to the Ancient Edition of the Great Learning" see WYMQJ, vol. 1, 5:242. The *Commentary to the Ancient Edition of the Great Learning* (*Da xue gu ben pang shi* 大學古本旁釋) is included in the *Xu xiu si ku quan shu, jing bu, si shu lei* 續修四庫全書, 經部, 四書類 (Shanghai guji chubanshe, 1995), 159:3.

together you may establish the practice of humanity and kindness."[234] That is how the individual comes to understand the axiom that the "mind is principle," as well as the methods for recovering this natural condition: "Preserving Heavenly principle, and expelling self-centered desires," and "being sincere about one's intentions." Most critically, as Wang points out in his "Preface to the Ancient Version of the Great Learning," this method includes acting upon that knowledge of the good that is always present as the very substance of the mind-heart. Upon realizing that one is in error, regret is natural, and that is the foundation for correcting mistakes, and for reform. The community covenant summed up this process: "If we can repent and change our ways, we shall gradually advance to the good."[235] Here is a self-reinforcing process grounded in the natural goodness that all possess, which is why Wang's advice to both his students and programs call for carrying this out both in private and public settings.

In more negative terms, in his *Instructions for Practical Living*, Wang repeatedly states that moral wrongdoing is the result of a certain deliberate choice not to take note of and act upon what one's good moral sense calls for: "The sense of right and wrong is something all have," but some fail to recognize and act upon it because "the will is not yet sincere or concrete." And, in a letter to his younger brothers, he attributed virtually every kind of character flaw anyone might have to a failure of will: "For any sprouting of the slightest bit of selfish desire, only chastise oneself for failing to exercise willpower." Such a failure to exercise willpower would be "like failing to plant the root and then merely going about cultivating and irrigating."[236]

In addition, Wang often resorted to a "failure of will" to explain what he saw as the manifest "evildoing" of the bandits, something that justified state intervention, whether that be in the form of campaigns of extermination or putting in place measures to facilitate the instantiation of an order of virtue. From those people he suspected of involvement with bandits, he demanded demonstration of sincere intentions as, for example, when he called upon elders and headmen to bring forward troublemakers: "[By so doing, you will], first of all, clearly demonstrate your sincere intention to do what is good and remove what is evil (*wei shan qu e zhi cheng*) and, secondly, weed out the henbane and bristle grass, preventing them from spreading and leaving behind trouble for such good and honest people as yourselves."[237]

---

234 Wang, "The Community Compact," 299.
235 Ibid., 306.
236 *WYMQJ*, vol. 1, 7:259.
237 Ibid., 16:538–39.

Likewise, the analogies Wang Yangming routinely drew upon to explain the process of recovering human nature, self-cultivation, and aligning with principles find broad parallels in his more general discussions of what was needful to restore social order. These included, for example, treatment of illness and plant growth. Regardless of his sympathy for those who turned to banditry out of desperation, such criminal conduct, especially in its more egregious forms, was best understood on the analogy of a festering ulcer that resists a cure or weeds that prevent the growth of good plants. He often claimed that failure to exterminate remnant bandits meant "the root of the weeds" yet remained and might "again sprout and spread." Also, he frequently spoke of incorrigible bandit bosses "planting the seeds of wickedness"; they "could be likened to ulcers" in need of aggressive treatment.[238] By the same token, he also frequently analogized desire (for power, wealth, or sex, for example), moral failure, and simple wrongdoing to weeds and disease. In both cases, whether bandits or errant desire, they needed to be "eliminated" and "cleaned out"—uprooted once and for all, so that they would not again sprout or, as a disease, recur. Thus, as much as his military response was shaped by the bloodshed he was faced with, it is also not incorrect to conclude that Wang resorted to violence in part because there was potentially some degree of violence in the metaphors used in his virtue ethics. Such metaphors, therefore, constrained the range of solutions he might have pursued.

To be sure, one might also find a great deal of irony in the fact that while carrying out such clearly violent campaigns, Wang was also dedicating as much time as he could to discoursing on his philosophy of mind to his literati friends and students.[239] Yet this judgment is too hasty, especially when we keep in mind that Wang appears to be free of any charge of acting on anything other than what he felt was right in light of the circumstances before him. Certainly, from a Marxist point of view, or from a point of view that privileges exposing how moral conventions serve interests, irony abounds. The metaphors and rhetorical strategies he employed could indeed be cynically dismissed as lacking any other meaningful referent than power. But the issues at hand hold more complexity than that, should we consider the idea that a superior form of social order can only be realized by an assertive authority backed by a philosophy of human nature and a hierarchy of values that are grounded in reason, however this term may be defined. In the final analysis, Wang believed he was doing what was necessary to bring about a better society grounded in an order

---

238   *WYMQJ*, vol. 2, 27:1003.

239   Zou Shouyi 鄒守益. *Wang Yangming xiansheng tu pu* 王陽明先生圖譜 [Illustrated Biography of Sir Wang Yangming] (Beijing: Beijing chubanshe, 2000), 17:479.

of virtue, an order in harmony with the natural moral order, with human nature. Hence, his campaigns and policies were to lay the foundations for the actualization of a hierarchy of ends, the telos for which was his conception of the good.

Nevertheless, in retrospect, we should question the way Wang Yangming simply accepted local elites' and officials' characterization of conditions and the demonization of those engaging in armed disturbances. No one today would accept the notion that thousands of peoples living in hundreds of settlements were deliberately choosing to engage in evildoing for hardly any other reason than the fact that they had become accustomed to wrongdoing. The bar allowing for claims of victimization and sympathetic understanding is far lower today than it was during Wang Yangming's time. What appeared to him as chaos and wickedness appears to us today as a characteristically pre-modern response to injustice rooted in complicated social, economic, and ethnic tensions, tensions that such a limited state presence could not possibly manage. Confronted as he was with a situation where the state had limited ability to mediate local conflicts and recognize patterns of migration and their economic and social consequences, Wang Yangming at first fell back on rhetoric and turned to violence, and then relied upon established residents of local communities to work with authorities in extending the reach of the state into lawless regions at the subcounty level.

For his accomplishments in southern China, Wang was, in mid-1518, promoted to vice-censor-in-chief on the right as well as awarded a minor hereditary title for his son and later descendents.[240] But continuing to suffer as he was from chronic illness, as well as wishing to return to his hometown to see his father and grandmother, he both declined the honor and repeatedly requested leave from office. Indeed, in the hopes he might find support in this regard, he also repeatedly dispatched letters to Wang Qiong, the minister of war who had given him his commission. In them, Wang Yangming not only apprised the minister of developments during his campaigns and thanked him for his assistance in empowering him as superintendent of military affairs, but also pleaded with him for permission to return home due to his physical condition, family matters, and personal wishes.[241]

But the minister of war nevertheless kept his empowered grand coordinator down in Ganzhou, with those broad discretionary powers granted to him in his additional capacity as superintendent of military affairs. And the reason for this was that Wang Qiong had witnessed trouble brewing in the northern half

---

240   *NP*, 34:1258.
241   Ibid., 34:1258–59.

of the province for several years, and believed Wang Yangming might be needed to confront it. Thus it was that he remained in Ganzhou for another year, till
mid-1519, at which time he would indeed be forced to take action. It is to that
campaign that we now turn.

CHAPTER 3

The Prince and the Sage

As of early 1519 Wang Yangming was still residing in southern Jiangxi. As grand coordinator and vice-censor in chief, he was the highest official in this region, responsible for effecting measures to maintain peace and security after nearly two years of campaigning. He was, however, petitioning to leave office, for he suffered from chronic illness and wished to visit his aging father. But his requests were repeatedly denied, for his ardent supporter at the head of the Ministry of War—Wang Qiong—wanted him to stay put. Having long suspected that a much more serious threat loomed over the Ming dynasty, he needed Wang Yangming to counter it. Indeed, this unsettling issue was very likely the real reason the minister had helped Wang Yangming gain broader discretionary powers—and the title of superintendent of military affairs—in the first place, something Wang Yangming was well aware of.[1] This threat was the Prince of Ning Zhu Chenhao 寧王朱宸濠 (1478–1521), the great-great-grandson of the Ming dynasty's founding emperor's seventeenth son, Prince Xian of Ning.[2]

Though the prince lived during roughly the same period as Wang Yangming, he led a very different life: as imperial nobility, he would have been allowed to reside in (and was largely confined to) one of the many princely establishments granted to senior lines descended from the founding emperor's children. However, not unlike certain other princes in the history of the Ming, the Prince of Ning harbored high aspirations.[3] But being already a prince, what higher status could he achieve?

---

1 Huang, "Shi de ji," 38:1416.
2 *Ming shi* 明史 [Ming History], ed. Zhang Tingyu 張廷玉 (Beijing: Zhonghua shuju, 1974), 117:3593. Hereafter, MS.
3 The exemplar for rebellious Ming princes who believed they had a claim to the throne was the Yongle 永樂 emperor Zhu Di 朱棣. With the assistance of the Prince of Ning, Zhu Di usurped the throne from his nephew Zhu Yunwen 朱允炆 in 1399. For a biography see the *Dictionary of Ming Biography*, ed. L. Carrington Goodrich and Chaoying Fang (New York: Columbia University Press, 1976), 1:355. Also notable is that as recently as 1510 the Prince of Anhua had led an uprising in the northwestern corner of the empire. For a thorough study, see David Robinson, "Princes of the Polity: The Anhua Prince's Uprising of 1510," *Ming Studies* 65 (May 2012): 1–12. No doubt, these rebellions conditioned the perception of officials throughout the empire, including Wang Yangming, although he does not refer to this particular rebellion in his communications. In general, scholarship on Ming princes and imperial clansmen has exploded since an earlier version of this chapter appeared in 2008. For an overview see

However, Zhu Chenhao's attempt to displace the Zhengde emperor from the throne would fail clamorously. As the great Ming literatus Feng Menglong explained in his semi-fictional account of Wang Yangming's life, "From the day he raised the rebellion . . . to the day he was captured . . . the total was a mere forty-two days. From the day Wang Yangming departed Ji'an . . . to the day he succeeded at defeating the prince . . . the total was only fourteen days. Since ancient times never has there been a case of such marvelously swift suppression of a rebellion as this."[4] As we shall see, for the prince this must have been a rather humiliating conclusion to years of grandiose designs and preparation. But as for Wang Yangming, his victory became the fodder for a great deal of celebratory writing, beginning with the earliest biographical accounts of his life. The enigmatic late-Ming scholar and student of Wang Yangming's philosophy Li Zhi 李贄 (1527–1602) claimed, "Those who performed exceptionally meritorious services in ancient times were indeed many. However, never has there been a case of [someone], even prior to requesting troops or provisions, capturing a rebel within ten days. This only our master could have achieved."[5]

Much scholarship addresses the relationship between Wang Yangming's experiences during this time and the further development of his thought. Zuo Dongling believes that "if [we] should wish to answer the question as to just why Wang Yangming proposed, around the fifteenth year of the reign of the Zhengde emperor [1520], the 'extension of the innate knowledge of the good' then we must understand the relation between Sir Yangming's bitter experiences and his state of mind."[6] In this regard, Zuo is less focused on the campaign itself than he is with the ensuing course of events. For after Wang captured the prince, the emperor, at the behest of his circle of close confidantes, chose personally to lead a campaign, and following their advice ordered the release of the prince around a lake in northern Jiangxi (Lake Poyang 鄱陽湖) so that he could reenact the prince's victorious capture, the glory for which would redound to him and his courtiers. Because Wang Yangming refused to obey, his life was at stake for months, and not least because some of

---

David Robinson, "Princely Courts of the Ming Dynasty," *Ming Studies* 65 (May 2012): 1–12. For my article, see Larry Israel, "The Prince and the Sage: Concerning Wang Yangming's 'Effortless' Suppression of the Ning Princely Establishment Rebellion," *Late Imperial China*, vol. 29, no. 2 (December, 2008): 68–128.

4   Feng, "Huang Ming da ru Wang Yangming," 176.

5   Li Zhi 李贄, *Xu cang shu* 續藏書 [Books Concealed Continued], in *Mingdai zhuanji congkan* 明代傳記叢刊, ed. Zhou Junfu (Ming wen shuju, 1991), 106:269.

6   Zuo Dongling 左東嶺, *Wang xue yu zhong wan ming shi ren xintai* 王學與中晚明士人心態 [The Relationship between Wang's Learning and the State of Mind of Mid- to Late-Ming Scholars] (Beijing: Renmin wenxue chubanshe, 2006), 211.

these confidantes were making every effort to have him executed. Thus, he weathered both a difficult campaign and a farce which nearly cost him his life. For Zuo, Wang's ability to navigate such challenges not only tells us something about his character but also helps us to understand how he came to what most scholars consider to be his final teaching: the extension of the innate knowledge of the good (*zhi liangzhi* 致良知).[7]

Similarly, Xu Fuguan has attempted to give serious consideration to his "meritorious achievements" in light of his philosophy. He points out that those who hold Wang Yangming's achievements in high esteem typically point to his rapid suppression of the Prince of Ning's rebellion. With this he is largely in agreement:

> The rapidity with which he assembled troops, the resourcefulness and decisiveness with which he deployed the military, and [the fact] that within less than two months and seven days he pacified the rebellion, this naturally is a very striking achievement.[8] Yet this is something a skilled general could have achieved. But amidst dangerous suspicion and shocking [circumstances], the clarity with which he saw principle, the decisiveness with which he judged matters and, after his success, [his ability] to evade suspicion and distance danger, remain unfettered by concern for his safety, and look indifferently upon worldly honor and official rank—this is not something a skilled general could have accomplished.[9]

Xu in fact believes that what was most impressive about this campaign was Wang Yangming's ability to maneuver through harrowing difficulties and yet remain largely unmoved, and he proposes to further our understanding of Wang's statesmanship and this campaign in particular by drawing a distinction between the purely pragmatic politician and the principled politician. Whereas the former is largely motivated by the desire for power and recognition and views politics as an arena of competing interests, the latter takes cues from the principles laid down by Confucian sages, and is concerned solely with "what

---

7   Ibid.

8   Xu Fuguan's timeframe is incorrect. The rebellion began 6/14 according to the Chinese calendar and the prince was captured the following month on 7/26.

9   Xu Fuguan 徐復觀, "Wang Yangming sixiang bu lun 王陽明思想補論 [Supplemental discussion of Wang Yangming's thought]," in *Zhongguo sixiangshi lunji xubian* 中國思想史論集續編 (Taipei: Wen qun yinshua youxian gongsi, 1982), 506–507.

must be the case for the mind-heart of humanity and righteousness."[10] Here we have a piece of Socratic wisdom: A man worth anything at all does not concern himself with whether his course of action endangers his life, and rather considers only whether or not what he does is just.

On many occasions, Wang Yangming spoke of just such ideals; in a letter written in reply to a student, he stated, "What is taken as virtue in recent times is in reality nothing more than [the desire for] honor and official rank: 'The man of humanity acts justly and does not seek utilitarian profit, manifests the Way but does not look for meritorious recognition.'"[11] According to Xu, Wang's greatness lies in the fact that he acted strictly on the basis of transcendent principles irreducible to narrow personal interest: "Wang Yangming's political actions and meritorious achievement all derived from his self-cultivated humanity, which is also to say from his giving full scope to innate knowledge of the good."[12]

According to Wang's doctrine, to say that his actions were in accord with innate knowledge of the good is to say that he had unified knowledge and action.[13] For him, extension of innate knowledge of the good meant acting upon knowledge rooted in what Mencius conceptualized as universal moral mind, from whence springs naturally given knowledge-cum-sentiment of right and wrong, or what Philip Ivanhoe refers to as "innate" or "nascent moral sense."[14]

---

10 Ibid., 496.

11 *WYMQJ*, vol. 1, 4:161.

12 Xu, "Wang Yangming sixiang bu lun," 497.

13 See, for example, Wang, *Instructions for Practical Living*, 250.

14 Ivanhoe, *Ethics in the Confucian Tradition*, 19. For a discussion of the relation between Mencius's "four beginnings" and Wang Yangming's thought, see Chen, *You wu zhi jing*, 166. For *liangzhi*, see also A.S. Cua, "Between Commitment and Realization: Wang Yang-ming's Vision of the Universe as a Moral Community," in *Philosophy East and West* 43, no. 4 (October 1993): 611–47. Throughout this book, I retain Wing-tsit Chan's translation of *liangzhi* as "innate knowledge of the good." In his "Inquiry on the *Great Learning*", perhaps the most definitive statement of his teachings, Wang states that innate knowledge of the good is the sense of right and wrong which–following Mencius–"requires no deliberation to know, nor does it depend on learning to function" (Wang Yangming, *Instructions for Practical Living*, trans. Wing Tsit-Chan, 278). Ivanhoe's translation of *liangzhi* as "pure knowing" leaves the moral import of such knowing underemphasized. Also, Chan's translation is not meant to imply a body of knowledge; as A.S. Cua points out, *liangzhi* is not a "repository of universal principles or rules to guide the perplexed agent" (632). For him, it is better understood as, variously translated, "moral sense," "moral discrimination," and "moral consciousness." I would also agree with Cua that *liangzhi*, as the locus where *tianli* (Heavenly reason) naturally and clearly reveals itself in consciousness, has an "implicit volitional character" and therefore "the will to its actualization" (631).

For Mencius, to know this mind is to know human nature and therefore to know Heaven.[15] Consequently, to actualize such knowledge in one's political conduct is to actualize a transcendent moral force, to bring the political order in line with a natural order of right. According to Julia Ching, one who is able to achieve this has become a paradigmatic human being, one who mediates between the human and natural or cosmic orders.[16] Such a person is therefore one who exemplifies the Confucian political ideal of sageliness within and kingliness without, who demonstrates the inseparability of virtue and just political praxis. Very much in a Socratic sense, these are the natural leaders of society.

The accounts indeed present this story not so much as the mere suppression of a rebel prince as much as a powerful manifestation of a great mind. Wang Yangming's brilliant campaign and ability to cope with the dreadful aftermath were seen as testimony to the validity of his subsequent teaching—the innate knowledge of the good. Indeed, Xu Fuguan goes so far as to suggest that he had acted effortlessly, comparing this to an ancient ideal: "The sages and worthies in principle take as their cause saving people from danger and death, while themselves remaining totally without concern for recognition; at its highest, this is comparable to what Confucius spoke of as 'Shun and Yu holding possession of the empire as if it were nothing to them.'"[17]

This was a time and a world woven of moral fabric, nothing like, say, the post-foundational position, whereby, in the words of Alasdair Macintyre, "there are and can be no valid rational justification for any claims that objective and impersonal moral standards exist."[18] As opposed to being grounded in a natural order, moral principles stem rather from contextually relative reasoning, sentiments, or interests. From this perspective, the discourse on sagehood should be bracketed and analyzed as something other than what it takes itself to be, and therefore as an unreflected background horizon of normative notions particular to a time and place. According to Julia Ching, Wang Yangming understood "sagehood as culminating in an experience of oneness with Heaven and Earth and all things, an experience which permeates the sages' thinking and being and acting, which becomes identified with *xin* 心 [mind]

---

15   Mencius, *Mengzi yi zhu* 孟子譯注 [Mencius, Translated and Annotated], trans. Jin Liang-nian 金良年 (Shanghai: Shanghai guji chubanshe, 2005), 271.

16   Julia Ching, *Mysticism and Kingship in China: The Heart of Chinese Wisdom* (Cambridge: Cambridge University Press, 2000), 106.

17   Xu, "Wang Yangming sixiang bu lun," 496. Xu is quoting the *Analects*, 8:18.

18   Alasdair Macintyre, *After Virtue: A Study in Moral Theory* (University of Notre Dame Press, 2007), 19.

or *liangzhi* 良知 [innate knowledge of the good] or *benti* 本體 [original sub-stance], overflowing into a concrete awareness of his social and political responsibilities."[19] Of course, a post-foundationalist would question the extent to which social and political action can be grounded in such a transcendent order. Yet Wang Yangming and his contemporaries were troubled by no such postmodern dissection: an unquestioned concept of morality was at the heart of Wang Yangming's doctrine of the unity of knowledge and action, as well as his new teaching in the wake of the rebellion, which called for extending, or acting upon, innate knowledge of the good.

To be sure, the idea that the political world had become an arena of compet-ing interests was something clearly conceptualized in Wang Yangming's politi-cal philosophy: this fallen political world reflected the growing hegemony of all-too-human desire, of self-centeredness resulting from the obscuration of pure moral knowing. But the notion that the political was not part of a higher order transcending such interests and defining their true end would have been incomprehensible. For him, political community is not something that comes about merely through the rational organization of desire. Ultimately, a politi-cal order aims to inspire the individual, through the cultivation of various vir-tues and prohibition of various vices, to pass beyond the promptings of narrow self-interest and the desire for power to promptings of a higher nature—the teleological draw of human nature, the wellspring of fundamental goodness (*zhi shan* 至善). Wang believed that such promptings are available to the clear-minded, and that because their interest—the original interest of mind attuned to nature (*xing* 性) and therefore to higher moral principle (*li* 理)—is human-ity as a whole (the one substance of humanity *yi ti zhi ren* 一體之仁), because they point beyond the individual to society as a whole—served by the politi-cal—they could in no way be unmasked or deconstructed as a sign for any-thing other than the good.

But regardless of how we judge the broader validity of Wang's political phi-losophy and virtue ethics, we don't necessarily need to reconstruct the cam-paign against the Prince of Ning solely within the framework of the abovementioned philosophical terms; after all, these concepts arose in a real, historical setting. In fact, some level of post-foundational bracketing might even, as a kind of heuristic device, serve to further our understanding of just what the key terminology in Wang's philosophy and ethics meant in actual practice, without necessarily denying their universal import.

For my purposes, because the philosophical meaning of the innate knowl-edge of the good has already received much attention, I believe it a useful

19   Ching, *To Acquire Wisdom*, 126.

exercise to undertake an historical inquiry into its normative import. For Wang, the innate knowledge of the good was "what is referred to as the 'great foundation of all under Heaven,'" and to act in accord with this was "what is referred to as "all under Heaven attaining the Way.'"[20] In other words, the ideal social and political order is one fully in accord with human nature, and therefore with innate knowledge of the good. To follow such knowledge is to return the world to the Way, and this is what he appears to have believed he was doing throughout the suppression of the rebellion. Indeed, in 1520, not long after the end of the campaign, while still residing in Ganzhou, Wang explained to his student Chen Jiuchuan 陳九川 (1495–1562), "Your innate knowledge of the good is your own standard. When you direct your thought your innate knowledge knows that it is right if it is right and wrong if it is wrong. You cannot keep anything from it. Just don't try to deceive it but sincerely and truly follow it in whatever you do.... I have only in recent years realized this through personal experience and become so clear about it."[21]

In Wang's "Inquiry on the *Great Learning*"—which Wing-tsit Chan calls his "most important writing"[22]—he explains that innate knowledge of the good is "the sense of right and wrong common to all men."[23] Those who sincerely wish to do so and who do not deceive themselves can become aware of this sense and further it, over time becoming increasingly able to will the good through their actions. But those for whom such knowledge is obscured, and who are therefore willing both good and evil, might still become resolved to clarify such knowledge for themselves and thereby redirect their misguided willing in the direction of the good. It is perhaps for this reason, among others, that A.S. Cua defines *liangzhi* as "moral sense" with an "implicit volitional character."[24]

But just what exactly was it for Wang Yangming that counted as good and evil, and what exactly is this thing called "common sense"? In answering this question, I have taken cues from Charles Taylor's notion of the social imaginary, that is, "the way people imagine their social existence, how they fit together, how things go on between them and their fellows, the expectations that are normally met, and the deeper normative notions and images that underlie these expectations."[25] By creating a dense description of Wang's political

---

20   *WYMQJ*, vol. 1, 8:279.

21   Wang, *Instructions for Practical Living*, 193.

22   Ibid., 271.

23   Ibid., 278.

24   Cua, "Between Commitment and Realization," 631.

25   Taylor, *Modern Social Imaginaries*, 23.

actions at this particular phase of his life, I hope to make a preliminary stab at reconstructing his social imaginary, thereby giving further definition to moral knowledge as he understood it. If for no other reason, such an inquiry reveals the extent to which the meaning of his key philosophical notion was very much tied to its time, and hardly comprehensible apart from it.

In this chapter, the broader political context for the rebellion will be reconstructed in order to acquire some understanding as to just why the prince was able to conceive of usurping the throne and some insight into the attitudes of political elites towards the contemporary political environment. By so doing, I believe we can deepen our understanding of Wang Yangming's claim that defeating the prince was nothing more than acting upon *liangzhi*. Following, I will recount the course of events during his military campaign and discuss how Wang and commentators explained such a rapid victory, an interpretation inseparable from the powerful contemporary idea of sagehood.

The next chapter picks up with the aftermath of the campaign, when Wang Yangming implemented measures to restore order in the region and appropriately to reward or punish those officials and civilians who had, respectively, either assisted him or followed the traitor. The latter will be particularly important, for it is possible from his judgments and recommendations to the court to tease out more precisely just what justice meant for him in practice. Following, I will discuss the challenges Wang faced in the wake of the emperor's decision to lead a mock campaign of his own, experiences often said to be the impetus for his final formulation of the theory of the "extension of the innate knowledge of the good." I will also explain how his teaching addressed the problem of official conduct in a time of decline, as well as elucidating the role of the innate knowledge of the good in restoring a better world.

The Rise of the Prince of Ning

What was the broader political setting in which Wang Yangming was operating, and how could it have fostered the ambitions of a minor prince to rebel against the very emperor of China? Ultimately, for Wang, the blame for the rebellion fell on the emperor, something he made very clear in two memorials he sent while suppressing it. A statement from one of these indicates concisely just how this prince, over a period of several years, had been able to amass political and economic power in the local and national arenas, as well as a potent military force. Wang believed that, more than anything else, the main problem was that the proper routines of government were being obstructed by imperial favorites who acted outside the bounds of their authority and misled the emperor into engaging in certain improprieties. In this regard, his criticism falls squarely within the parameters of what Zhang Fentian believes to be central to political culture in general and the consciousness of political elites in particular during the entire imperial period: individual emperors might be praised and blamed, revered and excoriated, but the need for an emperor was almost never doubted.[26] What is perhaps more characteristic of the Zhengde emperor's reign was the degree to which his actions were construed as a parody of the ideal and how therefore some officials, including Wang Yangming, responded by following the dictum that the Way transcends the ruler, the minister is responsible for the Way, and he should therefore take things into his own hands, modeling in his conduct the ideal of sageliness within and kingliness without. This is just what Wang Yangming did: he used the authority given him to the fullest possible extent in order to take control of the situation, even when this meant using powers granted him to disobey direct orders from the emperor himself.

Wang Yangming composed the following indictment just days after the prince first raised his rebellion, and after having received documents from the prince's establishment denouncing the emperor and declaring a new reign. He forwarded these to his ruler, and added:

> Your servant has heard that trials and tribulations regenerate a dynasty and serious hardship awakens a sage. Your majesty has held the throne for fourteen years, repeatedly passing through catastrophes and uprisings, and the minds and hearts of the people are in turmoil. And yet [your majesty] still goes on imperial tours without cease, leading some in the imperial family to plot to take up arms, with the hope of usurping the great treasure [the throne]. Furthermore, as for unwarranted aspirations, are these harbored only by the Prince of Ning? And as for the treacherous pretenders under Heaven, is it to be believed that these are only to be found in the imperial family? When my words and thoughts come to this, I become terrified and alarmed.... I hold out the hope that your majesty should deeply reproach himself, and change and alter his ways; cashier the treacherous and fawning, in order to win the hearts and minds of all the heroic under Heaven; and, in order to put an end to the aspirations of

---

26   Zhang Fentian 張分田, *Zhongguo diwang guannian: shehui pubian yishi zhong de "zui jun—zun jun" wenhua fashi* 中國帝王觀念: 社會普遍意識中的罪軍尊軍文化法式 [The Concept of the Emperor in China: the Cultural Norm of Praising and Blaming the Emperor as an Ideology Widely-held throughout Society] (Beijing: Zhongguo renmin daxue chubanshe), 552.

the treacherous pretenders, cease touring, definitively establish the foundations of the state, and exert yourself to govern the country well. Then
the great peace might yet be realized, and all officials unimaginably
blessed.[27]

In 1519, it would have been obvious to every scholar-official throughout the
empire just who "the treacherous and fawning" were, just as it would have been
to the "treacherous and fawning" themselves when at least some read this memorial. The Zhengde emperor had throughout his reign made a farce of the
Confucian sage-king ideal by surrounding himself with individuals—mostly
eunuchs and military officials—who had little interest in the style of governance advocated by the scholar-official class, and whose appeal to the emperor
was their conveniently shared enthusiasm for the martial arts, warfare, enter-
tainment, and travel.[28] He owned such a long history of allowing the reins of
power to come under the control of eunuchs or other favorites that Wang
Yangming's call for change counted as no more than a drop in an ocean of pro-
tests in the ultimately tragic hope that the emperor should "awaken" to his central role in the higher cosmic order.

Undoubtedly, the emperor's egregious behavior had spawned widespread
disillusionment and apathy among officials, which is precisely what Wang
Yangming was signaling when he called for him to win back their support.
What is perhaps most astonishing about the Zhengde emperor's reign as a
whole, though, is the fact that in spite of both his deliberate efforts to frustrate
officials and frequent brutal treatment of them, many nonetheless continued
to do everything they could to get him to change his ways. One episode among
his many charades captures well Ming officials' predicament at the very time
they were confronting the prince's increasingly manifest designs on the throne.

During the spring of 1519, a few months prior to the rebellion, the emperor
pulled a stunt he surely knew would thoroughly incense officialdom. At this
time, he returned from yet another tour of the northern garrisons that had
taken him nearly four hundred miles from the capital, only to announce to
court officials his wish that they should prepare for a tour of inspection in the

---

27   *WYMQJ*, vol. 1, 12:396.
28   For an account of these vices during the Zhengde emperor's reign, see James Geiss, "The
     Leopard Quarter during the Cheng-te Reign," *Ming Studies* 27 (1987): 1–38. According to
     him, the Zhengde emperor was attempting to revive an essentially martial vision of
     emperorship, while his officials insisted that he adhere to their understanding of a civil
     vision, whereby the emperor remains as a passive symbolic figure confined to the inner
     quarters of the imperial palace following the advice of his advisors (19).

South. This caused an immediate outcry among ministry officials, some of whom had been or would later become students of Wang Yangming. Because they remonstrated, on April 18, 1519, Minister of War Huang Gong 黃鞏, Ministry of War Vice Director Lu Zhen 陸震, Ministry of Personnel Vice Director Xia Liangsheng 夏良勝, Ministry of Rites Secretary Wan Chao 萬潮, and Erudite for the Court of Imperial Sacrifices Chen Jiuchuan were all imprisoned in the Embroidered Uniform Guard Prison. Huang Gong and Lu Zhen had submitted a memorial entitled "Six Matters Concerning Effective Rule," in which they reiterated the very issues about which officials had been voicing their concerns for several years. First, because the emperor completely ignored his duties and ceremonial protocol, they called for him to "revere the learning of the sages." Second, because he never heeded the counsel of his advisors and allowed the traffic of official communications to be handled by his court eunuchs and imperial favorites, they called for him to "open up avenues for criticism." Third, because he was going by the title "Awesome and Martial General-in-Chief, the Duke of Zhenguo," they demanded that he "rectify names." Fourth, because he was continuing to pass his days on imperial pleasure tours, they called for him to cease these. Fifth, because he was making his decisions based solely on the advice of imperial favorites, they called for their removal. Finally, because the emperor had as of that time failed to appoint an heir to the throne, they urged him to do so.[29]

All of these recommendations were aimed at rectifying the emperor's derelictions of duty, which had, they believed, also allowed the Prince of Ning to accumulate power and pose a threat to the security of the region and potentially the entire country. Hanlin Compilers Shu Fen 舒芬 and Cui Tong 崔桐 clarified this connection in a memorial to the throne when they wrote, "Because of recent events, we shed bitter tears of blood, having that which we must speak of before the emperor. There is a rebellion on the horizon at the princely establishment in Jiangxi. High officials harbor the heart of a Feng Dao 馮道,[30] taking emolument and rank as an entitlement, positions in the court

---

29   Tan, *Guo que*, 51:3170.

30   Feng Dao (882–954) lived during the Five Dynasties period and served five different courts and eleven emperors. For this reason, the implication is that officials were loyal only to their self-preservation. See *Zhongguo lidai renming da cidian* 中國歷代人名大詞典 [Great Biographical Dictionary of China] (Shanghai: Shanghai guji chubanshe, 1999), 1:465. However, it should be noted that Feng Dao only became a symbol of disloyalty during the Song Dynasty, and was not viewed as such during his time. For a study, see Wang Gung-wu, "Feng Tao: An Essay on Confucian Loyalty," in *Confucian Personalities*, ed. Arthur F. Wright and Denis Twitchett (Stanford: Stanford University Press, 1962), 123–45.

as a marketplace, and the emperor as a chess piece."[31] In a similar vein, Xia Liangsheng, Wan Chao, and Chen Jiuchuan warned the emperor of the dangers of imperial tours, failure to select an heir, and assuming improper aliases: they "fear[ed] that these would give rise to unwarranted aspirations."[32]

For giving their honest opinions on these matters, most of these officials were beaten and imprisoned, but this only set off yet another round of remonstration involving over one hundred ministry officials. In response, an edict was issued accusing them of exceeding their status, speaking lies, and levying malicious accusations. Yet, in spite of the fact that these officials were forced to kneel before a gate to the imperial palace for five days straight from dawn to dusk, the clash continued unabated for several days as more capital officials memorialized calling for lenient treatment and cancellation of the tour. They too were arrested, interrogated, and forced to wear the cangue. In the end, all of these officials were beaten, several were relegated to minor posts outside the capital, others had their salaries withheld for months, some were demoted to commoner status, and a few even died.[33]

Although the emperor would, against personal precedent, finally give in to the unrelenting pressure, the impact of these events was tremendous. A future disciple of Wang Yangming, Luo Hongxian 羅洪先 (1504–1564), appraised the outcome:

> In the court of Emperor Wuzong, the eunuchs Liu Jin and Jiang Bin successively controlled the reins of power. Officials who remonstrated would always as a result meet their deaths. Critics believed this was of no benefit to the situation, only making obvious to all the faults of the ruler, something not appropriate for an official to do. As for their meeting a pointless death, these commentators also believed it was the outcome of acting precipitously on the passion of the moment, of agitating and as a result meeting their doom. Truly, though, they could not help themselves. At that time, gentry maintained a circumspect silence in order to avoid such deadly clashes, and yet no one would criticize them. Alas! At the time Jiang Bin was encouraging the emperor to undertake a southern tour ... which would have devastated the central territories. And yet the rebellious Zhu Chenhao was plotting to have his eldest son usurp the throne, relying on Jiang Bin as his collaborator. The edict announcing the tour was issued ... and everyone just looked at each other, not daring to

---

31   Tan, *Guo Que*, 51:3170.
32   Ibid.
33   This account is drawn from Tan, *Guo Que*, 51:3170–73.

call this into question. But because these gentlemen remonstrated with their lives, the plans for a southern tour were surprisingly dropped. Alas! Having resulted in this, were their actions truly without any benefit?[34]

Such then was the broader political environment Wang Yangming was confronting when the uprising began: although the emperor's deplorable conduct might have inspired heroic resistance in some officials, many were adopting a posture of indifference.

Also with regard to the prince's suspicious conduct, the result was largely apathy. As Zuo Dongling has pointed out, the lesson of the fates of Fang Xiaoru, Huang Zicheng, Lian Zining, and Yu Qian was likely on their minds: officials who dare to get involved in the internal affairs of the imperial family do so at their own risk.[35] This is likely what Luo Hongxian meant when he claimed officials were harboring the heart of Feng Dao: they would serve whoever happened to be in power so long as that ensured self-preservation. In his historical notes, Zheng Xiao provides a telling anecdote:

> When the Prince of Ning rebelled, I was twenty-one years old and on my way to take the provincial examination in Hangzhou. I saw many military communications along the way, and none dared directly to state that it was Chenhao who had rebelled. Some merely stated there was an unexpected turn of events in the provincial capital of Jiangxi, some that there was an extremely urgent situation in Jiangxi's provincial capital, some that a serious situation had arisen from the murder of the grand coordinator, and some that soldiers, horses, and troops had suddenly amassed in Nanchang, that word was that there was a rebellion.[36]

Only one person, he noted, had the courage to report things as they really were: "Only Yangming submitted a report, clearly stating that the Prince of Ning in Jiangxi was plotting rebellion."[37]

But prior to looking at the grand coordinator's resolute response, what remains to be explained is the exact connection between the emperor's behavior, the havoc wrought by imperial favorites, and the rise of the Prince of Ning. It is

---

34   Ibid., 51:3172.
35   All of these scholar-officials were executed for their involvement in imperial clan politics.
36   Zheng Xiao 鄭曉, *Jin yan* 今言 [Speaking of Our Times] (Beijing: Zhonghu shuju, 1997), 4:175.
37   Ibid.

to more specific factors and background events leading up to the rebellion that we now turn.

The Origins of the Rebellion

The brewing of events leading up to the rebellion can be pieced together from various records, especially the deposition prepared during the succeeding reign by the ministries of justice during interrogation of various menials in the service of the prince. These largely confirm what Wang Yangming observed in a victory memorial:

> The Prince of Ning is utterly dissolute, treacherous, and cruel. His rank odor permeates everywhere. He maims and kills good people, exploits and harms commoners; calculating his crimes, never before has there been something of this magnitude. He has been plotting treachery now for over twelve years, and the area over which he domineers through his mounting power extends everywhere. The gentry, although over a thousand miles away, all cover their eyes and wave their hands, none daring to reveal his crimes. The people, even should they reside in the remote countryside, keep their mouths shut and swallow their fury, and dare not plead their grievances. Furthermore, he summons fugitives, and lures in powerful bandit leaders such as Wu Shisan and Ling Shiyi, drawing in a mob of several thousand. He enlists brave and fearless men accomplished in the martial arts from all directions, and those who are able to uproot trees and knock down gates also number over ten thousand. Furthermore, he has men in his gang such as Wang Chun deliver gold and silver amounting to over ten thousand taels [for bribes and rewards]. . . . On the day he incited the revolt, he had his escort guard and other close imperial relatives follow him, linked together his gang and personal clique, and drove about and coerced merchants, soldiers, and civilians. He sent out officials under his control and confidantes, having them conscript mercenaries to follow along, the largest [group] numbering in the thousands, the smallest in the hundreds. Sails covered the river, numbering some eighteen thousand. Those following who headed east downriver in fact numbered no less than eighty to ninety thousand. What's more, he falsified confidential decrees to intimidate those near and far, and promulgated fake proclamations to confuse the people. Therefore, not much more than one month after [the prince] had raised an army and initiated an uprising, [people] everywhere were overawed and recoiling in fear, all saying this great affair had already been decided, and no one dared to come out and resist, to pit their strength against him. Those who valued

their integrity only fortified city walls and defended themselves, while those infuriated by their strong feeling of loyalty only assembled soldiers to await the opportune moment. It was not the case that there was a lack of men capable in strategy or having the virtues of righteousness and loyalty, but rather that his [the prince's] sheer bluster and power to domineer caused this state of affairs.[38]

In this summary assessment, Wang Yangming identifies conditions that had permitted the Prince of Ning's "rotting stench and pollution" to spread. It is worthwhile elaborating upon some of these in order to better understand how the prince became such a threat, in particular, looking at how the prince influenced those close to the emperor, the tactics he used to silence officials, and his sources of power and wealth in the local arena.

In order to gain the upper hand in Jiangxi as well as to amass the resources required to stage a rebellion, the Prince of Ning first needed to gain some influence over those imperial favorites surrounding the emperor who handled the majority of administrative routines. That way, he could both prevent indictments of his conduct from coming to the attention of the emperor and also obtain edicts granting his wishes. And the way he achieved this was fairly straightforward: bribery. Bribery could be effective because the emperor put much of the administrative machinery at the imperial court in the hands of his inner court.

The story as to just how the prince was able to recover his escort guard—a key element of his military—is exemplary of how he achieved a number of ends that officials repeatedly opposed. Escort guards were assigned to princely establishments for protection, but were on occasion removed as a form of punishment to princes, especially if their loyalty was in question.[39] This was the case for the Prince of Ning, although his guard had actually been removed during the Tianshun 天順 reign (second reign of Zhu Qizhen 朱祁鎮, 1457–64), at which time the prince's grandfather Zhu Dianpei was implicated in a case of treason.[40] When Wang stated that the prince had been plotting treachery for over twelve years, he may have been aware that Zhu Chenhao had first petitioned to recover the guard in 1507. The petition was eventually granted, despite the fact that the Ministry of War recommended denying it, because the powerful eunuch director Liu Jin 劉瑾 accepted a hefty bribe and secretly ma-

---

neuvered to make it happen.[41] When Liu Jin was executed, the ministry immediately memorialized calling for the guard to be placed directly under Jiangxi
provincial officials' control as the Nanchang Left Guard, which is indeed what
happened.[42]

This change of status, however, was not to last very long. In the meantime,
the emperor had assembled another group of favorites who were equally open
to accepting money from the prince. The key figure here was fawning favorite
Qian Ning 錢寧, who began his stellar career as a mere servant in a eunuch
director's household. After coming to the emperor's attention via Liu Jin and
winning his friendship in part through a shared passion for the military arts, he
was eventually appointed to the powerful position of commander of the Embroidered Uniform Guard.[43] By bringing in actors and monks to entertain the
emperor, playing a key role in the construction of the Leopard Quarters and
encouraging the emperor to travel incognito, the commander gained his confidence as well as power over much of the internal political machinery.[44] "When
the emperor was intoxicated," states the *Ming History*, "he would frequently
sleep in Ning's bed. So when officials arrived in the morning and were awaiting
an audience, but did not know the whereabouts of the emperor or when he
would appear, they would first search for Ning, for should Ning arrive they
knew the emperor would soon follow."[45]

In 1514, when the prince again decided to use every means at his disposal to
have his escort guard returned, he relied on two channels. The first was Zang
Xian—a favorite musician to the emperor who came to his attention via Qian
Ning.[46] But prior to that, a relative to Zang had been punished with service in
the Nanchang Left Guard and had already helped the prince establish a connection to him.[47] In early 1514, the prince ordered several of his staff to depart
for the capital with cartloads of silver, gold, and other valuable goods. According to the confession of one of the prince's eunuchs, they first proceeded to
Zang's home and gave him ten thousand taels. He in turn was to send five thousand taels to Qian Ning, and Qian would in turn send three thousand to the
powerful Director of Ceremonials Zhang Xiong 張雄 and one thousand to the

---

41   Gu Yingtai 谷應泰, *Ming shi ji shi ben mo* 明史紀事本末 [Record of Events in the Ming
      History from Beginning to End] (Taipei: Sanmin shuju, 1963), 47:479. Hereafter, *MSJSBM*.

42   Ibid.

43   *MS*, 307:7891.

44   Ibid., 195:7890–91.

45   Ibid., 307:7891–92.

46   Ibid., 195:7891.

47   Chen Hongmo 陳洪謨, *Ji shi ji wen* 繼事紀文 [A Record of Things Heard Concerning
      What Was Transmitted from the Ancestors] (Beijing: Zhonghua shuju), 5:102.

Director of the Eastern Depot Zhang Rui 張銳.[48] This amounted to making substantial gifts to the majority of the imperial favorites, who at the time were serving in the Leopard Quarters and "controlling the reins of power;"[49] this also meant influencing and gaining the favor of the two most powerful eunuchs serving the emperor. Because Zhang Rui was in charge of the Eastern Depot and Qian Ning the commander, they were in control of the emperor's personal and much-feared security and intelligence-gathering apparatus.[50] Likewise, Zhang Xiong's position as director of ceremonials meant that he would play the role of surrogate of an inattentive emperor, handling the flow of state documents within the inner court, authorized as he would have been to convey imperial sanctions by "giving the red ink."[51] Thereafter, this would be a channel regularly exploited by the Prince of Ning. Putting it more simply, the *Ming History* biography for Qian Ning states, "All of those in the service of Chenhao who came to present bribes at the capital would stay at the actor Zang Xian's home and, via [Qian] Ning, reach those close to the emperor."[52]

The prince's second channel was an official by the name of Lu Wan 陸完, whom he befriended when Lu was serving as surveillance commissioner in Jiangxi.[53] When Lu became the minister of war in 1513, the prince saw this as the perfect opportunity to recover his escort guard, and made overtures to him in the form of gifts and recollections of the good old days when Lu was serving back in Jiangxi. At the very moment the prince was bribing imperial favorites, he also dispatched a petition to the ministry requesting that his guard be returned, and Lu appended an endorsement, which in turn was forwarded to the grand secretariat. With the cooperation of Grand Secretary Yang Tinghe 楊廷和, a draft was prepared by the chancellery and sent to Zhang Xiong for approval. A decree was then issued by eunuchs in the palace secretariat and during the third month of 1514 both the escort guard and military farming colonies were placed back under the control of the Prince of Ning, effectively taking them out of the hands of provincial commission officials.[54]

---

48   Xie Fen 謝蕡, "Ning fu zhao you 寧府招由 [Deposition of the Ning Princely Establishment]," in Deng Shilong 鄧士龍, *Guo chao dian gu* 國朝典故, ed. Xu Daling 許大齡 and Wang Tianyou 王天有 (Beijing: Beijing daxue chubanshe), 108:2206.

49   *MS*, 304:7795.

50   Henry Shi-Shan Tsai, *The Eunuchs in the Ming Dynasty* (New York: State University of New York Press, 1996), 104.

51   Ibid., 227.

52   *MS*, 307:7891–92.

53   Chen, *Ji shi ji wen*, 5:102.

54   *MSJSBM*, 47:480.

This same process would be repeated on several other occasions when the prince needed to obtain something from the capital, including having his eldest son brought there, in the hopes that he would come to the attention of the emperor. Throughout his reign, the Zhengde emperor had received numerous memorials pleading for him to select an heir, primarily to put an end to the "aspirations of treacherous pretenders." The prince was very likely biding time because he somehow believed his son would be adopted by the emperor as his heir. Thus, in the spring of 1516 he again sent cartloads of silver to the capital— forty thousand taels—to bribe Qian Ning and Zang Xian. He requested that they arrange to have his eldest son invited to the capital for the purpose of conducting ritual offerings of incense at the Grand Temple, effectively placing him in the role of heir apparent. Qian Ning sent the prince's agents back to his establishment with several gifts, such as a jade belt and gemstone, deceptively claiming they were bestowed on the prince by the emperor. The prince was told to await further orders, orders that were not to come until the spring of 1519.[55] At that point, Qian Ning managed to have the emperor approve the prince's petition, having the order written on "colored dragon paper" normally reserved for communications from the Protector of the State. This effectively meant that the prince would mistakenly come to believe he was to be charged with the duty of acting in the emperor's stead should there be no heir apparent upon the emperor's death.[56] According to most sources, this all took place behind the emperor's back.

Why would Qian Ning, who was close enough to the emperor to have him as a bedfellow, act like this? His and the actions of those assisting him in the inner court would seem to support what the *Ming History* suggests concerning his motive: for years Qian Ning's wealth and status were at a peak, but seeing that the emperor was heirless, he decided to hook up with a strong prince to secure his future, and for this reason had been assisting the Prince of Ning for years.[57] Likewise, according to Feng Menglong, "Emperor Wuzong was without a son, and Chenhao schemed to have his own son designated heir apparent. Zhu [Qian] Ning and Zang Xian, along with many powerful eunuchs, did much to help him realize this design, but there were also many officials among the Six Ministries, Nine Ministers, supervising secretaries, and censors who collaborated. Because the matter was so serious, they dared not speak."[58] Given Luo Hongxian's belief that many officials were looking upon yet another conflict

---

55   Xie, "Ning fu zhao you," 108:2208.
56   Geiss, "The Cheng-te Reign," 426.
57   *MS*, 307:7891.
58   Feng, "Huang Ming da ru Wang Yangming," 121.

within the imperial family with studied indifference, Feng Menglong's account seems highly probable. Indeed, the prince's outrageous criminal behavior failed to alarm the emperor for the very reason that, as Wang Yangming stated, the Zhu Chenhao conspiracy and the alienation caused by the emperor's egregious conduct ran so deep that few dared to reveal the prince's crimes.

The prince's connections at the highest levels were thus vital for keeping officials silent both at the local and national levels. Throughout the Zhengde emperor's reign, but especially after 1514, local officials and censors in Nanjing regularly memorialized concerning not only the prince's aspirations, but also his illegal seizures of land, taxation and extortion of wealthy households, efforts to cow local authorities,[59] and usurpation of the prerogatives of the emperor—for example, by calling his establishment an imperial palace, referring to himself as ruler, and issuing edicts.[60]

Yet perhaps most significant was the prince's success in silencing Assistant Surveillance Commissioner Hu Shining 胡世寧 (1469–1530). In a memorial dispatched to the Ministry of War, the commissioner described how the prince had, ever since regaining his escort guard, harassed the people and managed to gain the upper hand over officials and clerks in such a way that "rites and music and imperial commands" were no longer emanating from the court alone. He made it clear that the dangers in Jiangxi did not end with bandits, who were in any case plundering throughout the region at his behest. The ministry responded by ordering the prince to rectify his conduct and control his subordinates. But although the prince was at first alarmed, he made good use of his connections, dispatching a memorial claiming that Hu Shining, by levying such malicious accusations, was attempting to sow discord in the imperial family. Naturally, this memorial was accompanied by substantial bribes for Qian Ning, Zang Xian, Zhang Xiong, and others.[61] As a result, Commissioner Hu was imprisoned, interrogated, beaten, and finally exiled to a border garrison. "Thereafter," a confession by one of the prince's staff reads, "[Prince Zhu Chen]hao became ever more brazen in his conduct, trumping up charges against grand coordinators, regional inspectors, and officials from the three provincial administration commissions; through accusing them of misconduct he controlled them, forcing them to swallow the humiliation and quietly bear this."[62]

---

59   Geiss, "The Cheng-te Reign," 424.
60   *MSJSBM*, 46:480–481.
61   Xie, "Ning fu zhao you," 108:2207.
62   Ibid.

In addition, by having his princely establishment staff form connections with sub-official functionaries in official yamens in Nanchang, Zhu Chenhao was able to control the flow of documents leaving the province. Combined with his tactics of intimidation, this meant in effect that "his boundless criminal activities would not come to the attention of the emperor."[63] Furthermore, he also stationed agents pretending to be merchants in towns along the routes to Beijing just so that he could more quickly receive news from the capital. In the spring of 1519, Grand Coordinator and Censor in Chief Sun Sui memorialized seven times concerning the depredations and intent of the prince, but all of these were intercepted by the prince's agents.[64]

Other key elements of the prince's power were manpower and financial resources. While sources repeatedly mention marginal characters somehow connected with the Prince of Ning—a clerk, a diviner, a geomancer, a provincial graduate, a soldier, some distant descendants of the imperial family—by far his greatest sources of strength were bandits, his escort and other regional guards. In order to foster close ties with bandits, the prince would rely heavily on his establishment staff to make connections and bring them to his palace. As early as 1514, the prince "secretly ordered [eunuch attendant Liu] Ji and others to draw in powerful bandits experienced in the military arts." These men were ordered to "emerge frequently and plunder, return to the establishment, and divide up the booty."[65]

At the same time, apparently concerned that he lacked the requisite military skills and was also short of commanders, the prince invited to his palace a provincial examination graduate known both for his literary accomplishments and knowledge of the military arts. This scholar, Liu Yangzheng, would become one of his key advisors, along with a retired censor-in-chief by the name of Li Shishi. Aside from the prince's gifts of silver, the motivation behind these two men's support of the prince remains obscure. According to Feng Menglong, "After failing the metropolitan exam, Liu Yangzheng donned the clothing of a recluse and, because of his achievements in writing poetry and prose, acted arrogantly. Provincial officials acted beneath their dignity by calling on him, and took gaining audience with him as a great fortune."[66] The prince won his friendship though a constant stream of gifts and inquiries, and when Liu went to the establishment in 1515, he praised the prince as having "the ability to

---

63   Ibid., 108:2208.
64   Ibid., 108:2210.
65   Ibid.
66   Feng, "Huang Ming da ru Wang Yangming," 120. Cf. *MSJSBM*, 47:481.

bring order out of chaos."[67] As for Li Shishi, in addition to styling himself as a great military strategist, he was also related to Zhu Chenhao through the marriage of their children.[68] Chenhao had befriended him when Li was serving as an official in Nanchang early on during the Zhengde reign and had been involved in his promotion to the rank of censor-in-chief. After retirement, Li would play a key role in advising him during the rebellion.[69]

Throughout 1517 the prince's efforts to forge ties with criminal elements continued apace. While getting ready to rule "all under Heaven," the prince and these two advisors realized they needed more men experienced at warfare, so Chenhao invited what amounted to a long list of bandit bosses and their followers to the establishment. Furthermore, he had his staff summon and gather together from every direction fugitives, thieves, hangers-on, as well as those who had had their death sentence remitted to penal servitude or exile.[70] This motley crew was concealed in nearby mountains, but also given free rein to plunder civilian property, granaries, treasuries, merchant vessels, and wealthy households. These were at least some sources for the income the prince needed to fund his bribes.

In addition, for years the prince had already been ordering his staff and supporters to use any and all means possible to swell his coffers by forcibly seizing property, using his authority to dominate various forms of commerce (such as selling salt and pepper), selling government grain at extortionate prices, occupying publicly owned lakes, and seizing property from locals who had commended it to him for the purpose of having it fall off tax registers.[71] Aside from requiring this revenue for his extensive networks of bribery, he also needed it in order to send large sums of money to native officials in Guangxi and their "wolf troops,"[72] as well as to "barbarian" *man* 蠻 settlements in southern Jiangxi and southwest Fujian. In addition, he would send his men throughout the region to gather materials for manufacturing weapons and other military equipment, including hides from Guangdong for making leather armor, as well as craftsmen who could manufacture lances, daggers, armor, and helmets. Per-

---

67   Xie, "Ning fu zhao you," 108:2207.

68   Feng, "Huang Ming da ru Wang Yangming," 120.

69   Chen, *Ji shi ji wen*, 5:101.

70   Xie, "Ning fu zhao you," 108:2208.

71   Ibid.

72   *Lang bing* were usually non-Chinese troops under the control of Zhuang native chieftains.

haps most famously, in 1517, the prince obtained Portuguese breech-loaders 佛郎機銃.[73]

Given the extent of the prince's criminal activities over the preceding ten years, it is astonishing that he was never stopped. In fact, the only thing that put an end to the ongoing collaboration and cover-up by imperial favorites was their own internal rivalry. In fact, sources inform us of a fairly complex political dynamic, the end result of which was the emperor finally coming to the realization that an inquiry into the prince could not be avoided. According to Chen Hongmo, it all began with a certain guard in the Eastern Depot and a censor from Nanchang, who both hated the prince for various reasons. Thus, when the prince had a memorial drawn up praising his own filial conduct, the guard and the censor jumped on this as an opportunity to question his motives. Apparently, they proceeded to convince Grand Secretary Yang Tinghe and Director Zhang Rui that their previous connections with the prince could be a grave liability. Wishing now to fully distance himself from the prince, Zhang Rui hooked up with eunuch Jiang Bin and Director Zhang Zhong—both of whom in any case desired to alienate the emperor from imperial favorites Qian Ning and Zang Xian— and persuaded them to go with him before the emperor to speak of the prince's egregious conduct. About the same time, Grand Secretary Yang had the guard and censor convey Zhang Rui's intention to a censor by the name of Xiao Huai so that he would submit a memorial indicting the prince's conduct on a variety of counts.[74] When the emperor showed the memorial to his grand secretaries, Yang Tinghe's recommendation was that the court should, in accordance with a precedent set during the Xuande 宣德 emperor's reign (Zhu Zhanji 朱瞻基, r. 1426–36), commission a high dignitary and high official to take a letter to the prince proclaiming the emperor's sincere intent to

---

73   Xie, "Ningfu zhao you," 108:2208. According to Zhou Weiqiang's analysis, the prince's
      agents' acquisition of a Portuguese breech-loader in the third lunar month of 1517 is the
      first record for the introduction of this weapon into China. He speculates that this was a
      result of the prince's agents' involvement with networks of foreign trade on the southeast
      coast (where the Portuguese first arrived in the 1510s) during this time, and also that the
      prince would then attempt to manufacture these guns within his compound because they
      were commonly used on vessels for amphibious warfare. When the prince rebelled in
      1519, the scholar-official Lin Jun, who had personally experimented with one of these, sent
      a tin copy of the gun to Wang Yangming, but it did not arrive until the first of the eighth
      month of 1519, after he had already suppressed the rebellion. Wang did, however, make a
      record of this. For his analysis, see Zhou Weiqiang 周維強 "Folangji chong yu Chenhao
      zhi pan 佛朗機銃與宸濠之叛 [The *Folangji* Gun and Chenhao's Rebellion]," in Dong
      Wu lishi xuebao 8 (2002): 93–127.
74   Chen, *Ji shi ji wen*, 5:103.

preserve the imperial clan, and ordering him to reform his errant ways and turn over a new leaf. Consequently, Eunuch Director Lai Yi, Censor-in-Chief Yan Yishou, and Commandant-Escort Cui Yuan were ordered to travel to the establishment to instruct and admonish the Prince of Ning.[75]

The Prince Rebels

Unfortunately for the prince, however, his channels for receiving speedy information from the capital failed to work as intended. After the court had made its decision, an agent of the prince residing in the capital—Lin Hua—misunderstood the reason these high officials were making their way to Jiangxi. Under the impression that the purpose of this visit was to arrest the prince, he hurried back to the establishment with the urgent report. Based on his familiarity with dynastic law, whereby whenever a prince was to be arrested and his property confiscated a commandant-escort and high official were to be dispatched, the prince did indeed fully expect that the intent of these two was to arrest him.[76]

The day Lin Hua arrived at the palace just happened to be the prince's birthday, and as befitted such an occasion, officials from all over the province had come to offer their congratulations and join his banquet. Upon hearing of the impending visit of a high dignitary and high official, the prince assumed the worst—that his plans for rebellion had been divulged. He therefore brought the banquet to a close and summoned his loyal retinue, including establishment personnel, two provincial graduates, regional military commissioners, commandants, bandit leaders, and commanders. He informed them of the dire situation: "As of now officials are being sent to investigate the affairs of my establishment and to remove the escort guard, and if we do not act, the result will not be good."[77]

The two key figures with whom he consulted closely throughout this night were the now clearly traitorous military advisor Li Shishi and Liu Ji, the former advising him he should begin immediate preparations to launch a rebellion. The plan was, at such time as officials had returned to the princely establishment in the morning to take leave (in the wake of the birthday celebration), to confront them with his grand designs and arrest any of them refusing to give their allegiance. Thereafter, the prince hurried to complete his reproduction of an imperial court, to manifest what he believed himself destined to become. He therefore immediately began making his key appointments: Liu Ji, for

---

75   Tan, *Guo Que*, 51:3175.

76   Chen, *Ji shi ji wen*, 5:104.

77   Xie, "Ning fu zhao you," 108:2211.

example, was to become his eunuch director, Li Shishi the preceptor of state. From this time on, the prince would continue making such appointments, as well as promising high rank and emoluments for those supporting his ascent to the throne.[78]

Just what all these illegally appointed high-ranking officials and dignitaries must have been thinking of their rise in status is something lost in the sources which, of course, flatly condemn them for this most heinous of crimes. They acted in some ways like those marginalized individuals in early modern Europe who carried out a ritualized overturning of authority, which they believed was withholding the status, recognition, and justice legitimately owed to them.[79] Rebellions in imperial China often followed a theatrical course with similar plot lines, which primarily called for denouncing those in power while mimicking their bureaucratic hierarchy of ranks and offices. The two powers would soon meet face to face: one real, and one a façade; one legitimate, the other denounced; one a manifestation of Heavenly Principle and therefore a cause for righteous support, the other a manifestation of misguided and ultimately evil desire and therefore a cause for righteous extermination.

However, if we look at such ritualized forms of social violence as disempowered social groups demanding just governance, then it is entirely conceivable that a large number of those involved in the rebellion may really have believed they were participating in something righteous, no matter how villainous the key leaders are made out to be in standard histories written by the scholar-official class. In fact, sources recount the efforts he made to win over public opinion and recognition from the court through bogus displays of filial piety—for example, through carrying mourning to extremes, and dilettantish literary pursuits.[80] In addition, Daoist technicians are said to have read his destiny from his physiognomy and were pleased to inform him he had the appearance of an emperor.[81] Furthermore, the prince would spy on the court, and when he heard of the emperor being slandered he was elated, but when he heard of praise he would become angry.[82] These did paint a picture of a rather conniving individual, but as for those immediately surrounding the prince, he very likely cultivated relations with them in such a way that they may have truly

---

78   Ibid., 108:2211–12.

79   Cf. Keith Wrightson, *English Society, 1580–1680* (New Brunswick, N.J.: Rutgers University Press, 1982), 63, 174.

80   Tan, *Guo Que*, 51:3174.

81   Xie, "Ning fu zhao you," 108:2205.

82   Jiao Hong 焦竑 ed., *Guo chao xian zheng lu* 國朝獻征錄 [Record of the Evidence for the Worthies of Our Dynasty], in *Mingdai zhuanji congkan* 明代傳記叢刊, ed. Zhou Junfu, vol. 109–14 (Ming wen shuju, 1991), 47.

believed they were participating in a righteous cause. Therefore, when they took on their new roles in the mock court, they were simply enacting in whatever way they could the imperial political ideal, and it would not be hard to imagine that their utterances amongst each other were at times scripted according to a language of honor and loyalty common to "the Way of the ruler" (*jundao* 君道). In any case, their reproduced imperial microcosm was about to be crushed by the real one.

All these anecdotes raise the question as to how much of what was claimed about the prince's conduct was manufactured by scholar-official elites who had unpleasant encounters with him. On the contrary, Craig Clunas' study of Ming princes (whom he calls kings) amply demonstrates that they were deeply involved with the social, economic, and cultural life of their local societies. That is why the Prince of Ning's cultural pursuits and patronage of scholars were hardly unusual, and perhaps only made to look so in the aftermath of his rebellion.[83] In a similar vein, Richard Wang notes that local officials often conflicted with princes whose establishments were located in administrative units under their jurisdiction, one reason being that local yamens delivered their stipends and collected rents on princely estates. He finds that, if the conflict was of an economic nature, the princes were usually favored. However, should officials succeed in branding the prince as a political careerist with greater ambitions, then the prince risked severe punishment.[84] For this reason, any claims against them by officials could easily be manufactured or exaggerated.

The truth about the prince's conduct probably lies somewhere in the middle. Nevertheless, given the level and frequency of the charges leading up to 1519, it would not be difficult to imagine a situation whereby we have a prince who, though marginal on the national political scene, did indeed have inordinate fantasies as to his destiny, and that these were fanned by sycophants, the farcical conduct of the emperor, and a telling precedent in the Jianwen usurpation. For this reason, Wang Yangming had no problems branding him as a careerist and demonizing him for his depravity.

When provincial officials returned the morning of July 10, 1519, to pay their respects and take leave, they found themselves surrounded by armed supporters of the prince, and what followed was a confrontation with Zhu Chenhao that became the occasion for both stunning heroism and shameful cowardice.

---

83   Craig Clunas, *Screen of Kings: Royal Art and Power in Ming China* (Honolulu: University of Hawaii Press, 2013), 170.

84   Richard Wang, *The Ming Prince and Daoism: Institutional Patronage of an Elite* (Oxford: Oxford University Press, 2012), 17.

The prince notified these officials that he had received a secret edict from the empress dowager proclaiming the illegitimate birth of Emperor Wuzong and ordering him to raise a rebellion, and that he was now calling for their support for his great righteous cause (*da yi* 大義). In response, Grand Coordinator Sun Sui and Surveillance Commissioner Xu Da displayed their "staunch loyalty" by engaging in a shouting match and excoriating the impostor, only to end up beheaded.[85] Their heads were hung above the city walls, as a lesson to the crowd. Indeed, some thirty provincial civilian and military officials, "fearing for their lives, and failing to be courageous enough to hold to the righteous and resist," submitted to the prince.[86] Bound, they were forced to acclaim their new emperor, and then imprisoned. After this, the prince's key supporters assembled over a hundred men—mostly other distant imperial family clan members and establishment staff—and brought them before the prince so they could shout "*wan sui* 萬歲"—"Long live (the emperor)!"[87]

Over the next few days, the prince's preparations proceeded apace. In need of funds, he had already ordered his eunuch attendant Xu Qin and other establishment personnel to fan out over nearby provincial, prefectural, and county yamens.[88] They were also to release prisoners—more potential manpower. The prince further dispatched a summons to imperial clansmen and officials "near and far" proclaiming, "Today I am launching a great enterprise, and you should each fully exert yourself in supporting it; after succeeding in this matter, imperial clansmen will receive high titles and rank, and officials will receive promotion."[89]

Others were preparing "imperial" vessels and commandeering official and civilian boats. All were ordered to be ready to depart for Nanjing (the southern capital) on July 13. According to the eunuch Liu Ji, on the evening of the tenth, bandit bosses Ling Shiyi, Min Niansi, Wu Shisan, and Yang Qing were at the prince's side assuring him that "the emperor should relax, for even with only us four, you can rest assured that the city of Nanjing will be defeated."[90] The prince then appointed as commanders these and several other bandit leaders, regional military commissioners, and commanders, ordering them to lead four contingents numbering some two thousand soldiers each. These new appointees were then commanded, along with key eunuch attendants, to board over

---

85   Xie, "Ning fu zhao you," 108:2212.
86   Ibid.
87   Ibid.
88   Ibid.
89   Ibid., 108:2213.
90   Ibid., 108:2214.

two hundred commandeered boats and head downriver to attack two major Yangtze port cities, Jiujiang 九江 and Nankang 南康.[91] According to Wang Yangming's summary of reports he had received, on the evening of July 12, some one thousand stolen vessels filled with rebel bandits charged into Nankang Prefecture. Because the city walls and moats were still under construction, and the local militia small, most officials fled to nearby Mount Lu, but later joined other officials sent by Wang Yangming in what would become a successful attempt to recover the city about a month later.[92]

On the morning of the fourteenth, Xu Qin's forces arrived at the gates of Jiujiang in two hundred vessels and, using a combination of incendiary warfare (fire lances and flaming arrows), guns and cannons, and scaling ladders, were able to penetrate a weak defense, enter, and take control of the city. Civil and military officials fled. In all cases, occupation of these areas was followed by widespread looting and burning. There were similar attacks on county seats in the prefectures of these two towns and elsewhere throughout northern Jiangxi, with varying levels of defense put up by local civil and military officials and supportive civilians.[93]

In addition to raiding treasuries, the prince's agents were also ordered to conscript more mercenary soldiers. One eunuch attendant, for instance, was to assemble rebel-bandits and local stalwarts (*kuai shou* 快手) to attack prefectures and counties. Several guard, battalion, and hundreds commanders were to draw men from military farming colonies, but they apparently fled and did not do so. Other establishment personnel were dispatched to nearby counties to enlist mercenaries, but the magistrates in some of these areas were able to head up a defense, intercept, and kill them.[94] Some of these magistrates, such as Gu Bi in Fengcheng, would soon lead reinforcements to assist Wang Yangming.

On July 12, his key advisor, Liu Yangzheng, arrived at the provincial capital, and so important was this scholar to Zhu Chenhao that the prince personally came out to a local postal station to greet him and escort him into the princely establishment. He immediately appointed him military supervisor, and assured him that once he had attained his goal, he would promote Liu to the high post of grand councilor. Furthermore, the prince informed his confidantes of his intention to declare a new reign, changing it to Shun De 順德 (Conforming

91   Ibid.
92   *WYMQJ*, vol. 1, 12:423.
93   Ibid., 12:421–22.
94   Xie, "Ning fu zhao you," 108:2215.

to Virtue). Liu, however, advised him to await arrival in Nanjing before doing so.[95]

The prince then ordered his eunuch Liu Ji to verify the number of soldiers in his ceremonial guard and the Front and Left Guards in Nanchang, in preparation for departure. These eight thousand soldiers, along with some twenty-five thousand bandits and civilians residing respectively in Western Mountain (just to the west of Nanchang) and the provincial capital, were all to be provisioned with armor, incendiary weapons, and equipment from the guard and civilian manufactories.[96] In addition to preparing his forces for the march to Nanjing, the prince also worked closely with his literati advisors for the purpose of sending out proclamations denouncing the emperor and guaranteeing the people relief from taxes and labor service. At the same time, using provincial administration commission seals, they sent out communications to offices throughout the empire, calling for them to surrender allegiance and join his cause. Through various forms of coercion, the prince managed to have some imprisoned officials carry these falsified documents throughout Jiangxi and Guangdong. This included Ji'an Prefecture 吉安府, where Wang Yangming was then stationed.[97] The official charged to bring the document to him was an administrative vice commissioner of Guangxi by the name of Ji Xue, who had formerly served under Wang Yangming during his campaigns in the southern Gan region. He and the establishment guards escorting him were captured by Wang's soldiers while en route and brought before the grand coordinator, who had them promptly imprisoned.[98] Thus it was that, several days later, Wang would dispatch the memorial cited earlier, in which he called for the emperor to cashier the treacherous and fawning in order to win back support from the righteous, enclosing these falsified documents.

If, as the confession of his eunuch Liu Ji suggests, the prince had indeed intended to march to Nanjing on July 13, he most certainly did not do so. The above preparations and planning took place between July 10, the first day of the uprising, and July 26, at which time he would finally lead forces to the southern capital, Nanjing. The reason for this delay was that Zhu Chenhao was succumbing to Wang Yangming's psychological warfare and stratagem, and was hesitant to depart because intelligence had led him to believe doing so might be a dangerous move. But in order to understand why this was so, we

---

95   Ibid.
96   Ibid.
97   *WYMQJ*, vol. 1, 12:395.
98   Ibid.

now turn to Wang Yangming's response to reports of the rebellion and the impending march to Nanjing.

A Righteous Cause

In the aftermath of his victorious campaign to defeat the prince's rebellion, Wang Yangming insisted that credit for his success must first and foremost go to the high court officials who had made advance preparations. In particular, he was referring to Minister of War Wang Qiong, who had shown great foresight in charging him to quell a minor uprising in a guard unit located in Fujian. In fact, as the minister observed to one of his secretaries, the disturbance in Fujian was almost too trivial to bother the grand coordinator with, but he had ulterior motives: to allow Wang Yangming to retain broad discretionary powers for handling any kind of disorder.[99] And that disorder would soon arise, when the minister received a memorial reporting the rebellion. Immediately, he called for high officials to meet at the Zuo Shun Gate of the imperial palace. In a clear sign of the state of mind of other high officials, everyone was said to act indifferently, not daring to denounce the Prince of Ning. Only Wang Qiong was outspoken, excoriating the prince for his reprehensible conduct. But he informed the other officials they need not feel cause for alarm: "When I appointed Boan [Wang Yangming] to Ganzhou, it was specifically for this moment: the bandits, within a mere day and night, will be captured."[100]

Wang Yangming departed Ganzhou on July 5, 1519, sailed north along the Gan River, arriving some 120 *li* south of Nanchang in Fengcheng 豐城 on July 11. There he was greeted by the local magistrate, Gu Bi, as well as commanders of the local militia, who immediately notified him of the rebellion and reports that the prince had dispatched over one thousand soldiers to pursue him.[101] These men were well aware of the grand coordinator's recent campaigns in southern Jiangxi, and that he would have the wherewithal to muster and lead forces, so they urged Wang to lead the way. And thus it was that he changed course and decided to head straight back to the prefectural seat in Ji'an.

Wang's response appears to have been quite impassioned. When he decided to turn back, he took an oath together with three aides: they vowed to serve with their lives, launch forces, and lead a punitive campaign against the

---

99   *NP*, 34:1262.
100   Ibid., 34:1261.
101   *WYMQJ*, vol. 1, 17:571.

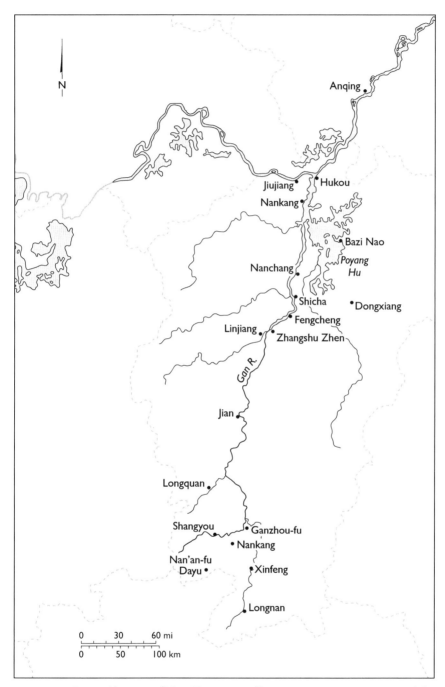

MAP 2   *Principal locations of Wang Yangming and his campaigns in Jiangxi Province while he waged war on the Prince of Ning in 1519.*

prince.[102] Something of the moral force behind this act can be gleaned from an official communication sent to the supreme commander of Guangxi and Guangdong, as well as his first urgent report to the court concerning the matter, both written upon arriving in Ji'an on July 14. In these, he stated both the reasons for his actions and initial estimation of strategic conditions:

> Of all the affairs under Heaven, none is more urgent than a ruler or father's dire predicament. Should the prince head downstream with the current, and the southern capital fail in its defensive preparations and suffer an attack by him, he could then ride on his victory and drive north, shaking the capital environs. That being the case, it remained unclear what direction calculations of victory or defeat would take, and this was therefore the critical moment deciding the security or endangerment of all under Heaven. When my fears and concerns reached this point, my heart was pained and bones chilled, and in all righteousness I could not bear to leave this behind and depart [from Fengcheng for Fujian].[103]

Similar concerns were conveyed in a letter to his ailing father written a few days later. In this, he expressed his deep regret at having to forgo the opportunity to visit him on the way to Fujian, but explained that "when what is right for an official comes to this, how could one then seek an easy way out or avoid involvement?"[104]

After taking the oath, Wang quickly returned to Ji'an, a location he believed best suited to effecting his strategy, which was now starting to take form. As he told one of his aides, the best strategy would be to draw back and send out communications with a call to arms, raise forces, and punish the rebel.[105] Wang was, however, facing dire circumstances, for the prince had dispatched soldiers to pursue him in Fengcheng, and on top of that winds were unfavorable for sailing upriver to Ji'an. The terrified helmsman expressed his reservations to Wang Yangming and insisted they wait to sail until the southerly winds had ceased. But for Wang there was no other choice. According to an account penned by Long Guang, a vice magistrate who accompanied him during much of this time, Wang ordered his aides Lei Ji and Xiao Yu to bring him incense so that he could burn it on the bow of the boat. In an act of piety, facing north and repeatedly prostrating himself, he wailed and pleaded, stating, "Should Heaven

---

102   *WYMQJ*, vol. 2, 39:1468.
103   *WYMQJ*, vol. 1, 17:572.
104   Ibid., 26:985.
105   Feng, "Huang Ming da ru Wang Yangming," 138.

take pity upon the people, then permit Wang Shouren to come to the aid of the country; I only wish that the wind should change directions. If Heaven should be of a mind to assist the rebel, such that the people meet calamitous suffering, then Shouren is willing first to drown, with no wish to live any longer."[106] Some of the hands on deck became excited, indicating the wind had died down, so his two aides carried burning incense to the upper deck to test which way the wind was blowing. Indeed, it was changing directions, and the north wind soon picked up.[107] Nevertheless, at the very time the prince's soldiers were approaching, it became evident this vessel was too large to quickly return to Ji'an, so Wang changed into commoner clothing and, along with his aides, boarded a small fishing boat, leaving behind Xiao Yu wearing his cap and gown to act as a decoy.[108]

On his way to Ji'an, Wang Yangming already knew what he needed to do: since there were no forces ready for an orthodox head-on battle with the prince, he had to engage in diversionary tactics. He first stopped over at Linjiang 臨江, where he was greeted by Prefect Dai Deru, who urged him to quickly take charge of matters in the city and begin preparations for a confrontation with the prince. But Wang believed that because Linjiang was situated dangerously close to the provincial capital and also served as a commercial hub located on the Gan River, stationing his forces in the city would leave him open to an indefensible attack by the prince. His strategy, as he explained it at this time, would be based on predicting the prince's possible moves: should Zhu Chenhao implement a superior strategy, and take advantage of his momentum by doing the unexpected and marching directly to Beijing, then the country would be in serious danger; should he pursue an average strategy and march directly to the southern capital (Nanjing), then the territories north and south of the river would be divided and suffer great harm; but should he merely occupy the provincial capital of Jiangxi and remain confined to this region, then forces coming to the aid of the emperor would have time to assemble in all directions. "Like a fish swimming in a cauldron, even if he does not die what could he achieve?"[109] In other words, the prince's fate would be sealed.

Upon further inquiry from Prefect Dai, Wang Yangming surmised that the prince, inexperienced in warfare as he was, would most likely recoil from the

---

106   Qian Dehong 錢德洪, "Zheng Chenhao fan jian yi shi 征宸濠反间遗事 [Stories Concerning the Use of Stratagem While Waging War on Chenhao]," in *WYMQJ*, 39:1472.

107   Ibid.

108   Huang, "Shi de ji," 38:1417.

109   Feng, "Huang Ming da ru Wang Yangming," 141.

battlefront should he become alarmed.[110] For this reason, all Wang needed to do was to compose a bogus Ministry of War communication that would give the impression that an attack on Nanchang was imminent, thereby causing the prince to remain and defend it. Since he had no forces with which to face the prince directly, Wang believed his only option was to stall the prince's departure. This would give the two capitals not only time to make defensive preparations, but also time for imperial troops and regional forces—including his own—to assemble and launch an assault. Thus, at this point, he believed his role would be to engage in diversionary tactics, thereafter becoming part of a larger concerted campaign.

Employing Stratagem

But how could Wang Yangming stall the prince, who intended to launch the attack on Nanjing while Wang was still en route to Ji'an, on July 13? His only choice was to employ stratagem and engage in psychological warfare, primarily for the purpose of sowing discord within the prince's ranks but also to cause enough suspicion to delay his enemy's plans. Soon after leaving Fengcheng, Wang Yangming conceived a scheme to have a falsified urgent communication from the supreme commander of Guangxi and Guangdong taken into Nanchang and intercepted by the prince's agents. This "confidential" communication would have given the prince the impression that the court had already been making preparations for a possible uprising, and therefore ordered the supreme commander to secretly assemble a massive force in the region. In fact, the communication stated that the supreme commander had already departed with his troops from Guangzhou Prefecture and was advancing towards Nanchang.[111]

According to Long Guang 龍光, who was accompanying Wang Yangming while he was composing and preparing to send out these fake orders, his aide Lei Ji voiced his concern that "when the Prince of Ning sees this, I fear he may not fall for it." To this, the master strategist raised another possibility: "He may not believe it, but might he not become suspicious?" Lei Ji confirmed that suspicion would be inevitable, so Wang only smiled and stated, "Should he become suspicious for only a moment, then his cause will be over."[112]

Thus, the grand coordinator believed this was all he needed to achieve his strategic objective: sow just one seed of doubt. He had only to manipulate appearances and the prince would be defeated in advance. Certainly, with hind-

---

110   Ibid.
111   Qian, "Zheng Chenhao fan jian yi shi," 39:1468–69.
112   Ibid., 39:1471.

sight, later admirers would point to his ability to handle so deftly the given strategic configuration of power through such subtle manipulations as being the key to his military greatness. But, in the moment, how could Wang Yangming be so sure this clever stratagem would hit the mark? At the conclusion of this conversation with Lei, he added:

> Chenhao has for long been depraved in his conduct, cruelly harming the people, and although for the moment those who follow him in his rebellion today are many, it is surely not their true intention, but rather merely a matter of being coerced or enticed by profit—of temporary shared interests. Even if he sends out a motivated force, with a righteous army I will call the prince to account for his crimes and pursue him slowly from behind; the strategic power deriving from allegiance and rebellion will be separated, and victory and defeat can be known in advance. However, if the rebel-bandit troops pass over the area early on, they will devastate the lives of the people. If the tiger or rhino gets out of the cage, they will be difficult to trap and return. As for the strategy for now, for every day that we delay Chenhao, all under Heaven will truly receive the good blessings of another day.[113]

Such being the case, he needed to bide time principally for the purpose of separating out the righteous from the unrighteous among the prince's followers, through psychological warfare and by wearing down their spirit. Also, he needed to raise forces whose strategic power would lie in the soldiers' natural response to the cause. That is, all he had to do was to buy enough time to speak to people's nascent moral sense and persuade them to do what was right, something the prince was unable to do because he had lost the confidence of the people. Manipulation through stratagem could be effective in its subtlety only insofar as it accorded with deeper, naturally correcting normative tendencies.

When Wang Yangming arrived in Ji'an, he was met by cheering crowds and greeted by Prefect Wu Wending 伍文定, at least after guards, upon seeing the grand coordinator's vessel, raised the gates of a city now under martial law.[114] Wu had already served under Wang Yangming during his campaigns in the southern Gan region, but even prior to this had earned a reputation for martial vigor as well as for being upright to the point of intolerance.[115] When Prefect

---

113   Ibid.
114   *MTJ*, 48:1485.
115   *MS*, 200:5281.

Wu greeted the grand coordinator, he immediately called for him to take charge of mobilizing forces, stating, "This rebel-bandit is violent, cruel, and immoral, and has already for long lost the trust of the people. You, sir, have always been of noble character and held in high esteem. Furthermore, you have control of the armed forces, so as for the matter of bringing forces to rescue the emperor, this can now be achieved."[116] Of course, Wang Yangming did consent to the prefect's wishes for, as he would soon inform the court in an urgent memorial reporting the rebellion, "Victory or defeat cannot be predicted, so this is truly the critical moment deciding the security and danger to all under Heaven."[117] Thus, he entered the city and comforted the soldiers and civilians and oversaw the mustering of soldiers and provisions, "summoning the righteous and courageous."[118]

Wang Yangming also explained to the court that the strategic balance of power was indeed overwhelmingly in favor of the prince, for he had been planning for this moment for over ten years, assembled some twenty thousand "dare-to-die" soldiers, lured in over ten thousand bandits, and gained control over his escort and other regional guards.[119] This effectively gave him a force numbering over sixty to seventy thousand soldiers. Such was their power that, on the day of his arrival, Wang was receiving urgent reports from officials in several Jiangxi counties concerning looting and plundering by rebels swarming all over these areas.[120] In contrast, at a time when, as he informed the court, "soldiers and civilians have fallen under the coercive influence of the Prince of Ning's expanding power, and thus were everywhere serving as his eyes and ears while not daring to speak out," all he had was "a few hundred weak and fatigued soldiers."[121] That is why he had no choice but to withdraw into a defensive posture and engage in diversionary tactics.

Realizing these tactics could be effective in delaying the prince only for so long, Wang proceeded to implement a two-pronged approach for defeating him. On the one hand, with the aim of causing the prince to "miss the opportune moment" and his supporters to "lose their fighting spirit," he would continue deploying stratagem and psychological warfare; on the other, he would raise forces for an orthodox confrontation. In other words, his principal concern was not only to give capital officials time to make preparations, but also

116   *MTJ*, 48:1485.
117   *WYMQJ*, vol. 1, 12:392.
118   Ibid.
119   Ibid., 12:397.
120   Ibid., 17:572.
121   Ibid., 12:397.

simply to deflate what he saw as a very fragile "high" among followers of the prince, whose support was ultimately hollow because lacking in righteous motivating factors. The strategy in the end worked. According to Long Guang, because the prince kept postponing his campaign, those rebel-bandits awaiting orders while stationed on vessels all over the lakes and rivers became increasingly doubtful, as well as dispirited and unmotivated; as a result, over several days their strategic power disintegrated and some began to scatter.[122] As was ideally the case for the military strategist, the enemy was simply being defeated in advance.

Another ruse Wang Yangming employed to bring about this result was indeed the counterfeit communication, dispatched to the court and intercepted by the prince's agents, in which he pretended he was responding to orders from the Ministry of War. According to these supposed orders, forces were being mobilized and would soon arrive in the region to strike Nanchang.[123] He confirmed that he had taken due note of the ministry's detailed plan for implementing a strategy for "attacking where the enemy is unprepared," but nevertheless had some important information that might call for a change in plans: the prince had sent large forces downstream. In light of these new conditions on the ground, Wang advised the court that those hundreds of thousands of government troops launching from all directions and preparing to attack (and he offered much detail here) had better advance slowly and wait for the prince's rebel forces to leave Jiangxi, in the hopes of drawing them out and cutting them off. What he most feared, Wang stated in no uncertain terms, was a decision on the part of the prince to remain in Nanchang and stage a defense, something that would wear down troops not accustomed to local conditions. Wang also added that the prince's chief strategists, Li Shishi and Liu Yangzheng, had sent confidential letters conveying their intention to requite the court with meritorious service. In conclusion, he confidently explained, "Should Chenhao depart precipitously from Jiangxi, and should we jump on this opportune moment and attack from all sides, given inevitable mutinies within his ranks, victory shall come easily."[124] Wang then ordered his aide Lei Ji to select a runner in his service and have him deliver this memorial to the court. This runner, however, was to have no inkling that the document was a ruse, and Lei was to order him to proceed under cover and conceal his tracks while en route to Nanjing.[125]

---

122   Qian, "Zheng Chenhao fan jian yi shi," 39:1470.
123   Ibid., 39:1469.
124   Ibid.
125   Ibid.

To ensure this runner would be intercepted, Lei paid a visit to someone who had long been in communication with the prince, and somehow managed to have him secretly proceed to the establishment and inform the prince of the memorial. When the prince heard of this, he immediately dispatched agents to find and capture the messenger, and after doing so, he was so distressed by the bogus communication that he beat the runner during an interrogation, hoping he would reveal the nature of the deception. But all this was, of course, to no avail, and the runner died.[126]

Although this communication might easily have appeared far-fetched, perhaps the reason Wang Yangming succeeded in sowing "just one doubt" was that he also paid a large number of actors to dress up as soldiers and lie in ambush in areas where the prince might have expected—based on the intercepted documents—to find troops. But in addition, with the help of Long Guang, he composed counterfeit replies to letters supposedly received from Li Shishi and Liu Yangzheng, the prince's chief military advisors. In these cleverly worded documents, he made it clear to them that he understood why they were at first forced to follow the prince, but also that their willingness to divulge the prince's plot and serve as infiltrators plainly demonstrated their "original mind of boundless loyalty and desire to requite the court."[127] Should the prince intercept these letters, he would be led to believe that these two were indeed colluding with Wang Yangming, but that they were merely biding their time until imperial forces deemed it the opportune moment to attack.

Wang's aides found a way to have the letter for Li delivered to Liu and vice versa, as well as to have them intercepted by the prince. Once again, the runners captured by the prince were slain, but the letters did have the intended effect of inciting suspicion between them. As Long Guang would later explain, "As a result superiors and inferiors became suspicious and fearful, and the strategic power of the military therefore daily waned."[128] According to one account, when the two strategists did in fact advise the prince that he should depart as quickly as possible and march to Nanjing, the prince interpreted this as advice fed to them through Wang Yangming's letters: by suggesting he go to Nanjing, these "traitors" were sending him right into a trap.

Of course, there was no such trap, and the last thing Wang wanted was for the prince to depart for Nanjing, which is precisely why his stratagem aimed at convincing him to do so. The grand coordinator and superintendent of military affairs had thus managed to buy himself time to mobilize forces, plan provi-

---

126   Ibid.
127   Ibid., 39:1470.
128   Ibid.

sions, disperse grain and rewards, manufacture weapons, and amass vessels. But equally as important, Wang had also bought time to engage in psychological warfare and mobilize popular support for his cause, as well as to pry people away from the temptation of getting caught up in the uprising. In particular, he and his aides composed and pasted up over a thousand proclamations, placards, and banners instructing the populace in the felicities and calamities that would result from either maintaining their allegiance or joining in the rebellion. According to Long, "When [we] pasted up proclamations and hung banners and wooden placards, it was during the middle of the night when it was dark, and we braved the wind and rain, traveled over places difficult of access, going in and out of bandit fortresses, managing to survive ten thousand deaths."[129]

One of the proclamations his aides may have been pasting up survives today. Wang Yangming's "Proclamation to Comfort and Settle the People" captures his efforts to maintain calm and stir up popular support for his cause:

> Proclamation to instruct soldiers and civilians in towns and villages near and far: recently evildoers calling for rebellion have on high violated the way of Heaven, and below lost the support of the people. This official has stationed himself here and has a definitive plan. Troops coming to save the emperor are assembling in all directions. I expect each of you to live in peace and pursue your livelihoods. Do not become alarmed and suspicious, and dare on your own authority to move. If, as a result of doing so, you incite and cause turmoil, local hundreds captains and tithing heads shall bind you and send you to the military headquarters, and you shall be punished according to military law. If amongst you there are loyal and righteous heroes able to contribute plans and render service, and willing to join the righteous armies and attack the traitors, you should come to the military headquarters.[130]

Although we have no direct evidence as to the effect of these proclamations, it is nevertheless reasonable to conjecture that the prince's domineering behavior throughout the province had earned him enough popular enmity for such proclamations to prevent civilians from supporting him and to recruit soldiers for Wang's campaign. And as we shall see, local officials from surrounding prefectures would soon arrive with thousands of recruits both from regional military units and the civilian population.

---

129   Ibid., 39:1472.
130   *WYMQJ*, vol. 2, 31:1127.

Rallying Troops

While the facts concerning Wang Yangming's stratagem come primarily from a
later account composed by his close disciple Qian Dehong, information concerning the other prong to his strategy—assembling forces for a campaign—
can be pieced together from a flurry of official communications he dispatched
from Ji'an. Since he knew the prince would eventually depart for Nanjing, he
had to raise a force to confront him, at first by occupying his "lair" (Nanchang)
and thereafter by going out to battle him as soon as he returned to recover his
base.[131] This is the task Wang undertook from the day he arrived in Ji'an until
he met with other Jiangxi officials and their forces in Linjiang on August 9, 1519.

According to his urgent report to the court, "After entering the city [of Ji'an,
on July 14], I offered consolation to the soldiers and civilians and, along with
Prefect Wu Wending, supervised the mobilization of soldiers and the implementation of a strategy, reining in people's demoralized state of mind, and inspiring in them a spirit of righteousness and loyalty."[132] As a result, officials
present "were roused with enthusiasm, thinking only of rendering service by
punishing the criminals, in order to requite [the blessings] of the court."[133]
They then proceeded "to dispatch calls to arms near and far, proclaiming the
deep humanity of the court and unveiling the crimes of the Prince of Ning,"
with the result that "the heroic responded to the call, people became inspired
and energized, and within a few days of planning soldiers gradually gathered
from all directions."[134]

On many other occasions, Wang Yangming explained to officials the importance of inspiring people to take action, encouraging them "out of righteousness to capture the cruelly violent and apply the straight to the crooked."[135] In
an official communication sent to Yongxin, a mountainous county in the western part of Jiangxi, where one might expect to find rustic and hardy subjects,
he praised those "capable and dauntless" men who could be relied upon
at times such as these because "when they see what is right they become
courageous."[136] And July 23, in an official communication praising the prefect
of Ruizhou and his soldiers for their actions in capturing rebels, Wang legitimated the virtuousness of their conduct by stating that such sentiments and
actions accorded with Heaven's intent and the will of the people: "Whereas the

---

131   *WYMQJ*, vol. 1, 12:398.
132   Ibid., 17:572.
133   Ibid.
134   Ibid.
135   *WYMQJ*, vol. 2, 31:1127.
136   Ibid.

traitor bandits are calling for an uprising, Heaven is angered and the people aggrieved, and execution and destruction won't be long in coming; but today the blaze [of the prince's] strategic power is spreading, and this official alone has been able to arouse loyalty and courage, dealing a setback to the vanguard. Those near and far have heard of this, their righteous *qi* naturally increasing."[137] Wang therefore stated that they would be rewarded "in order to further encourage people's good intentions."

Yet perhaps Wang Yangming's most forceful call to arms can be found in the orders he sent to prefectures throughout Jiangxi, where he would find most of his soldiers. In these, we find both concrete instructions as well as a description of the nature of the threat:

> The greatest evil under Heaven is rebellion, and the greatest righteousness punishing traitors. The most distinguished of rites is the conferring of a princely establishment, for the favor (*en de* 恩德) is solemn and profound; and yet the prince dares in just this way to harbor treacherous intent ... on high violating the Way of Heaven, and below treading upon the anger of the masses. The moment of his destruction can be expected to arrive within days. As for this official, although not specifically appointed [for this], how could I sit on the side and watch when there is this dangerous threat? Relying on the allegiant to punish the rebel, rousing and leading the loyal and righteous, heroes arise in all directions, together implementing a plan and combining strength. Aside from ordering Ji'an and other prefectures and counties to mobilize local militia and guard their areas, and ordering Guangdong, Fujian, Huguang, and others to muster forces and plan for taking coordinated action ... each prefecture shall have those counties, guards, and battalions under their jurisdiction mobilize government troops and militia to protect and guard the cities and moats, in order to maintain security in the area. Each shall respectively mobilize local militia and allocate them among the passes, in order to head off [enemy]. Each shall select and enlist fearless and brave crack troops, approximately four to five thousand in large counties and two to three thousand in small counties, each coming fitted with sharp weapons and provisions, as well as choose and commission a competent, brave, and strong official to lead, train, and drill.... Those near the river banks shall each prepare vessels and await this official to dispatch an official holding the warrant banners and warrant cards (*ling qi*

---

137   *WYMQJ*, vol. 1, 17:575.

ling pai 令旗令牌),*[138]* and then immediately in accordance with the set time launch your forces and attack.... The day has come for the minister and son to exert their filiality to the utmost with their lives, and for each it is fitting to arouse your sense of righteousness, to motivate the soldiers and people, in order together to achieve the glorious merit of destroying the traitors, as well as to exert to the full your one thought of requiting your country.[139]

This official communication did in fact circulate throughout Jiangxi, and within a few days, as explained below, Wang Yangming would meet up with a number of prefects and magistrates and the forces they had managed to assemble.

Undoubtedly, the reason Wang Yangming felt confident he would succeed was the fact that he believed his actions to be just—that is, they were in accord with the will of Heaven and the will of the people. By the very nature of things, such a heinous affront to moral principle as this rebellion would simply be incapable of overwhelming a power anchored to a transcendent order. Here, Charles Taylor's observations of what retribution means within the Platonic-Aristotelian concept of an ontologically-secured hierarchical moral order apply equally to how Wang Yangming conceptualized what he expected to take place:

> We have an order that tends to impose itself by the course of things; violations are met with a backlash that transcends the merely human realm. This seems to be a very common feature in premodern ideas of moral order.... Anaximander likens any deviation from the course of nature to injustice, and says that whatever resists the course of nature must eventually "pay penalty and retribution to each other for their injustice according to the assessment of time."... In these cases, it is very clear that a moral order is more than just a set of norms; it also contains what we might call an "ontic" component, identifying features of the world that make the norms realizable.[140]

For Wang Yangming, the "ontic" component was Heavenly endowed nature (*xing* 性), the source of people's inner sense of justice, of naturally occurring sentiments of right and wrong. If people are thinking clearly, they will naturally be moved to action by their direct apprehension of sentiments according

---

138   The cards and banners were imperial warrants signifying and authorizing imperial orders.
139   *WYMQJ*, vol. 1, 17:573–74.
140   Taylor, *Modern Social Imaginaries*, 10.

with the principle of loyalty. As he stated in one of his many conversations with his students, "When the mind is free from the obscuration caused by self-centered desires, it embodies Heavenly principle (*tianli* 天理), which requires not an iota added from the outside. When this mind is pure in Heavenly principle and manifests itself in serving parents, there is filial piety. When it manifests itself in serving the ruler, there is loyalty. And when it manifests itself in dealing with friends or in governing the people, there are faithfulness and humanity."[141]

But while Wang Yangming was assembling forces in Ji'an and other prefects and magistrates throughout Jiangxi were doing the same in their respective locales, Prince Zhu Chenhao, based on intelligence, had come to the realization that he had indeed been duped, and therefore immediately prepared his forces to march on the southern capital. Meanwhile, Wang Yangming initiated his plan for recovering Nanchang and confronting the prince in battle.

Applying the Straight to the Crooked

During the time between his commanders' successful occupation of Jiujiang on July 14, 1519, and his final departure for Nanjing twelve days later on July 27, the prince had continued to amass and organize a considerable army. Establishment personnel and cooperating officials trained and reviewed troops made up of bandits, town ruffians, guards, and "coerced" civilians. This motley crew was in turn organized into five contingents with 140 columns each. These contingents were to be led by a number of mostly minor cooperating military officials drawn from the guards as well as from establishment personnel. At the same time, to safeguard Nanchang, the prince left behind other loyal establishment personnel, officers, and a few close relatives of minor imperial nobility, along with some ten thousand troops. On July 27, 1519, the prince and his commanders made their final preparations and the now massive force of over sixty thousand soldiers began to move down the Yangtze River in the direction of the southern capital.[142] While some local government officials would remain under guard in their yamens in Nanchang, others were forced to accompany the prince on his vessel, where they may very well have encountered his consorts and other descendents of collateral lines from the Ning Establishment.

But instead of sailing straight to Nanjing, the prince decided to stop off at Anqing 安慶, located about halfway downriver to his prize. Xu Qin and his contingent had already laid siege to this city, where they were now held up

---

141   Wang, *Instructions for Practical Living*, 7.
142   Xie, "Ning fu zhao you," 108:2219.

waiting for the prince, who indeed arrived on August 3.[143] Just why the prince would insist, when Prefect Zhang Wenjin and Regional Military Commissioner Cui Wen were staging what would later become a much-celebrated defense, on first defeating Anqing is somewhat unclear. Against the advice of his literati strategists, who believed he should go straight to Nanjing without delay, Zhu Chenhao apparently was either taunted into continuing the siege by large numbers of civilians and officers cursing him from atop the city's walls, or because he simply felt that if they could not succeed here then they had no chance of overall success. In any case, while accounts of the rebellion and its suppression attribute most of the credit to Wang Yangming and his key commander Wu Wending, several do, however, mention the key role of the heroic defense staged by officials at Anqing in giving Wang Yangming a crucial window of opportunity for occupying Nanchang before the prince's forces could reach the southern capital.[144]

Prior to the rebellion, these local officials had already made defensive preparations, including repairing city walls, dredging the moats, and amassing grain and other provisions. Although they had few soldiers at their disposal, upon being confronted with rebel forces, they were able to mobilize a militia and other assistance from the resident population. With such support, they deployed clever tactics and technology to resist the siege warfare of their opponents, including dropping stones and pouring boiling water on the rebels' heads, and burning their scaling ladders and towers.[145] Because they were so successful in repelling Chenhao's assault, the prince was held up in Anqing until August 9, at which time he received word of the impending attack on Nanchang by Wang Yangming's forces.[146] Once again, against his strategists' advice—and as Wang had foreseen—the prince insisted on turning back.

All the while the prince was held up in Anqing, Wang Yangming had been preparing to depart for a garrison post north of Linjiang on the Gan River, where he would meet up with all those civil officials-turned-commanders and their contingents on August 9.[147] According to his victory memorial, some fourteen prefectural and county officials arrived with nearly thirty-five thousand troops.[148] From Linjiang, Wang Yangming's now fully assembled army

---

143   Ibid.
144   Tan, *Guo Que*, 51:3183.
145   *MSLWZSL*, 176:3419.
146   Feng, "Huang ming da ru Wang Yangming," 162.
147   *WYMQJ*, vol. 1, 12:401.
148   Ibid., 17:579–80.

moved upriver to Fengcheng, where they would make final preparations for the assault on Nanchang.

Wang did face some resistance to his plans at this point—one official believed Nanchang to be impregnable and further insisted that the prince's soldiers would be so dispirited from a long and failed siege at Anqing that it would be better to press straight there and defeat him head on; after that, Nanchang would easily follow. His commander, however, disagreed:

> If our troops were to reach Anqing, the rebel-bandits would turn and fight to the death. The forces in Anqing are merely able to fend for themselves, and would not be able to supply reinforcements for us while we are on the river. Further, the troops in Nanchang would cut off our supply lines, and the rebels in Jiujiang and Nankang would combine their strategic power, cut us off, and follow from behind. With no hope for reinforcements from any direction, we would become hard pressed. But today these contingents have assembled rapidly, making their first show of awesome strength, such that those within the provincial capital will surely be terror-stricken. Under these conditions, to unite our forces and rapidly attack—with such strategic power—their defense will surely fail. The consequence of occupying Nanchang will be the destruction of the rebels' courage and deflation of their will to fight, for this is their base. By the very nature of this strategic state of affairs, they will surely return. In this way the Anqing encirclement cannot but be withdrawn, and the Prince of Ning's capture is inevitable.[149]

By August 13, all of Wang Yangming's commanders and their forces had advanced to Shicha 市汊[150] and were now poised to attack and recover the prefectural capital.[151] Early the next day, each contingent was to proceed to a predetermined city gate, penetrate defenses, and enter and occupy key strategic locations, including official yamens, military compounds, and the princely establishment itself.[152]

Just prior to the assault, to ensure that soldiers and civilians within the city would neither flee nor be lured into joining the resistance expected from the prince's forces, Wang Yangming also had agents infiltrate the city and disseminate proclamations to the people. In these he made it clear he was soon to

---

149   Ibid., 12:401.
150   Shicha was located halfway between Fengcheng and Nanchang on the Gan River.
151   *WYMQJ*, vol. 1, 12:401.
152   Ibid., 17:579–580.

arrive with a massive force, and that anyone contributing to the "treachery" through their "evildoing" would be killed without mercy. But by the same token, he expressed deep sympathy for the plight of those whose lives had been thrown into turmoil as a result of the prince's actions. He assured them he felt confident that even should they have cooperated with the prince or maintained silence this could not have been "their true intention," and having thus understood the nature of the wrong done to them, he was coming with over two hundred thousand soldiers "for no other reason than to redress the injustice done to the people, to call to account for their crimes the principal evildoers."[153] "As for those good soldiers and civilians who choose decisively to expel evil and turn toward the good," his proclamation stated, "your lineages will not suffer destruction."[154]

On August 13, 1519 all contingents departed Shicha, arriving at their designated locations at dawn the next day. Wang Yangming reported to the emperor that just prior to departure, "I took a solemn oath with all the soldiers, proclaiming the awesomeness of the court, and again unveiling the crimes of the Prince of Ning. [I instructed them that] each general was, upon the first drumbeat, to draw close to the city and, upon the second, to ascend. If after the third drumbeat they were not yet defeated, then some within the ranks were to be executed, and if upon the fourth they were not yet defeated then commanders were to be executed. After swearing the oath, there were none whom were not grinding their teeth and deeply pained in their hearts, jumping about with enthusiasm and rage."[155] But his efforts to work up his soldiers' courage did not stop there. Wang then gave orders for the execution of several soldiers accused of failing to follow his commands, presumably as a lesson for those soldiers not yet focused on the task at hand. This whole act was, however, somewhat of a ruse, for these soldiers were in reality the very ones that had earlier been dispatched by the prince to escort captured officials ordered to carry false proclamations throughout the province. It would appear that Wang Yangming had long before decided to have them brought along for some such purpose.[156]

According to the victory memorial, although those supporters of the prince who remained behind to protect the city had fortified it with rolling logs, ash bottles, (gunpowder) bombs, and other equipment, when the various contingents reached the city gates they put up little resistance. These supporters were already deeply distressed, "their fighting spirit snatched away (*duo qi* 奪氣)," so

153   Ibid., 17:581.
154   Ibid.
155   Ibid., 12:398.
156   *NP*, 34:1266.

when confronted with thousands of soldiers crying out and charging they dropped their weapons and fled. Some city gates were already open, while others were either hacked down or opened up from within by soldiers who had penetrated with scaling ladders and ropes.[157] This lack of resistance suggests that Wang Yangming's estimate that the prince had at this point little support within the city was indeed accurate.

Upon entering the prefectural capital, Wang Yangming was mainly concerned with restoring order and strategizing for the prince's imminent return. On August 16, he received reports that the prince had five days earlier withdrawn the failed siege at Anqing and moved his forces, berthing at Ruanzi Jiang 阮子江.[158] Zhu Chenhao's plan for recovering his home base was first to send a force of twenty thousand selected from among his best troops. They were to pass over Lake Poyang and enter Nanchang, after which time he himself would return with a larger force. In spite of the fact that many had fled over the course of the last month, due both to the delays caused by Wang Yangming's ruses and to the failure of the siege at Anqing, the prince's forces remained potent enough to give Wang Yangming's commanders cause for concern. According to Wang's report to the court, his commanders contended that they must withdraw into a defensive posture because, "drawing energy from their anger and fury, should they [the prince's forces] unite their strength and quickly strike, we will be at a strategic disadvantage and unable to match them."[159] The grand coordinator, however, contended that the enemy's forces, far from being substantial, were in reality vacuous:

> Although the strength of his military is indeed formidable, and his vanguard possesses a strong fighting spirit, nevertheless wherever they go they rely only on [intimidation], overawing those near and far, through inflicting suffering by burning, plundering, slaughtering, and killing. But they have yet to confront a formidable enemy, who will deploy the orthodox and unorthodox when fighting. Furthermore, the means by which he motivates and incites his subordinates are promises of titles and rank. Add to this the fact that within a month they have already been forced to return, the officers' state of mind must be dispirited, so if we first send out crack troops, and take advantage of their slow return, meeting them with

---

157   *WYMQJ*, vol. 1, 12:401.
158   Ibid.
159   Ibid.

a surprise attack, in order to deal a blow to their vanguard, the many generals will be routed prior to even having fought.[160]

Fundamentally unimpressed by his opponent, Wang Yangming commanded his officers to divide up into several contingents and prepare for departure.

Although he recovered the prince's former base with little difficulty, Wang nevertheless faced some immediate challenges within the city. In his report to the court, he explained how he implemented a number of measures directed at restoring order so as to diminish support for the prince, an approach that falls more broadly under his understanding that success in campaigns ultimately revolved around winning the passive and active assent and support of the local public.[161] For this reason, his measures were often designed to appeal to what he took to be the moral compass of the masses. For example, some soldiers within his contingents failed to uphold discipline, indiscriminately killing innocent civilians. Presumably, they believed that taking more heads would, in terms of concrete rewards, redound to their merit. This was. in any case. a fairly common practice, one routinely faced by commanders. In addition, some of these soldiers were recently resettled bandits from Ganzhou known for their martial ferocity. Wang's solution was to have several of them executed as a lesson to the others. In addition, he also made it clear that within the city soldiers would now only receive rewards for those captured alive, and that heads would no longer be counted. So important was this measure that, according to some accounts, news of this brought calm throughout the city.[162]

Many other measures followed. After determining how troops were to be deployed to confront the imminent arrival of the prince's forces, he ordered officials to provide massive relief to soldiers and civilians. They were also to have residents and local guides spread the news that those coerced into supporting the prince would be pardoned, even those whom had illegally arrogated official titles and ranks.[163] But his other major concern was the minor nobility in Nanchang, such as commandery-princes and their juniors, who might yet continue to collaborate with the prince. Likely believing their fate was sealed, Wang Yangming chose personally to pay a visit to them and provide reassuring words in order to take them out of the strategic equation.[164]

---

160   Ibid.
161   Ibid.
162   *MSJSBM*, 47:488.
163   *WYMQJ*, vol. 1, 17:582.
164   Huang, "Shi de ji," 38:1420.

When the grand coordinator entered the city, imperial concubines who failed to receive Wang's reassuring proclamations prior to the assault had already immolated themselves within the palace, triggering a blaze that spread beyond the establishment to neighboring areas. On the second day, accompanied by other officials, Wang visited the palace, and found that most buildings lay in ashes, save for some warehouses that he promptly had sealed up. As for the remaining bodies of the palace women, he explained to the court, "Although the Prince of Ning is a traitor, and his crimes can never be forgiven, nevertheless there is no place where the sincere and peaceful humanity of the court fails to penetrate."[165] Therefore, he ordered a proper burial.

On August 17, Wang Yangming received reports that the first wave of the prince's forces, led by his loyal rebel-bandit supporters, had reached Qiaoshe 樵舍.[166] Innumerable sails were said to be covering the river for dozens of *li*. That evening Wang's armies—primarily those same officers and soldiers who had retaken Nanchang—were ordered to advance north in preparation for a direct assault. At dawn, Prefect Wu Wending formed an "orthodox" front formation, with support from behind by Regional Military Commissioner Yu En's forces. Prefect Xing Xun was to circle around and drive forward from behind the enemy's forces, and Prefects Xu Lian and Dai Deru were to form flanks. With approximately five hundred crack troops each, these contingents were put in a formation that aimed to disperse the enemy's strategic power. Unfortunately, accounts of three ensuing major battles, which took place on and around the environs of Lake Poyang and ended on August 20, 1519, with the capture of the prince, offer only a skeleton outline of the locations of the conflict and the strategies pursued. The records speak of cannons, guns, swords, armor, other weaponry, and incendiary warfare, but with so little detail that we can only make a rough sketch of Wang Yangming's tactics during what was predominantly amphibious combat.

On the morning of August 18, the rebel forces advanced to Huang Jia Crossing, approximately twenty *li* from Nanchang, confronting Wu Wending and Yu En's forces. Although they suffered a slight setback, these two commanders had advanced to the north specifically in order to lure the enemy into making a precipitously rapid advance that would draw out their forces. This allowed Xing Xun to drive right into the middle of their ranks while the remaining contingents attacked from all directions. Such a sudden onslaught from all directions threw the rebel forces into a state of disarray, and several thousand surviving troops were forced to withdraw into a defensive posture at Bazi Nao

165   *WYMQJ*, vol. 1, 17:582–83.
166   Qiaoshe was a town located, during the Ming, in Xinjian County.

八字腦.[167] According to Wang Yangming, in this first confrontation, over two thousand were killed or captured, with innumerable drowning.[168]

Prior to the next confrontation the following day, the prince moved to counter this setback both by motivating his officers with hefty rewards of silver taels, but also by ordering forces occupying Jiujiang and Nankang to come with reinforcements. It was at this point that Wang commanded several prefects to lead contingents to these cities and recover them, something they did successfully. That same day, the rebel-bandit forces took advantage of a favorable north wind to charge forward on the river with "a ferocious spirit," meeting Wu Wending's forces at the battlefront, and dealing them a setback wherein several dozen soldiers died. Concerned with signs that his commanders intended to draw back, Wang sent officers under his command to the front lines with orders that anyone seen retreating would be immediately executed. This apparently inspired some considerable heroics by some, especially Wu, who is said to have had his whiskers burned while charging the front lines at the stern of his boat, standing amidst firing cannons. With the arrival of other imperial contingents, and bombs coming in reach of his boat, the prince and his forces were again forced to draw back, this time to Qiaoshe, where they linked their boats up into a square array. Again, during this battle, thousands were killed and captured, and countless drowned.[169]

Aware that the prince had now withdrawn into a vulnerable formation, during that evening Wang Yangming oversaw the preparation of incendiary weapons. His plan was to have Prefect Wu advance in small vessels filled with combustible materials and set the enemy's fleet on fire, while simultaneously sending out signals to have forces lying in ambush attack from multiple directions. On August 20, while Prince Zhu Chenhao was busy reproaching his officers and compliant officials and threatening to behead them for their failure to fight to the death, Wang's forces rapidly approached and attacked, setting a fire that was spread by gusting winds. The prince was forced to flee his boat, leaving behind his wife and concubines, who subsequently committed suicide by drowning themselves in the river. According to one account, after changing into commoner clothing so he could flee incognito, the prince boarded another boat, only to find himself captured by a magistrate by the name of Wang Mian 王冕, who, at Wang Yangming's instructions, was pretending to be a fisherman waiting amidst reeds in a fishing boat. When the unsuspecting prince offered money for his assistance, the magistrate sounded a sharp

---

167   Bazi Nao is located to the west of Poyang County, on the southern shore of the Po River.

168   *WYMQJ*, vol, 1, 12:402.

169   Ibid.; see also Feng, "Huang Ming da ru Wang Yangming," 170.

whistle, and several official vessels appeared. The prince, seeing no way out, also attempted to drown himself, only to find himself fished out by a long poll. Thus it was that he was captured along with his principal conspirators, although for the next two days remnant forces were also pursued and destroyed. Wang Yangming estimated that three thousand more were killed and captured, while over thirty thousand drowned. As he described the scene, "the discarded armor, weaponry, property, and floating corpses covered the river like a sandbar."[170] All that remained was to pursue rebels that had taken flight.

According to Long Guang's account, among those factors that contributed to this victory during these three days of campaigning was Wang Yangming's ongoing use of psychological warfare for the purpose of simply getting rebel-bandit forces to fly the coop but also to reduce their fighting spirit (qi 氣). In fact, on the day of the first battle, prior to intercepting the rebels on Lake Poyang, Wang arranged to have some one hundred thousand wooden placards floated downriver, upon which were engraved a brief proclamation pardoning from execution all who would surrender. The enemy troops, seeing the turn things were taking with the fall of the provincial capital, and in any case likely feeling compelled to take flight, when they saw these they are said to have fought to get their hands on one in order to float their way to safety.[171]

According to another anecdote, during the battle the next day, when Wu Wending's forces were fighting to the death (or be executed for retreating), Wang Yangming also arranged to have large placards raised up high for all to see, with the words: "The Prince of Ning has been captured, our troops shall not wantonly kill."[172] Much of the rebel force was thrown into a state of panic and confusion, and for that reason quickly routed. Whatever else all this and other deception may have had on the outcome of these battles, Long Guang claimed that such brilliant foresight was clear evidence of Wang Yangming's "wondrous resourcefulness" (*ying bian zhi shen* 應變之神), and his divine good fortune (*shen yun* 神運).[173]

Interpreting Victory

How did Wang Yangming interpret the meaning of his victory, and explain his success? As might be expected, in his victory memorials Wang Yangming

---

170   *WYMQJ*, vol. 1, 12:403.
171   Qian, "Zheng Chenhao fan jian yi shi," 39:1472.
172   Ibid.
173   Ibid.

named each of his loyal supporters and requested that they receive due recognition and rewards for their commendable service, while also duly noting other elements critical to this achievement:

> When this rebellion began, with a frail constitution ridden by multiple diseases, less than mediocre ability, and knowledge that is always impractical, your servitor immediately risked failure in undertaking his appointed duties, and while away traveling, with only a few hundred soldiers, advocated raising an army amidst great hardship, danger, and suspicion. Within a month, [we] were able to recover fortified cities and take prisoner the principal evildoers. Defeating a mass of one hundred thousand powerful bandits with just over ten thousand soldiers—this truly is the hidden virtue of Heaven, the silent blessing of the ancestors and gods of grain and earth, and the divine martialness of the emperor. But also those court officials involved in planning and deliberations dispersed the calamity before it sprouted and made advance preparations; [they] discerned the signs before any movement and covertly put in place controls. They changed my commission to superintendent of military affairs, allowing me to gain control from the upper reaches and possess the power to strike fear, like lions and leopards in the mountains. The law was proclaimed. Men were led on their own initiative to battle, and in a united way what appeared was completely harmonized action [lit.: the mutual causation of arm and finger]. Your servitor was ordered to arrive in time with reinforcements, without limits on location, and therefore covertly held the strategic power of the head and tail of the snake of Chang Mountain.[174] Thus, I was able, without awaiting the promulgation of an edict, to assemble forces from several prefectures. And people from several prefectures, also prior to being supervised in accordance with the orders of an edict, of their own accord came to the rescue of the endangered country, driving long distances and crossing territories, directly striking and exhaustively pursuing, and not concerning themselves with dereliction of appointed duties.[175]

---

174   Wang Yangming is alluding to the legendary snake of Changshan, whose head and tail could come to the rescue of each other. The idea is that if the head of a battle formation were to come under duress, the tail would immediately be there to provide reinforcements, and vice versa. See *Hanyu da cidian* 漢語大詞典 [Comprehensive Chinese Dictionary] (Shanghai: Hanyu da cidian chubanshe, 1989), 3:734.

175   *WYMQJ*, vol. 1, 12:404–405.

Here Wang mentions very briefly such intangible forces as the emperor, ancestors, and Heaven while clearly emphasizing what were for him two of the three key factors determining the outcome: the foresight of high officials who empowered him with the discretionary power he needed to take action as he saw fit, and the way in which so many officials, soldiers, and civilians in the region rose to the occasion.

The third factor—one discussed only with close friends—was his own ability to remain "unmoved" throughout the conflict, such that his judgment was unimpeded and he could respond efficaciously to the changing course of events. This is what Long Guang referred to as his "wondrous resourcefulness," but the implication here was that this "resourcefulness" was inextricably tied up with his virtue. Therefore, it is worthwhile to look at how, in more practical terms, Wang Yangming himself interpreted his victory.

As explained earlier, because many officials both inside and outside the emperor's court were cowed into silence by a prince with powerful connections, little could be done to stop his criminal actions in the local arena. Yet there were some officials in crucial positions of power who were quietly implementing measures in preparation for what they saw as the inevitable—a rebellion. The individual to whom Wang Yangming gave so much credit was Minister of War Wang Qiong, the man he routinely praised for his foresight in pushing for him to be granted the power he needed to take the actions he did.

With this discretionary power, Wang Yangming became authorized to implement military planning and apply rewards and punishments as he saw fit, without having first to request permission or concern himself with interference from superiors. With regard to conducting warfare, such empowerment was particularly vital. Long before, in his *Commentary on the Seven Military Classics*, Wang had already blended generalship with the Confucian ideal of sagehood by commenting on how the ideal general should embody a combination of virtue and efficacy. Though he would later renounce his pursuits during this early period of his life as frivolity, here as elsewhere the impact of his military studies would remain potent. And one key theme that emerges in his annotations is the pivotal role of the general given complete latitude to act as he deemed appropriate. Wang, for example, highlighted the statement in the *Art of War* that "one whose general is capable and not interfered with by the ruler will be victorious."[176]

What stands out during his period of service in Ganzhou was that he believed anything could be accomplished should virtuous and capable officials

---

176   Wang, *Wang Yangming pi wu jing qi shu*, 11. This translation of the *Sunzi* is taken from
         Sawyer, *Seven Military Classics*, 161.

be given the proper autonomy and leeway, and not only when there was a military crisis. Yu Yingshi has pointed out that an important trend in Ming political culture was a growing emphasis on the exercise of authority in local affairs as control at the national level was increasingly lost to and endangered by incompetent emperors and their surrogates.[177] Certainly, this would fall in line with Wang's general thinking as a whole: to restore a more ideal world, there needed to be a temporary de-emphasis on the role of the sage-king and elevation of the role of virtuous individuals—individuals who exemplified in their conduct sagely ideals.

Another important factor influencing the outcome of the conflict has to do with the psychology of warfare. Ralph Sawyer explains that the military classics stress the significance of developing a disciplined, spirited, and highly motivated force, as well as the crucial role of vital energy (qi 氣) in attaining this goal.[178] Wang Yangming's communications are shot through with precisely these concerns, and frequently suggest that he believed his forces' spirited response to a dispirited enemy made for rapid success. In his commentary to the *Art of War*, he also wrote, "One who excels at deploying the soldiers of the Three Armies 'leads them by the hand as if they were only one man,' and further as if they are of one mind, causing them all to have the heart 'to be cast into positions from which there is nowhere to go,' and thus during combat there are none who won't fight to the death, such that before even engaging in battle, victory is already achieved."[179]

But how is a general to achieve such an aim? For Wang, if the cause were both righteous and a matter of life and death for emperor and country, then individuals should rise to the occasion without coercion. This was simply the natural response of people's sentiments of right and wrong (*shi fei zhi xin* 是非之心) rising in solidarity in the face of an imminent threat to "the whole," not in the modern sense of "nation," but rather in the very Confucian sense of that fabric of personally meaningful social order that was most exemplified through devotion to one's ruler. On the other hand, should the enemy's cause be misguided, and driven by materialistic or selfish interests (*gongli zhi xin* 功利之心), then it would be easy to snatch away their fighting spirit. His annotations to the *Art of War* reverberate throughout his strategy during this campaign: "the qi of the three armies can be snatched away," "the commanding general's mind can be seized."[180]

---

177   Yu, *Song Ming lixue*, 275.

178   Sawyer, *Seven Military Classics*, 155.

179   *WYMQJ*, vol. 2, 32:1186.

180   Wang, *Wang Yangming pi wu jing qi shu*, 31. For this translation of the *Sunzi* see Sawyer, *Seven Military Classics*, 170.

For Wang Yangming, the mind of right and wrong, or the moral mind (*yi li zhi xin* 義理之心), is the innate knowledge of the good, and it is to this that Wang Yangming believed himself to be appealing from the beginning. In this regard, Wang Ji 王畿 (1498–1583)—an important student of Wang Yangming— recorded a fascinating statement from his teacher a few months after the conflict had ended:

> Chenhao's traitorous plot had already been developing for some time, and officials within and without [the court] were cooperating and assisting him.... Therefore, some were saying that this great enterprise was already a fait accompli and no one again dared to oppose the spearhead of his attack. As for our teacher returning to Ji'an by boat, advocating the righteous and raising forces, all believed he was either foolish or bluffing. At the time, Zou Qianzhi was present at his military headquarters and, seeing that people all around were in a state of turmoil, he entered and spoke with our teacher. Our teacher, with a stern look, replied, "There is no place amidst Heaven and Earth to which one could flee in order to escape this righteous cause. Even should all under Heaven choose to follow the Prince of Ning, I would still, though all alone, act precisely in this way. All people have this innate knowledge of the good (*liangzhi*), so how could it be the case that no others will respond to the call and come? As for consideration of the end result or, put differently, victory and defeat, this is not something for which I plan."[181]

Thus, with a just cause on his side, he was able to guide circumstances to their natural conclusion.

Aside from discretionary power and a just cause, the one remaining element necessary to ensure victory was leadership by a skilled general. Although he attributed victory to others in his official statements, enigmatic statements made to his students suggest that Wang Yangming also believed it was his own ability to effortlessly master an unfolding situation that brought about the result it did. Likewise, because the skill and ease with which he so rapidly subjugated the prince seemed to his followers to exemplify a key attribute of sagehood—"effortless action"—much of the record left by them amount to anecdotes illustrative of this ideal.

---

181 Wang Ji 王畿, "Du xian shi zai bao Hai Riweng Ji'an qi bing shu xu 讀先師再報海日翁 吉安起兵書序 [Preface Composed Upon Reading My Former Master's Second Letter Reporting Mobilizing Armies in Ji'an to Hairi Weng]," in *WYMQJ*, vol. 2, 41:1599.

In his account of Wang Yangming's stratagem, Qian Dehong noted that throughout the eight years that he followed his teacher, every time Wang was questioned about his military campaigns he would become silent, a stance he also took in his memorials. As Long Guang explained to Qian, "When our master composed his victory memorial he worried it would be needlessly long-winded, and he therefore left out everything pertaining to the strategy of sowing discord and suspicion; but also because stratagem and deception are not affairs the virtuous man engages in by choice, he wished not to explain this clearly to others."[182] Nevertheless, even after his teacher passed away, Qian continued to make inquiries because, although he was able from his official communications to outline the course of events, "as for this matter of employing spies (yong jian 用間), I only once heard the gist of it, but the official documents did not mention this."[183]

In 1535, six years after Wang Yangming had passed away, Qian paid a visit to Long Guang, who, as a vice-magistrate in Jiangxi, had played an important role in assisting Wang during the initial phases of his strategic maneuvering. Fortunately, Long had kept copies or drafts of the many covert and counterfeit communications Wang had used during the campaign. Combining information from these and recollections from others involved, Qian was able to compose a detailed account of both Wang's stratagem and some of his remarks regarding his experiences throughout the campaign, these last being particularly crucial for understanding what Wang believed were the keys to his victory.[184]

To clarify this, his strategy should be placed firstly within the context of his learning in the military arts, and secondly within the broader framework of his discourse on the mind. His commentary to the first chapter of the *Art of War* not only pulls together his thinking on strategy, but also delineates the conceptual horizon within which his plans for containing the prince's rebellion were formed. Wang wrote that "in speaking of warfare, [Sunzi] always states, 'Warfare is the way of deception, always achieving victory through hidden plans.' . . . People's eyes are unable to see though my plans. This is because there is a mastery of factors prior to warfare. When Sunzi first opens his mouth, he immediately states, 'Evaluate it comparatively through estimations, and seek out its true nature.'"[185] A complete mastery of factors prior to waging war and achieving victory by employing deception: this for him was undoubtedly the key to this victory. Wang Yangming anticipated the prince's evolving plans every step

---

182   Qian, "Zheng Chenhao fan jian yi shi," 39:1471.
183   Ibid., 39:1474.
184   Ibid.
185   *WYMQJ*, vol. 2, 32:1185.

of the way, and formulated corresponding strategies to defeat them, largely by undermining the prince's confidence and the support of those following him so that fighting could be reduced to the bare minimum. In this regard, his actions were fully in keeping with what he highlighted in his notes on the *Sunzi*: "The highest realization of warfare is to attack the enemy's plans."[186]

But what are the requisite qualifications for being able to achieve such mastery? For Wang, this was not so much about the military arts themselves as it was about the Confucian cultivation of effortless action, the inner virtue necessary for efficacious military leadership. Qian recounted the following conversation between Wang and one of his students:

> Someone asked, "Is there an art to employment of the military instrument?" Master replied, "Just what art could there be to employing the military instrument? Only if in learning one is pure and serious, and cultivates their mind so that they remain unmoved, that is the art. The wisdom and capacity of average people are not all that far apart, and victory and defeat need not await divination at the battlefront; these only revolve around whether this mind remains moved or unmoved."[187]

Wang Yangming illustrated what he meant by recounting the reaction of some of his high officers when forces suffered a setback at the front lines and he was in the midst of ordering them to prepare for incendiary warfare. Apparently, they were caught by surprise and repeatedly reported the urgency of the situation to him. Though the account does not explain exactly why, Wang told his students his "ears were as if they had heard nothing."[188] Very likely, these unnamed officials were calling for a change of plans, or withdrawal. But whatever the case may have been, the lesson was clear: "These individuals are all very well known today, and in normal times how could they be deficient in wisdom and strategy? But to lose their footing so fast in the face of crisis, how could they possibly implement their wisdom and strategy?"[189]

The "unmoved mind (*bu dong xin* 不動心)," a concept discussed by the pre-Qin Warring States philosopher Mencius, was later adopted by Song and Ming Dynasty Neo-Confucian philosophers to designate a state of mind attained

---

186   Wang, *Wang Yangming pi wu jing qi shu*, 9. This translation of the *Sunzi* is taken from Sawyer, *Seven Military Classics*, 161.

187   Qian, "Zheng Chenhao fan jian yi shi," 39:1473.

188   Ibid.

189   Ibid.

through various methods of self-cultivation.[190] The essence of such a state is that the silence, calm, and quiescence won through quiet-sitting or other forms of meditation becomes available and is carried throughout all activity in such a way that the individual achieves a degree of detachment from personal considerations and is therefore able to act "effortlessly."[191] Perhaps what stood out most for those students present during the campaigns was just this element of serene detachment. According to Zou Shouyi 鄒守益 (1491–1562):

> Formerly our master, while waging war with the Prince of Ning, was together with two or three of his friends seated in the military headquarters lecturing. A scout brought him a report stating that the front lines had suffered a setback, and those around him all appeared alarmed. But our master merely exited the room to speak with the scout, and returned and again took his seat, the expression on his face unchanged. Later, a scout hurried in with a report that the rebel-bandit soldiers had been totally routed, and those around him all became animated with joy. Our teacher again exited to speak with the scout, returned, and sat down, continuing to lecture as before, his expression unchanged.[192]

In a conversation he held with his student Chen Jiuchuan regarding how effectively to command forces and confront the enemy, Wang drew out the theoretical implications of what must have been evident to Zou from this conduct: "If one truly is willing to apply their innate knowledge of the good, such that they are always clear, wise, and unobscured by desire, then they will be able naturally, when confronting affairs, to remain unperturbed—the unmoved true essence is able without a word naturally to respond to change."[193] In this case, the affair was a rebellion and the response its suppression. The military arts were therefore seamlessly woven together with Wang's philosophy of mind.

One important condition, however, would have had to be met for Wang Yangming's claims to make any sense in the context of his thought, and for his

---

190   The phrase *bu dong xin* can be found in *Mengzi* 2:A:2. For an analysis of "effortless action" see Edward Slingerland, *Effortless Action: Wu-wei as Conceptual Metaphor and Spiritual Ideal in Early China* (Oxford: Oxford University Press, 2003), 4. He translates *bu dong xin* as "the heart/mind that does not stir."

191   For a similar analysis of the relation between contemplation/stillness and action in Zhu Xi's religious thought, see Julia Ching, *The Religious Thought of Chu Hsi* (Oxford: Oxford University Press, 2000), 122.

192   Qian, "Zheng Chenhao fan jian yi shi," 39:1473.

193   Ibid.

followers to be able to celebrate this clear manifestation of his learning, this irrefutable demonstration of how his inner sageliness translated into truly virtuous practice: his actions would had to have been just and therefore in accord with moral principle. As he would inform one of his disciples in 1520, "If you use this little thing [innate knowledge] clearly, no matter how much and how eloquently one may talk, all right and wrong, sincerity and insincerity in what he says are manifested right in front of it. What is in accord with it is right and what is not in accord with it is wrong."[194] That is, extending innate knowledge of the good means translating immediate moral knowledge into practice, and that is what confers calm even amidst a storm.

In more general terms, Wang frequently spoke with his disciples of the connection between the unperturbed mind, principle, and their daily lives: "Self-cultivation and governance have never been two separate Ways. Even when official business is pressing, it is the concrete place for study and inquiry. . . . In the practice of our daily lives there is nothing that is not the ongoing manifestation of Heavenly principle. Should this mind be preserved and not lost, moral principles will mature naturally. This is what Mencius referred to as 'neither forgetting nor assisting, inquiring deeply and realizing it for oneself.'"[195] For Wang Yangming, an individual can realize just such an unperturbed state, or achieve the serenity and stillness of the Buddhist who has wiped away all thought and reflection, simply by "accumulating righteousness," or "according with principle" even while amidst "the myriad changing affairs of social life."[196] In his study of "effortless action" as a discourse common to all emerging philosophical traditions in early China, Edward Slingerland explains the normative dimension of the Confucian appropriation of this ideal phenomenological state, stating, "The culmination of knowledge is understood not in terms of a grasp of abstract principles but rather as an ability to move through the world and human society in a manner that is completely spontaneous and yet still fully in harmony with the normative order of the natural and human worlds— the Dao or 'Way.'"[197]

Generally speaking, this link between the natural and the normative also legitimated authority and all that this might imply, including the need to resort to violence to keep order. In this regard, I believe we find ourselves at odds with the past: in just what sense can the reasoning and sentiments expressed throughout this campaign be considered natural? Even for Wang Yangming

---

194   Wang, *Instructions for Practical Living*, 194.
195   *WYMQJ*, vol. 1, 4:145.
196   Wang, *Instructions for Practical Living*, 203.
197   Slingerland, *Effortless Action*, 4.

there was certainly much that did not fit very clearly within his claim that this was all a matter of, as he told Wang Ji, "innate knowledge of the good responding to phenomena (*liangzhi ying ji* 良知應機), like clouds in the sky floating past one's eyes."[198] He was, for instance, reticent about discussing stratagem. It is also not surprising to find that he was throughout this time deeply troubled by all that was happening, including the need to resort to force. Even in the military classics, employing the military instrument is generally considered a last resort when more ideal, and typically Confucian, means for resolving conflict have failed. Wang once highlighted this in his annotations to *The Methods of the Sima*: "When uprightness failed to attain the desired objective, [the ancients] resorted to authority (*quan* 權)."[199] But after suppressing this rebellion, and with reference to his years of campaigning against bandits in southern Jiangxi, he explained to a student why he believed the use of force sometimes becomes a necessity:

> Formerly someone asked, "If a person were to cultivate his mind until it becomes immoveable, then could they deploy troops with you?" The master stated, "They also must have learned through experience. This is a matter of blades facing off and killing people; how can it [be learned through] imagination? One must have practiced this matter personally, and when lines of command gradually become clear, and wisdom well rounded, only then can one win trust throughout the land. There is no such thing as one who has not personally experienced this but is nevertheless able to grasp the implicit principles—this is the error of later generations' theory of the investigation of things. Confucius himself said that he had not studied the matter of warfare, and this was not just modesty. However, only if the sage were to take office and realize his aspirations would he have the way of dispersing rebellion before it takes shape. They therefore did not need to employ [the military instrument]. Later generations speak of governing, but never once discuss the root and origin, always beginning only from the halfway point, and therefore turning things upside down. If one were to discuss seeking the root and origin, then how could there be a rationale whereby one must first slaughter people and only thereafter settle them? Ever since I was dispatched to campaign in Ganzhou, the court has repeatedly caused me to be involved in affairs requiring killing people. How could I bear this piercing [of my heart by a knife]? It is only because things have come to this. [This state

198   Wang, "Du xian shi zai bao Hai Riweng Ji'an qi bing shu xu," 41:1600.

199   Wang, *Wang Yangming pi wu jing qi shu*, 113.

of affairs] can be likened to a person who has taken ill—first unhealthy environmental influences must be brought under control, and only then can the original vital energy be recovered.[200]

No other statement captures more clearly Wang Yangming's political predicament as he understood it, and I believe we here detect a degree of fatalism in his tone regarding the resort to force as sometimes being a necessary evil. Indeed, we may have to reassess Xu Fuguan's claim that Wang Yangming's actions all derived from his cultivated humanity and extension of the innate knowledge of the good and Julia Ching's that he was throughout this time following "the promptings of the human heart and its desire for good." These statements may not accurately represent his campaigns up to this point, given his view of such a solidly gray political maelstrom, as well as his belief that sometimes achieving justice required forcibly removing unhealthy environmental influences *on the periphery* that, according to his own analysis, had deeper systemic origins at the center.

Conclusion

Chen Lai observes that the fundamental import of the extension of the innate knowledge of the good (*zhi liangzhi*) is that one must act according to such knowledge.[201] In this regard, Wang Yangming united his earlier theory of the unity of knowledge and action (*zhi xing he yi* 知行合一) with extension of the innate knowledge of the good. Chen further offers a lucid interpretation of just what this meant: "Innate knowledge of the good is intrinsic moral standards . . . to extend innate knowledge of the good is to prosecute these standards in practice; interpreted along these lines, 'to extend' is to act."[202]

In this chapter I have attempted to argue that because theory and practice were never divided in Wang Yangming's thought, and because he repeatedly stated that his philosophy of *liangzhi* was thoroughly verified as a result of his experiences during his campaign to crush the rebellion by the Ning Princely Establishment, an historical inquiry into Wang Yangming's conduct throughout this time, as well as the normative import of his teaching, becomes topical. Thus, I have shifted the focus from largely ahistorical readings of his philosophy of moral self-cultivation to his political practice. By so doing, I believe we

200   Qian, "Zheng Chenhao fan jian yi shi," 39:1474.
201   Chen, *You wu zhi jing*, 180.
202   Ibid., 182.

gain insight not only into just how Wang Yangming sought to restore "all under Heaven" to the Way—beyond just some schedule of Confucian norms—but also into the moral ambiguities he confronted throughout this time. Such ambiguities are absent from the received biographical accounts that seek to highlight how his conduct accorded with exemplary paradigms for sagehood, as well as from much secondary scholarship, the focus of which has been the philosophical fruits of Wang's meditations on "inner sageliness." Thus, I have tried, for example, to highlight the seeming irony of his unflagging commitment to his ruler, even when that ruler's conduct was no more admirable than that of the prince he so thoroughly demonized; also, it is difficult to align waging war and the use of deception and intrigue against the many followers of the prince with his subsequent claims to have been extending moral knowledge throughout this time. In short, it seems evident that what was supposed to be universal knowledge was in fact historically specific and replete with contradictions; indeed, it might not be going too far to suggest that the discourse on sagehood (and innate knowledge of the good) itself played a role in creating the very drama that served to prove itself right. The rebellion by the prince was an excellent opportunity to demonstrate commitment to unifying knowledge and action, and melded well with the sentiments of those many regional officials and commoners who turned out to support him. In the next chapter, I shall continue with these reflections and expand upon them further.

Sageliness Within, Kingliness Without

The challenges Wang Yangming confronted in Jiangxi were hardly to end with his rapid suppression of the prince's rebellion, and by some accounts what he had just overcome paled in comparison with what he would face over the course of the next year. During this time, the emperor and his circle of favorites traveled to the region for the purpose of reenacting and stealing the credit for a rebellion now dead in the water. Censor Li Long's judgments capture well the predicament he faced:

> What was difficult about suppressing the prince's rebellion wasn't suc-ceeding at it but rather rallying the righteous. This is because the traitor-ous prince's rebellion had indeed found collaboration from within [the Ming court], and people wished only to look on from the sidelines. And yet at this time those officials who came to the aid of the emperor were all willing to risk their lives and destruction of their families in order to save their country. Thereafter, the jealous tried to bring them down by spreading rumors and wished to steal the credit for their achievement. On what basis will people in their hearts remain loyally obedient? Should in the future there be some unforeseen turn of events, who will be willing to rise to the occasion?[1]

The jealous to whom Li refers were at first two of the emperor's closest com-panions—Eunuch Director Zhang Zhong 張忠 and the Earl of Anbian Xu Tai 許泰. The threat they posed to Wang Yangming became so serious that death was a constant prospect for many months, and it is for this reason that Wang's principal biographer Qian Dehong took issue with the censor's assessment: "As for the events surrounding the suppression of the rebellion, it was not hard to rally the righteous but rather extremely difficult to handle the turn of events initiated by Zhang Zhong and Xu Tai."[2]

The period of time covered here begins when Wang Yangming returned from Hukou to Jiangxi's provincial capital (Nanchang) on August 21, 1519, and ends with his departure for Beijing on July 23, 1521, when he was summoned by the emperor for the purpose of conferring honors and possibly high office. For

---

1   *NP*, 34:1275.
2   Ibid.

those two years between capturing the prince and being called to Beijing, Wang Yangming was largely residing in Jiangxi as grand coordinator. It was during this same period of time that the Zhengde emperor, abetted by the border commander Jiang Bin 江彬 and other close companions, departed with a large expeditionary force and several generals in order to lead his own campaign against the prince and rewrite the history of the rebellion. These imperial favorites plotted against Wang Yangming and accused him of crimes. In many moments Wang feared for his life, and that of his entire lineage.

As explained in Chapter Two, scholarship on Wang Yangming has stressed how important these trials and tribulations were to his unveiling of the doctrine of the extension of the innate knowledge of the good (*zhi liangzhi* 致良知). Okada Takehiko, for instance, believes that while suppressing banditry in southern Jiangxi and then the prince's rebellion, Wang became more fully aware and convinced that what he was witnessing and acting upon was "the mysterious operation of the unobstructed mind (*mushin no myōyō* 無心の妙用)" or, in other words, the natural functioning of innate knowledge.[3]

There is ample evidence to support this interpretation of Wang's philosophical development. In the middle of 1520, while residing in southern Jiangxi's Ganzhou Prefecture, he informed his close disciples that his guiding light during this time, when he had very much to stand on his own and weather the constant threat of death, was innate knowledge of the good. He also explained that these experiences caused this knowing to become more lucid.[4] According to his disciple Qian Dehong, "After the campaign against the Ning Princely Establishment, he suffered hardship caused by Zhang and Xu, his life hanging by a thread. He was tempered one hundred times and polished a thousand, and yet the radiance shined through, and he came only further to trust in the goodness of this knowledge. [Following its] spiritual transformations and wondrous responses, without ever flowing towards excess, transparent and still to the depths, silent without falling into emptiness, [this knowledge] could be verified with a thousand sages and be shown to be without error."[5]

But in addition to correlating his philosophical development with his life experiences, there is another side to Wang Yangming's claims that should also be explored. His assertion that innate knowledge of the good was sufficient to handle all of the difficulties he confronted also implies that his actions throughout this time were in some sense the result of his having moved a step forward

---

3   Okada, *Ō Yōmei taiden*, 3:277–78.

4   Cf. Wang, *Instructions for Practical Living*, 193.

5   Qian Dehong, "Yangming xiansheng nianpu xu 陽明先生年譜序 [Preface to the Chronological Biography of Sir Yangming]," in *WYMQJ*, vol. 2, 37:1357.

with, or extended, this knowledge. Thus, rather than taking the history of these events and his personal experiences in broad outline as material for analyzing the evolution of his philosophy, it will be useful to look more carefully at his political practice. That is, I propose to take under consideration just how his notions of justice—as a dimension of the moral knowledge given by *liang-zhi*—provided the standards for achieving right relations within the community in which he acted, as well as how he drew upon the institutions available to him to achieve those ends.

While it is true that for Wang Yangming justice is ultimately a property of persons—in that they have the capacity and clarity to become aware of and act upon knowledge of right and wrong (*shi fei zhi xin* 是非之心) —it is also true that, in order for such knowledge to be considered genuine, it must be "extended (*zhi* 致)." In this regard, he was only giving a modified version of his lifelong teaching of the unity of knowledge and action.[6] In his "Inquiry on the *Great Learning*", Wang explains that, as people go about their lives, thoughts and desires continuously emerge as a manifestation of will; some of these might be good (a manifestation of Heavenly principle) and some not. And yet, when unobscured, Heavenly endowed nature enables people to know which thoughts and desires are good and which are not, as well inspiring them to love what is good and hate what is not, thereby setting them on a path towards a genuine life without self-deception, a life consisting of good purposes and sound motives. This is the meaning of extending the innate knowledge of the good.[7]

Furthermore, in terms of connecting this process to action, when willing manifests as thought and desire this naturally entails something real, the object of willing, some affair or event. This is precisely where Wang Yangming's interpretation of the very first step towards learning in the eight-step program in the *Great Learning* comes into play. For him, to "investigate things (*ge wu* 格物)" means to "rectify affairs": "It is to rectify that which is incorrect so it can return to its original correctness."[8] That is how moral life is linked with political life. Because "to rectify that which is not correct is to get rid of evil (*qu e* 去惡),

---

6 For an analysis, see Chen, *You wu zhi jing*, 180–81.

7 Wang, "Inquiry on the *Great Learning*," 278–79.

8 Ibid., 279. The eight steps, in order, are the investigation of things, extension of knowledge, making the will sincere, rectifying the mind, cultivating one's personal life, regulating the family, ordering the state, and peace throughout the world. Each step depends on the prior one. Therefore, the first–the investigation of things–is the critical starting point. For a discussion and translation of the *Great Learning* see Chan, *A Sourcebook in Chinese Philosophy*, 84–94.

and to return to correctness is to do good (*wei shan* 為善),"[9] it follows that "investigating things" is essentially about achieving justice. Wang further links moral personhood with action when he states, "If as we come into contact with the thing to which the will is directed, we really do the good and get rid of the evil to the utmost which is known by the innate faculty, then everything will be investigated and what is known by our innate faculty will not be deficient or obscured but will be extended to the utmost."[10] It therefore follows that because he consistently mobilized the institutions available to him to eradicate injustice, he must have believed they could in fact serve that end. Thus, justice, if properly employed, can also be a property of institutions. In short, the state had a role to play in encouraging individuals to do good and rid themselves of evil. That is how Wang's philosophy was implicated in his political practice, and analysis of his memorials and actions during this time therefore shows how "sageliness within, kingliness without" fit together in this historical context.

In the first section of this chapter, I draw on official communications from Wang's period of service in Jiangxi to explain his understanding of the nature of justice and the role of the state in securing and upholding it. Geoffrey MacCormack, in his monograph on law in traditional China, notes that although we have very little in the way of formal treatises analyzing the function of punishment, it is nevertheless feasible to tease this out from officials' legal reasoning in particular cases.[11] This also holds true for Wang Yangming, for although he provides no formal treatises on law and the function of rewards and punishments, the existing collection of his official communications can easily be viewed as exercises in the application of justice.

The second section reconstructs the challenging course of events weathered by Wang in the aftermath of his campaigns. The goal here is to set the stage for providing a description of what moral knowledge and practice, or applying *liangzhi*, meant in the context of the setting in which these ideas arose. Finally, in the remaining two sections, I attempt to show that, with regard to his political practice, it is not enough to examine Wang's ethics as articulated in his more programmatic philosophical statements. Rather, I paint a more complete picture of what he considered to be virtuous conduct, thereby filling out our understanding of the "spirit" of Wang Yangming's philosophy as it per-

---

9   Ibid.

10   Ibid., 279–80.

11   Geoffrey MacCormack, *The Spirit of Traditional Chinese Law* (Athens, GA: University of Georgia Press, 1996), 188.

tained not only to his own life and his followers but also to the ongoing political community in which he lived.

Rewards and Punishments

When Wang Yangming returned to the Investigation Bureau in Nanchang, he brought along those principal leaders taken prisoner during the battles on Lake Poyang, among which were the Prince of Ning, his eldest son, other members of the prince's branch of the imperial clan, and officials who supported him. All had temporarily enjoyed high ranks bestowed by their hopeful leader—grand steward, preceptor of state, marshal, grand adjutant, and commissioner-in-chief—only to find themselves now imprisoned. With Grand Co-ordinator of Jiangxi Sun Sui beheaded and many provincial and local officials compromised by active involvement in or passive acquiescence to the prince's designs, Wang Yangming found that, despite being officially the grand coordinator charged with quelling disturbances in Southern Gan, much of the responsibility for governing the area also fell upon his shoulders. He therefore remained in the provincial capital for a little over a month, restoring order to the region and dealing with those caught up in the rebellion.

Aside from his two victory memorials, we also have other communications addressing a number of pressing matters, including tax relief for Jiangxi, selling off the prince's property for revenue, making proper arrangements for his concubines, implementing measures to restore order to the region, and taking steps to ensure that those who had meritoriously served the state receive due recognition while those guilty of crimes would be punished. Of particular interest here are memorials where he provides his judgments to the court regarding the application of rewards and punishments. These give us some insight into his understanding of the nature of distributive justice, of how each is to be rendered his due. For Wang Yangming, as was the case with schools and academies, state institutions should serve to promote and encourage the perfection of virtue while at the same time discouraging vice. This could be achieved in part through just punishments and rewards. With regard to rewards, two examples will suffice.

In concluding his victory memorials, Wang petitioned the court to recognize the virtuous conduct of those officials who assisted him in this cause by properly rewarding them. Highlighting the magnitude of their achievement and its implications for the country, Wang stated:

Whereas the Prince of Ning's blazing rebellion gathered powerful momentum, with a mass of 180,000 massacring the inhabitants of captured cities and destroying prefectures, people near and far were cowed with fear. Until today his violence had continued for over a month, and yet not one of those divisions that should have come to the rescue has yet responded. As for the aforementioned officials who commanded the armies, army-inspecting censors, and those officials who were at the time recuperating from illness, in mourning, or retired, they all followed this official and arose during a time of dire emergency and great disorder, uniting in mind and cooperating in planning, leading the righteous and courageous, breaking into the enemy ranks as the vanguard, in order to defeat and destroy this fortified city, and occupy his lair. Although this is what should be the case for one whose status is that of an official, it was the outcome of their genuine vehement passion and bitter anger. At a time when popular sentiment is alienated, of two minds, and wavering, without rewards and punishments there is no way to raise the morale of the literati.... I wish that the emperor should expediently deploy the means at his disposal to manage this disaster, by immediately promoting and rewarding the above mentioned officials, in order to motivate those near and far.[12]

Whatever else may have been the real motives of those who chose to assist him in this campaign of suppression, for Wang Yangming the one most worthy of recognition was the outpouring of loyal and righteous indignation. This was a forceful expression in sentiment and action not only of the very values that could reinvigorate the country, but also ideally of natural and spontaneous moral knowing.

Rewarding those whose conduct evidenced action based on principled sentiments is a consistent theme in his communications. When elders in Qingjiang County 清江縣 requested the construction of a memorial temple in honor of a former prefect, Wang replied with his approval, writing of the man, who had also served under him during his campaigns:

Since Dai has always been a prefect of stainless reputation, long recognized for his just governance, today, upon the occasion of his retiring from office, residents of this prefecture will build a memorial temple to requite his virtue (*bao de* 報德). From this, one can discern the presence of the principle of Heaven (*tianli* 天理) in people's hearts, something that cannot be overlooked. Officials of this prefecture and county shall therefore acknowledge the people's sentiments, and allocate someone to guard this, for not only will this encourage later generations, it will also foster a revival. Furthermore, this will promote the cultivation of people's virtue, and draw them back to sound morals.[13]

Thus, behind this external political act is "Heavenly principle," in this case the desire to requite virtue, and institutions can be engaged to promote such moral knowledge. The emperor, by giving due recognition to meritorious conduct on the part of officials, and in turn officials, by giving due recognition to worthy conduct on the part of the people, could manifest a benevolent, paternal, and fostering care that ideally served to encourage knowledge of principle and therefore the possibility of self-transcendence through perfection in virtue. Rewards encouraged cultivation of the mind-heart by fostering knowledge arising from human nature (*xing* 性). This brings Wang's political practice directly in line with his teaching:

> Knowledge is the original substance of the mind. The mind is naturally able to know. When it perceives the parent, it naturally knows that one should be filial. When it perceives the elder brother, it naturally knows that one should be respectful. And when it perceives a child fallen into a well, it naturally knows that one should be commiserative. This is innate knowledge of good and need not be sought outside.... However, the ordinary man is not free from the obstruction of selfish ideas. He therefore requires the effort of the extension of knowledge and the investigation of things in order to overcome selfish ideas and restore principle.[14]

Likewise, such obstruction to moral knowing might also be removed by the state through a just application of rewards and punishments.

In sum, Wang Yangming believed the political order must be founded on a justice of merit and desert. Political institutions should give due recognition to those who act virtuously, in light of the higher good. The paradox here is only that those who act justly should not be doing so out of a desire to obtain such rewards and recognition. I propose here to further our understanding of Wang's underlying notions of justice through a comparison with post-Homeric Greek conceptions of justice defined in terms of desert, as outlined by Alasdair MacIntyre. According to his analysis, a fundamental distinction is drawn between

---

13   Ibid., 17:597.
14   Wang, *Instructions for Practical Living*, 15.

the goods and qualities of excellence (internal goods) and the goods and qualities of effectiveness (external goods).[15] Internal goods are implicitly rewarding goods that a person gains by participating in and mastering some form of systematic activity (for example, philosophy, farming, sustenance of communities). The qualities of excellence are those virtues necessary for achievement in such activity. The goods of effectiveness, conversely, are the external—institutionally secured—rewards of riches, power, status, and prestige. The qualities of effectiveness are qualities of body, mind, and character enabling a person to secure those goods.[16]

For MacIntyre, aside from being implicitly rewarding, internal goods are available to anyone who chooses to participate in a practice, and generally benefit the community as a whole. They don't have to be divided up. External goods, on the other hand, usually do, as not everyone can enjoy wealth, power, and prestige. Ideally, though, the systematic pursuit of excellence is in some way compatible with the goods of effectiveness: on the basis of a given set of principles about how goods are to be ordered into a way of life, the political order rewards those who deserve to be rewarded. Such is a justice of merit and desert.[17] On the other hand, a justice defined only in terms of the goods of effectiveness—that is, riches and prestige—would merely entail establishing a set of ground rules and sound expectations, social rules to be followed as if fulfilling a contract, for the purpose of advancing the interests of all parties with the maximum fairness. MacIntyre believes that justice defined in this way is inferior and leads to an amoral, competitive society where cheating and exploitation abound.[18]

Likewise, for Wang Yangming, who followed a long tradition of discourse differentiating between principle and profit, a fundamental distinction must be drawn between just acts based on principled intentions (*yi li zhi xin* 義理之心), and acts based on utilitarian considerations, that is, those done for fame and profit (*gong li zhi xin* 功利之心).[19] An order of justice constructed around the former is the way of the sage-kings, while one built around the latter would be the politics of the hegemons and men who believe only in the utilitarian

15   Alasdair MacIntyre, *Whose Justice? Which Rationality?* (London: Duckworth, 1988), 32.

16   Ibid.

17   Ibid., 34.

18   For a discussion, see Ted Clayton, "Political Philosophy of Alasdair MacIntyre," *Internet Encyclopedia of Philosophy*, last modified December 21, 2005, accessed January 30, 2014, http://www.iep.utm.edu/p-macint/.

19   For a discussion of the origins of this distinction in Confucius and Mencius, see Taylor, *Religious Dimensions of Confucianism*, 11–22.

pursuit of self-interest.[20] The latter was anathema to him, a symptom of divorce of the political order from virtue. He clearly believed that justice required fairness, in the sense that each person had to be accorded what he or she merited based on external goods of effectiveness, but whether an action deserved reward or not depended on whether it was considered virtuous from the standpoint of the internal goods of excellence. For him, those goods are determined by human nature. In other words, justice required a standard by which relative achievement could be appraised and relative desert apportioned, but this standard was ideally one that ran deep, as an expression of a unitary order forming the basis of human life itself. Prior to 1520, Wang usually referred to this order as the principle of Heaven, while from that year he often pointed to the innate knowledge of the good. At an individual level, whether one is preserving Heavenly principles or extending innate knowledge of the good, the reward is an internal good. Virtue is its own reward. Nonetheless, imperial institutions could legitimately serve the purpose of distributing external goods in accordance with such a unitary order, thereby drawing the social and political world into closer correspondence with their true nature. This is the logic that runs through all of Wang Yangming's political practice, including his recommendations for the distribution of rewards.

MacIntyre further explains that a system of justice based on the goods of effectiveness and one based on merit and desert differ also in terms of the binding force of their rules. In a system of justice where goods of effectiveness can be secured merely by fulfilling a reciprocal contract, acts of injustice harm oneself only insofar as they are recognized (or caught) by others.[21] In other words, people obey the rules only because it is in their interest to do so. In such a social order, punishment primarily serves as a deterrent. But in the case of a justice of excellence, or a justice of merit and desert, someone who breaks the rules primarily harms him- or herself, in the sense that such individuals deprive themselves of some opportunity to achieve the goods at which they were aiming. Accordingly, "the discipline of punishment within such a scheme is only justifiable because and in so far as the punishment educates those upon whom it is inflicted; it has to be the kind of punishment which they are able to learn to recognize as being to their own benefit."[22] A justice of desert has primarily a reformative function, and in fact in those cases wherein the offender

---

20 In his letter to Gu Dongqiao, Wang Yangming discusses this distinction and the process of decline in detail. See "Da Gu Dongqiao 答顧東橋書 [Letter in reply to Gu Dongqiao]," in *WYMQJ*, vol. 1, 2:55.

21 Macintyre, *Whose Justice? Which Rationality?*, 37.

22 Ibid.

does not yet see the end involved, it may have to be enforced by those who administer justice.[23]

If Wang Yangming conceived of the role of the distribution of the goods of rewards and recognition in terms of merit and desert, did he also conceive of the role of punishment solely in terms of its educational or reformative purpose? Close study of his memorials suggests that his understanding of the purpose of punishment was more complicated. Geoffrey MacCormack proposes that the object of a penal code is to secure compliance with certain standards of conduct through the threat of punishment, but that this doesn't necessarily tell us anything about the ulterior purposes of punishment. These purposes could be summarized as deterrence, retribution, and reform. MacCormack believes that "the Legalists had been interested only in the deterrent, whereas the Confucianists not only had stressed in addition its reformative possibilities, but had also used language hinting at the desirability of retribution."[24] Wang Yangming's legal judgments evidence all three purposes, each explicable within the framework of his background notions of moral order.

In a memorial entitled "Lenience in the Application of Heavy Punishments In Order To Replenish the Ranks," Wang Yangming forwarded a recommendation to the court from the Jiangxi Surveillance Commission, to which he had appended his own judgment. At issue was the criminal conduct of a large number of civilians and soldiers who, upon being offered silver taels and rice, served the Prince of Ning during his attacks on Anqing. Following the commission's recommendation, Wang determined:

> Because Qiu Liangfu and the others all once followed the traitor, they should be sentenced to execution. However, this commission states that because the Prince of Ning was in the past so domineering, wicked and cruel, among people of both high and low station there were none who were not intimidated. On the basis of the law (*fa* 法) [such criminal conduct] should not be tolerated, but in seeking out the circumstances (*qing* 情) it is also the case that they had no choice. To pardon them would be overly lenient, but to execute them seems overly severe. Therefore, it is necessary to take into consideration the sentiments of the people. I request that the respective ministries review this and give due consideration, perhaps having these criminals' sentence of capital punishment remitted to permanent service as soldiers. In this way, not only will the

---

23   Ibid.
24   MacCormack, *Spirit of Traditional Chinese Law*, 16.

requirements of circumstances and law both be fully met, but also the ranks of the military will not be depleted.[25]

In his analysis of the "spirit of traditional Chinese law," MacCormack notes that the "very essence of the penal codes was to define the conditions under which specific offenses were committed by individuals and to prescribe the punishments appropriate to the offense."[26] In general, judicial authorities sought to find a balance between the facts of the case and the laws (qing/fa 情/法), for only in this way would the sentence be equitable. Through harmonizing circumstances and principle (shi/li 事/理), punishments would serve the ideal aim of giving effect to some particular value or moral absolute, serving as a warning, promoting good morals, or repressing wickedness and debauchery.[27] His analysis captures well the balance Wang Yangming was seeking in his judgments.

Yet there is little in this routine document to indicate why this punishment was appropriate for these particular individuals and whether or not Wang really believed the ends (filling the ranks of the military) justified the means. Presumably, he believed release from execution was a big enough show of clemency. Other memorials allow for more precise insight, suggesting that he often judged cases largely within the horizon of broader concerns, as opposed to concern strictly for the fates of those individuals being punished. In one entitled "Disposition of Officials Who Joined the Traitor," he deliberated upon just punishment for a number of officials caught up in the rebellion. These included high officials and regional supervisors from the province's three commissions who happened to be present at the prince's court that day. Although all were initially arrested by the prince, as the rebellion progressed some were released and actually assisted the rebel prince. When the prince departed Nanchang, some officials were left behind—albeit under guard—to manage affairs, while others were made to accompany him on his vessel. Determining just why they chose to assist him—their individual motives and mental states—was a crucial element in Wang Yangming's deliberations. In general, he believed that righteous conduct called for resistance or suicide; the failure of these officials to act as such constituted their crime, but was also likely the result of fear for their own lives or the wellbeing of their families.

Basing his investigation on their written statements as well as statements from the prince's establishment personnel, Wang Yangming determined that

---

25   *WYMQJ*, vol. 1, 12:413.

26   MacCormack, *Spirit of Traditional Chinese Law*, 212.

27   Ibid., 198.

these officials' criminal acts could be broken down into three different catego-
ries based on degree of culpability. The most serious crimes were committed
by those who willingly served in an advisory role to the prince.[28] Less serous
were the crimes of those who remained in Nanchang in an official capacity:
"Although circumstances were such that they were forced to do so, this is nevertheless a matter touching upon willing compliance." Least serious were the
crimes of those who were imprisoned either in the city or held under guard
during the march to Nanjing: "Although this is a matter of willing compliance,
the circumstances were such that this truly was a matter of being coerced to do
so." Having determined the extent of criminal liability, Wang concluded:

> The aforementioned officials willingly permitted themselves to be taken
> as prisoners, and were incapable of committing suicide. They willingly
> accepted bribes from the rebel-bandits and dared not refuse. If they were
> to be admonished with the moral integrity proper to an official, then they
> are all not without failings. Yet in terms of the seriousness of their
> offences, there cannot but be degrees. I wish that the emperor should
> aggressively enforce his authority, and for those guilty of manifestly seri-
> ous crimes, execute them in accordance with the law, thereby providing a
> warning to officials who should choose not to be loyal. Take into consid-
> eration those whose true intentions can stir pity by having them cashiered
> or exiled, in order to preserve the humanity of lenient punishment where
> the seriousness of the crime is in doubt. Then perhaps the treacherous
> and fawning will take note and be alarmed, and the laws of the country
> clarified.[29]

Once again, Wang's judgments in this case were based on his prudent assessment of the correct balance between circumstances and the law, as well as on
his understanding of the mental states, or motives, of the accused. With regard
to the latter, the underlying moral norm against which he interpreted their
behavior as well as the application of the law was, of course, conscientious
service to one's ruler.

However, as with the previous memorial, we find little indicating the purpose of such punishment strictly with respect to those receiving it. Deterrence
and retribution largely overshadow reform, and for this reason external forces
largely overshadowed individuals, making their punishments symbolic. At
least to some extent, Wang may indeed have believed that demotion and exile

---

28   *WYMQJ*, vol. 1, 12:417–18.
29   Ibid., 12:418.

might not only give those guilty of less serious crimes a chance for reflection and expiation, but also—perhaps more importantly—allow them to escape potentially bloody retaliation by a vengeful emperor. Nevertheless, it is difficult to determine if their individual fates were uppermost in his mind, especially since all indications suggest otherwise, that is, that their fates mattered only inasmuch as they served as a lesson to others, demonstrated the powers of the court as dispenser of justice, or contributed to the restoration of moral principles in a time of decline.

Although deterrence and retribution are often considered to be Legalist in origin, such motives for punishment could also be legitimated strictly within the normative horizon of Confucianism. In fact, Wang Yangming did not conceive of the legal order as being solely in the service of the power of the state, nor did he see as its aim the contractual securing of the diverse interests of individuals or parties. Rather, he understood the law in the circumscribed sense in which MacCormack defines natural law: codified law is natural law because it forms part of the natural order of things and therefore accords both with human nature and the will of Heaven.[30] No doubt, Wang believed the threat of severe consequences for official misconduct was an unfortunate but necessary corrective to the extraordinary deviance from the ideal he envisaged.

One of the clearest statements on the purposes of punishment comes at the end of a memorial reporting officials' failure to stage an adequate defense when attacked by the Prince of Ning's rebel-bandits. For the most part, these were civil and military officials with jurisdiction over the prefectures of Jiujiang and Nankang and their respective counties. Wang outlined in some detail how it was that they had failed to maintain proper defensive preparations in normal times and therefore were unable to fulfill their duty of protecting their territory, or had simply fled at the sight of marauding rebel-bandits, or fled but attempted to rally forces and return to fight the rebel. Only a few had actually stood up to and chased them off.[31] Although he requested that for the time being these officials should be allowed to remain in office so as not to leave these areas bereft of leadership, he did spell out just why they should be held accountable for their crimes:

> As for the above officials, in seeking out the circumstances it is true that there are degrees of seriousness, but in terms of assessing what in prin-

---

30 Geoffrey MacCormack, *Traditional Chinese Penal Law* (Edinburgh: Edinburgh University Press, 1990), 40.

31 *WYMQJ*, vol. 1, 12:421–25.

ciple is right they have all violated articles of the law. Although there are those who earned merit afterwards, it is difficult to overlook their initial omissions. Furthermore, because tolerance is repeatedly practiced, and methods for boosting [morale] fail to be implemented, in recent years the morale of scholar-officials has ebbed, and military discipline has become lax. Those who merely plot for advantage and shy away from danger escape punishment, while those who choose to exert themselves in service are not tolerated. Therefore, lazy indifference has become the habitual practice, and integrity and loyalty are rarely commended. I wish that the emperor should aggressively enforce his authority, strictly enforce the law, and [therefore] petition to release an edict to the judicial offices, ordering them thoroughly to investigate the degree of liability for these crimes, and to punish these officials according to the statutes ... and then perhaps there will be the springs of renewal, sufficient to serve as a warning for the future.[32]

"Justice and coercion," the philosopher Leo Strauss writes, "are not mutually exclusive; in fact, it is not altogether wrong to describe justice as a kind of benevolent coercion."[33] Strauss draws this conclusion from his observation that restraint is as natural to people as freedom: "Man is so built that he cannot achieve the perfection of his humanity except by keeping down his lower impulses."[34] Assuming that those who administer and enforce justice are themselves just, and especially because they understand the relation between the rules of justice and those higher ends to which they subscribe, it follows that they may have to exercise such punitive powers over others in order to achieve reformative ends. Such benevolent paternalism is also a key element of Wang Yangming's political practice.[35] Clearly, however, although he sought to reform errant individuals, he also believed that they must sometimes be sacrificed for the benefit of reforming the political whole, of alerting others to the springs of renewal. In addition, the state held the authority to determine what counted as virtuous conduct and to reward and punish accordingly. Ideally, the state reshapes society to bring it closer in line with natural moral order.

Such, then, were Wang Yangming's recommendations to the respective ministries for disposing of those who became embroiled in the rebellion. However, at this time, he was faced with a more urgent matter: the disposition of the

---

32   Ibid., 12:425.

33   Leo Strauss, *Natural Right and History* (Chicago: University of Chicago Press, 1965), 133.

34   Ibid., 132–33.

35   For a full discussion of benevolent paternalism, see Chapter Five.

now imprisoned prince and his principal accomplices, as well as the emperor's plan to lead armies and campaign against the rebel-bandits. Wang's success in navigating these dire predicaments would eventually become for him the real-life verification of his teachings on the origins of virtue, as well as the impetus for its reformulation. Moreover, this success supplied evidence for his biographers of the extraordinary character of their teacher, and of his imperturbable inner freedom.

Steering Oar in Hand, Navigating the Rapids

On July 15, 1519, when Wang Yangming dispatched his first urgent report to the court concerning the rebellion, he clearly hoped and expected that the emperor would immediately commission generals to deploy armies and proceed to the region.[36] Shortly thereafter, in early August, at the urging of Minister of War Wang Qiong, court officials made the same recommendation, but by this time rumors were already afoot that the emperor and his favorites had something else in mind.[37] In a futile attempt to forestall the inevitable, Chief Grand Secretary Yang Tinghe 楊廷和 (1459–1529) voiced his concerns to the emperor over the dangers of leaving the capital and borrowing forces from the northern border. Nevertheless, court officials soon received a reply confirming their worst suspicions: the emperor would personally command the "Six Armies," obviating the need to commission generals. Rather, orders were to be drafted for the "Awesome and Militant General in Chief, the Duke of Zhenguo" to command a small number of generals appointed directly from his circle of favorites for the purpose of leading capital and border troops to the region to crush the traitor prince. The Marquis of Anbian Xu Tai was to serve as a vice-general, Eunuch Director Zhang Zhong as a superintendent of military affairs and general for the pacification of rebel-bandits, Commissioner-in-Chief Liu Hui 劉暉 also as general for the pacification of rebel-bandits, while another eunuch director, Zhang Yong 張永, was made a superintendent of military affairs.[38]

Ironically enough, just fifteen days after the edict announcing the imperial campaign was released, Wang Yangming already had the principal traitors in custody and was preparing to escort them to the capital to be presented to the emperor. But his victory memorial, composed on August 24, did not reach the emperor until September 19, four days after he and his royal entourage had

---

36 *WYMQJ*, vol. 1, 12:393.
37 *MSLWZSL*, 176:3415.
38 Ibid.

departed. Undoubtedly, by this time they already knew of the victory, for on September 6 Nanjing censors had submitted a memorial praising the emperor for the solemnity of his laudable achievement: before even initiating his personal campaign, the emperor's awesomeness had already led to the subjugation of the evildoers. It was therefore incumbent upon him to take into consideration the terrible devastation from natural disasters and warfare in the region, and bring his plans for a campaign to a halt.[39]

As for Wang Yangming, when he submitted the victory memorial he appears only to have believed that seasoned generals, uninformed of the victory, might still be preparing to head for the region. Apparently, enough rumors about an impending imperial campaign were circulating to cause widespread panic. Hence, on that same day Wang also dispatched a communication to local civil and military officials, ordering them to urge those soldiers and civilians under their respective jurisdictions to remain calm and prepare to assist him at such time as he should pass through with the prisoners. But these orders to officials stationed in yamens and courier stations along the routes to the south also suggest that he had not yet come to believe there was substance to the rumors. Given that that the prince had been captured and security restored—he asked them—why would capital troops march such long distances for no reason? These officials were therefore to inform alarmed people of the falsity of these rumors, but also to be on the alert for capital troops moving down from the north that might still be unaware that the prince was in custody.[40]

In fact, at some point during the month of September, the emperor ordered Zhang Zhong, Xu Tai, and Liu Hui to take their armies and proceed in advance to Nanchang.[41] The grand coordinator certainly could not have imagined that his initial plea for military assistance in the wake of reports of the rebellion would evolve into a massive charade. As he would soon discover, the real intention of these imperial favorites was to order him to place the prince in their custody so that they could re-enact the campaign upon the emperor's arrival. Given that the prince was to be released somewhere around Lake Poyang for this purpose, local residents had every reason to panic.

In response to this alarming turn of events, on September 10, while residing in Jiangxi's capital, Wang Yangming submitted another memorial stating that he had the traitors in hand, but also warning the emperor of danger should he choose to travel through areas where the prince might yet have sympathizers.

---

39   Ibid., 177:3451.
40   *WYMQJ*, vol. 1, 17:587.
41   *MTJ*, 48:1491.

Most importantly, he announced his decision to depart Jiangxi in order to deliver the prince in person:

> When first initiating his plot, [the prince] fully expected the emperor might personally lead a campaign and hence in advance placed members of his treacherous clique along the routes to lie in ambush. He thus hoped to pull off the strategy of a Bolang or Jingke.[42] But now this rebel, faster than a spin of a heel, has already been captured, and according to the law shall be sent to the gate of the imperial palace, in order to manifest the punitive power of Heaven. I wished to entrust [these prisoners] to subordinates for escorting, but I fear hidden accomplices might yet be around and take advantage of any opportunity to attack, perhaps leading to some great misfortune. Should I die it would be with this regret. Therefore, while pacifying rebel-bandits and presenting prisoners of war is the established proper ceremony of the country, it is also my duty. So I will depart on the fourth of October, overseeing government troops and personally escorting Chenhao and those criminals guilty of serious crimes to the imperial palace.[43]

Although it is uncertain when or even if the emperor received this hopeless plea, what is clear is that he and his generals, upon arriving at a location just south of the capital, did receive Wang's first victory memorial on September 19. According to the *Veritable Records*, the emperor chose to conceal it because he wanted this battle for himself.[44]

The dire implications of having thousands of troops stationed in Nanchang to quell a nonexistent rebellion were all too clear to Wang Yangming: it meant throwing the whole of northern Jiangxi into a state of chaos. As grand coordinator, in fact, he was unwilling to go along with this charade, even though it would mean disobeying orders and placing his life at risk. Thus, on October 4, he departed the provincial capital with the prince and his principal accomplices, determined to take them under secure escort directly to the emperor, who was at that point making his way down to Nanjing.[45]

When Wang Yangming realized that two of the emperor's most trusted companions, Eunuch Director Zhang Zhong and Marquis of Anbian Xu Tai, were due to arrive in Nanchang with their forces, he decided to evade them by

---

42   These were two assassins who made an attempt on the life of the First Emperor of Qin.
43   *WYMQJ*, vol.1, 12:409.
44   *MSLWZSL*, 177:3467.
45   Tan, *Guo Que*, 51:3192.

taking an indirect route towards the emperor's provisional palace in Nanjing. But although he managed to leave just prior to their arrival, Wang found himself nonetheless pursued by their agents, who caught up with him while he was passing through Guangxin 廣信, Jiangxi. On at least two different occasions they conveyed orders for him to turn back immediately to the provincial capital and hand over the prisoners. Naturally, Wang refused, and in order to secure himself against accusations of directly disobeying orders, he also dispatched a communication to the Ministry of War calling into question the authenticity of these documents: "Since this official has perhaps recklessly shouldered the heavy responsibility for a war that touches directly upon issues of security and danger of the region, and the life and death of the three armies, with regard to all confidential matters, unless I receive an imperial order with the imperial seal or properly sealed Ministry of War communications, I dare not lightly believe them."[46] Indeed, since the above orders were not in accord with proper procedure, he had legitimate reasons to suspect they were the work of accomplices of the prince attempting to set a trap; at least, that is how he reported the matter to likely sympathetic readers at the ministry. Instead of obeying such orders, fearing he would be unable to evade his pursuers, he departed that night, arriving the next day at a postal station in Yu Mountain 玉山. Afterwards, he hurried on —with his prisoners—towards Hangzhou.

Yet while it may have been relatively easy for Wang Yangming to evade these orders, he was confronted with a more serious challenge upon arriving in Zhejiang. It was at this time, with provincial officials present, that he also turned away an officer from the Embroidered Uniform Guard sent directly by the emperor with orders from the "Awesome and Militant Commander-in-Chief, the Duke of Zhenguo" to hand over the prisoners. Wang at first refused to see the guard, but when those officials present urged him to comply, fearing he would be accused of crimes if he did not, he told them that he did not in his official capacity fall under the authority of a commander-in-chief. He went further, instructing them as to how an official is to deal with an errant ruler: "As for a child confronting instructions from parents he knows to be wrong, if he is able to inform them of this, he should follow them in tears. How could he bear to willingly please them?"[47]

Nevertheless, the grand coordinator eventually permitted the guard to enter, even though he would send him back to the emperor empty-handed. Prior to the guard's departure, a colleague asked whether or not Wang should, as prescribed by etiquette, present the guard with a gift. So Wang had someone

46   *WYMQJ*, vol. 1, 17:590.
47   *NP*, 34:1269.

bring him an insignificant and humiliating sum of money, which the insulted guard refused. The next day, when the guard came to take leave, the grand co-ordinator took his hand and said:

> During the Zhengde reign, I spent a considerable amount of time in the Embroidered Uniform Guard Prison, and I never once came across some-one like you, who looks so lightly upon money and so values righteous-ness. Yesterday your refusal to accept the gift and demand full and proper etiquette was beyond my expectations. When I heard you refused it, I was taken aback. Aside from being able to write characters, I really have no other abilities. On another day I will certainly write a memorial com-mending you, so that other Embroidered Uniform guards shall know that there is someone like you.[48]

Back in Nanchang, when news of Wang Yangming's obstructionism reached Zhang and Xu, they began to spread malicious rumors: the grand coordinator, they were claiming, had initially colluded with the prince, but when he real-ized the rebellion might fail, turned against him in order to hide his complicity. The biographical entry for Xu Tai in the *Ming History* details just what these two generals and their soldiers were up to in the provincial capital:

> Chenhao had already been captured by Wang Shouren. [Xu] Tai wanted to take the credit for his achievement, and therefore hurried to Nanchang. [He and his forces] carried out an exhaustive search for remaining rebels, framing cases against incalculable numbers of literati and commoners. The extent of the extortion and blackmail, as well as numbers dead, exceeded that of the rebellion of Chenhao. Being jealous of the achieve-ment of Shouren, they sought in a hundred different ways to have him pushed out. They detained Wu Wending and humiliated him in the extreme.[49]

Prefect Wu, it will be recalled, had been second-in-command during much of the campaign against the prince, and given his close ties to the grand coordina-tor, he was not about to allow himself to be cowed by the marquis and eunuch director into giving false incriminating evidence against him. Upon being bound up by the two and enduring beatings, he excoriated them: "Without concern for nine generations [of our ancestors and descendants], we subju-

---

48   Ibid.
49   *MS*, 307:7890.

gated the great traitor to our country. What crime is there in this? You are confidantes of the emperor, and yet you dare to shame and humiliate the righteous and loyal in order to get revenge on the bandit rebel. For your crimes you ought to be executed."[50]

While the emperor's favorites were busy throwing Nanchang into a state of turmoil, Wang Yangming finally arrived in Hangzhou and directly sought out the other eunuch director, Zhang Yong, who had been sent there by the emperor to persuade Wang to hand over custody of the prince. According to one account, "Yong at first refused to see him, and Shouren denounced those at the gate, went straight in, and yelled, 'I am Wang Shouren, and I have come to speak with you of the affairs of the country, so how could you refuse me!' Yong was intimidated, and Shouren therefore spoke of the extreme suffering and devastation in Jiangxi."[51]

Apparently, Wang approached the eunuch director because of his reputation for integrity, but also in the hopes that he might play a role in persuading the emperor to halt his plans. He told Zhang:

> The people of Jiangxi have for long suffered the poisonous presence of Zhu Chenhao, and now they have passed through a great rebellion, followed by drought, and now the burden of provisioning government troops from the capital and border garrisons. Their hardship is extreme, and they have no choice but to flee to and gather in the mountains and valleys and resist. Formerly those who helped Chenhao were coerced into doing so, and now today they are being incited by all of these unbearable pressures. As a result, treacherous cliques are arising in great numbers, and all under Heaven is falling into a state of collapse. Under such circumstances, won't it be difficult to raise forces to pacify disorder?[52]

In reply, Zhang Yong claimed that, far from desiring to take credit for the grand coordinator's achievement, he had come along only to look after the wellbeing of the emperor, who was surrounded by a cabal. He further warned Wang that the emperor would not change his mind about the campaign-cum-tour: should he go against his wishes, this would only provoke those surrounding him and lead to even worse problems. Whatever else may have transpired during their conversation, Wang was convinced that Zhang Yong's motives were reasonably

---

50   Ibid., 200:5280.
51   Ibid., 304:7793.
52   *NP*, 34:1268.

sound, and possibly saw no other way out of the impasse. Wang thus entrusted him with the prisoners.

Afterwards, sometime in November 1519, Wang retired to Jingci Temple 淨 慈寺 by the West Lake 西湖 in Hangzhou. Hoping to remain, he submitted a memorial requesting leave on account of illness, albeit unsuccessfully.[53] Indeed, this brief period of respite was hardly to last, for he found the news concerning the imperial expedition intolerable, and therefore journeyed to the emperor's provisional military headquarters to protest. But prior to reaching his destination, just south of Nanjing, he was intercepted by Grand Secretary Yang Yiqing 楊一清 (1454–1530), who conveyed orders appointing him grand coordinator of Jiangxi, and convinced him to give up his plan. At this point, Wang Yangming returned to Nanchang, arriving there late in 1519. He thus took over the post formerly occupied Sun Sui, the grand coordinator executed by Zhu Chenhao.[54]

His troubles, however, were hardly to end with handing over the prince, for returning to Nanchang meant coming face to face with the very individuals who would attempt to have him framed for the crime of rebellion. Zhang Yong too arrived in the provincial capital, with the prisoners, having been ordered to carry out a full investigation into the rebellion and assemble a list of all involved. He may also have sought to restrain Zhang Zhong and Xu Tai, who were yet seeking evidence implicating the grand coordinator. In this effort, however, they failed, after which they returned to the emperor's headquarters. The compilers of his *Chronological Biography* ascribe this outcome to Wang's deft handling of the situation:

> At the time, Zhong and the others were coercing Chenhao into helping them search all over [for the evidence]. [Their] soldiers and horses filled up the city and overflowed into the streets and alleys such that no one could even travel. [Censor] Xu and [Secretary of Scrutiny] Lun saw the turn things were taking and joined the cabal in the rumor-mongering, and what was being said was totally unjust. Our teacher returned to Nanchang, and at the instigation of their superiors, the northern forces willfully sat around and cursed at him, some even going so far as to obstruct his movements and incite quarrels. Our teacher was, however, totally unfazed by this and treated them with the utmost deference. Prior, he had already ordered local police to move city residents to the countryside, and to have the elderly and frail greet the soldiers at the gates. At

---

53 Huang, "Shi de ji," in *WYMQJ*, vol. 1, 38:1423.
54 *NP*, 34:1269.

first he wished to feast and reward the troops, but Xu Tai and the others forbade this, and ordered them not to accept. Then he sent out proclamations both within and outside the city, describing the hardship faced by northern troops forced to leave their homes, and requesting that residents should treat them with the courtesies normally extended to guests. When he went out and came across soldiers grieving [over a fallen comrade], he would stop and inquire, and generously provided them with a coffin, sympathize with them, and depart. After some time, the soldiers all felt touched. During the winter solstice, he ordered the city to make offerings. The people had only just gone through the rebellion, so wailing and offerings of libations could be heard without cease. The northern soldiers all thought of their homes, lamenting and wishing to return. Without yielding to them in any way, our teacher spoke with Zhong and Tai, and they began to fear him.[55]

Indeed, by the end of 1519—in part because of the impact that Wang Yangming's conduct and proclamations had on the soldiers—Commanders Zhang and Xu, as well as Zhang Yong, departed with the prince and his accomplices, mooring them on the Yangtze in the southern capital early the next year.

On January 26, 1520, with the prince due to arrive, grand secretaries present at the emperor's provisional palace in the southern capital were ordered to deliberate over proper protocols for disposing of the prince.[56] Their efforts, however, did not in the short term bring closure to this case. Although they recommended that Emperor Wuzong immediately withdraw forces and return to Beijing, announce victory to Heaven and Earth, the ancestors, and the gods of soil and grain, as well as have court officials and other princes further deliberate upon a fitting punishment for the prince, the emperor refused to even receive the imprisoned Zhu Chenhao, thus carrying on the farce by pretending the prince had not yet been captured. Their advice was patently ignored and, while the prince and his cohorts languished in a vessel on the Yangtze River, the emperor lingered on in Nanjing for eight more months.

In the meantime, Wang Yangming's trials continued unabated. Upon returning to Nanjing, Zhang Zhong and Xu Tai, along with Jiang Bin, claimed before the emperor that Wang was once an accomplice to the prince. They even alleged he was plotting a rebellion himself. Skeptical, Emperor Wuzong demanded evidence, at which point the three urged him to summon the grand coordinator in person, claiming he would refuse to come. In actual fact, they

55   Ibid.
56   *MTJ*, 48:1497.

planned to block his access to the emperor. When the summons arrived, Wang Yangming knew it was legitimate because Zhang Yong had also dispatched a messenger to verify the emperor's wishes and urge him to depart immediately. Wang indeed left without hesitation, but while he was passing through a customs outpost on his way to Nanjing, he was blocked by agents of the imperial favorites and returned to Wuhu 蕪湖 County in Anhui Province. Their malicious plan had worked. Sometime in late January, having likely given up on gaining access to the emperor, Wang changed into commoner clothing, donned a blue-ribboned silk kerchief, and visited a Buddhist retreat in Jiuhua Mountain 九華山, in the same province where he was now stranded.[57]

While up in the mountains, Wang Yangming certainly had every reason to believe he still faced retaliation. Indeed, it appears that the only reason he escaped execution was the support of Eunuch Director Zhang Yong, who throughout this time attested to Wang's staunch loyalty before the emperor. Even the emperor is said to have admitted to Zhang that "Wang Shouren is a man learned in the Way, and hearing of my summons he would certainly come immediately, so how can it be, as is said, that he will not?"[58] Zhang explained to him that some were attempting to steal the glory for Wang's achievement, so the emperor dispatched an agent to scout out his whereabouts and report back to him. After learning that Wang was awaiting his fate in the mountains, the emperor likely had Zhang convey his intention that Wang should return to Jiangxi and finally take up his new post as grand coordinator of that province.

Thus it was that on February 18, 1520 Wang Yangming made his way back to Nanchang, where he would remain until July, implementing measures to restore stability to the region and spending further time engaging his growing following of students. His problems at the Zhengde emperor's provisional headquarters, however, were hardly over. While in the southern capital, the imperial companions continued to vie for meritorious recognition, and specifically wished to be the ones to present the prisoners to the emperor, as if they had indeed captured them. It may once again have been the intervention of Zhang Yong that mitigated any potential damage they might have caused. He is said to have informed them, "Absolutely not. Before we departed from the capital, Chenhao had already been captured. When he was being escorted north for presentation, they passed over Yu Mountain and crossed over Qiantang. People witnessed this, so the credit cannot be taken."[59] Nonetheless, to satisfy their demands, in his self-appointed capacity as "Awesome and Martial

57   *NP*, 34:1270.
58   *MTJ*, 48:1498.
59   *NP*, 34:1274.

General-in-Chief, the Duke of Zhenguo," Wuzong dispatched a military com-
muniqué to Wang Yangming, ordering him to resubmit the victory memorial.
This time, however, Wang was to include the names of the emperor's commanders, attributing the credit for the success to them.

By the time he received these orders, Wang Yangming had already decided
to leave Nanchang and spend time traveling down the Gan River 贛江 to Ganzhou in southern Jiangxi, where he had previously been stationed for two years
as grand coordinator. Very likely he wished to escape the stifling political atmosphere in Nanchang as well as attend to official matters in other parts of the
province. While there, he also chose to review the military and spend time
training officers and soldiers in the arts of war, something that not surprisingly
raised eyebrows, given that the rumors about his supposed complicity in the
rebellion were yet rife, and Jiang Bin had dispatched someone to spy on him.[60]
In his study of Wang's political life, Dong Ping speculates that he was making
these moves simply to show his disapproval of the emperor's conduct, but also
perhaps because he feared that Jiang might be planning to attempt a coup
d'état.[61]

So dangerous were his actions that Wang's close friends counseled him to
return to Nanchang and avoid bringing further suspicion upon himself, advice
he roundly refused: "I am here [doing nothing but] intoning poetry and practicing ritual with children. What is there to be suspicious of?" To Chen Jiuchuan 陳九川, who had proffered this advice, he resolutely stated, "Sir, why
are you not engaged in learning through holding discussions? When I was formerly in the provincial capital with the powerful palace eunuchs, danger was
confronting me right before my eyes, and yet I was also serene, for should there
have been some terrible unforeseen turn of events, I would not have been able
to escape it. There is deep reflection behind the reasons for my not acting
rashly."[62]

When he complied by resubmitting his victory memorial on July 31, 1520,
Wang Yangming met the demands of his ruler but in fact gave little credit to his
courtiers. Rather, he composed a summary account of his campaigns explicitly
acknowledging the roles of his commanders, as well as calling for their com-
mendation. Although he mentioned by name Zhang Zhong, the Duke of Anbian Xu Tai, and Eunuch Director Zhang Yong, he merely stated that they had
arrived in the area to investigate and campaign. Likewise, as for the "Duke of

---

60   Ibid.
61   Dong, *Wang Yangming de shenghuo shijie*, 148.
62   *NP*, 34:1274.

Zhenguo," Wang stated that he had, upon being commanded by Heaven to lead a punitive expedition, brought the "Six Armies" to Nanjing, but that was all.

Yet it must have been sufficient, for shortly after receiving this memorial the Zhengde emperor finally decided to receive the prisoners and prepare to return to the capital. On August 13, 1520, well aware that the emperor's companions were encouraging him to remain throughout the fall and tour Zhejiang, Grand Secretaries Liang Chu 梁儲 and Jiang Mian 蔣冕 submitted a memorial pleading with him to return to Beijing. Supposedly because they insisted on kneeling and wailing at the gate to the emperor's residence until such time as they received an edict granting their wishes, Wuzong chose to give in to their demands.[63] On September 19, 1520, the emperor ordered the construction of a broad public square for the victory ceremony. It was to be surrounded with troops, some carrying large military banners. While the emperor sat donned in his military attire, the prince was to have his shackles removed and freed, so that he could be recaptured and shackled to the sound of beating drums and gongs. Thereafter, he was presented to the emperor. A few days later, with the prisoners caged up in vessels following from behind, the imperial entourage began the journey back to the capital. Wang Yangming, finally feeling some sense of relief that the end of the charade was near, soon returned to Nanchang.

Sageliness Within

How is a gentleman to conduct himself as an official when serving his ruler under such trying circumstances? In such settings, what virtues—inner dispositions and character traits—will evolve out of openness to the voice within, to one's moral conscience and knowing? This would seem to be the question Wang Yangming was addressing on those many occasions when, in the presence of colleagues or students, he spoke of such issues or modeled such composure and serenity. We have already seen, for instance, how he claimed that while campaigning against the prince, he had in his own view acted quite effortlessly, and fully expected support from others because "all people have this innate knowledge of the good, so how could it be the case that no others will respond to the call and come?"[64]

Likewise, while Wang was away in Ganzhou, his friends were urging him to return to the southern capital, yet he remained unperturbed by the threat

---

63   *MTJ*, 49:1501.
64   *WYMQJ*, vol. 2, 41:1599.

posed by Jiang Bin and others surrounding the Zhengde emperor. It was during
that time that Wang wrote what would become one of his more famous poems,
the "Song of Weeping":

> The wise are without perplexity, the humane without worry;
> Why should the gentleman be distraught, eyebrows knitted with concern?
> Wherever we should wander all is a level path, relying on Heaven to judge
> what is before us, this is not human calculation.
> Shooting a small bird with a pearl worth a thousand *jin* of gold, why go to
> the trouble of digging the soil with a precious sword?
> To serve when called upon, to retire when dismissed, this body floating
> upon turbulent waters in a ship without a captain;
> With poise and grace does a man confront a world turned upside down;
> why look upon constraints like an impoverished convict?
> Does not the gentleman see that when the old man in the east side of the
> house had taken measures to prevent danger posed by tigers, a tiger
> entered during the night and bit off his head?
> While on the west side of the house, a child, knowing nothing of tigers,
> chased it off with a pole as if driving a water buffalo.
> The wise, having choked, discard food; the ignorant, fearing drowning,
> first jump in.
> When one comes to know their destiny in life they are liberated; why be
> fearful of slander, fleeing calamities, only lamenting?[65]

According to Okada Takehiko, this poem is significant because it expresses the
sentiments of a Confucian who was liberated (*satuo* 灑脫) and joyfully according with what is decreed by Heaven (*letian* 樂天), thus showing the maturing
of Wang's learning of the mind-heart.[66]

Another anecdote, recorded by Wang Ji 王畿 (1498–1583), a disciple of Wang
Yangming, provides further material for reflection on the virtues his teacher
considered of utmost importance for managing a challenging political world.
According to Ji, after handing over the prisoners and in the midst of confrontation with the emperor's favorites, his teacher simply awaited his fate. At one
point he gathered students around and informed them, "Ever since employing
the military instrument, [I] have come increasingly to feel that this effort of
extending the innate knowledge of the good and investigating matters is even

---

65   *WYMQJ*, vol. 1, 20:784.
66   Okada, *Ō Yōmei Taiden*, 4:276.

more refined and penetrating."⁶⁷ Wang Ji observed that some students felt that, given how difficult and pressing times of war can be, his response was rather eccentric. But their teacher explained:

> The extension of the innate knowledge of the good relies upon the investigation of things—this means truly responding to stimuli when confronting phenomena, and is where one's efforts should be placed. In normal times, one is idle and relaxed and therefore without much in the way of inquiry. But when amidst the demands of warfare, when preservation and destruction may be decided in the time required to take one breath, the endangerment or security of the country is tied to one's total spirit. Just one subtle thought, reflecting and discriminating, without the slightest need for caution or control, without permitting any excess, neither deceiving nor forgetting, confronting the critical moment and spiritually responding: this is the wondrous functioning of the innate knowledge of the good, which accords with the natural state of all things. Yet I remained detached from it all.... Since weathering and passing through this affair so full of potential for great achievement or failure, honor or disgrace, all the gains and losses [that I have experienced], all the glory and shame, have been just like a light breeze passing by my ears and nothing more, so how could they be capable of moving even one thought of mine? Although today I have succeeded in this meritorious act, it is nothing more than one instance of the innate knowledge of the good responding to the occasion, and like a cloud that has just passed by my eyes, I have already forgotten about it.⁶⁸

For Wang Ji, the lesson was of great consequence: "To die amidst affairs under Heaven is easy, but to succeed at affairs under Heaven is difficult; to succeed at some affair under Heaven is easy, but to go without receiving the credit for meritorious accomplishment is difficult; not to receive the credit is easy, but to be able to forget about it altogether is hard—this is the true path of the learning of the sages of ancient times, and also the painstaking effort with which our teacher took on responsibility for the Way throughout his whole life."⁶⁹

Wang Ji believed that his teacher had donned the mantle of sagehood because his spiritual attainments allowed for detachment from the personal consequences of the fruits of his actions. Critical for understanding this point is

---

67   Wang, "Du xian shi zai bao Hai Riweng Ji'an qi bing shu xu," 41:1600.
68   Ibid.
69   Ibid.

Wang Yangming's statement that the entire event amounted to nothing more than "innate knowledge of the good responding to the occasion (*liang zhi ying ji* 良知應跡)." Analysis of this statement will help clarify his doctrine that knowledge and action are ultimately one, forming a seamless whole. It will also take us into the heart of his Confucian discourse on the relation between the development of personal virtue and governance (*xiu ji zhi ren* 修己治人).[70] The connection between the two lies in Wang's interpretation of the term "investigating things" (*ge wu* 格物) for, as he explains, "When the principle of Heaven in the innate knowledge of my mind is extended to all things, all things will attain their principle. To extend the innate knowledge of my mind is the matter of the extension of knowledge, and for all things to attain their principle is the matter of the investigation of things."[71]

In the "Inquiry on the *Great Learning*," Wang interprets the investigation of things as rectifying or correcting affairs (*zheng shi* 正事).[72] By affairs, he means that towards which willing or thoughts are directed. Thinking about or willing an affair will naturally bring forth a judgment by one's innate knowledge designating whether it is right or wrong, good or bad, thereby supplying the basis for action. Put more simply, no matter what a person may be conscious of, there will be a moral tone to that consciousness. Because willing and thinking (as another form of willing) may either be insincere or sincere, correct or incorrect, and as a result lead either to right or wrong action, a standard is required to rectify will and thought, and this standard is the innate knowledge of the good, extension of which leads to right action. Insofar as the mind is unbeclouded by self-centered considerations, this knowledge and the capacity to recognize and act upon it becomes increasingly self-evident, refined, and pure, eventually reaching the point where the process of rectifying affairs becomes completely natural. This would seem to be the implication of Wang Yangming's remarks to Wang Ji.

Here, "natural" implies more than simply acting on conscience or moral intuition. Within Wang's philosophical discourse we find a number of paired terms pointing to differing, though dialectically related, goals of self-development. On the one hand, through quiet-sitting and calming the mind, the student of the Way should be able to attain what Julia Ching refers to as "pure consciousness," a state of mind essentially devoid of emotions, images, and

---

70   In a letter to Xu Chengzhi, Wang Yangming states that "self-cultivation and governance were originally never two separate Ways." (*WYMQJ*, vol. 1, 4:145)

71   Wang, *Instructions for Practical Living*, 99.

72   *WYMQJ*, vol. 2, 26:972.

form.[73] In Wang Yangming's terminology, this state is referred to as the mean prior to the rise of emotions (*wei fa zhi zhong* 未發之中) or as quiescent and unmoved (*ji ran bu dong* 寂然不動), and he does not hesitate on occasion to compare this to the liberating "nonbeing" of the Daoists or "emptiness" of the Buddhists.[74] Achievement of this goal amounts to a kind of enlightenment because this pure unadulterated awareness, often analogized to a mirror, is none other than the principle of Heaven or the innate knowledge of the good.[75]

This enlightening apprehension, however, cannot be considered the final goal of self-cultivation, for the referent of *wei fa zhi zhong* and *ji ran bu dong* must be brought into, integrated, and realized in the midst of everyday life. In other words, contemplation and stillness must be united with action.[76] In Wang Yangming's terminology, all of which is drawn from classical sources, this goal is referred to variously as the "harmony after the rise of emotions (*fa er jie zhong jie wei zhi he* 發而皆中節謂之和),"[77] "when acted upon, it immediately penetrates all things (*gan er sui tong* 感而遂通),"[78] "one must always be doing something (*bi you shi yan* 必有事焉),"[79] and "the feelings of the sage are in accord with creation and yet he has no feelings of his own (*qing shun wan wu er wu qing* 情順萬物而無情)."[80] Thus, when Wang's student Qian

---

73 Ching, *Religious Thought of Chu Hsi*, 116.

74 Ibid., 116. For the influence of Buddhism on Wang Yangming, see Chan, "How Buddhistic is Wang Yang-ming," *Philosophy East and West*, vol. 12 (1962): 203–15; Chen, *You wu zhi jing*, 218–22. According to Wang Yangming, "Innate knowledge is the equilibrium before the feelings are aroused [*wei fa zhi zhong*]. It is the state of broadness and extreme impartiality. It is the original substance that is absolutely quiet and inactive [*ji ran bu dong*]." (*Instructions for Practical Living*, 134) The classical locus is the *Doctrine of the Mean*. For a translation, see Chan, *Sourcebook in Chinese Philosophy*, 98.

75 According to Wang Yangming, "Innate knowledge is the equilibrium before the feelings are aroused [*wei fa zhi zhong*]. It is the state of broadness and extreme impartiality. It is the original substance that is absolutely quiet and inactive [*ji ran bu dong*]." (*Instructions for Practical Living*, 134) The classical locus is the *Doctrine of the Mean*. For a translation, see Chan, *Sourcebook in Chinese Philosophy*, 98.

76 Cf. Julia Ching's analysis of these concepts in Zhu Xi's philosophy (*Religious Thought of Chu Hsi*, 122.)

77 Wang Yangming is citing the *Doctrine of the Mean*. For a different translation, see Chan, *A Sourcebook in Chinese Philosophy*, 98.

78 Wang Yangming is citing the *Book of Changes*. For a translation, see "Appended Remarks," in *Yi King*, trans. James Legge, pt. 1, ch. 10, 370.

79 The classical locus for this term is *Mencius* 2:A:2. For a translation see Chan, *A Sourcebook in Chinese Philosophy*, 63.

80 Cheng Yi 程颐 and Cheng Hao 程颢, *Er cheng ji* 二程集 [Collected Works of Cheng Yi and Cheng Hao], vol. 2 (Beijing: Zhonghua shuju, 1981), 2:460.

Dehong stated that throughout this time Wang Yangming was still and abiding in silence, and when he himself stated he was without involvement and unmoved, this is precisely the kind of spiritual attainment to which they were referring. This is also the implication of his statement, as recorded by Wang Ji, that innate knowledge of the good conforms naturally to all things.

As for the connection with action, what is most characteristic of Wang's philosophy is that, whether it be *wei fa* 未發 (the mean prior to the rise of emotion) or *yi fa* 以發 (harmony after the rise of emotion), such spiritual attainments are of utmost ethical significance because cultivation of the mean allows for direct contact with the very springs of moral knowing. More to the point, it is precisely through acting upon moral knowing that one remains quiescent. As he told an individual who had sought his instruction, the stillness and quiescence of mind derives from the reality that it is always accumulating righteousness, which is why "following [Heavenly] principle is called quiescence."[81]

I think that we here find the broader discursive context for Wang Ji's record, although we have indeed arrived at some very unfamiliar territory. Wang Yangming claimed that he was completely free of self-interest because he was abiding in "the eternally illuminating (*heng zhao* 恆照)" ontological ground (*ben ti* 本體) that is innate knowledge of the good, and that because he was free of self-interest he was able naturally to bring affairs to completion, in accord with the Way (*da dao* 達道).[82] This is truly difficult to understand by any contemporary theoretical measure, but it is precisely what Wang Yangming stated in so many ways, and why his followers believed he had managed to embody the ideal of sageliness within and kingliness without: he had throughout this time united contemplation with action, direct moral knowing with the affairs of the body politic. This is also perhaps why such scholars as Julia Ching and Chen Lai have resorted to terming this a kind of mysticism.[83] Likewise, in Chinese scholarship, one often finds the terms "spiritual realm (*jingshen jingjie* 精神境界)" to describe such elevated awareness. And yet, that said, we are still left to wonder just what more precisely and concretely counted as the kind of moral knowing that brought such peace of mind.

---

81   *WYMQJ*, vol. 1, 2:182.

82   In his edition of *Instructions for Practical Living*, Wing-tsit Chan translates this as: "Innate knowledge of the good is the original substance of the mind, or what I have just referred to as that which is always shining." (132) In "Shu Zhu Shouqian juan 書朱守乾卷," Wang Yangming states that innate knowledge of the good is "the foundation of all under Heaven," and that to act according to the innate knowledge of the good is what is called "all under Heaven reaching the Way" (*WYMQJ*, vol. 1, 8:279).

83   Cf. Chen, *You wu zhi jing*, 380–413; Ching, *Mysticism and Kingship*, 174.

Fin de siècle Virtue

At some point during the first half of 1519, prior to the rebellion, Wang Yang-ming replied to a letter from a student by the name of Cai Xiyuan 蔡希淵 with advice that in retrospect appears all too premonitory. In this, he informed Cai that he had heard from a mutual friend that he, Cai, was at odds with some individuals currently in power, but that he was nonetheless confident these were not problems Cai had brought upon himself; hence, he could not be held responsible for them. Thus, he encouraged Cai with a promising approach to this challenging situation: "Xiyuan is by nature modest, generous, of a mild disposition, and looks upon worldly matters of honor and shame, and the changing attitudes of those of differing status, no differently than he looks upon a gust of wind or hazy day. So how could he harbor ill feelings amidst all this?" Citing the wisdom of Mencius, Wang proceeded to discourse on the importance of adopting a posture of humility:

> When someone treats him rudely and unreasonably, the gentleman should look within and tell himself, 'I must have been impolite.' If upon reflection he finds that he indeed showed proper etiquette, he should take another look at himself and say, 'I must have been disloyal.'" Xiyuan, your efforts at self-transcendence are daily more refined and incisive, so how could you look upon yourself as unfailingly conscientious? In years past when I was exiled to an official post in Guizhou, there was not a month that did not go by when I was not confronted with barbaric and irrational treatment. But now, reflecting upon this, I see this was the most effective way to steel my character.[84]

The perverse treatment to which Wang Yangming was referring was the humiliating beating he suffered at court in 1507 at the hands of the powerful eunuch Liu Jin, as well as his subsequent exile to a courier station in a remote region of southwest China. At the time the Zhengde emperor had allowed the reins of power to fall in this eunuch director's hand, and for years he terrorized officialdom. When Wang submitted a memorial calling for the release of two officials he believed to have been unjustly imprisoned, he criticized this deviant state of affairs. As a result, even after the beatings and exile, he was still pursued by the eunuch's agents, and for months could never be certain of survival. But far from succumbing to the pressure, he turned these circumstances

---

84   *WYMQJ*, vol. 1, 4:159.

into material for self-cultivation, directly confronting his own fear of death by building a coffin for himself and engaging in meditation.[85]

From one angle, we can read this advice in a historical light, as the "contemporary significance" of his moral philosophy. That is, in a time of crisis, perhaps first and foremost for the purpose of maintaining sanity and clarity in an unpredictable and sometimes dangerous political system and culture, it was necessary to yield a principle of freedom, of autonomy from all those fears within and without that might impede principled and conscientious conduct. Over the course of a decade, he had frequently observed to his students that learning to maintain integrity in a time of decline and in the face of relentless attacks upon one's person by directly confronting and weathering them was essential to building a virtuous disposition and developing practical wisdom:

> When living in times of peace, one really does not gain much insight, something that only comes when beset by gains and losses, weathering misfortune, and confronting adversity and humiliation. Should one have the ability not to become angered over those things that in normal times would anger one; should one not become distressed to the point of losing one's footing over something that could cause one to do so—this is also the place to put forth effort. Although under Heaven there might be ten thousand changes, [it is natural that] the way in which I respond does not go beyond happiness, anger, grief, and joy, these four emotions. This is the essence of learning, and governance is also to be found here.[86]

To explain how adversity benefits the growth of virtue, Wang Yangming distinguishes true self (*zhen wu* 真吾) and false or artificial self (*wei ji* 偽己). The difference between the two was for him ontological, in the sense that the former is real, identified with the highest good, and acts naturally according to truth, whereas the latter is unreal, attached to phenomena, and moved by erroneous thoughts and desire. The roller coaster of the sociopolitical is the place of true learning because moral conflicts provide the experiential material for tempering and steeling, and hence for furthering, the will to unidentify with the false self and become centered in the true self. In an essay composed for a friend, he explained that "when you are attached to the desires of the false self, then you will be simultaneously attacked by fears over profit and harm, controlled by anxiety over praise and blame, [thoughts of] gains and losses

---

85   *NP*, 33:1227.
86   *WYMQJ*, vol. 1, 4:154–55.

continuously forming before you. You are therefore bound by honor and dis-grace."[87]

Finding the courage, confidence, and moral autonomy necessary to tran-scend trying circumstances, and grounding such freedom in a higher self, na-ture, or principles, is of course not a new theme in Confucianism. Yet it is here that we find the transcendent reference point creating tension with and pre-venting conformity to society, something which Max Weber claimed to be non-existent in the Confucian tradition.[88] Nor is this freedom a new theme in the history of the world: parallels can be found in Stoicism, the four noble truths of Buddhism, or the karma-yoga of the Bhagavad Gita. It is just that Wang Yang-ming's personal travails were particularly challenging and he was able to ar-ticulate very carefully how practical life related to his teaching of virtue. According to Qian Ming, "As he came increasingly to lose hope over politics and reality, he sank deeper into the realm of natural transcendence; his subjec-tive consciousness also further expanded and, what is more, he further came firmly to trust that he had won his own independent character and absolute power of self-determination."[89]

As explained earlier, it was just after the psychologically challenging after-math to the campaign that Wang Yangming began to teach this self-determin-ing power of the innate knowledge of the good, something he claimed was verified throughout that time. In a letter to Zou Shouyi 鄒守益 (1491–1562) composed in 1521, he points to the intimate connection between the evolution of his moral philosophy and his political experiences over the prior two years. Wang states, "Recently I have come to believe that the three characters *zhi li-ang zhi* 致良知 (extension of the innate knowledge of the good) are truly the 'treasure of the orthodox dharma-eye' of the teaching of the sages. In prior years I had not fully exhausted my doubts, but now ever since being occupied with so many affairs I have come to realize that this innate knowledge of the good is completely sufficient."[90] Wang compared the guidance of *liangzhi* to having a steering oar in hand: despite the dangers posed by treacherous waters and fierce winds, all goes as smoothly as one might wish.

---

87   Ibid., 7:261.

88   Max Weber's view of Confucianism as an "ethics of accommodation"–to borrow Heiner
      Roetz's description–may be found in his *The Religion of China*, trans. Hans H. Gerth (New
      York: Free Press, 1951), 260. For a discussion of the limitations of Weber's characterization,
      see Heiner Roetz, *Confucian Ethics in the Axial Age: A Reconstruction under the Aspect of
      the Breakthrough toward Postconventional Thinking* (Albany: State University of New York
      Press), 1993.

89   Qian, *Yangming xue de xingcheng yu fazhan*, 76.

90   *NP*, 34:1278.

This steering oar can also be interpreted in light of his earlier teaching on the "mean" and "harmony" (*zhong he* 中和). For Wang Yangming, although the innate knowledge of the good is equivalent to the mean before feelings are aroused (*wei fa zhi zhong* 未發之中), this does not imply that such a state is present only while quiet-sitting. He also claims that this knowledge "is neither before nor after any state and is neither internal nor external but is one substance without differentiation."[91] That is why "the task is a continuous and unified one," and "one must be trained and polished in the actual affairs of daily life."[92] This training and polishing requires sustaining a collected and concentrated mind amidst activity, so that—following the Song Dynasty philosopher Cheng Hao—"the nature is calm whether it is in a state of activity or state of tranquility."[93]

Arriving at the mean is the key to confronting affairs because it yields a disposition where sentiments are balanced. Hence, one is neither overly reactive nor overly detached and indifferent. As such, any response to affairs and things becomes natural, as opposed to deriving from personal considerations. In the *Instructions* Wang states, "There is no event outside of human feelings and human affairs. Are pleasure, anger, sorrow, and joy not human feelings? Seeking, hearing, speaking, acting, wealth and noble station, poverty and humble station, misfortune, calamity, death and life are all human affairs. Human affairs are all within the realm of human feelings. The important point is to achieve the state of equilibrium [the mean] and harmony (*zhong he*)."[94] Having arrived at the mean, it becomes possible to accord with the changing flow of events and to respond to them appropriately: "It is necessary for a person fully to realize this substance of his own mind and then its functions will be found in its midst. If one should nourish the essence of his own mind so that there is really equilibrium before the feelings are aroused, then naturally when they are aroused they will attain harmony in due measure and degree, and wherever it may be applied it will be correct."[95]

Yet, even as Wang Yangming pointed to these most sublime of virtues, he was also repeatedly pointing to others particularly suited to the times. In another letter to Cai Xiyuan written in 1512, some nine years prior to the rebellion, he addressed the issue of the best way to conduct oneself vis-à-vis a political world in a time of decline. He explained, "When sages and worthies live during

91   Wang, *Instructions for Practical Living*, 136.
92   Ibid., 192.
93   Cheng Yi and Cheng Hao, *Er cheng ji*, vol. 2, 2:461.
94   Wang, *Instructions for Practical Living*, 34.
95   Ibid., 47.

the *fin de siècle* (*mo shi* 末世), although at certain times their conduct towards others and handling of affairs might be compromising, their way is always upright. Should one regard oneself as a person of integrity and yet treat others as if they are trivial, this is not the conscientiousness, empathy, and compassion of the humane person. Xiyuan may find my advice far too tactical, and yet this is in fact reasonable."⁹⁶

For Wang Yangming, the exemplar for such a humble and tactically compromising posture was Confucius's student Yan Hui 顏回. In a letter written in 1513 to another student, he explained:

> When the noble man dwells among mean men, there is no reasoning by which he would readily subscribe to their views. If he should unfortunately find himself pressed to the limit by circumstances after having exhausted all reason and suffered harm from them, then he must remain content and that is all. If in handling such circumstances one does not act so wholly in accord with the Way, perhaps becoming excessive in one's hatred for the wicked, or perhaps harming oneself with furious indignation, it will be of no help in the matter, and only incur their hatred and vengeance. Consequently, this is all a mistake on the part of the gentleman. There is an old saying: "As long as the matter is not detrimental to what is right, it is acceptable to go along with convention." [But] how could the noble man heedlessly go along with convention? It is just that he doesn't make a point of going against convention. "Live among the wicked as if one is wearing courtly attire while sitting among mud and ashes." This is the purity of Boyi. "Although you stand by my side with breast and arms bare, or with your body naked, how can you defile me?" This is the mildness of Liu Xiahui. The noble man's learning is to transform the physical self, and therefore in principle the mildness of [Confucius's student] Hui seems to me to be the appropriate attitude to adopt.⁹⁷

Serene detachment and a prudence born of humility characterized by tactical yielding: this was the spirit of Wang Yangming's political practice throughout

---

96   *WYMQJ*, vol. 1, 4:157.
97   Ibid., 4:161. Both the legendary Boyi 伯夷, said to have lived during the transition from the Shang to Zhou dynasties, and Liu Xiahui 柳下惠, an official in the service of the state of Lu during the early Eastern Zhou, are frequently cited by Confucians as worthies for reason of their virtuous conduct. The quotes are from *Mengzi* 2.9, where he discusses these two worthies. See Mencius, *Mengzi yi zhu*, 76–77.

the Ning campaign and the aftermath, and one that had matured after dealing with Ming political life now for over a decade.

Committed Detachment

Given such repeated claims in biographical sources of Wang's supposed serene detachment, dispassionate response to the problems he confronted, and imperturbable inner freedom, we might yet question why Wang ever felt it necessary to become involved in politics at all. To be sure, his commitment to his duties might be explained by his claim to have been acting upon what was given naturally—on a rational and an emotional level—by innate knowledge of the good, by knowledge of right and wrong. Yet the paradox of his simultaneous tranquility and commitment to the aims and ends of the Ming state as he understood them, a commitment often requiring strong intervention, remains an important enigma worthy of inquiry.

At one level, Wang Yangming's serenity could be seen as resulting from his contemplative practices, which—as he claimed—had led him to a place free of personal consideration, while his passionate involvement could be seen as his according, as a result of his spiritual attainments, with the Way, what is called "the sage's feelings accord with creation and yet he has no feelings of his own." In this sense, Wang's feelings about the events surrounding the princely rebellion were not personal highs and lows related to the dramatic moments of the campaign, but were rather feelings in harmony with principles at a higher level. It is thus not surprising that he told Zou Shouyi that he remained deeply troubled from the moment he had heard of the rebellion till its conclusion.[98] Likewise, according to one story, when he was stationed at his military headquarters in Nanchang during the battles with Zhu Chenhao's forces, Wang received a report stating that the prince had been defeated. Although those around him were excited by the news, the grand coordinator is said not to have shared their joy. On the contrary, when asked why he appeared so unexcited, he stated, "When I heard the Prince of Ning was captured I did not believe this to be untrue; it was just that those injured and killed were many."[99] Finally, Qian Dehong notes that when Wang received news that the emperor's imperial entourage had finally returned to the palace in Beijing, "he only then began to feel relieved of his worries."[100]

On another level, the apparent contradiction between serene detachment and deep concern and emotion may indeed be nothing more than a matter of

---

98   Feng, "Huang Ming da ru Wang Yangming," 177.
99   *NP*, 34:1267.
100   Ibid., 34:1278.

what Lin Jiping calls "contributing to worldly causes with the attitude [that one] is beyond the world."[101] This was in fact a theme invoked by Wang when he compared Buddhists to Confucians so as to highlight what made Confucians unique:

> The Buddhists are afraid of the burden of the relationship between father and son and therefore escape from it. They are afraid of the relationship between ruler and minister and therefore escape from it.... In all cases, because the relationships between ruler and minister, father and son, involve attachment to phenomena, they have to escape from them. We Confucians accept the relationship between father and son and fulfill it with the humanity it deserves. We accept the relationship between ruler and minister and fulfill it with the righteousness it deserves... When have we been attached to these relations?[102]

However, anecdotal accounts suggest Wang's seemingly koan-like reading of the paradoxical union of transcendent non-attachment and worldly engagement is not to be taken at face value. As explained further in the next section, throughout this time Wang Yangming was concerned about his father's health and repeatedly petitioned to return home to visit him. After the campaign, Wang received news that his father's condition had become grave and hence wished to depart immediately. But having later received another report of improvement, he chose to remain. With regard to his conduct, he once inquired of his students, "When I wished to return home, why did not any of you encourage me to do so?" To this a student replied, "Master's one thought of returning home appears to be [an instance] of attachment to phenomena." But Wang called into question his student's lack of dialectical imagination, stating, "How could I not but be attached to this phenomena?"[103]

Does the same dialectic regarding Wang Yangming's single-minded thought of his father—a clear instance of the operation of the innate knowledge of the good—apply to his single-minded thought of coming to the rescue of his endangered emperor and country? I here again refer to the record by Wang Ji, where his master is said to have stated that his response to the rebellion, his

---

101 Lin Jiping 林繼平, *Wang xue tan wei shi jiang* 王學談微十講 [Discussing Subtle Dimensions of Wang's learning: Ten Lectures] (Taipei: Lantai chubanshe, 2002), 185.

102 Wang, *Instructions for Practical Living*, 205. Of course, this is Wang Yangming's characterization of Buddhists, and it is probably best understood as serving a rhetorical purpose rather than as an accurate description.

103 *NP*, 34:1277.

call to action, was "nothing more than, at one moment, the innate knowledge of the good responding to the occasion," and the outcome of one subtle thought "confronting the opportune moment and spiritually responding." And although the thought drifted along like a cloud in the sky, so confident was Wang Yangming in the validity of this knowledge that he concluded, "There is no place amidst Heaven and Earth to which one could flee in order to escape this righteous cause. Even should all under Heaven choose to follow the Prince of Ning I would still, though all alone, act precisely in this way. All people have this innate knowledge of the good, so how could it be that there will be no others who will respond to the call and come?"[104]

Seemingly beyond the world and yet at the same time very much in it—perhaps this is the greatest paradox of all. Somehow innate knowledge of the good tipped Wang Yangming's leaning towards being present in that world, drawing him deeply into a commitment to the whole Confucian project of political life and personal transformation. It is perhaps here that we find a rather mysterious clue as to just how Wang Yangming's campaign against the prince ever got off the ground in the first place.

Kingliness Without

During those roughly two years Wang Yangming spent in Jiangxi as grand coordinator after having captured the rebel prince, he also dealt with other official matters. How he handled these matters gives us further insight into his moral compass and, therefore, into the meaning of innate knowledge of the good. For him this meant, according to Julia Ching, "simply the great principle, to do always in one's life what one's mind-and-heart says is right and good."[105] She further explains how this practice evolves: "Throughout his life, a man's effort to cultivate virtue is to consist only of one task. From youth to old age, from dawn to dusk, he has only to extend his *liangzhi* in response to things and affairs and circumstances as they arise, and so to render his *xin* [mind-heart] ever more sincere and transparent, open to life and its challenges, to the calls of responsibility which bind him to others in a society which is fundamentally a moral order."[106]

Indeed, this is the very call which rings throughout Wang Yangming's official career as well as his political vision as a whole, and yet Ching rightly raises the

---

104   Wang, "Du xian shi zai bao Hai Riweng Ji'an qi bing shu xu," 41:1600.
105   Ching, *To Acquire Wisdom*, 115.
106   Ibid., 120.

point that "he says remarkably little about how it is to be extended and realized."[107] However, it is possible to reply to this conundrum. Through further analysis of Wang Yangming's political praxis, we gain insight into how innate knowledge of the good is to be extended in a society that is fundamentally a moral order, an order to which all are called in responsibility by the promptings of the self-transcending mind-heart.

Loyal Official

After he was blocked from access to the emperor by Zhang Zhong and Xu Tai early in 1520, Wang Yangming returned to Nanchang, where he would remain until he journeyed downriver to southern Jiangxi during the summer. While in the provincial capital, he was preoccupied with restoring order and reviving the livelihood of the region in the wake of the havoc wreaked not only by the Prince of Ning, but also by ongoing banditry and inclement weather.[108] To this end, he petitioned to have the province exempted from grain taxation, sought to bring tax relief to the region by redistributing land and other assets confiscated by the prince, and ordered officials to pursue remnant brigands and implement the household registration system for the purpose of shoring up local security.[109]

However, in addition to these relief measures, on May 31, 1520, Wang composed a self-impeachment memorial, indicting himself for poor performance as an official. The occasion for this was a massive flood in Jiangxi during the previous month and the resulting widespread devastation and suffering. According to his *Chronological Biography*, "At the time Wuzong was yet residing at the southern capital, so [Wang Yangming], unable to remonstrate, chose for the time being to describe the unusual disaster in the region and impeach himself because of it, in the hopes that the mind and heart of the emperor would be awakened and he would turn his attention to the people."[110]

Wang's tactic was interesting if not somewhat unconventional. More routinely, owing to an entrenched belief in resonances between the universe and political order, an official might call on the emperor to examine himself on the occasion of cosmic irregularities. The emperor should then accept blame as necessary and release edicts with policies designed to ameliorate suffering. This political notion that the emperor is ultimately responsible for what befalls all under Heaven is an ancient one. According to Zhang Fentian, "'Taking the

---

107 Ibid., 115.
108 *WYMQJ*, vol. 1, 13:429.
109 The series of communications addressing these matters are in *WYMQJ*, vol. 2, 31: 1151–54.
110 *NP*, 34:1272.

blame (*zui ji* 罪己) [for misgovernment and natural disasters]' became a type of important cultural concept for evaluating the emperor-king."[111] He further explains that "'[the story of how the sage-kings] Yu and Tang accepted blame as opposed to how Jie and Zhou blamed others reflects this kind of notion regarding the emperor-king and the discourse on the Way of the ruler: since the emperor is omni-competent in his authority, he should accept complete responsibility; because the emperor-king exercises absolute authority, he should accept absolute responsibility."[112]

Wang Yangming was well aware of historical precedents where emperors released edicts accepting blame for problems arising in their empires. Two were cited in the memorial he dispatched to the emperor during the initial phases of the rebellion, when he called for Wuzong to inspire heroism by reproaching himself and changing course.[113] On this occasion, however, he applied the same logic to himself, apparently hoping that through an emotionally powerful, exemplary demonstration of this political practice, Wuzong's conscience would be awakened and he would consequently take action:

> Because your servitor has no ability, he was mistakenly entrusted with the office of the grand coordinator of Jiangxi. For several months up to the present, I have been unable even once to implement administrative measures beneficial to the people. And because with each passing day the region suffers more calamities, the people's hardship worsens daily and they are increasingly impoverished with each new day. Natural disasters occur daily and calamities burden them daily. From spring to early summer rain has fallen continuously. For months the rivers and lakes have been overflowing and swelling without receding.... As for all those [Jiangxi] prefectures along the [Gan and Yangtze] rivers, there are none that haven't been damaged. Sprouts have been drowned, and houses and huts are floating about on the water. The residents of Yubiao have gathered and are perched atop trees, merchants' and travelers' vessels are passing through the alleyways, and [city] walls are collapsing and boundaries have been breached. A thousand miles [of land] have become like a ravine, smoke has been extinguished, and only the sound of wailing is heard. Inquiring among elders, they all claim that there has been nothing

---

111   Zhang, *Zhongguo de di wang guannian*, 647.

112   Ibid., 648. According to traditional Chinese historical accounts, Yu and Tang are model rulers from the Xia and Shang Dynasties, while Jie and Zhou are their antithesis dating from those same dynasties.

113   *WYMQJ*, vol. 1, 12:396.

like this for several decades. All provincial, prefectural, subprefectural, and county officials have been ordered to rectify themselves and engage in introspection, survey their respective territories, and memorialize. In addition, because calamities don't come from out of nowhere, and are rather the result of governance; because governance is not by nature corrupt but rather so as a result of officials; and because official incompetence in fact begins with me, how can I avoid blame? ... Quietly reflecting upon this, this servitor's crimes are indeed many! What are these? When Chenhao rebelled, your servitor was residing on the frontier and unable to contain the problem before it arose. Thus, violence suddenly broke out, startling and alarming those near and far, and troubling the emperor into having to lead a punitive expedition. Armies terrorized the countryside and the people were endangered along the routes. Consequently, the commands of the court have been obstructed, and everywhere hardship and fatigue have increased daily. This constitutes your servitor's first great crime. Merely in order to avoid incurring displeasure over appearances, I carelessly planned only for my self-preservation, and indirectly condoned and looked on from the sidelines, hoping that with some luck [I might] escape calamity. My being incapable of speaking frankly and remonstrate forcefully in order to make the emperor understand—this constitutes your servitor's second great crime. Counting currying favor and chiming in with the crowd as loyalty, I fail to realize that every day I fall deeper into error. Expediently taking and leaving office and pandering, I don't realize that with each passing day I bring more disorder to long-established laws and institutions. Mistaking cleaning up messes and bringing false charges against others as ability, I remain unaware that I have day after day further departed from the minds and hearts of all under Heaven. And merely taking gathering taxes and pursuing levies as good planning, [I] don't realize that the grievances of the people accumulate daily. This is my third great crime. On a higher level unable to be of benefit to the country, and on a lower level unable to help the people, I just sit and look upon the dire hardship, as [the people] drown in it. This is my fourth great crime. ... Should an official be guilty of just one of these four great crimes, this is sufficient to summon a disaster and lead to an unexpected turn of events. But what if it is of all of [the crimes]? This is why the anger of Heaven and the gods has been incurred, the rage of the people deepened, to the point that portentous calamities have accumulated. What doubt can there be about this?[114]

---

114   Ibid., 7:431–32.

In conclusion, Wang Yangming expressed his wish that the emperor should both provide relief and select a competent official to replace him. But he also insisted that Wuzong make an example of him before officialdom and "all under Heaven," by executing him for his crimes. If the emperor was unwilling to do so, he should at least cashier him. In this way, Wang explained, "those in positions of power will be warned, the hardships of the people brought to rest, the people's anger vented, and Heavenly-induced disasters quelled." "Even should I die," he proclaimed, "it will be without regret."[115]

Certainly, given the fact that this emperor had behaved so abominably— according to Wang's standards—during his fifteen years on the throne, it is difficult to fathom why Wang Yangming would have seen any point in submitting this appeal to the emperor's conscience. It may be the case that he deliberately intended a degree of bitterness and sarcasm. Nevertheless, we also catch a glimpse of the political implication of extending the innate knowledge of the good, or what he otherwise refers to as "clarifying bright virtue and loving the people (ming de qin min 明德親民)."[116] We catch a glimpse of his sense of responsibility for the people he was charged to govern, and of the conscience of an official standing before his own, Heaven's, and the people's moral compass. Such, ultimately, were the standards to which Wang Yangming held both the emperor and officialdom, as he placed the onus on virtue, the overriding prerequisite for justice and, therefore, for a better world.

Filial Son

After having done so several times in prior years for similar reasons, between 1519 and 1521 Wang Yangming submitted five memorials to the court requesting leave to visit his ailing father and reinter his deceased grandmother. The first was written early in 1519 after the conclusion to the campaigns on the bandits in southern Jiangxi, but was denied because the Minister of War Wang Qiong sensed the impending threat posed by the Prince of Ning. In the second, dated July 17, 1519, he requested permission to stop over while en route to Fujian for the purpose of managing unrest in a military unit.[117] Naturally, Wang dropped this plan when he learned of the prince's rebellion. The third request, dated September 18, 1519, was dispatched just prior to his escorting the captured prince to the emperor's provisional palace, but was denied because he was needed in the region to manage ongoing banditry in the aftermath of the

---

115   Ibid., 7:432.
116   This interpretation of the innate knowledge of the good is found in his *Inquiry on the Great Learning (Da xue wen* 大學問). See *WYMQJ*, vol. 2, 26:969.
117   *WYMQJ*, vol. 1, 12:394.

rebellion.[118] The fourth request, dated October 1, 1520, was composed while he was in southern Jiangxi attending to official duties as grand coordinator and holding discussions with students,[119] while the last was written in July 1521. Throughout this series of memorials, Wang Yangming's pleas became increasingly impassioned, reaching the point where he decided to inform the court that, should his request not be approved, he would depart without regard for the consequences.

The last two petitions are particularly helpful for understanding his justification. In the one composed while residing in southern Jiangxi, he took care to explain why his intention was not to use this visit as a pretext to evade official duties and pursue a life of solitude. Rather, since he had already conscientiously carried out his responsibilities and settled affairs in the region, he merely wished that the court should honor his request to temporarily return and see his aging and critically ill father. Not to do so, he informed them, would be to "harm the mind-heart of the filial son":

> The suffering of your servitor cuts to the bone and gouges out the heart. Serious illness has overtaken me, and death has become my neighbor. This, however, is not even worth discussing. My father's health worsens daily from serious illness. While bedridden, he chants, thinking of seeing me just once, wailing day and night. Each time I receive a letter from home, I cry out in grief, pass out and collapse, one moment regaining consciousness and the next losing it. Even beasts as wicked as tigers and wolves yet know of the bond between father and son, and such small birds as the crow yet cherish thoughts of returning to nurture their parents. Today my father's illness has reached this critical state, and he only desires to see me return just once. Yet this official is reluctant to part from his covetous desire for official rank, and unable decisively to flee and return home. This does not even measure up to the standards of the birds and beasts, so how [dare I] stand between Heaven and Earth? The greatest of ethical relationships for a human being are, privately, that between father and son and, publicly, that between official and ruler. The ruler is to be served conscientiously and the father filially; not to be conscientious and filial is the greatest shame under Heaven. Even should I be fortunate enough to escape [punishment according to] the laws of the country, I am still more shameful than a beast, and it would be better to die rather than live.... Prior, during the rebellion at the Ning Princely

---

118   Ibid., 12:414.
119   Ibid., 13:436–37.

Establishment, I desired to return home to visit my father in his time of illness. But there was urgent danger to the country, and in the moment required for just one breath, preservation or destruction could not be determined. Thus, I abandoned nine generations to possible execution, sacrificing my life for the preservation of the dynasty. At the time, what was in principle of greater importance was the rightness of relations between ruler and official. But now that the danger to the dynasty has been pacified, warfare has ceased. . . . When an official gives his life to rescue his ruler from danger he doesn't think twice about sacrificing nine generations to execution. And when [he] becomes deeply worried about endangerment to his father's life, he also risks execution without a second thought. At this time, should orders [granting my wish] again fail to arrive, then I will risk death and flee home.[120]

Although this second-to-last request was denied, Wang Yangming did wait for some time, for he would not return home for nearly a year. Perhaps he was receiving news that his father's health had stabilized and was therefore still holding out for official permission. But this was only to come after the Zhengde emperor had died—from an illness contracted from falling from his boat into the Grand Canal—and a new emperor had come to the throne: the Jiajing emperor, Wuzong's cousin, Zhu Houcong 朱厚熜 (r. 1521–1567, temple name Shizong). In recognition of Wang Yangming's achievements, Shizong sent an imperial edict requesting his presence in the capital for appointment to a potentially prestigious position. In his reply memorial, Wang informed the emperor that he was already en route to Beijing, having departed on July 23, and that he intended to pass through his hometown and visit his father along the way.[121]

In this last memorial, written in late July 1521, while en route, Wang explained that uppermost in his mind was his desire to balance his determination to visit his ill father with his wish to respond immediately to the newly enthroned Jiajing emperor's gracious summons. He suggested that in the past there really was no such moral conflict because he was suffering attacks from imperial favorites and simply desired to flee politics. But now that his sovereign was showing such promise for bringing about a renaissance and had furthermore redressed the wrong done to him by removing his predecessor's circle of favorites from power:

---

120   Ibid., 13:438.
121   Ibid., 13:451.

How could I not wish to depart in the morning and arrive in the evening? ... But my father is both old and ill.... Furthermore, the love between father and son derives from the nature bestowed by Heaven (*tian xing* 天性), and is only further intensified by the suffering that comes with thinking of each other during years of separation. Thus, my risking committing a crime in order to return home during this journey of mine is what must be the case, given moral sentiment and principle. On the one hand, however, if I don't openly petition for this from the court and just depart secretly on my own authority, this would be to deceive the emperor. On the other, if out of fear over incurring shame for delaying [responding to the summons], I allow feelings for the one who gave me life to be severed, this would be to forget one's father. To deceive the emperor is disloyal; to forget one's father is unfilial. It is true that in this world there has never been one who is unfilial towards his father and yet able to be loyal to his ruler. Thus I risk committing crime and therefore send this petition.[122]

For Wang Yangming, the innate knowledge of the good is the principle of Heaven (*tian li* 天理) naturally revealing itself to awareness, and to extend the innate knowledge of the good is to unify knowledge and action. So we here see his philosophy brought to life, its emotional import. There can be no doubt that Wang Yangming was both a devoted son and a loyal official. His feelings in this regard were deep and of great personal importance to him because they served as confirmation of those moral intuitions that he believed to be innate and that went to the heart of his philosophical vision. It was indeed these moral sentiments (*qing* 情) arising from nature (*xing* 性) that defined justice. Ironically, however, he never would have to honor the call of his ruler, for while en route he was forced by court politics to return home, thus in the end having his request fulfilled under unexpected circumstances.

Rewarding his Comrades at Arms

Even with the seemingly hopeful transition from Wuzong to Shizong, fallout from the campaign against the Prince of Ning and its aftermath continued to plague Wang Yangming. After the Zhengde emperor had fallen ill and then passed away on April 19, 1521, Chief Grand Secretary Yang Tinghe engineered a housecleaning at court and managed to have this cousin to the deceased ruler designated as heir to the throne. Up to this point, although some of Wang Yangming's subordinate commanders had received minor promotions, delibera-

---

tions on the proper recognition for him had not yet taken place. But the future Jiajing emperor had been aware of the grand coordinator's meritorious service. Hence, upon ascending the throne, he summoned him to the capital for the purpose of conferring honors and high office.[123] The imperial command, which arrived on July 15, 1521, stated, "Formerly, you succeeded in attacking and pacifying the rebel-bandits and bringing peace to the region. At this time when a new reign is poised to commence, it is appropriate to summon you for appointment. When the imperial command arrives, you should come quickly along the courier routes."[124] But although Wang departed for the capital four days later, he never did have the opportunity to hold an audience with or serve as a high official for the newly enthroned emperor, for whom he held such high hopes.

The reason for this must be traced to the actions of Chief Grand Secretary Yang Tinghe and thereafter to other mostly unnamed high officials who were jealous of the grand coordinator. By all accounts, the powerful grand secretary resented the fact that, every time Wang memorialized regarding his victories, he attributed much of the credit for his success to the foresight of one of Yang's political adversaries, the Minister of War Wang Qiong, while never mentioning the role of the grand secretary.[125] He thus provided a pretext for those seeking the favor of the grand secretary to attack him. As a result, Yang and possibly other officials close to the emperor instructed remonstrating officials to submit memorials arguing that, because expenses were manifold in a time of national mourning, it was inappropriate to hold banquets and dispense rewards.[126] For this reason, Wang turned back while on his way to Beijing, and although he received the supernumerary post of Nanjing minister of war, he returned to Zhejiang, thereafter remaining in retirement in his hometown for six years.

Later that year, however, at the urging of the Ministry of War, this issue of recognition and rewards was raised again, and the emperor ordered officials to deliberate. The outcome was an imperial decree bestowing a number of honors on Wang, the most important of which was the noble title Earl of Xinjian 新建伯. In addition, he was to receive the prestige title Grand Master for

123   *MTJ*, 49:1523.

124   Huang, "Shi de ji," in *WYMQJ*, vol. 1, 38:1424.

125   Wang Shizhen 王世貞, "Xinjian bo Wang Wencheng gong Shouren zhuan 新建伯王文成公守仁傳 [Biography of the Earl of Xinjian Sir Wang Wencheng Shouren]," in *Guo chao xian zheng lu* 國朝獻徵錄, ed. Jiao Hong 焦竑, in *Mingdai zhuanji congkan* 明代傳記叢刊, ed. Zhou Junfu, vol. 109 (Ming wen shuju, 1991), 109:323.

126   Huang, "Shi de ji," in *WYMQJ*, vol. 2, 38:1424.

Splendid Happiness, the merit title Pillar of State, a yearly disbursement of grain, and a patent by command. These were all to be inherited by his descendants.[127] A runner was dispatched with the decree and rewards, and arrived at his home on January 6, 1522, at the very moment that he was celebrating his father's birthday.

However, far from being pleased, in the first of two memorials declining all recognition, Wang Yangming informed the court that "when I heard these commands I was alarmed and at a loss as to how to proceed."[128] The burning issue for him was the fact that those who served under him had received no recognition; indeed, the most prominent officials had been variously demoted, cashiered, or reduced to commoner status.[129] One reason for this was the enmity he had earned from Yang Tinghe, but also important was how his rising status—as measured by the recognition he had received for his military accomplishments and by the swelling numbers of students intrigued by his unorthodox doctrines—was incurring the displeasure and envy of powerful officials. Indeed, according to Huang Wan, Wang's subordinates' achievements were being suppressed and volumes recording their merit revised at the very time that "remonstrating officials pandered to the interests of those in power and impeached him for false learning."[130]

Although he twice attempted to decline the honors, all but the grain and patent by command were bestowed. His arguments before the court once again bring to focus Wang Yangming's overriding concern with justice, his conviction that everyone must receive their due according to their contributions to society. In his first memorial, dated February 6, 1522, he enumerated four reasons why he dared not accept any such titles. Firstly, he explained that the Prince of Ning's plot had developed over ten years and yet, amazingly enough, was defeated within a month. This was something "that could not have come about through human effort alone."[131] Rather, the credit here went to the will of Heaven, which "hates disorder and thinks of order, and was to awaken a sagely emperor, to bring about a renaissance and great peace. Thus, his plot was foiled and his spirit snatched away." Hence, he humbly asserted that "should your loyal servitor wish rashly to receive this [honor], this would amount to taking the credit for the meritorious achievement of Heaven."[132]

127 Ibid.
128 *WYMQJ*, vol. 1, 13:453.
129 Huang, "Shi de ji," in *WYMQJ*, vol. 1, 38:1424.
130 Ibid.
131 *WYMQJ*, vol. 1, 13:453.
132 Ibid.

Two additional reasons concerned his superiors and subordinates, those at court who had made advance preparations for the rebellion by giving him broad discretionary powers, and those officials in Jiangxi who had served him during the military campaigns. For him to accept honors when others weren't receiving recognition would be to "conceal others' good" and snatch away credit due to them.[133] Finally, he stated in no uncertain terms that judging from his health and the degree of competence with which he carried out his duties, he deserved no recognition whatsoever.[134]

Wang concluded this list with his overall judgment, which I believe gives us a great deal of insight into what for him counted as manifestly unjust and therefore positively evil:

> As for calamities, there is none greater than undeservedly receiving the credit for Heaven's meritorious achievement; as for crimes, there is none more serious than concealing the good done by others; as for evil, there is none deeper than stealing credit for the competence of subordinates; and as for humiliation, there is none greater than forgetting one's sense of shame. When these four are taken together the calamity is complete, and therefore this official dares not accept this title.[135]

For Wang Yangming any of the above actions could only have derived from the false self in pursuit of prestige and profit (*gong li zhi xin* 功利之心), something the political order should never recognize, for this would be to foster vice and therefore to further worsen the darkened state into which the imperium had fallen.

Further, he stated that if he were to receive rewards when others hadn't, the result could only be "all under Heaven becoming resentful over an unjust distribution of desert (*bu jun* 不均)."[136] Here, as was the case with his attribution of success to Heaven, we find that Wang Yangming believed himself to be living in a cosmos and social order embodying notions of moral order whose violation would result in retribution, both from above and below. He did not live in a disenchanted universe. Rather, the cosmos was pregnant with forces upholding the deeper notions for normative social and political order that he held to be so sacred, and which were commonly shared by the good sense of

---

133   Ibid.
134   Ibid., 13:454.
135   Ibid.
136   Ibid., 13:456.

others like himself. The institutions of the empire were simply to chime in with, if not assist in, the fulfillment of these norms.

On the other hand, in a memorial entitled "Declining Conferral of the Title of Nobility and Broadly Bestowing Generous Rewards In Order To Make Manifest to All the Institutions of the Dynasty," he does provide positive reasons why honors must be justly distributed. In addition to pointing out that the ancients always bestowed rewards in timely fashion in order "to quickly requite good works," he also explained that the goal was not only fairness but also to "arouse and raise the ethos of scholar-officials," "invigorate the spirit of scholar-officials,"[137] and "encourage demonstrations of loyalty through participating in righteous causes (效忠赴義)."[138] As he had already stated on so many occasions, this was the reason why laws for rewards and punishments had to be clarified. Promoting excellence in some members of the community benefits the community as a whole. More generally, fostering those virtues innate to human nature was essential to the purposes of governance and, given a new emperor on the throne showing such promise, this was an excellent time to do so.

In addition to explaining why he himself must not be rewarded, Wang Yangming also vividly portrayed the appalling disparity between, on the one hand, the great virtue exemplified by the conduct of his subordinates and, on the other, their treatment at the hands of the court. Firstly, he explained that regardless of their past behavior and reputations, "they all possess the achievement of demonstrating loyalty by giving their lives in service and uniting their efforts to save the emperor, what is referred to as one group sharing the same praiseworthy accomplishment."[139] Secondly, their conduct must be understood in context:

> At the time [of the rebellion], should it have been the case that these prefectural and county officials merely harbored a fear of death and a desire to survive, given the fact that there were no imperial orders, each of them could have used this as a pretext for protecting only their respective jurisdictions. What could I have done? Nevertheless, hearing my call for mobilization, they all, out of a sense of indebtedness [to the emperor], became enthusiastic and spirited, some raising troops and arriving, some standing up and coming forthwith. This being the case, should they really not have had the intention of giving their lives in

---

137   Ibid., 13:456–57.
138   Ibid., 13:455.
139   Ibid., 13:454.

service to their endangered ruler and of requiting their ruler through a concerted demonstration of loyalty, why would they have been willing to commit themselves to a calamity that could only result in their bones being ground to dust and the extermination of their lineage? Or why, out of hope for a one in ten thousand chance that they would receive meritorious recognition, tread on deadly ground? Therefore, all who served together with this official are truly sincere in their loyalty and righteousness.[140]

Thus, it was only fair that they should be given full recognition, for "if those below, in response to the call for the righteous, risk dangers over which they would surely lose their lives, then those above, in order to requite them for meritorious achievement, should bestow rewards upon them."[141] The institutions of the state were to promote action motivated by loyalty, loyalty buttressed by sentiments of gratitude, by rewarding with a fostering benevolence from above. In this way, the state would be able to circulate moral awareness through the political body, which was ultimately the key to recovering order.

Conclusion

In his lifetime, Wang Yangming never saw most who served him receive the recognition he felt they deserved. As for him, the title of nobility and other honors he received were most unwelcome, and indeed there is little evidence to suggest he had much desire to serve at the Ming court. Between his poor health, his wish to spend time with his father, and his love for teaching while in retirement, he had many good reasons not to be disappointed that he was turned back while en route to Beijing and his petition to visit his father was unexpectedly approved. In September 1521 he returned to his home in the city of Yue, Shaoxing Prefecture, and would thereafter spend time here and traveling to his ancestral and childhood home in the neighboring county of Yuyao. Should he have had any intention of taking office in Nanjing, he did not do so, likely because his father passed away the following spring. He thus began to observe a period of mourning.

In any case, it was looking less and less likely that Wang Yangming would be appointed to serve the newly enthroned Shizong. There were a number of reasons for this, and they all seemed to converge in 1522 and 1523, at the very time

---

140   Ibid., 13:456.
141   Ibid.

he was in mourning. Although Chief Grand Secretary Yang Tinghe managed to have those men who slandered Wang and sought to steal the credit for his victory removed from power, as well as to restore a sense of normalcy to the Ming court during the interim, he also engaged in vendettas with officials who displeased or opposed him. That included Minister of War Wang Qiong, who may have been poised to move into the grand secretariat. Yang directed men in his faction to frame Wang Qiong for collaboration with the treacherous eunuchs and military men he had just removed from power, bringing upon him a death sentence.[142] But although this sentence was commuted to exile to a border garrison, given his ties with Wang Yangming, the accusations would only have made the many rumors about Wang look even more plausible. And the Ming court, with Chief Grand Secretary Yang at the helm, did nothing to dampen these, because he and other powerful officials effectively did not want Wang working alongside them.

Apparently, the grand secretary had willing assistance from other Ming officials early on because some were leery of Wang's rising fame, as well as the growing popularity of his unorthodox teachings. According to Wang Shizhen:

> Those envious of him rose in a swarm, viewing him as a teacher of false doctrines. They also stated that when he occupied Nanchang he permitted his officers to plunder and take gold, valuables, and children from the Ning mansions. Some even stated that he had colluded with [Prince Zhu] Chenhao in the plot but later broke with him, violating their agreement. What was said was extremely ugly and unbearable to hear.[143]

Some of these rumors even found their way into the *Veritable Records* for Wuzong's reign, compilation of which began late in 1521 under the direction of Yang Tinghe. In the entries concerning Wang's suppression of the prince's rebellion, we find it alleged that he had no intention of attacking Nanchang until convinced to do so by Prefect Wu Wending. Wu supposedly engineered the occupation of Nanchang, only to be followed by the grand coordinator, who staged a leisurely entrance while ringing bells. Furthermore, upon entering the city, Wang purportedly allowed his soldiers—former bandits whom he had reformed—to rapaciously plunder the city: "Residents died in great numbers on their beds.... The stench of corpses filled the streets." [144]

---

142   *MSLWZSL*, Zhengde 14/7/20 正德十四年秋七月辛亥 (August 14, 1519) entry.

143   Wang, "Xinjian bo Wang Wencheng gong Shouren zhuan," 109:320.

144   *MS*, 198:5231.

Most of these rumors came to a head in 1522 when a censor and secretary of scrutiny, doing the bidding of the powerful grand secretary, submitted a memorial calling for a thorough investigation of Wang Yangming, as well as for his impeachment. By far the most damaging accusation was their claim that the prince had sent a letter to his accomplice, the Minister of War Lu Wan, calling for the removal of Grand Coordinator Sun Sui and replacing him with some other named individuals more favorably disposed towards him, including Wang Yangming. This letter had supposedly fallen into the hands of a local magistrate in Jiangxi, who reported this matter to them. On the grounds of this at best selectively quoted letter, these officials charged that Wang had secretly collaborated with the prince only to then seek laurels. Consequently, he was mistakenly awarded the title of nobility for what only appeared to be a stunning victory.[145]

A record of this preposterous memorial was conveniently retained in the *Veritable Records*, but it is from a memorial penned by a student of Wang Yangming that we learn of just how many rumors were afoot. In a heated defense, Lu Cheng 陸澄 showed up the absurdity of several claims about his teacher: that a letter from Chenhao stating that he is "also okay" implied collusion; that his sending one of his students to lecture to the prince also implied collusion; that he was planning to visit the prince to offer congratulations on the occasion of his birthday; that he only mobilized troops to attack the prince because he was urged to do so by other officials; that when he occupied Nanchang, his soldiers wantonly burned and plundered; that his defeating the prince was something any magistrate could easily have accomplished; and lastly, that his victory memorial thoroughly exaggerated what he had achieved.[146]

Other memorials both defending and attacking Wang Yangming followed, but the emperor halted the controversy and any further deliberation. "As soon as Shouren heard of the rebellion by Chenhao," Shizong advised, "he adhered to justice, raised an army, and prevented a huge disaster. To reward him for his great and worthy achievement, he was specially honored with a title of nobility. There is no need for further deliberation."[147] Wang also avoided becoming further embroiled in controversy, instructing his student Lu to desist from defending him. His letter to Lu reveals that a central reason for the efforts to defame him was the apparent cause célèbre caused by what for many literati seemed like blatantly unorthodox teachings. "Can we possibly win all these debates?" he asked his student. Rather, here was an opportunity for learning

---

145   *MSLSZSL*, Jiajing 1/9/3 嘉靖元年九月丙午 (September 9, 1522) entry.
146   Lu Cheng 陸澄, "Bian zhong chan yi ding guo shi shu," in *WYMQJ*, vol. 2, 39:1458.
147   *MSLSZSL*, Jiajing 1/9/3 嘉靖元年九月丙午 (September 9, 1522) entry.

how to maintain composure: "One should engage in introspection, and if what they are saying has some merit to it, and I am not completely confident of my own position, then I should seek to understand theirs, as opposed to merely adhering to my own convictions and negating others. If what they have to say is wrong, and I am fully confident in my own position, then I should demonstrate the soundness of what I know in my actions, basing my effort on humility."[148]

In a calculated gesture of just such humility, Wang proposed that these men may really mean him no personal harm and have many good reasons for their actions. Having blamed himself for the swarming criticism and warned his students that they must first take note of the logs in their own eyes, he stated confidently, "The noble men of former times, even should the whole world oppose them, they would not heed it, or a thousand generations oppose them, they would not heed it, but only seek the truth and that is all. How could the praise and blame of one moment suffice to change their minds? However, if I have not fully clarified things for myself, how could I then say that what others allege is altogether false?"[149]

In concluding his discourse on the virtue of fearless humility, Wang linked it to his now principal doctrine of the extension of the innate knowledge of the good and his long-espoused belief that theory and praxis must be unified:

> Mencius states, "The mind of right and wrong is knowledge." "All have the mind of right and wrong." This is what is referred to as innate knowledge of the good (*liangzhi*). Who lacks this knowledge? It is only that they are unable to extend it. The *Classic of Change* states, "Knowledge arrives, apply it." Knowledge arriving is knowledge [innate knowledge of the good]; applying this knowledge is the extension of the innate knowledge of the good. This is why knowledge and action are unified.[150]

Yet, for Wang Yangming, between *liangzhi* and action there were a number of intervening principles and considerations that required a considerable amount of reflection and weighing. None of these can really be considered apart from the historical situatedness in which he "extended" or "acted." We need not accept at face value his claim that *liangzhi* by its own nature discriminates right and wrong. Among these intervening factors we have seen that, with regard to punishments, political conditions being what they were in a time of decline,

---

148   *WYMQJ*, vol. 1, 5:188.
149   Ibid., 5:189.
150   Ibid.

the ideal of reform had to be weighed against the need for deterrence. More-over, in some cases the measure of evil of some individuals was so great that, in order to accord with the order of things, retribution was necessary. Indeed, in addition to elaborating upon virtues suited to the political conditions of the time, Wang constantly drew attention to considerations such as public senti-ment and the need to balance principle and circumstances. That is why pru-dent compromise may have to prevail over rigid adherence to principle. This goes a long way, for instance, towards explaining why he chose to hand the prince over to the eunuch Zhang Yong and later took Yang Yiqing's advice that he drop his plans to speak before the emperor and return to Jiangxi. It also sheds light on why he felt justified in manipulating people who potentially had power over him but whom he saw as misguided inferiors—for example, the Embroidered Uniform Guard, and Zhang Zhong and Xu Tai.

To be sure, all of these considerations were interpreted within the broader horizon of the normative Confucian social and political order as he saw it, and in light of his overarching interest in fostering the cultivation of virtue in a moral-political order so that the people living in it could lead a good and just life. These are the ethics and ends that are key to understanding his justice of merit and desert. They also key to understanding just how Wang Yangming, as an official, repeatedly went about the task of determining and assigning (good and bad, commendable and deplorable) motives to all those whom he was charged to govern and mobilized the institutions at hand to promote virtue and eliminate vice.

Benevolence on the Border

Until recent times, Western scholarship has interpreted military strategy and international relations in realist paradigms. Structural realism, or realpolitik, privileges an anarchic structure and accepts the premise that states are basically rational actors engaging in a competition for power, which explains why strategic thinking is largely tied to relative capabilities.[1] In recent decades, however, largely out of dissatisfaction with realism, military historians have adopted cultural approaches to account for the foreign and security policies of states.[2] This strategic cultural approach privileges the role that ideational variables play in determining strategy. According to Jack Snyder, strategic culture is "the body of attitudes and beliefs that guides and circumscribes thought on strategic questions, influences the way strategic issues are formulated, and sets the vocabulary and conceptual parameters of strategic debate."[3] Most fundamentally, these attitudes and beliefs—the result of unique historical circumstances and experiences—are held by elites within the security community, and heavily condition how they think about the use of force for political ends.

While this perspective constitutes a fresh take on Western military history, the strategic cultural approach has long been employed in interpreting its Chinese counterpart, seen specifically in the idea that Confucian elites were averse to militarism and inclined towards deterrence and pacifism. Early studies, such as the standard *Chinese Ways of Warfare*, stressed the role of the Confucian culture and ideology of the scholar-official class in fostering an aversion to force when resolving conflicts.[4] The preferred strategies for handling security threats were assumed to be diplomacy, accommodation, stratagem and maneuver, and achieving the voluntary submission of the enemy through moral suasion and cultural influence. According to Alistair Johnston, characteristics

---

1   Wang Yuangang, "Power Politics in Confucian China" (Ph.D. diss., University of Chicago, 2001),17.

2   John S. Duffield, "Political Culture and State Behavior: Why Germany Confounds Neo-Realism," *International Organization* 73, no. 4 (September 1999): 765.

3   Jack Snyder, *The Soviet Strategic Culture: Implications for Limited Nuclear Options* (Washington, D.C.: Rand, 1977), 9.

4   John K. Fairbank, "Varieties of Chinese Military Experience," in *Chinese Ways of Warfare*, ed. Edward L. Dreyer, John K. Fairbank, and Frank A. Klierman (Cambridge, MA: Harvard University Press, 1974), 1–24.

© KONINKLIJKE BRILL NV, LEIDEN, 2014 | DOI 10.1163/9789004280106_007

of this type of strategic culture include a theoretical and practical preference for strategic defense and limited warfare, and an apparently low estimation of the efficacy of violence.[5] The latter characteristic is exemplified by Sunzi's oft-cited proposition: "Not-fighting and subduing the enemy is the supreme level of skill."[6]

Nevertheless, more recently, other theorists have cast doubt on this interpretation, arguing for a complete reassessment of Chinese security behavior from imperial times to the present.[7] According to Swaine and Tellis, "Even though the pacifistic views of Confucius and Mencius as espoused by the practitioners of Confucian statecraft have at times influenced strategic decisions concerning whether, and to what degree, force should be employed, a cursory examination of the security behavior of the Chinese state suggests that Chinese rulers have frequently resorted to violence to attain their national security objectives. In fact, one could argue that the use of force has been endemic in Chinese history."[8] For these scholars, policies that appear to reflect antimilitarist cultural influences, such as static defense and accommodation, are rather to be explained as a response to the realities of the distribution of power between the dynasty and its adversaries.[9]

The most powerful attack on the supposed pacifist nature of Chinese strategic culture has come from Alastair Johnston. Through a careful study of the *Seven Military Classics* and Ming memorials addressing security on the northern border, he believes he has found a consistent Chinese strategic culture.[10] Elites involved in matters of security collectively shared grand strategic preferences deriving from central paradigmatic assumptions about the nature of conflict and the enemy, and these preferences and assumptions constituted a dominant strategic culture. However, Johnston sees a distinction between how security decisions were made and how operational strategy actually worked out in practice. He believes there is an immense disjuncture between the assumptions behind this operational strategy and the idealized Confucian-Mencian discourse in which it was often couched:

---

5   Alastair Iain Johnston, *Cultural Realism: Strategic Culture and Grand Strategy in Chinese History* (Princeton: Princeton University Press, 1995), 25.

6   Ibid., 93.

7   A good example of scholarship that questions this paradigm is the collection of articles in *Warfare in Chinese History*, ed. Hans van de Ven (Leiden: Brill, 2000).

8   Michael D. Swaine and Ashley J. Tellis, *Interpreting China's Grand Strategy: Past, Present, and Future* (Santa Monica: Rand, 2000), 46.

9   Wang, "Power Politics in Confucian China," 6.

10   Johnston, *Cultural Realism*, x.

I argue … that there is evidence of two Chinese strategic cultures, one a symbolized or idealized set of assumptions and ranked preferences, and one an operational set that had a nontrivial effect on strategic choice in the Ming period. The symbolic set, for the most part, is disconnected from the programmatic decision rules governing strategy, and appears mostly in a habitual discourse designed, in part, to justify behavior in culturally acceptable terms. The operational set reflects what I call a *parabellum* or realpolitik strategic culture that, in essence, argues that the best way of dealing with security threats is to eliminate them through the use of force.[11]

Johnston demonstrates that the dominance of this operational culture meant that the Ming dynasty was not only predisposed to violence towards its enemies but also acted more and more coercively towards them as relative capabilities became more favorable. In a slight theoretical twist, however, he prefers not to assume that this realpolitik can be considered the result of a-historical or a-cultural explanations such as system structure.[12] Rather, he believes that even realpolitik can be attributed to cultural assumptions, and therefore coined the term "cultural realism" to stress this conclusion. These assumptions include the enduring beliefs that warfare and conflict are relatively constant features of interstate affairs, that conflict with an enemy is zero-sum because enemies invariably have the worst intentions, and that violence is a highly efficacious means for dealing with conflict.[13]

Accordingly, there has been a necessary revision of earlier notions about the role of Confucian cultural norms in determining how the state behaved in matters of security. The idea that imperial China's scholar-official elites preferred policies of enculturation, of diminishing barbarian threats by spreading civil culture and displaying largesse, is trumped by the hard facts of strategic operational policy-making. Furthermore, as Arthur Waldron has demonstrated in his study of the history of the Great Wall, a Ming political culture of debilitating factionalism only further contributed to the dominance of what he terms "hardline" and "militant" attitudes towards the steppe peoples. He contrasts what he considered to be a generally successful and rational frontier policy of accommodation and strong defense with a culturally exclusivist "orthodox and righteous" approach that led to the erection of strict cultural boundaries and

---

11   Ibid.
12   Ibid., 28.
13   Ibid., 60.

frequent resort to offensive campaigns.[14] He considers those advocating the former to be a small intellectual constituency generally experienced in these matters and pragmatic in their outlook, whereas the latter were often playing a political game.[15] In this game, an uncompromising approach was smarter, politically speaking, because it "appealed to a broad constituency among the educated classes where philosophical ideas that rejected as demeaning any Chinese dealings with 'barbarians' were increasingly widespread."[16] In such a political environment, when an official advocated a policy of accommodation, he opened himself up to the charge of being an "appeaser."

However, just how the Confucian "symbolic" or ideological discourse should be appraised in light of this scholarship remains problematic, for most of it is specifically aimed at trouble at the northern border, where structural conditions—as Edward Dreyer and Frederick Mote have pointed out—were most suited to the invention of realpolitik.[17] Stark environmental and cultural differences created fertile ground for political and ethnic tensions along a border region that, historically speaking, had always endangered the integrity of the state. Accordingly, the strategic cultural assumptions regarding the use of force that Johnston highlights in this case cannot necessarily be taken as the norm for other situations of conflict. We might, for example, consider just what cultural factors conditioned how officials thought about violence when the conflict was, for example, a rebellion in loosely integrated frontier regions or border zones. Although establishment of control by the Ming state was, of course, always the end goal, both the definition of this goal and the means proposed to achieve it could vary considerably, leaving many unanswered questions. To what extent was "cultural realism"—those assumptions Johnston finds behind Chinese realpolitik—an outcome of the overwhelming pressure on officials to successfully control the territories under their jurisdiction, and to what extent does this pattern actually represent genuinely held beliefs and attitudes? Did officials generally prefer pragmatic accommodation and compromise, or were they more inclined to adopt a militant approach? Likewise, how did they go about legitimating their policy decisions and operational strategies? Would we too conclude that there is a disjuncture, as Johnston

---

14   Arthur Waldron, *The Great Wall of China: From History to Myth* (Cambridge: Cambridge University Press, 1990), 172–74.

15   Ibid., 109–10.

16   Ibid., 109.

17   Edward Dreyer, review of *Cultural Realism: Strategic Culture and Grand Strategy in Chinese History* by Alastair Iain Johnston, *The American Historical Review,* vol. 104, no. 2 (April 1999): 525–26; Mote, *Imperial China: 900–1800,* 702–703.

found, between an "idealized set of assumptions and ranked preferences"—
the garb of Confucian moral discourse—and the actual strategies employed,
with their underlying cultural assumptions?

To further complicate the picture, the strategic problems officials faced in
the South differed from those in the North.[18] Southern borders were not as
hard but were rather a fluid social environment with internal frontiers, where
the reach of the state was weak and dependent upon a variety of ad hoc political arrangements. When the state was confronted with security threats from
internal rebellions in these areas, these were frequently found to be led either
by disaffected Han residents and settlers, or by leaders of one of the many "barbarian" (*man yi* 蠻夷) populations with whom these diverse political arrangements had been struck. In such an environment, warfare could not so easily be
considered the best means for settling conflict, nor could the enemy be viewed
in simple zero-sum terms, as necessarily having only the worst intentions. In
the midst of these internal rebellions erupting on the periphery of the Chinese
state, where the setting was highly complex and ambiguous and the costs and
benefits of different courses of action were invariably uncertain, classically
trained scholar-officials were confronted with both practical dilemmas and
ethical issues that they could have more easily dismissed had they been dealing with aggressive external threats. The result during the Ming—as Geoffrey
Wade has so deftly summarized it in his overview of Chinese policies with regard to Southeast Asian states and to non-Chinese more generally in China's
Southwest—was a complex combination of military action, divide-and-rule
policies, intimidation through demands and threats, inducements by promises
of material and political rewards, enculturation through schools and examination, and use of non-Chinese to control other non-Chinese.[19]

---

18   For an overview of China's integration of southwestern regions into provinces, including
     secondary literature, see Mote, *Imperial China: 900–1800*, 702–717.
19   Geoffrey Wade, "The Ming Shi-lu (Veritable Records of the Ming Dynasty) as a Source for
     Southeast Asian History, 14th to 17th Centuries (Ph.D. diss., University of Hong Kong,
     1994), 172–206. Other more recent studies also include accounts of the management of
     uprisings and rebellions in specific southern or southwestern provinces and the complex
     array of attitudes and policies involved. For accounts of the expansion of Chinese admin-
     istration and strategies of imperial control for Guangxi, see Leo Shin, *The Making of the
     Chinese State: Ethnicity and Expansion on the Ming Borderlands* (Cambridge: Cambridge
     University Press, 2006); for Yunnan, see Bin Yang, *Between Winds and Clouds: The Making
     of Yunnan (Second Century BCE to Twentieth Century CE)* (New York: Columbia University
     Press, 2009), www.gutenberge-e.org/yang/index.html; and for Guizhou, see John Herman,
     Amid the Clouds and Mist: China's Colonization of Guizhou (Cambridge, MA: Harvard Uni-
     versity Press, 2007).

As we have seen, the rebellions Wang Yangming was assigned to manage throughout his career were internal ones in South China. The last two specifically involved non-Chinese in the southern province Guangxi, and they therefore provide enlightening case studies for addressing these very issues. In fact, his retirement in Zhejiang came to an abrupt end in 1527, when he was appointed supreme commander (*zongdu* 總督) and dispatched to Guangxi for the purpose of settling ongoing conflict between the Ming state and the native chieftaincies of Tianzhou 田州 and Sien 思恩. Prior to his arrival, the previous Supreme Commander Yao Mo 姚鏌 (js. 1493) had been pursuing a policy of subjugation, but Wang rapidly came to the conclusion that this approach was both ineffective and unjustified. Thus, he immediately sought to overturn Yao Mo's position by advocating a policy of accommodation, thereby bringing the conflict to a nonviolent conclusion. The documentation for this event is substantial enough to make it feasible—through the "interpretive lens of strategic culture"[20]—to delineate just how each of these supreme commanders defined the situation before him and why he chose the strategy he did, and thereby to interpret his moral reasoning.

To do so, some further definition of just how the term "culture" is being employed here is necessary to prevent terminological confusion. I propose to define culture as those shared background understandings providing the parameters within which strategic discourse is held, and through which strategic policy is legitimated. Because these understandings are constituted more specifically in the official discourse of political actors, this culture can be more narrowly confined to elite political culture. Above, strategic culture has been defined variously as "ideational influences," "attitudes and beliefs," and "preferences and assumptions." But political culture, defined as the semantic field of intersubjective meanings shared in common by a collectivity (in this case, scholar-official elites), conceptually comes even before all of these influences, beliefs and preferences. I am here drawing upon Jurgens Habermas's analysis of interpretive understanding in social inquiry. For him, social action depends on how the agent defines the situation, something that goes beyond personal motivations into the realm of intersubjective meanings—for example, institutionalized roles and social norms. These are the interpretive schema through which social action is mediated; in a sense, they establish the structure for, or constitute, social reality.[21]

---

20   Johnston, *Cultural Realism*, 1.

21   Jurgens Habermas, *Communication and the Evolution of Society*, trans. Thomas McCarthy (Boston: Beacon Press, 1979), xi.

Also helpful here is Charles Taylor's notion of the "social imaginary," which he defines as "that common understanding that makes possible common practices and a widely shared sense of legitimacy."[22] These are not just intellectual schemes but rather "the way people imagine their social existence, how they fit together, how things go on between them and their fellows, the expectations that are normally met, and the deeper normative notions and images that underlie these expectations."[23] These expectations include both a sense of how things usually go as well as an idea of how they ought to go, thereby providing a common understanding enabling the collective practices making up social life to be carried out.[24]

For Taylor, such social sense is formed within the horizon of a largely unstructured and unarticulated background understanding. It is within this horizon that particular features of our world show up for us with the meanings they have.[25] In this sense, everyone is more or less embedded within a given horizon, although such horizons naturally conflict and diverge under the impact of historical processes. However, on occasion this background understanding is conceptualized in terms of a political or moral order of society, such that "features of the world or divine action or human life that make certain norms right" are identified and these deeper normative notions and images are brought to the fore.

Furthermore, no matter what an individual might think about his or her social behavior, such reasoning is implicitly moral because it inevitably concerns just how other's claims are taken into account, which claims, in what way, and to what extent. Stephen Chilton refers to this as cultural moral reasoning: "When one decides how to behave in relation to others they are making a moral judgment.... Cultural moral reasoning is that which is shared, publicly common, and people must use this to communicate with and persuade each other in the context of their culture. The goal of such reasoning is to persuade or explain a desired course of action."[26]

I find this to be a useful approach for thinking about Ming memorials in general and Wang Yangming's and Yao Mo's in particular. Because officials were attempting to persuade the court and emperor to take a proposed course of action by establishing the grounds for claiming that it is right, they tapped

---

22   Taylor, *Modern Social Imaginaries*, 23.
23   Ibid.
24   Ibid., 24.
25   Ibid., 25.
26   Stephen Chilton, *Grounding Political Development* (Boulder: Lynne Rienner Publishers, 1991), 72.

into that usually unspoken normative horizon of cultural moral reasoning. Of course, officials invariably clashed over policy, probably due to individual beliefs and attitudes, personal predicaments and motivations, or subscription to certain policy goals and factional interests. However, what typically did not come into the discussion were the deeper ideas and norms providing the very basis for getting the discussion off the ground, what Charles Taylor refers to as "moral frameworks."[27] When clashes do occur at this deeper level, we can catch a rare glimpse into the background notions of moral and political order held within a given political culture, and therefore a glimpse into what makes up the identities of the political actors, how appropriate behavior is determined, and how the roles of political elites are conceptualized. Strategic behavior is nothing but social behavior and, as such, cannot be removed from the context of the shared social imaginary and the common moral framework in which it arises—even so-called realpolitik. Indeed, as Johnston hoped to prove, structural realism cannot escape the net of culture. However, such clashes over policy show that we are dealing with diverging political cultures, each with its own normative discourse for legitimating courses of action, and this would include strategic policy. In fact, we might hypothesize that conflicts within political culture as here defined may very well be an important variable in strategic decision making.

This brings us back to Wang Yangming's and Yao Mo's conflicting narratives (of the circumstances) and their opposing strategic policies. When Wang began to advocate accommodation as the best strategy for ending local resistance in Guangxi, his reasoning before the court suggests that he was deploying discourse characteristic of one type of political culture against another likely more dominant one.[28] I will attempt to show that when Wang Yangming argued against the use of force, he found it necessary to overturn not only a realist (in actual fact, a cultural realist) strategic argument regarding policy, but also a more ingrained cultural proclivity to resort to violence. In an attempt to alleviate some of the bloodshed caused by what he believed to be misguided moral reasoning, Wang appealed to the court's deeper sense of ethics, making the case that adopting the benevolent paternalism he espoused would serve not only moral principles but also the long-term strategic interests of the dynasty. It must be pointed out, however, that the peaceful settlement Wang

---

27   Charles Taylor, "Interpretation and the Sciences of Man," *Review of Metaphysics* 25, no. 1 (September 1971): 27.

28   According to Geoffrey Wade, voices advocating restraint and opposing the use of force in matters of expanding into and controlling unrest in frontier regions of the southwest were in the minority during the Ming (Wade, "Ming Shi-lu," 171).

proposed reflected an anti-militarist cultural disposition rooted in the now problematic notion of Confucian pacifism. Again, his policy was akin to what Waldron has called "pragmatic," while his predecessor's was "hardline." But the terms pragmatic and hardline imply both an ethics and diverging social imaginaries, and analysis of these will shed light on both Ming political culture and Wang Yangming's position within it. And most importantly, at a more abstract level, Wang's moral framework can be tied in with what Charles Taylor refers to as a conception of a political and moral order of society, or his understanding of "features of the world or divine action or human life that make certain norms right." For Wang Yangming, this is what politics was ultimately about. Thus, the connections between Wang's practical life and philosophical vision will also be explored.

Man Rebellions in Guangxi

In the sixth month of 1527, Wang Yangming, after having spent six years in much-longed-for retirement in his hometown in Zhejiang, was recalled by the court and appointed censor-in-chief and supreme commander of Guangxi and Guangdong.[29] On the surface, the reason for this appointment was the failure of Supreme Commander Yao Mo to achieve a lasting peace in the Right River Region of Guangxi, an area located in the northwestern part of the province and consisting largely of native chieftaincies that had been dominated by the Cen clan since the early Ming.[30] Although Commander Yao had in 1526 successfully defeated the rebellion led by Cen Meng (岑猛)—the native prefectural magistrate of Tianzhou—he nevertheless found himself facing ongoing resistance from two of his followers, Lu Su 陸蘇 and Wang Shou 王受. These native headmen had managed to incite a considerable uprising, the stated political purpose of which was both to change neighboring Sien Prefecture back to its former status as a native chieftaincy, and to reappoint one of Cen Meng's descendents as Tianzhou's native prefectural magistrate.[31] Yao Mo's response was, once again, to raise a large force to quell this uprising; however, while he was assembling one from several provinces, the court received scathing criticism of the commander. This memorial, calling for his impeachment, was from Regional Inspector Shi Jin, who claimed that Yao Mo, in an attempt to deceive the court, had memorialized victory prior to capturing all of the

---

29   *NP*, 35:1305.

30   *MS*, 200:5277.

31   *MS*, 318:8244.

principal rebel leaders.[32] He recommended that Wang Yangming be appointed to replace him, and with the endorsement of Grand Secretaries Gui E 桂萼 and Zhang Cong 張璁, the emperor assented, sending Yao Mo into temporary retirement.

Prior to arriving at the Office of the Supreme Commander in Wuzhou 梧州 in December 1527, Wang Yangming had already dispatched two memorials to the court, the first of which was a futile attempt to decline the commission, and the second a routine expression of gratitude for appointment to such a prestigious post. In these and in a flurry of communications to subordinates, he offered his initial assessment of the origins of the conflict as well as the best strategy for resolving it. For him, this uprising was largely the result of feuding between native officials, but it could still be managed, contrary to his predecessor's recommendations, without resorting to force.[33]

Wang began his journey in October 1527, and by the time he arrived in Wuzhou he had become even more convinced that his assessment had been accurate. As was the case with his management of conflict in southern Jiangxi, he believed it was his duty as an official to survey and interpret the opinion of local elites so as to balance it out with the immediate demands of the court and the long-term interests of the state. Thus, he noted, in a memorial composed shortly after arriving in the province, that he had along the way inquired among local gentry and travelers, and therefore believed he could already offer his "superficial" opinion concerning the origins of the conflict, the factors perpetuating it, and the best strategy for bringing it to an end.[34]

In the memorial, Wang first explained that the Office of the Supreme Commander in Guangxi and Guangdong had been established for the purpose of governing indigenous peoples—the Yao 瑤 and Zhuang 壯—as well as marauding bandits. The court had given this commission enough resources and discretionary power such that were the "formidability of the military presence here to be restored, this in itself would be sufficient to bring the barbarians (*man* 蠻) under control."[35] However, he also found that the regular military force had weakened over time, and this contributed in no small part both to ongoing local conflicts and to the adoption of misguided policies by officials who were not so much proactive as they were reactive:

---

32   MSLWZSL, 74:1697.

33   WYMQJ, vol. 1, 14:461.

34   Ibid., 14:462.

35   Ibid.

As a result of habitual patterns of negligent and lax behavior, military governance has gradually diminished. There are no competent generals that can be appointed as officers, and no soldiers suited for deployment as the rank and file. Thus, when emergencies arise, it has become necessary for officials to rely on the mobilization of local chieftains and their native *lang* 狼 (wolf) troops—as, for example, those under the command of Cen Meng—and only then are they able to act.[36]

But in Wang's observation, being relied on like this had led these local forces to feel resentful, exhausted as they were from constant mobilization.[37] Furthermore, the rewards for their meritorious deeds were being claimed by incompetent officers, who would lure them into treacherous acts only to then extort them, making them feel even more aggrieved. Under such conditions, the seeds of mistrust were sown, and while officials had increasingly to rely on deception and authority to coerce the chieftains into meeting their demands, these men had as a result become contemptuous and obstinate.[38]

It was just this kind of vicious cycle that had played a major role in the development of the conflict that officials first confronted with the bellicose native chieftain Cen Meng and thereafter the headmen Lu Su and Wang Shou. The blame was not simply to be placed on them, but rather on the system itself and all parties involved, including corrupt and incompetent officials:

> As for the wickedness they [Cen Meng and Cen Bangyan] have already displayed, to campaign against them for this surely is not excessive, but as for that which led them to act as they did, this also did not come about in one day. Self-reflection is therefore called for as to where to place the blame, and we should for the time being both admonish and encourage ourselves, rectify military governance, broadly proclaim our awesomeness and virtue, and appease our people, such that we are governed within and the barbarians are expelled without, and we therefore have an excess of strength. In this way, those near will be pleased and those afar cherished, and they [Cen Meng's followers, the headmen Lu Su and Wang

---

36   Ibid. Wang's observations appear to reflect what was in fact happening. For the decline of the *wei suo* (guards and battalions) system and decreasing numbers of soldiers in the regular military force from the mid-fifteenth century, see Shin, *Making of the Chinese State*, 37–40.

37   *WYMQJ*, vol. 1, 14:463.

38   Ibid.

Shou] will submit of their own accord, and they won't rebel, again arous-
ing our wrath.[39]

The court's displeasure, Wang believed, should only be directed at Cen Meng,
his son, and their wicked faction, but seeing as they had already been executed,
this should be sufficient to stop violence in the region and satisfy the court. On
the other hand, Lu Su and Wang Shou, he pointed out, did not have the reputation of being troublesome, and could therefore be dealt with leniently. Unfortunately, "as a result of [the state's] failure to overcome the anger directed at
these two local chieftains, the fate of over ten thousand innocents has been
ignored, the finances of two provinces exhausted, and troops from three provinces mobilized. Registered subjects have thus been prevented from farming
and women from weaving, and turmoil and suffering within a territory of several thousand *li* has continued for two years up to the present."[40] From his
perspective, these local leaders had simply been forced to flee for their lives
out of fear of punishment by officials, and had to be differentiated from those
common bandits roving about everywhere attacking fortified cities and plundering villages—those, that is, whom everyone wants executed.

On the contrary, what appears to have arisen in this case was a series of
complicated misunderstandings caused in no small part by officials' misguided policies, indignation, and excessive zeal.[41] Not only were they pursuing
measures that caused more hardship, they also failed to grasp the popular nature of this resistance movement. "To drive people who are experiencing hardship and exhaustion," he explained, "having them transport grain and weapons,
in order to campaign against someone who does not present a real threat to
the people, and who is not seen as an enemy and therefore for whom there is
no resentment—this is why in their hearts the people are not motivated, and
why this affair is so difficult to settle."[42] This was also why tens of thousands of
native and government troops had failed to defeat just over ten thousand rebels—the supporters of Cen Meng and the headmen. These rebels, being unjustly persecuted for what they believed to be righteous resistance, were able
"to withstand our troops by becoming more solidified in their will to fight to
the death."[43]

---

39   Ibid.
40   Ibid.
41   Ibid.
42   Ibid., 14:463–64.
43   Ibid., 14:464. In his record, Ji Ben 季本 (1485–1563) presents a similar picture of native
      headmen not normally regarded as troublemakers who were pressed by circumstances

Thus, at the outset of his instatement, to explain the origins of the impasse and formulate a strategy, Wang Yangming confidently surveyed the perspectives and sentiments of all parties involved in this conflict. But just who was it that had failed to grasp the big picture and persisted in a strategy of subjugation that perpetuated the devastating conflict? Clearly, he was referring in part to former Supreme Commander Yao Mo, whom he had at first stood up for, despite recommending a different strategy. While in the case of Cen Meng and his son, Yao's policy of suppression was justified to a degree, when it came to these headmen, Wang hinted that they may have had legitimate reason for resisting. Systemic problems with regional military institutions and reckless behavior on the part of regular officials were also to blame; under such circumstances, violent confrontation was unjust. His analysis, I would propose, also paints a picture of two alternatives within the spectrum of Ming strategic discourse on matters of pacifying internal rebellions and promoting lasting security and, by fleshing them out more fully, it becomes possible both to characterize this culture and also to position Wang Yangming within it. But to do so, it is necessary to further elucidate both the evolution of the conflict and the strategy he criticized, and which he called "shaking the lines of the net (*zhen ji gang* 振紀綱)."[44] This was the response exemplified by Yao Mo's policies, and in the following section we turn to his involvement in the conflict.

"Shaking the Lines of the Net"

When Wang Yangming began his journey from Zhejiang to Guangxi, he was well aware of the fact that he was going to be facing the complex world of local politics in the numerous native domains in this southwestern province. The prefecture of Tianzhou was just one among a mosaic of native administrative units, whose very existence hinted at the weakness of the state vis-à-vis local chieftains. When the generals of Zhu Yuanzhang 朱元璋, the Hongwu emperor 洪武帝, had succeeded in pacifying Guangxi in 1368, much of the original Yuan system of native chieftaincies was kept in place. This arrangement was

---

into rebelling. See Ji Ben 季本, "Tianzhou shi shi ji 田州事實記 [Record of the Facts Concerning Matters in Tianzhou]," in Ji Ben 季本, *Ji Pengshan xiansheng wenji* 季彭山先生文集 [Collected Works of Sir Ji Pengshan], in *Beijing tushuguan guji zhenben congkan* 北京圖書館古籍珍本叢刊, vol. 106 (Beijing: Shumu wenxian chubanshe), 875–77.

44   *Zhen ji gang* could also be translated, less literally, as "rectifying law and order." For this translation and a discussion, see John Dardess, *Confucianism and Autocracy: Professional Elites in the Founding of the Ming Dynasty* (Berkeley: University of California Press, 1983), 196.

the outcome of a kind of bargain struck between the expanding imperial state and local leaders of peoples that the state viewed as recalcitrant "barbarians." When the state lacked the wherewithal to extend its power into the southwest, the result was a kind of feudal arrangement, whereby in exchange for their nominal submission, these chieftains were granted official recognition and hereditary office, as well as a degree of freedom to rule their own domains as they wished.[45] The resulting normative system of rules and regulations was termed "the institution of native chieftaincies (*tusi zhidu* 土司制度)."[46]

From the perspective of the local chieftains, such recognition provided an opportunity to consolidate and legitimate their rule over local inhabitants, and there were thus high stakes involved in becoming a native official.[47] Partly for this reason, Ming official records are strewn with incidents of fighting both within and between powerful local clans—of intra- and inter-domainal feuding and internecine warfare. Thus, Wang Yangming had good reasons to believe that much of the trouble in the region was due to ongoing revenge killings. The specific conflict he was assigned to bring to an end related most immediately to a long history of warfare and intrigue between members of the Cen and other clans in the Right River Region of western Guangxi, where in general the reach of the state was weakest and there were very few regular administrative units.[48]

During the early Ming, of the forty-six major Yuan dynasty native chieftaincies that were reestablished, eight were governed by the powerful Cens.[49] Among these eight were the prefecture Tianzhou and the subprefecture Sien, where Wang Yangming confronted resistance from Cen Meng's followers Lu Su and Wang Shou. The Tianzhou chieftaincy was originally created during the Yuan, although the Cens probably emerged as local leaders during the Song. In 1368, Commander Cen Boyan surrendered to Zhu Yuanzhang's advancing forces, his route command was changed to a native prefecture, and he was granted a seal and appointed Tianzhou prefectural magistrate.[50] This hereditary

45   Leo Shin, "Tribalizing the Frontier: Barbarians, Settlers, and the State in Ming China" (Ph.D. diss., Princeton University, 1999), 51.

46   Fang Tie 方鐵, *Xinan tongshi* 西南通史 [A Comprehensive History of the Southwest Borderland] (Zhengzhou: Zhengzhou guji chubanshe, 2003), 623.

47   Jeffrey Barlow, "The Zhuang Minority in the Ming Era," *Ming Studies* 28 (1989): 19.

48   For other accounts of the evolution of this conflict, see Barlow, "The Zhuang Minority in the Ming Era;" Shin, "The Last Campaigns of Wang Yangming;" and Shin, *The Making of the Chinese State*, 85–90.

49   Shin, "Tribalizing the Frontier," 65.

50   Gong Yin 龔蔭, *Zhongguo tusi zhidu* 中國土司制度 [The Institution of Native Offices in China] (Kunming: Yunnan minzu chubanshe, 1992), 2004.

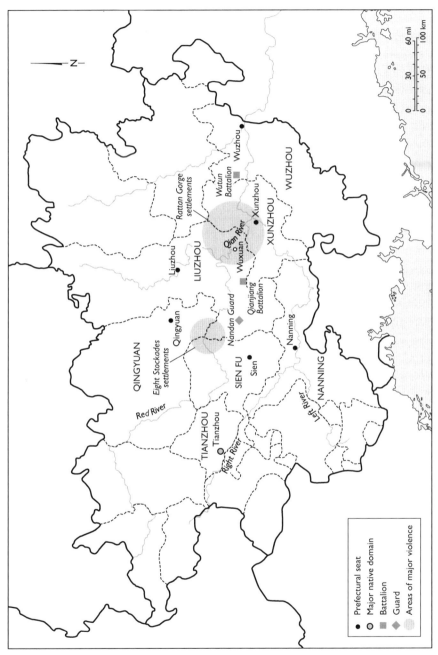

MAP 3   *Guangxi Province.*

chieftaincy maintained relatively harmonious relations with the court until troubles developed within the family of the thirteenth Cen to hold this office—Cen Pu. In 1493, Cen Pu's eldest son, Cen Hu, after supposedly falling out of favor with his father, had a servant kill him.[51] His four-year-old brother, Cen Meng, was thus appointed by provincial officials to succeed their father, under the protection and oversight of their paternal grandmother and Tianzhou local headmen. However, being a child and politically weak, he apparently fell victim to the political maneuvering of one of these deputies, who was colluding with the prefectural magistrate of Sien, a man by the name of Cen Jun, to take control of some of the young chieftain's territory.[52]

Sien was first established as a subprefecture during the Yuan, also under the leadership of Cen Boyan.[53] In 1369 Zhu Yuanzhang issued a seal reconfirming his status as Sien native subprefectural magistrate. In 1439, for his loyal service to the court, the fifth subprefect Cen Ying would see his domain upgraded to a prefecture.[54] In 1447, Sien was further changed into a native military-cum-civilian prefecture. After this time, of most immediate relevance are the records concerning the actions of the eighth prefect, Cen Jun, who was apparently far more aggressive than his predecessors in attempting to expand his local power. Shortly after four-year-old Cen Meng was appointed Tianzhou's prefectural magistrate, Jun was ordered to escort him to the prefectural seat. But in collusion with one of Meng's supposed supporters, he took advantage of Tianzhou intra-domainal conflicts and detained the boy in Sien.[55] Meng was eventually released when Supreme Commander Deng Tingzan threatened Jun with force, but Jun's attempt to domineer over the young chieftain is said to be the origin of what would become ongoing, devastating internecine warfare between the two prefectures. Cen Jun repeatedly attacked Tianzhou, until in 1502 he managed to occupy the prefectural seat, force Cen Meng to flee, and place a member of his own clan, Cen Yong, in charge of the prefecture.[56]

It was shortly after this time, in 1505, that the Supreme Commander of Guangxi and Guangdong Pan Fan, along with subordinate officials, began to

---

51   Huang Zuo 黃佐 and Lin Fu 林富, eds., *Guangxi tong zhi* 廣西通誌 [Comprehensive Gazetteer of Guangxi], 1531 ed., in *Beijing tushuguan guji zhenben congkan* 北京圖書館 古籍珍本叢刊, vol. 41 (Reprint, Beijing: Shumu wenxian chubanshe, 1988), 56:659.

52   Ibid.

53   Gong, *Zhongguo tusi zhidu*, 1086.

54   Ibid.

55   Tian Rucheng 田汝成, *Yan jiao ji wen* 炎徼紀聞 [Record of Things Heard on the Scorching Hot Frontier], in *Si ku quan shu* 四庫全書, vol. 352 (Shanghai: Shanghai guji chubanshe, 1987), 606.

56   Ibid., 606.

memorialize for permission to lead an expeditionary force against Cen Jun. Over one hundred thousand government and native troops from three provinces were mobilized for the campaign and achieved a quick victory over Jun.[57] When Jun committed suicide, the Ministry of War took advantage of the absence of a native official to change this native chieftaincy to a regular prefectural administrative unit (*gaitu guiliu* 改土歸流), a move that evoked a considerable amount of resistance. When Yao Mo requested approval for his strategy to quell the uprising led by the rebels Lu Su and Wang Shou, he cited reports from prefectural officials stating, "Ever since the prefecture was converted into a regular administrative unit, the area has repeatedly experienced rebellions, forcing the mobilization of government troops for campaigns of extermination, such that year after year there has been no peace even for one day."[58] The result of all the chaos and massacres, they claimed, had been "the flight of over half the residents."[59]

Cen Jun's defeat in 1505 also had serious implications for leadership in Tianzhou. For his unwitting involvement in the conflict, the now adolescent Cen Meng would lose his position as prefectural magistrate and be demoted to commander of a battalion in Fujian.[60] Tianzhou was also converted to a regular administrative unit, under the acting authority of the prefect of Sien. However, prefectural affairs remained in the hands of Cen Meng, who never did depart for Fujian but instead managed to gain an appointment as assistant prefectural magistrate, most likely by bribing cronies of the infamous eunuch and imperial favorite Liu Jin.[61] Over time, the power of his forces was revitalized to such an extent that he was able to nibble away at neighboring territories, encroaching on them and interfering with their politics.[62] But at least until 1525, when officials began to call for a campaign against him, officials may have remained restrained in their response because Meng had both made his forces an indispensable element in other government campaigns against rebel-bandits and also engaged in a good deal of bribery.[63]

The first sign of this changing attitude came when Cen Meng led his forces into neighboring Sicheng 泗城, seized several stockades, reached the subpre-

57   Huang and Lin, *Guangxi tong zhi*, 56:659.

58   Yao Mo 姚鏌, *Dongquan wenji* 東泉文集 [Collected Works of Yao Dongquan], in *Si ku quan shu cun mu congshu* 四庫全書存目叢書, vol. 46 (Jinan: Qi lu she chubanshe, 1997), 5:616.

59   Ibid.

60   *MS*, 318:8247.

61   Ibid., 318:8248.

62   Tian, *Yan jiao ji wen*, 606.

63   *MSJSBM*, 53:559.

fectural seat, and occupied it. Sicheng's subprefect Cen Jie immediately sent an urgent report to the Regional Military Commission, but Meng defended his actions by levying the charge that Jie was not a legitimate descendent of the Cen clan and had seized not only the chieftaincy but also ancestral property; therefore, he (Meng) merely wished to recover what was rightfully his.[64] Whatever merits his claim may have had, due to this conflict Cen Meng failed to respond to a summons for mobilization by Supreme Commander Zhang Ding, leading officials to come to the conclusion that Cen Meng's conduct had indeed become too "unbridled."

The two officials first responsible for memorializing to the court and initiating the process of waging war against Cen Meng were Supreme Commander Sheng Yingqi and Regional Inspector Xie Ruyi, the first to press charges against Cen. These accusations included refusing to obey orders, bribing officials, inciting disorder, and attacking neighboring native officials.[65] Their request was approved by the court and events were set into motion but, shortly thereafter, Sheng Yingqi was transferred and left his post, to be replaced by Supreme Commander Yao Mo.

According to Tian Rucheng (1530–1557), when Yao first arrived, he did not really believe that Cen Meng "intended to rebel," and suspected that much of the disorder was incited by officials in the region.[66] Also, another official involved in planning the campaign with Sheng Yingqi—Regional Inspector Shi Jin—"placed a considerable amount of the blame on the prior Supreme Commander Sheng Yingqi's having stirred up trouble and invited a conflict."[67] In fact, as Tan Qi has noted, with regard to the origins of this war, official histories are highly contradictory, and he convincingly demonstrates how each of the crimes for which Cen Meng was accused were largely fabricated, exaggerated, or in fact a direct result of official corruption: there were several officials attempting to ride on Cen Meng's successes as a native official and commander in many government-led regional campaigns by stealing the credit for his meritorious achievements, coercing him into campaigns he saw as unnecessary, or extorting him in every way possible when he displeased them. Apparently, the biggest offenders in this regard were in fact Supreme Commander Sheng Yingqi and Regional Inspector Xie Ruyi, but clearly also many other subordinate provincial civil and military officials were involved.[68]

---

64   *MSLWZSL*, 25:725.

65   *MS*, 318:8248. Yao Mo's memorials list out these crimes. See Yao, *Dongquan wenji*, 3:565–69.

66   Tian, *Yan jiao ji wen*, 606.

67   *MS*, 318:8249.

68   Tan Qi 談琪, "Cen Meng fanpan chaoting zhiyi 岑猛反叛朝廷質疑 [Questions Concerning Cen Meng's Rebellion against the Ming Dynasty]," in *Zhuangzu lun gao* 壯族論

Nevertheless, when he arrived in Nanning in the spring of 1526, Yao Mo immediately began to dispatch memorials with his plans for a large-scale campaign against Cen Meng, although whether he did so because he eventually concurred with prior officials' assessment of Meng's crimes—as his memorials definitively state—or for other personal reasons is difficult to determine. No doubt, he would have been under pressure from all those regional and local civil and military officials who had a stake in taking punitive action against Meng, especially Xie Ruyi. And yet, given the *Ming History* portrait of Yao Mo as a stickler in matters of protocol and adhering to lines of authority, the account by Tian Rucheng as to what went on behind the scenes may very well hold water. According to him, Xie Ruyi and Yao Mo fell afoul of each other, and when a letter to Yao from his son, Yao Lai—urging his father not to campaign against Meng—fell into Xie's hands, Xie fabricated the story that Lai had accepted a bribe from Meng.[69] Such a potentially damaging accusation assured that any appeasement on Yao Mo's part would have invited serious problems for both of them.

After memorializing three times, Yao's requests were approved, and what followed was a battle involving over one hundred thousand government and native troops assembled from three provinces. Cen Meng likely also raised a force of similar magnitude, divided them up into contingents, and dispatched them to various strategic passes and stockades around Tianzhou. However, Ji Ben (1485–1563), a student of Wang Yangming who came to Guangxi to assist him, penned an account suggesting this was purely defensive, for Meng had repeatedly, in a desperate effort to forestall the invasion, dispatched communications to Yao Mo and a memorial to the emperor pleading his case and requesting to atone for his crimes.[70] Nonetheless, Yao proceeded with the campaigns and within a matter of days Meng's forces were defeated, and both

---

搞, ed. Fang Honggui and Gu Youshi (Nanning: Guangxi renmin chubanshe, 1989), 275–83. Tan's conclusions receive support from Ji Ben's "Tianzhou shi shi ji." This follower of Wang Yangming was called to Wang's military headquarters in Wuzhou and was present during his period of tenure in Guangxi. He presents a picture of an upright and cultured native chieftain constantly exploited, extorted, and misrepresented by scheming local and provincial officials. The same applied to the two headmen who would rebel in the aftermath of Cen Meng's death (875–76). For Ji Ben's record of conduct and involvement, see Xu Wei 徐渭, "Shi chang sha gong xing zhuang" 師長沙公形狀, in *Xu Wei ji* 徐渭集 [Collected Works of Xu Wei], vol. 2 (Zhonghua shuju, 1983), 27:643–50.

69　Tian, *Yan jiao ji wen*, 606. Yao Mo's biography is included in the *Ming History* (200:5277–78).

70　Yao, *Dongquan wen ji*, 4:590. For Ji Ben's differing assessment, see "Tianzhou shi shi ji," 875–76.

he and his son Bangyan were killed. In the aftermath, the supreme commander petitioned to change Tianzhou into a regular administrative unit with a circulating official, along with some other proposals for reconstruction and the maintenance of long-term security. This included retaining a force of some ten thousand native troops from two pacification commissions located in Huguang, until such time as a lasting peace was achieved.

Regardless what his personal motives might have been, it is worthwhile examining how Yao Mo argued before the court in order to obtain approval to carry out this campaign, remove a native chieftaincy, and leave a standing force in its place. Just how he justified his actions and characterized Cen Meng is key, in that that similar discourse was used to rationalize the suppression of the ensuing uprising led by Meng's supporters Lu Su and Wang Shou. What is of interest here is that, although some officials at the time—and later Wang Yangming—would question the way in which Yao had judged the situation and the strategy he consequently adopted, the court nevertheless approved his recommendations. Therefore, his petition was worded in terms that clearly hit the mark.

In order to achieve his objective, in his memorials Yao Mo established his rationale as to why it was necessary to make a show of force, buttressing his argument by characterizing Cen Meng as wicked, arrogant, and impudent. In terms of his overall strategic objective, his assessment was that "without native officials, the Yao and Zhuang in Guangxi and Guangdong cannot be won over and ruled; without executing Cen Meng, the bellicosity of the native chieftains also cannot be contained and governed for our purposes."[71] According to his assessment, the "barbarians" in Guangxi would take advantage of any display of weakness on the part of the dynasty to advance their interests and exceed their allotted place, so the highest priority was simply for the court to marshal an overwhelming display of force in order to awe them into submission. The dynastic laws, he believed, were put in place precisely to achieve this objective: "The country has native officials because [we] rule over them. When inheriting office they must request approval, when deploying forces they must obey orders, and when submitting taxes they must do so on time ... When this is not the case ... then there is a violation [of the law] and they must be subjugated. This is the law of the dynasty."[72] After citing numerous instances where native chieftains were executed for violating these laws or rebelling, he explained, "They were all replaced with circulating officials. Although the uprisings could not immediately be ended, there were no cases in which crimes were commit-

71   Ibid., 4:586.
72   Ibid., 5:629.

ted and yet not rectified according to the law. This is because they must have something that instills fear in them [the state] and know that they must be on guard. In this way, [conflict with] native chieftains is prevented. If they are not completely restrained, and allowed to run rampant and uncontrolled, there is nothing they won't do."[73] Most urgently, any indication of weakness coming from the court had deeper implications for maintaining security in the region, for "at a time when all the barbarians (yi 夷) are looking on from the sidelines, if we were suddenly to recoil out of fear and cowardliness from the deployment of troops, only in order to pursue some policy of toleration and appeasement, then [I] fear the awesomeness of [the image of] the dynasty will be heavily damaged, the situation further aggravated, and [individuals as fierce as] tigers reared, leaving behind a catastrophe in the making."[74]

Yao Mo's express conviction that a campaign of extermination would be the only way both to bring down this unbridled chieftain and give other "barbarian" leaders an object lesson in imperial might was further hardened by those many accusations levied against Cen Meng in reports submitted by subordinate civilian and military officials, material he took full advantage of to further his arguments. Yao stresses how, from the very beginning, this arrogant youth made it clear that he would always act ungratefully towards his superiors and out of deliberate contempt for authority:

> Early on, when he was still young, politically weak, and ignorant, he was chased out [of Tianzhou] by Cen Jun, the prefectural magistrate of Sien. The court was thus troubled with having to raise an army numbering over one hundred thousand to attack Cen Jun and execute him, and only then could Meng be assured he would survive. At the time Meng was demoted to the post of commander of a battalion in Fujian. This was also very generous treatment. But he merely detected and took note of this generous treatment, and gradually spawned treacherous and clever schemes, thereafter raising forces to secure his status. The court fully values the righteousness of assisting the weak, and once again appointed Meng assistant prefectural magistrate, but from that time on Meng has trifled with the wishes of the court.[75]

According to this portrayal, Cen's crimes were the natural outcome of his fundamental contemptuousness and brazen arrogance. Yao pushes aside all other

---

73 Ibid.
74 Ibid.
75 Ibid.

evidence that the blame for the hostility resulted from constant mobilization of native forces and corrupt or incompetent officials and failing Ming institutions; rather, the fault lay with the ungrateful Cen Meng, for upon receiving so many charitable appointments, he only "toyed even more with the court" and his crimes "became even more wanton in their gross irreverence."[76]

In his memorials, the supreme commander marshaled a great deal of evidence to further his argument, claiming, for example, that after this time the aggressive chieftain began to poison officials and encroach upon neighboring native domains. "His savageness even reaches his own kind," Yao informed the court, "for he killed members from branches of his own clan."[77] But Cen Meng's actions reached the height of cruelty when he attacked the prefecture of Sicheng:

> With no orders from superiors, he mobilized tens of thousands of troops and, without any scruples whatsoever, attacked and surrounded Sicheng for three to four months. Although officials were sent to forbid and exhort him, Meng just haughtily disregarded them. In this subprefecture, half the people were cruelly victimized. He applied the hot pillar to Cen Jie. Flowing blood filled the fields, and dead bodies piled up as high as hills. What is more, he dug up and burned ancestral graves, such that anger reaches even to the depths of the earth. [He also] bound up women and children, spreading his poison through three generations. Following this, he ordered all the residents to disperse, and now all the towns and villages are desolate.[78]

For Yao Mo, Meng's crimes were so horrific simply because they had turned the world completely upside down.[79]

The supreme commander did eventually receive authorization to attack the wayward chieftain, but in the aftermath of his initial success, he failed to capture two of Meng's key supporters, Lu Su and Wang Shou. As he represented the case, these two had played a key role in Cen Meng's mobilization for defense against the onslaught of government forces, leading several thousand

---

76   Ibid.

77   Ibid.

78   Ibid., 3:571.

79   In his "Tianzhou shi shi ji," Ji Ben states that these claims against Meng were all fabricated and that in fact other native chieftains who had urged Cen Meng to join them in their attack on Cen Jie were responsible for his death and much of the destruction (875–76).

native troops at two different strategic locations.[80] Upon defeat, they escaped and proceeded to incite an uprising, the purpose of which was to force the dynasty to allow Tianzhou to retain its status as a native chieftaincy governed by the Cens, and to have a native official jointly govern Sien prefectural affairs. Yao Mo's response was once again to request authorization to raise a large force, and it was at this time that Regional Inspector Shi Jin submitted a memorial impeaching the commander and recommending that Wang Yangming take his place.

To justify another campaign of extermination, Yao first claimed that in the aftermath of the war with Cen Meng, he had returned to their livelihoods those forced into flight by or "coerced" into following the rebels. In spite of the fact that he had retained a force totaling over ten thousand troops in the region, a few wicked headmen (*e mu* 惡目) managed to escape his net and flee to the mountains and forests, something he pinned on the incompetence of subordinates:

> The wicked headman Lu Su manufactured a false seal and, in order to deceive the masses, fabricated rumors to the effect that Cen Meng was still alive and assembling a large force in Jiaozhi (northern Vietnam) to realize his plot to recover his office as [Tianzhou] native prefectural magistrate. The stupid and ignorant barbarian (*yi*) peoples believed him, and he proceeded to summon and link up with the tribal leaders Xing Xiang, Wang Dui, and others, who followed him in staging an uprising. People from all around responded to the call. On the twenty-eighth day of the eleventh month of the fifth year of the Jiajing reign [December 31, 1526], they led a mass of rebel-bandits and occupied the prefectural seat of Tianzhou, killing government troops and seizing the treasury.[81]

Yao claimed that the rebels, knowing full well that Cen Meng was in fact dead and by no means due to arrive with a large force, began to feel hard pressed and therefore sought amnesty. It was at this point that Lu Su dispatched a messenger to plead with officials for the opportunity to "repent of his errors" and "atone for his crimes through rendering the service of killing bandits."[82] Believing that the strategic balance of power was not yet in his favor, the supreme commander adopted the tactic of delaying them with appeasement.[83]

---

80   Yao, *Dongquan wen ji*, 3:577.
81   Ibid., 5:616.
82   Ibid.
83   Ibid.

Yao Mo, uninterested in Lu Su's offer, assumed that he was merely attempting to put into play the standard rituals for winning an amnesty only in order to further his devious interests. As evidence for this, he claimed that while biding time, Lu ordered Xing Xiang to collude with Wang Shou and others, raise a force, and occupy Sien. According to his account, they amassed a mob of over ten thousand, and on February 15, 1527, scaled the town's walls with over one hundred ladders, occupied it, took prisoner the prefectural magistrate and a battalion commander, and burned the yamen.[84] But after being excoriated by these officials—claimed Yao—Wang and others realized they were in for trouble and released them. Instead, they let it be known to the Office of the Supreme Commander that they wished to surrender in exchange for amnesty, and on the condition that a native headman be appointed to govern the area under the oversight of the prefectural magistrate. Indeed, some of Yao's subordinates appeared to believe that they should be offered amnesty. The supreme commander disagreed, explaining, "I am afraid some people nowadays hold a different opinion [from mine]. Some suggest that in the aftermath of devastation caused by so much warfare, it is appropriate to cease hostilities, recuperate, appease, and settle [the people]. [They would say that] since Wang Shou, Liang Di, and others have stated their wish to retain a circulating official on the condition that a native official be permitted to manage local affairs according to local customs, if we do not deign to follow their feelings on this matter, then [we must] fear that even more troubles will arise."[85]

In his rebuttal, Yao Mo claimed he was fully cognizant of this point of view, but that it was motivated by the corrupt personal interests and shortsightedness of the very individuals who were calling for his impeachment, including Regional Inspector Shi Jin.[86] "Because of just one temporary uprising," he informed the court, "they desire immediately to bend the law and give in to the wishes of some insignificant rebel tribal leader, but your servitor fears that this is a case of continuing the perfunctory governance of the Tang, and will leave behind a not insignificant danger from the native officials."[87] The bigger picture here was simply the terrible affront to law and order: "If we allow this trend to continue, then socio-moral norms, laws, decorum, and measures (*ji gang li fa* 紀綱禮法) will also be utterly destroyed one by one."[88] Besides, these native leaders simply had no intention of accepting an amnesty, and were

---

84   Ibid., 4:609.
85   Ibid., 4:610–11.
86   Ibid., 5:621.
87   Ibid.
88   Ibid., 5:629.

giving every indication to the contrary. "As of now," he informed the court, "the strategic power of the rebel-bandits is increasing, and their numbers growing; they are unfurling banners and giving commands, plundering villages and killing bulls, gathering masses and linking up with other barbarian bandits."[89] Finally, as if to soothe fears that the uprising was popular, Yao stated that "the people are not of the same mind, and only follow him because they are coerced into doing so."[90] For all these reasons, unless they are punished, other native officials' "ridicule and scorn will be further encouraged."[91]

As he had for the suppression of Cen Meng, Yao Mo did receive authorization to mobilize yet another army for this campaign, perhaps because he had the support of Grand Secretary Fei Hong, who may have been responsible for his appointment; also, he may have managed to convince his readers to accept his strategy by painting, in culturally-defined terms, a typical picture of a military threat that had to be contained. These terms are the social imaginary through which he constructed the identities and motivations of his adversaries, as well as the deeper normative notions underlying such an interpretive framework. His representations in both cases highlighted how these individuals grossly violated conventional expectations. These chieftains and headmen had, in other words, ignored or overturned the norms for acceptable mutual interpersonal behavior and relationships, and failed to live up to what was expected of them as subjects of the emperor. They must be harshly punished for their disloyalty, irreverence, and ingratitude, as well as their blatant flouting of the rules and regulations that cement social order. They had advanced their wicked and brazen selfish interests in utter disregard of shared agreements and expectations.

In general, there is nothing in Yao Mo's communications to suggest any way in which these native leaders' actions and the popular uprising supporting them might have been justified or rational. In fact, he made no effort whatsoever to portray their perspective, and systematically disregarded any evidence contradicting the moral correctness of his argument for waging war. In other words, the perspective of the adversary is both is overridden by Yao Mo's use of this type of normative imperial discourse: Cen Meng and his headman supporters appear as nothing more than the very opposite, the very shadow, of the ideal for principled conduct. For this reason, the commander repeatedly insisted "law and order must be rectified," and "the lines of the net shaken." It was only by means of violent suppression that these "unbridled" barbarians could

---

89   Ibid., 5:617.
90   Ibid., 4:610.
91   Ibid.

be awed into submission, forced to resume their status as obedient subjects of the emperor.

Now, it might be argued that what Yao Mo was really doing was quite different from the rhetoric he was spinning, that he was only referencing this moral framework in order instrumentally to advance a personal or political agenda, or to evade accusations of bribery and protect his son. But even should that have been the case, this does not explain why he chose the kind of rhetoric he did in order to promote his call for a campaign of extermination. Likewise, more generally, it might be argued that his discourse was simply the habitual means by which officials legitimated realpolitik. In moral terms, we might speculate that he shared with many other officials what might be called a kind of Hobbesian "tacit understanding" of the nature of justice, whereby justice is what results when self-interested individuals/groups negotiate with each other over relative ends based on the bargaining power they bring to the table. This is a justice of mutual advantage: conflicts of interest are decided based on a rationally prudent assessment of what one has to give up in order to secure the kind of cooperation from others necessary to pursue one's own ends.

However, I believe we must be very careful not to import a very modern commonsense understanding of persons and justice into this conflict; we should not assume that the moral vocabulary of Ming officials was merely a rhetorical flourish to embellish what was in reality a pragmatic compromise or a-cultural realpolitik. Instead, analysis of this language needs to be grounded within the context of the times. Within the world of Confucian discourse, a powerful distinction was drawn between those who act righteously and those who act for personal profit (*li* 利) or out of private desires (*sili* 私利), and scholar-officials always had a keen eye for the way in which people—and especially their political enemies—acted on the basis of the latter. But within the world of official discourse, there was simply no room for the concept of a society built around the legitimation of individuals or groups rationally pursuing their own interests, around a justice of mutual advantage. There was no typical self-reflexive process whereby such a tacit understanding was then translated into normative official discourse. That is why, within this horizon, structural realism invariably coincided rather directly with strategic culture, and why interests and culture appeared blurred—no deeper or prior context existed to explode the two apart in conceptual terms. Either such interests or pursuits were immediately invalidated along the lines that Yao Mo attacked his adversaries, or they were given some meaning and sense within the framework of a justice grounded in Confucian norms. This is, as we shall see, precisely what Wang Yangming attempted to do, according to a justice of impartiality grounded in his belief that all individuals bear an innate knowledge of the good. From this perspective, personal motives are a secondary issue.

But according to just what underlying moral norms did Yao Mo conceptualize the actions of the native leaders? Scholars of late imperial Chinese history have written extensively on the matter of the existence of a dominant moral orthodoxy during the Ming.[92] My translation of *zhen ji gang* 振紀綱 is taken directly from the work of John Dardess on the first Ming emperor's program— following the advice of his Confucian advisors—for the "psycho-behavioral reform of mankind." According to him, *ji* 紀 referred to a "leading thread" or norm; *gang* 綱, the "guiding rope of a net," a regulator, a rule, a law.[93] Thus, literally speaking, *zhen ji gang* could be translated as "shaking the lines of the net." In practice, this meant the imposition of centralized controls over the army, the bureaucracy, and society at large. What the nets and strings actually connoted was *liyi* 禮義, "decorum and righteousness," or "behavior required by one's given status."[94] But since *li* were often inadequate for controlling the behavior of people, a supporting system of "laws and measures (*fadu* 法度)" had to be formulated to provide the impetus for coercing people to behave with decorum.[95] Dardess explains that for the first Ming emperor, Ming Taizu, and his advisors, "the *ji gang* of human society was, then, its *lifa*."[96] Society was to be controlled by clarifying behavior required by given status (*li* 禮) and promulgating a supportive body of laws (*fa* 法), and the structure of *lifa* 禮法 was in turn the interlocking set of socio-moral principles commonly referred to as the three bonds and five constants. In essence, the founding emperor and his advisors set the stage for both the dominant form of moral orthodoxy, what I would term "membership discourse," and the means for backing it up by force, that is, a strict law-and-order orientation.

At least some of the emperor's advisors appeared to feel that the re-imposition of centralized controls—which for them meant the "the restoration of antiquity"—required an approach that differed greatly from what they took to be the norm for the Tang, Song, and Yuan. Dardess quotes Liu Sanwu's 1386 postface to the third series of Taizu's Great Announcements, to the effect that the Han, Jin, Tang, and Song dynasties had done no more than to "rule by

---

92 See, for example, Maram Epstein, *Competing Discourses: Orthodoxy, Authenticity, and Engendered Meanings in Late Imperial China* (Cambridge, MA: Harvard University Press, 2001), 13.

93 Dardess, *Confucianism and Autocracy*, 196.

94 Ibid., 197.

95 Ibid.

96 Ibid., 198.

accommodation."[97] In a similar vein, Wu Bozong wrote that late Yuan rulers had left the *ji gang* unshaken, a condition that the Ming must remedy through "sternness."[98] As we have seen, Yao Mo attempted to legitimate his rationale for using force precisely by appealing to this moral framework and social imaginary. He repeatedly attacked his adversaries for their desire to pursue a perfunctory and dangerous policy of appeasement, which could be likened to Tang accommodation. Yao claimed that accommodation would only violate law and order, which instead must be rectified, or the court would face serious consequences. And he believed that the only way to achieve stability was a display of might.

Obviously, there is a great distance in time between the first Ming emperor's court and Yao Mo's campaigns in the 1520's. But what I am trying to do here is to show how Yao Mo's practical reasoning in fact operates very much according to a pervasive normative structure for rational communication, and the precedent for this was set in the early Ming. In the most abstract of terms, this membership discourse and law-and-order orientation were hierarchically structured and authoritarian. In Neo-Confucian terms, the expectation was that, in order to secure a peaceful social order, the particularistic, desire-bound self would be sacrificed to a higher order in which self-identity is dependent on belonging to a group and one's role within it. In Yao Mo's memorials, as in most official and Neo-Confucian discourse, when the desire-bound self acted in a way that exceeded or violated norms of the group, it was typically considered unrestrained (*zong* 縱), domineering and willful, or unbridled (*fangzi* 放). Whenever the topic turned to the "barbarians," such willfulness was only exacerbated by the fact that, as Yao repeatedly stated, such peoples were by nature "ferocious," "savage," and "fearless." Thus, the balance of agency and communion envisioned in membership discourse and its supportive law-and-order orientation were in essence constructed on the grounds that without this order human behavior would degenerate into savagery. The signifiers for the latter were routinely projected upon various social groups, especially rebel-bandits and "barbarians," thereby obscuring the political, social, and economic origins of unrest. In this respect, this discourse—aptly employed by Yao Mo—is doubly powerful: it is both colonizing and violent, in the sense that it is at the very epistemic origins of acts of violence, such as campaigns of extermination.[99]

---

97   Ibid., 196.

98   Ibid.

99   For the relation between binary oppositions and social order, see Pierre Bourdieu, *Distinction: A Social Critique of the Judgment of Taste*, trans. Richard Nice (Cambridge, MA: Harvard University Press, 1984), 468. For Bourdieu, symbolic violence is the power to impose

To say that a discourse is "colonizing" implies that there exists some possibly superior hierarchy of values by which it can be judged, for if this were not the case, then we should have only a history of colonizations, but without anything of original meaning or value to be recovered, neither unjust hegemony nor just resistance. At best, one might—putting all other issues aside—entertain the thought that, given his description of Cen Meng's actions, Yao was simply attempting to show the court that here was a society rife with savage feuding, one that sorely needed a stable social order imposed upon it. However, the fact that Wang Yangming, still within the limits permitted by this overarching normative discourse, was able to settle this conflict peacefully suggests that there was indeed another solution. Edward Farmer, in his analysis of the "constitutional edifice of Ming despotism," explains:

> The desired modes of behavior and belief and the modes of enforcement generally subordinated the individual's interest to those of a collectivity. Little concern was shown for the individual's subjective side—for thought patterns, intentions, conscience, or freedom of action—but a great stress was placed on groupings, particularly hierarchical relationships, which were to keep the individual's actions within the proper bounds. The individual, it may be inferred, was assumed to have an identity defined primarily in terms of a nexus of social relations, the most important of which could be spelled out as specific obligations and responsibilities obtaining between subordinates and superiors.[100]

At first, with political support at the court, Yao Mo was certainly able to achieve his objectives by referring precisely to this legal and moral structure. His discourse evidences what William Rowe, in his study of Chen Hongmou, refers to as a "pervasive rhetoric of submission," the presupposition of which was a view of the person as the occupant of a variety of social roles, situated in a number

---

the meanings of such binary oppositions, and to assert their legitimacy, by concealing the power relations (political, economic, cultural) that are the underlying naked (and presumably more real) basis of its force. I am here, however, pointing out how symbolic violence, or the forms of domination prescribed by a particular discursive construction of social order and intersubjectivity, actually translates into real violence, beyond simply its more subtle institutionalizations and identity constructions. This is what I mean by the epistemic origins of violence. For further discussion, see David Swartz, *Culture and Power: The Sociology of Pierre Bourdieu* (Chicago: Chicago University Press, 1997), 89.

100   Edward Farmer, "Social Order in Early Ming China: Some Norms Codified in the Hung-wu Period," in *Law and State in Traditional East Asia*, ed. Brian E. McKnight (Honolulu: University of Hawaii Press, 1987), 10.

of intermeshing networks of mutual definition and reciprocal obligation.[101] For Yao Mo, Cen Meng and his deputies repeatedly violated the law and the most fundamental of moral norms not because they were acting on their consciences, or out of justifiable concerns, but because they were giving free reign to their self-centeredness. For him, and according to orthodox thought, the real sin was forgetting one's place in society.

But what if these men's actions were to be interpreted differently, without assuming that any anti-social or lawbreaking act necessarily derives from wanton desire, or from illegitimate personal or collective interests? What if they were, in fact, acting on their consciences, according to legitimate intentions and rationales—what Edward Farmer refers to as their "subjective side?" But to see these events in a different light, clearly at this time there would have to have been available a different conception of persons, as well as the political conditions and ethical impetus to conceptualize this conflict in different terms: only then could a peaceful resolution be found.

In fact, when Yao Mo was making preparations to go to war against the remaining rebellious deputies and memorializing concerning his plans, some at court apparently felt that this conflict might indeed allow for a different interpretation, and probably largely because of Regional Inspector Shi Jin's indictment, which deeply displeased the emperor and forced Yao to request that he be relieved of duty. According to Tian Rucheng, subordinates of Yao Mo were actively subverting his efforts to begin the attack on the native headmen by diverting orders and engaging in dilatory conduct; furthermore, in a memorial to the emperor, Yao claimed that Shi Jin was frustrating his mobilization efforts in numerous ways.[102] It is also the case that, as Tang Kwok-leong has proposed and Yao Mo's *Ming History* biography states, grand secretaries at the Ming court (particularly Gui E and Zhang Cong) who were enemies to the now retired Grand Secretary Fei Hong, were undermining his efforts because he was likely promoted by Fei and they saw his failure as another way to discredit Fei.[103] This may also have simply been the way genuine clashes over policy combined with personal vendettas at the court. Regardless, as Tang points out, at the very time Yao Mo was desperately attempting to salvage his reputation

---

101   William Rowe, *Saving the World: Chen Hongmou and Elite Consciousness in Eighteenth-Century China* (Stanford: Stanford University Press, 2001), 291–306.

102   Tian, *Yan jiao ji wen*, 607. For his indictment of Shi Jin's conduct, see Yao, *Dongquan wenji*, 6:629.

103   Tang Kwok-leong, "Tianzhou shi fei wo ben xin–Wang Shouren de Guangxi zhi yi 田州事非我本心—王守仁的廣西之役 [The Affair in Tianzhou Was Not What I Originally Intended—Wang Shouren's Campaigns in Guangxi]," *Qinghua xuebao*, vol. 40, no. 2 (2009), 270–71; *MS*, 200:5278.

and "atone for his crimes" by attacking the native headmen, orders had already gone out to Wang Yangming to proceed to the region and reassess the uprising, and other officials in the region therefore weren't by any means going to take action until his arrival.[104]

Imperial Magnanimity and "Willing Submission"

While it is true that Wang Yangming, in his initial plea to the court declining the appointment, suggested that Yao Mo was a perfectly capable official, and that he perhaps only needed unified support from the center, while on his way to Guangxi in late 1527, he dispatched a memorial to the court with extensive justification for offering amnesty to the accused, suggesting that he had changed his mind in the process. In this, he hinted at just what kinds of official practices were perpetuating the conflict, and also laid out his rationale as to just why "shaking the lines of the net" and annihilating the rebel-bandits was simply untenable from every conceivable perspective. "Some believe," he explained to the court, in clear reference to former Supreme Commander Yao Mo, "that if having already campaigned against them without defeating them, they were suddenly to be freed, then law and order might not be re-imposed."[105] To make his case, he presented a vivid picture of the suffering and devastation caused by warfare, addressed realpolitik strategic matters, argued for a response he believed best demonstrated the transformative power of the benevolent paternalism of the emperor and his officials, and cast the behavior of the rebel headmen in a more sympathetic light, one that is certainly more in accord with so much evidence suggesting that not only Cen Meng but also these headmen were grossly mistreated and misrepresented by regular officials.

"As for the campaign in Sien and Tianzhou," wrote Wang Yangming, "ongoing warfare has brought calamity upon two provinces, suffering and devastation has continued for over two years, the military's forces are exhausted on patrolling and defense, the people are exhausted from transporting provisions, and officials and clerks are worn out from endlessly running about."[106] He likened the region to a battered vessel floating amidst heavy winds and huge waves: the danger of capsizing and drowning lay right before the eyes. Military morale was so low that there was no will to fight and massive desertion, and not least because over ten to twenty thousand soldiers had died of pestilence

---

104   Ibid., 279
105   *WYMQJ*, vol. 1, 14:464.
106   Ibid., 14:470.

during the last year, with more dying every day. Drawing on commonplace statecraft maxims concerning government obligations to the people, Wang highlighted the snowballing effects of warfare: when women are prevented from weaving and men from farming, starvation and exposure to the elements ensues, forcing many to flee into the arms of the "desperadoes."[107]

Furthermore, officials were pursuing a policy that was not only devastating the region but that was also, in strategic terms, not at all conducive to the dynasty's long-term interests. He believed that because Tianzhou and Sien were close to the border of Jiaozhi 交趾 (northern Vietnam),[108] located in a mountainous region difficult of access and occupied by large numbers of Yao and Zhuang, it was necessary to retain the native chieftains for the purpose of providing a defensive screen.[109] Also, Tianzhou was important because it was a topographically level area located in the middle reaches of the Right River Region that could serve as a place to project power over the chieftaincies of Sicheng 泗城, Donglan 東蘭, and Zhen'an 鎮安. It would be correct to say, therefore, that Wang Yangming was hardly naïve in matters of realpolitik, and he certainly addressed the matter as to just whether or not a militant approach should be adopted. But he also completely re-conceptualized both long-term objectives and the best strategic means for realizing them within a different moral framework, and first of all by attacking the reasoning of his predecessors. Thus, in his relevant memorials, he repeatedly responded to a prevailing set of arguments by officials who wanted, in terms he used pejoratively, "to shake up the lines of the net" and get "retribution" by annihilating the rebels. "Today," he explained, "should it be absolutely necessary to engage in aggressive military action for the purpose of avenging anger, and in order to retain the rewards for prior successes, then it cannot be said that they won't be defeated; but even should we again defeat them, there are also ten dangers."[110] These dangers were the suffering, devastation, and strategically untenable consequences that would result from continued warfare.

Wang Yangming likened these officials' notion of "rectifying law and order" to the way of the hegemons (*wu ba* 五霸), under whom governance was an

---

107   Ibid.
108   Jiaozhi, a place name used since the Han and Tang, was an area in northern Vietnam incorporated into the Ming administrative system after a campaign was waged against Ho Quy Ly, who was accused of violating the tributary system and usurping the throne. In 1427, however, the territory was recovered by a Vietnamese leader. For an account, see John K. Whitmore, "Chiao-chih and Ming Confucianism: the Ming Attempt to Transform Vietnam," *Ming Studies* 4 (1977).
109   *WYMQJ*, vol. 1, 14:465.
110   Ibid.

oppressive hierarchy. For him, the fundamental purpose for which the state existed was to realize the ethical goods embedded in the benevolently paternalistic cosmic-moral order. This order was for him a non-oppressive hierarchy with soteriological import, at least in the sense that should it be functioning correctly it would draw people towards itself, and open them up to the good, specifically their ever-present though obscured original moral nature. Ideally speaking, the role of the emperor and his officials was not, as it were, to impose this order upon those acting outside its natural bounds, but rather to create the conditions most favorable for those teleological attractors (of the good) to work, drawing people naturally towards their proper place. Consequently, the idea that fighting some insignificant rascals out of spite and the desire for victory at all costs could be considered "shaking up the lines of the net" was simply untenable. As he pointed out, "The emperor's relationship with all people and things under Heaven is analogous to the way in which Heaven covers and the earth contains: there is nothing they don't wish to love and cultivate in order to preserve life. Is it possible that one should rather fight with some trivial mean person out of spite and the urge to win and still call this shaking up the lines of the net?"[111] In contrast, drawing upon an oft-cited, classical exemplar for governing the "barbarians," Wang Yangming explained that when recalcitrant Miao refused obedience, Yu 禹 was commissioned by Shun 舜 to lead a campaign, but after three decades the Miao still refused commands, and Yu withdrew forces. By contemporary standards, for these sages to have passed through three decades of campaigns, and then suddenly withdraw and return, constituted a serious failure "to shake up the lines of the net." But in the end the Miao "were reached and came" to the court in submission and for ten thousand generations Yao and Shun have been praised as sages. This is what was meant, in ancient times, by "shaking up the lines of the net."[112]

According to this story from the *Classic of Documents*, what happened was that Shun decided to win the Miao over by disseminating culture and manifesting virtue. Wang Yangming was here referencing what Alistair Johnston has labeled Confucian-Mencian strategic discourse: through pacifistic policies of cultural attraction, enculturation, and displays of largesse (such as offering amnesty), the dynasty could achieve the goal of bringing the enemy to submission without resorting to force. The essence of such discourse was to represent the surrender of the enemy as being the result of the magnanimity of the emperor and his representatives. Once the enemy began to understand that the

---

111   Ibid., 14:464.
112   This story derives from the "The Counsels of the Great Yu" in the *Classic of Documents*. See James Legge, *The Chinese Classics*, vol. 3, *The Shoo King*, 64–66.

emperor and his officials had only the best intentions, and that they were the emissaries of the one just and rational cosmic-moral order, then they would see that their former crimes may well be forgiven and begin to repent of their errors and turn over a new leaf. In the course of doing so, their unbridled behavior, their wanton arrogance, would be dissipated, and they would be able to find their place in the order of things and come within the orbit of the compassionate embrace offered by the universal empire.

The link between this broader notion of moral order and how Wang Yangming believed it could be put into political practice can be gleaned from statements he made concerning governing bandits in other areas of Guangxi. "Regarding the bandits in each area," he explained to officials of the Lingxi Circuit, "this is all a matter of appropriately appeasing and settling them, causing them to fear power and yet remember with gratitude the kindness and beneficence of their superiors, thereby yearly civilizing and monthly transforming, such that they of their own accord will not dare to do evil—this is a good policy."[113] Officials must therefore seriously rethink a "long-term strategy for appeasing, settling, placating, and cherishing."[114] Similarly, in a memorial written in reference to the "barbarian" problem as a whole, he raised concerns that competent officials weren't being appointed for longer enough periods of time to nurture this relationship: "If kind favors are not widely bestowed upon subjects, then the people will be without sincere affection and sentimental attachment; if benevolent power is not spread afar, then the barbarians won't develop an implicit faith and the aspiration to return to the righteous."[115]

Today, given our sensitivity to power and its manifestations—empire, colonialism, and hegemony—it is, of course, easy to view such statements with skepticism. The delicate balance of force and appeal to which Wang Yangming points certainly suggests the insidious operation of a colonizing logic impervious to itself. But what appeared to lead him to find a way to mitigate what he saw as an overzealous response in this case was not only his sensitivity to endemic violence and suffering, his moral intuition of the inherent value of saving innocent lives, and his assessment of strategic issues, but also the fact that he took the rebels' validity claims quite seriously, at least insofar as he attempted to redeem such individuals by giving them some provisional voice within the limits allowed by the benevolent paternalism it implied. And one reason for his being able to do so was his deep suspicion that official misconduct was the source of so many problems. He repeatedly impugned subordinates for

---

113   *WYMQJ*, vol. 1, 18:629.

114   Ibid.

115   Ibid., 18:630

aggravating and perpetuating the conflict. The crux of the problem here was that, as he explained to the Provincial Administrative Commission in Guangdong, "if everything under Heaven is ungoverned, then this is the result of incompetent service on the part of officials."[116] Not only were local officials and clerks passing their days in ease and comfort and putting forth no effort, even higher officials had no empathetic concern for the people, didn't bear in mind the territory they governed, nor did they teach by example or admonish simply by the excellence of their conduct.[117]

Furthermore, Wang Yangming also set forth interpretations of the conflict in such a way as to ask the court to see beyond the bounded intersubjective context afforded by membership discourse and its supportive law-and-order orientation (with its consequent strategic preferences). He wished that the actions of the rebels be viewed both situationally and psychologically, both from the perspective of their immediate circumstances and from the generalized perspective of the humane cosmic-social order the state was supposed to mirror. According to his way of thinking, the actions, motives, thoughts, and feelings of the rebels were at some level legitimate but not necessarily self-reflexively understood. They might, therefore, be doing the wrong thing for the right reason. Thus, he was in a sense positing an unconscious, which was none other than the obscured but always present innate knowledge of the good (*liangzhi* 良知). As opposed to judging these rebels according to the dictates of the external locus of rules and roles provided by membership discourse, he treated them as psychological agents responding to their own consciences. The duty of the official was simply to provide the conditions for restoring this knowledge, such that wayward subjects would be brought within the imperial fold, and social order returned to its natural state. As Yu Yingshi has pointed out, Wang Yangming's teaching of the extension of the innate knowledge of the good was inseparable from his plan for "realizing the Way through awakening the people (*jue min xing dao* 覺民行道)": he believed that if people could be taught to act upon *liangzhi,* then social order would be reconstructed from the ground up.[118]

As opposed to those officials who risked serious consequences in order to "shake up the lines of the net," Wang Yangming informed the court, "your loyal minister believes it is just to absolve these two chieftains of their crimes, and to give them the opportunity to renew themselves, but should they remain stubborn and unrepentant as before, then they shall be slaughtered without

---

116   Ibid.
117   Ibid.
118   Yu, *Song Ming lixue,* 304–305.

regret."[119] He called into question those who stubbornly insisted upon pursuing the rebels for their criminal acts:

> If [we] were able to accommodate [the rebels] then [we] also could, for the time being, place our efforts on bringing warfare to an end, stop the supply of provisions in order to rest and nourish the people suffering from devastation, halt the aspirations of the treacherous, and quell unpredictable uprisings. After the area is settled, and might and virtue are in harmony, the barbarians (*man yi* 蠻夷) will be genuinely convinced of our superiority and righteousness and therefore comply in earnest, and these two local chieftains will then be able to mend their wicked ways and turn over a new leaf. Why would there then be any need to pursue them for their crimes?[120]

Responding with force for the purpose of awing the rebels into submission, he believed, would only further harden them in their posture of resistance, leading to a spiraling cycle of violence. Wang was essentially suggesting that they were resisting because, from their perspective, the cause was just: "From the standpoint of officials, this is all just a matter of recalcitrant Miao rebels resisting their orders; but from the perspective of the *yi*, they all believe it is about the righteousness of loyal followers attempting to preserve the line of their beloved leader." As a result, the native chieftains of other subprefectures were suspicious of the court, and sympathetic to Lu Su and Wang Shou; this is why they were resisting mobilization, procrastinating, and looking on from the sidelines, unwilling to render service.[121] In such conditions, "to lose, merely out of anger over a small slight in a remote place, the hearts and minds of the native peoples in three provinces, here are hidden dangers and calamities difficult to state."[122]

In contrast, he contended that acts of largesse coming from the emperor would inspire confidence on the part of the native chieftains and lead them to surrender; in other words, should a benevolent hand be extended, this would be adequate to correct the systemic problems created by all parties involved, set the cycle of violence and injustice aright, and appeal to the rebels' innate good sense, causing them voluntarily to do the right thing. By "making brightly manifest the emperor's humane love for the living," and saving the lives of

---

119   *WYMQJ*, vol. 1, 14:463.
120   Ibid.
121   *WYMQJ*, vol. 1, 14:472.
122   Ibid.

thousands of innocents, as was the case with Yu and Shun's policies towards the Miao, "of the distant barbarians in the periphery of the empire, there will be none that won't be grateful and cherish our virtue."[123] If the hardship and suffering caused by warfare could only be avoided, soldiers would be able to realize their wish to return home, and subjects would be able to attend to their livelihoods with a glimmer of hope that they might yet survive. But more importantly, the native people's sympathy for the headmen's cause would be duly acknowledged and the chieftains' fears placated: "There are none who won't have their minds put at ease and their wills fixed, be enveloped by and cultivated with deep humanity, and touched by transforming virtue."[124] And along with subtly creating conditions whereby the leaders' minds would be encouraged to respond to the good, an amnesty would also reign in wayward inclinations. Wang Yangming proposed that demobilizing native troops and returning them home would make them preoccupied with local security, and their "arrogant and treacherous vital energy would be subtly dispersed, their desire to act recklessly outside the bounds of authority checked."[125] In the end, with an amnesty, the native peoples would all be "wholeheartedly convinced of the emperor's righteousness and therefore willingly submit."[126]

When Wang Yangming first submitted a memorial with his recommendations on January 2, 1527, the Minister of War Wang Shizhong appended a list of his reservations, and Wang was ordered to carry out further deliberations and report. But the supreme commander's next memorial would be both a response to these concerns and a victory report, for by the time he submitted this on February 22, 1528, he had already taken full advantage of the discretionary powers granted him as supreme commander and grand coordinator. He explained to the court that upon arriving in Nanning he ordered the demobilization of forces, in order to send a clear message to the rebel headmen that the court did not wish to exterminate them, but rather was opening up a path by which they could surrender. In an effort to win a measure of sympathy for their actions, he also portrayed to the court the straitened circumstances in which these rebels had found themselves—how they were pained by the fact that they had no way out, how after hearing that their leader Cen Meng was dead they felt they had nothing upon which to rely, and how they desired only to come forward and plead their case, but given that everywhere were troops preparing to execute them, they had no way to surrender.

---

123   Ibid.
124   Ibid.
125   Ibid.
126   Ibid.

After the demobilization commenced, Lu Su and Wang Shou, on January 28, 1528, sent several headmen to the military headquarters to plead their case. Since their statements seemed largely in keeping with what he had ascertained from his extensive inquiries and "truly worthy of pity," he sent them back to the rebel camp with a dispatch admonishing them for the crimes they had already committed and the suffering they had caused, but with due acknowledgement of both their reasons for committing them and their intentions, which Wang was prepared to recognize as ultimately sincere. These warranted an act of high-mindedness on the part of the emperor, and this was why Wang was giving them the opportunity to surrender.[127]

The supreme commander reported that approximately twenty days after receiving this, tribal leaders Lu Su and several others signed a joint petition and brought forward their case to his military headquarters, repenting of their crimes and surrendering, as well as explaining their circumstances and pleading for the emperor's largesse. In a clear act of ritual obeisance, they led some thirty thousand of their indigenous peoples to an area just outside Nanning's city walls and came forward, "prostrating themselves and pleading for pity for their lives, for remission of capital punishment in exchange for honorable service, in order to atone for past crimes."[128] The conflict was therefore brought peacefully to an end.

"Accommodating the *Yi*"

The fact that Wang Yangming's approach to settling this conflict, as well as his representation of those engaged in resistance, were so different from Yao Mo's raises the question as to just why this was the case. What I have attempted to demonstrate through analysis of their discourse is that each of these supreme commanders reached a very different conclusion regarding the situation before them, and assigned a very different constellation of motives to their adversaries, fundamentally because they did not share the same social imaginary and implicit notions about the normative moral and political order.

Furthermore, I have endeavored to draw out the connection between these diverging imaginaries and underlying implicit conceptualizations of moral order and the differing strategic preferences of the two commanders. In so doing, I am describing how political culture relates to strategic culture, but also explaining just why strategy is invariably linked to culture: strategic preferences

127   Ibid., 14:474–75.
128   Ibid., 14:468.

are always constituted within the moral reasoning of subjects who share more or less articulate background understandings of their social world. Yao Mo, for instance, did indeed appeal to at least two of those strategic cultural assumptions underlying the *parabellum* paradigm that Alastair Johnston believes to be characteristic of Ming grand strategy in the matter of the northern border: the enemy has the worst intentions, and violence is an effective means for achieving peace. In an attempt to suggest the epistemic origins of this kind of violence, I have linked this strategic culture to a more diffuse but pervasive and productive discourse on moral orthodoxy embedded in Ming political culture, and which I have termed "membership discourse" and a "strict law-and-order orientation." Wang Yangming explicitly characterized this position as a kind of bullying paternalism. Instead, he appealed to a situational prudence, into which he channeled his great ability to bring the rule- and role-bound normative perspective of this social system back to the basic principles that he believed were at its core, as well as his belief in the value of life, his concern over the long-term consequences of continued warfare, and his conviction that it was the role of the official to create the ideal conditions for guiding people towards the good.

He was able to express all of this without stepping outside the boundaries of the language of Ming officialdom. By repeatedly drawing from the routine ethical language of Confucian paternalism, especially insofar as this was the discursive means for legitimating policies of appeasement, Wang Yangming was able to represent the voice of the rebels in a faintly dialogical way, to permit them a degree of autonomy within the limits of his and what he clearly felt should be the court's benevolent paternalism. Thus, he referred in the strongest of terms to the principled sentiments that should guide the emperor as "Heaven" to the people, and that were in fact guiding the rebels, who could essentially be seen as wayward suffering innocents forced into an oppositional stance by circumstances partly beyond their control. Under these conditions, he went on to say, an act of appeasement at once demonstrates great largesse, or humanity descending from above, and at the same time assures a response of gratitude arising from the rebels' innate knowledge of the good, or adoration ascending from below, thereby bringing the alienated other into the grand unity by "dispersing their sense of distance and bringing about an understanding of the righteousness of relations between superiors and subordinates."[129]

Wang Yangming's thinking on this matter becomes clearer when viewed in light of his concrete plans for a viable political arrangement, for it is here that we can see the extent and the limitations of his ethical paternalism, as well as

---

129   Ibid., 14:476.

how his vision of social order shaped his strategic policies. When the headmen came forward and prostrated themselves, they apparently did so with a list of demands. Wang Yangming was willing to represent these to the court, and stated in a memorial that they "pleaded for pity for the fact that Cen Meng did not originally intend to commit the crime of rebellion, and for the preservation of his line and accommodation of the feelings of the barbarians (*yi*) on this matter."[130] He cited the jointly signed petition of eleven named leaders, which stated, "This prefecture was originally a native chieftaincy, but ever since it was changed to a regular administration, and subcounty administrative divisions were established, it has been in a state of chaos with no peace, because this change was not suited to native customs, and we lowly people are ignorant and dense and do not know the laws of the Han.... [We] further hope that [you] will stoop to accommodate the feelings of the *yi* on this matter, and reestablish the settlements of tribal headmen."[131] As we shall see, Wang Yangming would choose to meet them halfway in their demands, for while he may have been sympathetic to some of their concerns, he was by no means about to relinquish the upper hand or his long-term goal of integration.

The issue at stake here was just what kind of governance to establish within Sien and Tianzhou at both the higher and lower tiers. Wang Yangming's opinion was that it simply was not feasible to rapidly change these prefectures into regular administrative divisions. According to Jeffrey Barlow, the center of native Zhuang economic (and political) life was the *dong* 峒 (also *xiang* 鄉, *jia* 甲, "clusters of settlements," or "settlement"). Each *dong* was dominated by one lineage or clan consisting of kin and affines. The leaders of these lower tiers were the tribal headmen or deputies (*toumu* 頭目), while leaders with higher rankings in Zhuang political life would typically hold the *tuguan* 土官 titles, or native chieftaincies.[132] This political and geographic hierarchy did not necessarily correspond with the regular administrative system, as the demands of these headmen make clear, and thus instating such a system would more than likely result in both political and economic tensions. Wang Yangming became aware of this from his inquiries. As he explained to the court, "Ever since I received my orders, while en route I made inquiries among merchant travelers and questioned the local gentry, soldiers, and people, and there are none who don't believe that it is appropriate to follow the customs of the barbarians (*yi* 夷), and reestablish the native offices—perhaps then a long-lasting peace can

---

130   Ibid., 14:468.
131   Ibid.
132   Barlow, "The Zhuang Minority in the Ming Era," 20–21.

be obtained."[133] He contended that because the territories of Tianzhou and Sien were all originally occupied by Yao and Zhuang barbarians, who "can't be governed by the rites and laws of central territories (*zhong tu* 中土)," even should the court desire to establish a circulating official, they could not bear it.[134]

As was the case with his policy of appeasement, Wang Yangming found it necessary to fully justify his policy proposals because other unnamed officials were advocating the opposite. He referred to those involved in these deliberations who were insisting that a circulating official be permanently established, believing that failure to do so would not befit the dignity and authority of the throne or garner the proper attitude on the part of the native peoples. "Some believe," he stated, "that establishing circulating officials is the institution for governing central territories, and that removal of such an established post is undesirable because it means a loss of control; that the system of native chieftaincies is the custom of the barbarians, and reestablishing it will therefore mean giving in to their customs."[135] But Wang dismissed this argument by appealing to a higher principle: if establishing a circulating official throws these peoples into turmoil and leads to rebellions, why would the noble man (*junzi* 君子) insist upon doing so?

His solution to the problem was to grant these peoples enough autonomy so they wouldn't be forced into taking a posture of resistance (*genghua* 梗化), but also to keep them sufficiently (and paternally) contained so that they would eventually submit and become civilized (*xianghua* 向化). In other words, his institutional arrangements were designed to balance the coercive force necessary to dissipate and restrain wayward tendencies with the cultural influence necessary to cause the people to submit and transform of their own accord, according to the dictates of their innate knowledge of the good; these arrangements were, in other words, intended to be transitional. In this regard, Wang Yangming's strategic policies can be put into the category of what Steven Harrell refers to as a Confucian civilizing project.[136]

The issue, as Wang understood it, was how "to cause each person to obtain their proper place" when people have such varying temperaments conditioned

---

133   *WYMQJ*, vol. 1, 14:475–76.

134   Ibid., 14:477.

135   Ibid., 14:480.

136   Stevan Harrell, "Introduction: Civilizing Projects and the Reaction to them," in *Cultural Encounters on China's Ethnic Frontiers*, ed. Stevan Harrell (Seattle: University of Washington Press, 1995), 8.

by diverse environments, something that accounted for differences throughout the empire:

> Concerning the establishment of prefectures and counties under Heaven today, as for the difference between the large and small and the complicated and simple, the disparity between the middle country and the border regions, and the difference between circulating officials and hereditary chieftaincies, was there originally such variety? This is also a result of the different material ethers in broad valleys, large rivers, and local environments. When people are born amidst such [local conditions], the firmness or yielding, easygoingness or impetuousness of their disposition varies; their clothing, food, and material culture, likes, dislikes, and customs are of differing types. Therefore, accommodating their circumstances, and not violating their customs, acting in accordance with what they know and not against what is fitting—the crux here is to cause each person to find their proper place.[137]

When Wang speaks of not going against what is fitting according to the very nature of things (*yi* 宜) and of helping people find that place that not only feels right to them but also fits with the broader whole (*de qi suo* 得其所), he is clearly implying innate knowledge of the good. In a letter written while in retirement in Zhejiang, he once told a disciple, "What is right means what is fitting. When the mind attains what is fitting, it is called righteousness. If innate knowledge can be extended, the mind will attain what is fitting."[138] In the case of these native peoples, they are by nature rustic and wild (*guang ye* 獷野) and therefore, in guiding them towards recognizing this knowledge, they have to be treated delicately. His formula was to "reestablish the native chieftaincy in order to accommodate the feelings of the barbarians, divide up the native deputies (*tumu* 土目) in order to disperse their cliques, and establish a circulating official in order to control their strategic power."[139] He analogizes this delicate balance between autonomy and containment to caring for a wild deer:

> The disposition of the barbarians (*man yi* 蠻夷) can be likened to that of wild deer. To attempt to govern them with the system of regular administrations used in the central territories, and control them with the regulations for circulating officials, would be like herding deer into the main

137   *WYMQJ*, vol. 1, 14:479.
138   Ibid., 2:73.
139   Ibid., 14:481.

wing of a courtyard house and expecting them to be tame and docile. In the end, they merely knock over your sacrificial altars, overturn your tables, and dash about in frantic flight. Thus, they should be released in a large and spacious area suited to their rustic and wild disposition. Presently, the purpose of continuing the native chieftaincy is to suit their rustic and wild disposition. However, to allow them their native chieftaincies, without considering how to disperse their gangs and restrain their savagery (*chang jue* 猖獗), would be like releasing deer into the wilderness without the restraints provided by walls, without gelding the stallion and castrating the bear—in the end they will dash afar and stampede ahead, and there will be no way to rein them in. Today, the reason for fragmenting their settlements under separate deputies is to provide the limits of walls and to follow the way of gelding the stallion and castrating the bear. But to set up deputies without placing a superior and laws in their midst would be like herding deer in enclosed gardens without anyone to supervise them or guard the fences to prevent their goring and battling—in the end they will leap the fences, trample the crops, and chew through the fences, without anyone realizing it. Today, the purpose of establishing circulating officials is to provide just such supervisors of the enclosed park.[140]

According to Wang Yangming's scale of civilization, the more arrogant and violent a people's disposition may be—in other words, the closer they are to beasts—the more they are in need of coercive measures, so that they can be reined in and taught to take up their proper place in a higher social order.

The parallel here with his philosophy of desire and principle (*ren yu* 人欲, *tianli* 天理) is evident: such a disposition is simply one particularly striking manifestation of uncultured, potent desire. Without the right conditions, this material force (*qi* 氣) won't be dissipated, and the innate knowledge of the good will remain obscured. This aspect of the learning of the sages implies developmental levels: "All people have this innate knowledge. Only the sage preserves it completely and keeps it free from the least obscuration.... Only because with him the product of inborn knowledge is great, he is therefore said to be born with knowledge and to practice it easily. Ordinary people possess this innate knowledge in its entirety from infancy, except that it is much ob-

---

140   Ibid., 14:481. My translation is borrowed in part from Herold J. Wiens, *Han Chinese Expansion in South China* (Hamden, CT: Shoe String Press Inc., 1967), 219.

scured. But the knowledge of the original substance (of the mind) cannot be obliterated."[141]

On other occasions, Wang bemoans the decline of civilization, and how people's behavior has descended into savageness, akin to that of animals and barbarians, suggesting that his philosophy of self-cultivation and explanation for people's differing capacities for sagehood broadly parallel his scale for measuring levels of civilization.[142] The closer to sagehood an individual might be, or the more civilized a people, the more they can be expected and allowed to act as autonomous agents; the more obscured and less well-endowed an individual might be, or the more uncivilized a people, the more they will require various forms of legitimate coercion, or benevolent intervention.

But although Wang Yangming was advocating coercive measures to ensure stability, he was also taking into account behavior on the part of the headmen that was recognizably principled and in accord with norms. The reason he felt the native chieftaincy could be retained and local deputies appointed to manage lower tiers of governance—why, in short, their feelings on this matter could be accommodated—was that the Cen clan members had for generations governed Tianzhou loyally, and the local populace was deeply attached to them. He explained to the court that these native peoples were mourning over the loss of Cen Meng and his son and wished to see a Cen descendant placed in office. Given the people's pride over the clan's past contributions to the dynasty, and over the imperial patent conferred by the founding Ming emperor, and the fact that Cen Meng did not intend to rebel and even attempted to lay down arms and send a petition to the court, Wang believed their feelings on this matter could be respected.[143]

As Qian Ming has pointed out, later in his life Wang Yangming came increasingly to emphasize the importance of feeling and emotion in verifying truths obtained through extension of the innate knowledge of the good.[144] Therefore, that he was willing to accommodate the tribal headmen was very much in line with his philosophical development, for he granted the importance of allowing these peoples to act on their own sense of what was in accord with their feelings (qing 情), which was clearly an expression of moral sentiment, as well as the source of their resistance. In this regard, a de-emphasis on external forms and prescriptions and an emphasis on interiority and subjective intentions is a theme that runs throughout Wang Yangming's writings. However,

---

141   Wang, *Instructions for Practical Living*, 199.

142   Ibid., 118.

143   *WYMQJ*, vol. 1, 14:483.

144   Qian, *Yangming xue de xingcheng yu fazhan*, 80.

while granting the people their personal attachments—derived from their feeling of gratitude for the kindness of their leaders over generations—he never called into question whether or not this imagined community might in some way be incommensurable with his own, or simply with the greater unity of all under Heaven (*tianxia* 天下). That is, he assumed that their moral consideration must ultimately extend beyond the local community, that the binding power of innate knowledge of the good, as the "one substance of humanity (*yi ti zhi ren* 一體之仁)," would ultimately integrate them into the dynasty—the concrete reification of cosmic-moral order. He made every effort to identify signs demonstrating how this local community fit into the dynasty (expressions of loyalty, willingness to provide service, and demonstration of sincere intent to reform), and where he could find no such signs it became necessary to put controls into place in order to overcome antagonistic sentiments. So even though he was willing to allow local leaders to remain in office and to leave most of the settlements intact, this could only be done under the condition that serious measures be provided to manage them.

In Tianzhou, of the forty-eight clusters of settlements (*jia* 甲) that already existed, eight would be divided out, changed to a subprefecture, and placed directly under the jurisdiction of a descendent of Cen Meng. This descendant, however, would only receive the rank of clerk, but after years of loyal service would be allowed to advance through a series of ranks, and serve eventually as subprefectural magistrate. As for the remaining settlements, they were to be divided up into a lower-level tier of native police stations (*xun jian si* 巡檢司), each run by a respected local headman (*toumu* 頭目), who would be appointed by the court as local deputy. While these officials would be permitted to govern according to local customs, they would nevertheless fall under the supervision of the prefectural magistrate of Tianning 田寧, the new name for the regular administrative prefecture holding overall jurisdiction. As for Sien, Wang Yangming believed that because Cen Jun's descendants had already died there was no reason to reappoint a native prefect. He did, however, establish several native police stations, each falling under the jurisdiction of a native deputy. These would be accountable to a regular prefectural magistrate. All of the native offices could be held in hereditary perpetuity. In this way, competing vested interests would be created, thereby preventing any one particular individual from amassing power: "Each will understand that there is that upon which they depend, and won't dare to be of two minds."[145]

---

145   *WYMQJ*, vol. 1, 14:485. If Leo Shin is correct in his conclusion that Ming officials preferred to maintain order among native chieftaincies by dividing up their power, reducing the

In a statement capturing well just how he sought to strike a balance between limited autonomy and paternal containment, Wang explained that the purpose of his combination of native and circulating officials was to create a system of checks and balances. He was convinced that, as a result of the peaceful settlement, the "awesomeness and virtue" of the court was at a high point, and that peace was likely for some time to come. But he also expected that after several years, in Tianzhou and Sien, "as their numbers grow and amass, and as they become stronger, their aspirations will broaden, and then there will gradually arise the danger of willful domineering and annexation."[146] That is why regular officials must be posted nearby and take charge, and for four reasons. Firstly, even with differing administrative divisions, the people would submit annual taxes, "making them see that there are those to whom service is rendered." Secondly, because the court would hold the power to confer hereditary ranks and mobilize troops, they would understand that "there is an overarching structure of command." Thirdly, although the people would not be bound by conventional ritual etiquette, the institutions for attending court and paying tribute would "make them see that there is that which they must obey." Finally, although the laws of the central territory could not be strictly applied here, the native people would nevertheless understand that they could bring any grievances to the attention of the authorities. In the end, "through annual summer and winter petitions, and the event of special occasions to express congratulations and visit superiors, their sense of distance will be dispersed and they will come to understand the righteousness of relations between superior and inferior."[147] Thus, by envisioning them within the trajectory of a gradual process of acculturation that fit well with his ethical philosophy, and by proposing policies with sufficient constraints, Wang Yangming was able to convince the court to adopt his institutional measures.

Conclusion

As empirically sophisticated as Alastair Johnston's study of Chinese strategic culture might be, the overarching conclusions he draws for the northern border would benefit from the nuances of individual case studies, especially concerning internal conflicts in border zones of southern China. My intention in

---

size of their domains, and allowing their numbers to proliferate, then Wang's policy was in line with the norm. For Shin's argument, see his *Making of the Chinese State*, 95–99.

146   *WYMQJ*, vol. 1, 14:481.

147   Ibid.

this chapter has been both to examine such a case, as well as to add to our understanding of the historical context for Wang Yangming's service during this
time. By so doing, I hope I have deepened our understanding of what Johnston
refers to as two Chinese strategic cultures: "one a symbolized or idealized set of
assumptions and ranked preferences, and one an operational set." In this study
of the conflict in Tianzhou and Sien, Yao Mo's definition of the conflict and
strategic preferences belonged to the operational set, while Wang Yangming's
belonged to the symbolic. What I have attempted to do here is to explicate
more fully just how each achieved such a definition and how this, in turn, was
related both to the broader ends they envisioned and the means they believed
necessary to achieve them. That is, I have tried to bring to the fore the underlying moral frameworks through which their respective strategies were legitimated.

There are, however, two important limitations to this study, which raise
what are perhaps unanswerable questions. Having analyzed the discourse in
the official communications of these two supreme commanders and placed it
in historical context, are we able to say that they truly believed in the policies
they were arguing for, or rather that they used these policies and the rhetoric
justifying them simply for some ulterior motive, such as personal reputation or
political factionalism? Should the latter be the case, their moral reasoning before the court was again nothing more than a rhetorical overlay, at best the
accepted idiom for putting military options on the table.

Although this chapter has not been conceptualized along the lines of the
aims of empirical social sciences, I nevertheless believe it is very likely that
both Yao Mo's and Wang Yangming's cultural and moral reasoning did in fact
influence their policy choices. Nonetheless, there is solid evidence to suggest
that Yao Mo chose the policy he did because he was attempting to vindicate his
son of potentially damaging accusations of connections to Cen Meng, something that compelled him to shift from possible appeasement to a hardline
approach.[148] As for Wang Yangming, there is some evidence to suggest that the
policies he presented in his official communications were not only the outcome of his personal reasoning, but also a response to the broader political
scene. Tang Kwok-leong, for instance, goes so far as to claim that Wang may
have preferred to continue with Yao Mo's policies but did not because he believed he would have insufficient support from the Ming court.[149] Should that

---

148   See p. 247.
149   Tang, "Tianzhou shi fei wo benxin," 276–79. Tang's compelling argument is based on
       important circumstantial evidence. However, I believe that to draw the conclusions he
       does from it, most of what Wang's letters and communications say, as recounted in this

have been the case, though, it would be difficult to tally this behavior with his other military campaigns, when he took action without prior approval from the court or at least arrogated to himself an unusual amount of authority. Besides, if he was doing the bidding of the court and protecting the interests of followers in positions of power, then it is hard to see why he did not, as Grand Secretary Gui E hoped, take forces into Annam (northern Vietnam) for a punitive campaign and why he also left Guangxi without prior approval. At best,

---

chapter, would have to be dismissed. In fact, much of Tang's evidence can be interpreted in a different light to bring it more in line with what the majority of the evidence says. One enigmatic piece of evidence is recorded by Wei Jun about an official named Weng Wanda, who was present at Wang's side in the aftermath of the campaigns and near the time of his death. Wang supposedly stated to him that "the affair in Tianzhou was not what I originally intended; in later generations who will forgive me?" Taken out of context, this suggests that indeed Wang may have wanted to attack the headmen. But the notes Wei Jun subsequently provide cast serious doubt on this interpretation. Wei notes that in a memorial to the court (*xie en shu* 謝恩疏), Wang insists that there was no need to send in the military to execute the headmen or to remove the native officials: that is why when he entered Guangxi he dispatched someone to summon them. Wei then mistakenly states that Wang arrived in Wuzhou during the tenth month of 1527 but then slowly made his way to Nanning in order to alleviate suspicion, arriving there in the seventh month of the following year, some ten months later. In actual fact, he arrived in Wuzhou late in the eleventh month and then in Nanning during the first month of 1528. Wei then recounts a story according to which, when Wang was lecturing to students and staff in his headquarters, someone questioned whether such dilatory conduct might be indulging the enemy's hostility, wondering if Wang had some kind of secret plan at work. Wang responded, "The frontiers of Ling (Guangxi and Guangdong) have for long suffered the hardship of war. I have indeed summoned them and it is not the case that I am luring them into a trap." Furthermore, Wei states that the headmen and native officials then obediently accepted orders but that "mean persons" tried to extort them, so they became angry and suspicious, giving Wang Yangming no choice but to give in to their petitions. Thereafter, however, they served under him in successfully attacking Eight Stockades and the Rattan Gorge. And most importantly, Wei states that it was after Wang departed and under his successors that these headmen then became unruly and unmanageable; but even then, Wei places much of the blame on those officials. Therefore, major inaccuracies in this account aside, what it suggests is that if indeed Wang really stated that "the affair in Tianzhou was not what I had originally intended," then he was probably expressing regret about problems that arose in the aftermath. This interpretation makes sense in light of the fact that communications dispatched after the campaigns point to his frustration with the native headmen (Cf. Chapter 6 of the present work). For Wei's account, see Wei Jun 魏濬, *Xi shi er* 西事珥 [Miscellanea of Guangxi], in *Si ku quan shu cun mu congshu* 四庫全書存目叢書, shi bu 史部, vol. 247 (Jinan: Jilu shushe chubanshe, 1996), 784–85.

Wang may have later regretted his decision to pursue a policy of appeasement with the headmen of Tianzhou because the outcome was not as ideal as he had hoped.

In any case, whatever the truth may be about the motivations of the two supreme commanders, I would propose that their differing policies pointed to two conflicting moral frameworks for defining situations of conflict and strategic choices, and that regardless of motives or interests we simply don't find any other notions of moral and political order in Ming times which could have served as a background for conceiving of and expressing alternative ideas in official discourse. In other words, Yao Mo and Wang Yangming may well have been perfectly capable of adopting or arguing against the reasoning of the other, but they both nevertheless always remained within the parameters of their chosen moral frameworks. In fact, it was precisely the ferocity of both supreme commanders' defense of their respective standpoints that led me to conclude that the clashing moral frameworks to which they appealed in the policy discussion provided a background horizon that has ramifications throughout Ming political culture as a whole.

Another issue is just how the policy discussion here compares to others during the Ming. As stated in the opening to this chapter, far more research has been done on the primary concern of strategic studies—external conflicts— and the overwhelming conclusion has recently been that some kind of cultural or structural realism prevailed. But what of the ambiguities of internal resistance and rebellions, especially those involving non-Han ethnic groups? The literature on this topic is indeed vast but as of yet there is no systematic study synthesizing the findings from the perspective of strategic culture comparable to the study of the northern border by Johnston. Nevertheless, Herold Wiens long ago concluded that as an advocate of pacification, Wang Yangming was an exception, and more recent studies seem to confirm that suspicion. He believes that "[f]or the most part, when an uprising occurred, pacification measures were first attempted. These might be described as a mixture of negotiation, denunciation, propaganda, and threats of dread punishments, together with military maneuverings and the use of force."[150] However, if these measures failed, then armies would be raised for the purposes of subjugation. Likewise, although more recent studies on the establishment of provinces in southwest China bring out the complex give and take between the Ming state and indigenous forces, as well as how the two shaped each other, they also stress the confidence of the Ming dynasty and its increasing power to integrate the periphery through political, military, and educational administrative hierarchies.

---

150   Wiens, *Han Chinese Expansion in South China*, 221.

In his study of the creation of Yunnan, for example, Bin Yang seemingly echoes Alastair Johnston when he states, "As soon as the imperial state felt strong enough, it was determined to transform frontier society into another Chinese society."[151] According to him, the overall trend during the Ming and Qing is the weakening, suppression, and subjugation of native regimes.[152]

However, some curious facts about the events in Tianzhou might be kept in mind when studying other internal uprisings or armed disturbances, especially those involving groups defined as "barbarians." Firstly, Yao Mo may not have believed at first that force was necessary, and had to memorialize three times before the court approved his plans to attack Cen Meng. Secondly, a complex process of ongoing negotiations (often referred to as appeasement and exhortation, *fuyu* 撫諭) at the local level involving lower civil and military officials is alluded to in both Wang Yangming's and Yao Mo's memorials and official communications. This suggests that what leaves a record behind are those cases in which these negotiations simply broke down, and where the use of force became necessary. As we have seen, others involved also did not wish to attack Cen Meng or the chieftains, and their reasoning appears to be based on some level of principle and not solely on weakness. Finally, Wang Yangming insisted repeatedly that local gentry, soldiers, and people sympathized with these "barbarian" peoples, and believed that the unrest was the result of the policies of misguided officials. Given all these factors, even though the general trend during the late imperial period was towards firmer political integration of peripheral regions, this should not obscure the local dynamics in particular cases, and the complex ways in which differing attitudes in Ming political culture may have played a role in their resolution.

---

151 Bin Yang, *Between Winds and Clouds*, accessed February 1, 2014, www.gutenberge-e.org/yang/index.html, 4.3.

152 Leo Shin, on the other hand, in his definitive study of Guangxi during the Ming, argues that the preferred solution to bringing the unruly western half of Guangxi under control was not to reduce the number of native chieftaincies but rather to create smaller ones and allow the number to proliferate. See his discussion in *The Making of the Chinese State*, 58–105.

Subduing and Civilizing the Yao

Wang Yangming took no credit for the peaceful conclusion to the conflict in Tianzhou, which for him demonstrated instead the "authority and virtue of the [Ming] court."[1] According to his analysis, the court, concerned that justice had not been served and those natives "obstructing change (*geng hua* 梗化)" might rightly be aggrieved, had appointed him supreme commander. His duty had thus been to investigate the circumstances behind the rebellion and possibly open up a path by which the native headmen might come forward with sincere intentions, surrender, and offer allegiance, thereby obtaining a pardon for their crimes.[2] All of this had been achieved. In a memorial submitted on March 3, 1528, drawing amply upon the standard rhetoric praising the all-encompassing Jiajing emperor, Wang stated that such an ideal outcome to this conflict was the result of these natives (*man yi* 蠻夷) realizing the emperor was greatly concerned for their wellbeing.[3] In a bid to win their voluntary submission, he had let it be known to the headmen that the emperor "has extended the most pious humanity, loving the people as he would his own children, and out of fear that even just one thing might not find its due place." Indeed, "even should it be the sentence of just one man, yet concerned that he has been wronged, [the emperor] personally presides and judges."[4] Given such extraordinary concern for one, Wang asked, "should thousands be involved, how could [the emperor] lightly annihilate all of you?"[5]

So pleased was Wang Yangming with the outcome that he left testimony in Tianzhou in the form of a commemorative stone inscription:

> During the summer of the *bingxu* year [1526] of the Jiajing emperor's reign, imperial armies attacked Tianzhou, and then clashed with the peoples of Sien, inciting resistance. Troops from four provinces were assembled and the turmoil carried on for years. At the time the emperor, out of pity and concern, asked, "Is it acceptable to permit the innocent among

---

1 *WYMQJ*, vol. 1, 14:493.
2 Ibid., 14:474.
3 For a study of this universalist rhetoric as it appeared in the *Ming Veritable Records*, see Wade, "Ming Shi-lu," 43–56.
4 *WYMQJ*, vol. 1, 14:474.
5 Ibid., 14:474–5.

the people to die?" So he commanded the Marquis of Xinjian Wang Shouren, "Go forth and oversee the armies! Placate with virtue, don't slaughter with the military instrument." Troops were withdrawn and good faith generously proclaimed. The native peoples were touched with admiration and, within ten days, bound themselves and came forward to surrender, numbering seventy-one thousand. They were all freed and returned to their fields, and security was therefore restored to the two provinces.[6]

The only task that remained now, he stated in a March 3 memorial, was to appoint competent officials "thoroughly familiar with the local customs and conditions of the people" to oversee the implementation of his measures for reconstruction and resettlement in the now devastated regions of Tianzhou and Sien.[7] For this, Wang turned to Lin Fu 林富, a provincial administrative commissioner he had long known, and petitioned the court to grant him the discretionary powers necessary to "comfort and settle" the area. As he would later inform Commissioner Lin, "After Si[en] and Tian[zhou] came forward to surrender, and I was making plans for settling and bringing peace, I knew full well that I must find someone magnanimous, generous, benevolent, and empathetic, and whose virtue and authority had for long earned the confidence of the natives, to approach them as a father and nurture them as a mother, knowing [they] could not be controlled for an extended period of time by force and cunning without in the long run causing an uprising. In this regard, there was no one more qualified then [Lin] Xingwu."[8]

Such were the events of spring 1528, after which time Wang Yangming might very well have once again petitioned for leave on account of his ongoing illness, which, judging by his symptoms, was probably pulmonary tuberculosis. As he would inform his friends in letters dispatched from Guangxi, he had become so weakened from his disease that he could hardly breathe and could barely get out of bed. Nevertheless, the supreme commander chose to remain in the region and address other chronic disturbances in Guangxi about which he had been receiving repeated reports. "Because the suffering in this region had reached extremes," he explained to a colleague, "I had no choice but to act to rescue the people from adversity."[9] This adversity was banditry, specifically the rampant plundering by what he referred to as "Yao bandits (Yao zei 瑤賊)"

---

6   Ibid., 25:948.
7   Ibid., 14:466–67.
8   Ibid., 22:883.
9   Ibid.

hiding out in remote, mountainous regions of Eight Stockades (Bazhai 八寨) and Chopped Rattan Gorge (Duan Tengxia 斷藤峽).

Wang Yangming had told the native headmen that clearly his patience had limits, and that should the bandits in their territories delay surrendering and fail to "mend their wicked ways and follow the good (*gai e cong shan* 改惡從善)," imperial armies would arrive to carry out the righteous will of Heaven (*tian tao* 天討).[10] Wang made a vast distinction between the headmen and these so-called Yao bandits, whose intentions, he felt, were entirely different. In his first memorial to the court, entitled "Attack and Destroy the Incorrigible Yao Bandits," he made his case for taking military action:

> The court's authority and virtue have been proclaimed and whether a foreign country or a distant barbarian, all understand awe and respect before it, presenting gifts and paying tribute. And yet these Yao bandits alone dare, with the support of thousands, to fan out in all directions and plunder the villages in and around Wuyuan and other areas, killing people and setting fires, without the slightest scruples. . . . While your servitor has been stationed at Nanning, commoners have come forward again and again to pour out their woes, and to plead for troops to speedily rescue them from their misery, for when it is dawn they dare not plan for dusk. The measure of wickedness of the bandits is great, the gods are angered and people aggrieved, and it shall not be easy once again [for these bandits] to escape execution.[11]

By the time he dispatched this memorial—on May 3, 1528—Wang had already begun campaigning in the two regions. He had called upon Commissioner Lin Fu and Regional Military Commander Zhang You to lead the headmen of Tianzhou and Sien and their native troops to the Eight Stockades, for at the very moment they had surrendered they had also promised to "requite the court" by killing bandits. As for the Rattan Gorge, he also ordered Guangxi Right River Circuit military officials to lead native troops from the neighboring province of Huguang that had originally been mobilized by Wang's relieved predecessor Yao Mo for the purpose of suppressing disorder in Tianzhou.

Thousands of "Yao bandits"—to borrow the label commonly employed by representatives of the Ming state—perished during these campaigns, and just as is the case for the peaceful settlement of unrest in Tianzhou and Sien, there is a great deal of material concerning these, as well as Wang Yangming's

---

10   Ibid., 14:475.
11   Ibid., 15:493–94.

recommendations for maintaining security in the region and advancing the cause of civilization. To be sure, it is difficult to put a finger on the identity of those labeled "Yao bandits," save from the perspective offered in records left by him and other Ming officials. Although scholars have tried to trace a coherent genealogy linking these Yao to what is referred to as the Yao ethnic minority group 瑤族 in China today, others have cast doubt upon such continuity.[12] To simplify matters, we can assume that these peoples were considered one category of non-Chinese natives (*man yi* 蠻夷) because they were not registered subjects of the state, they had a different language, culture, and customs, and they were often at odds with registered Chinese and politically integrated indigenes.

Compared to the peoples of Tianzhou and Sien, Wang Yangming had little sympathy for the Yao and therefore felt justified in leading campaigns of extermination against peoples whose character he deemed incorrigible. Even though he occasionally acknowledged that local social dynamics and systemic institutional problems played a role in fostering banditry, he primarily attributed such conduct to willful wrongdoing. His solution was a theorized combination of measures involving applying military force and implementing policies aimed at persuading the resisting Yao to recognize the legitimate authority of the Ming state. More specifically, Wang identified two different types of Yao settlements and correspondingly developed two different but related sets of policies targeting each population. For those he believed could not become integrated as law-abiding subjects and therefore he deemed as incorrigible, he implemented the "path of exhortation through rewards and setting an example through punishments (*quan cheng zhi dao* 勸懲之道)" by using the military. For those for whom it could be determined that there might yet be "the signs of a change of heart and embracing of civilized ways (*hui xin xiang hua zhi ji* 回心向化之機)," he implemented the long-term policy of appeasing, settling, soothing, and subduing (*fu chu sui rou zhi chang ce* 扶處綏柔之長策).

Accordingly, Wang Yangming first carried out two major punitive campaigns to exterminate those beyond the pale but followed up with a series of measures aimed at bringing about the willing submission of the remaining Yao.

---

12   See, for example, Leo Shin, *The Making of the Chinese State*, 16–17. For a discussion of the distinctions between "Yao" and *min* subjects in Guangxi, see David Faure, "The Yao Wars of the Mid-Ming and Their Impact on Yao Ethnicity," in *Empire at the Margins: Culture, Ethnicity, and Frontier in Early Modern China*, eds. Pamela Kyle Crossley, Helen F. Siu, and Donald S. Sutton (Berkeley: University of California Press, 2006), 186. He calls the Rattan Gorge an "internal frontier."

This will be the subject of this chapter. I propose to unpack Wang Yangming's policies by first outlining how he achieved a description of the peoples he was dealing with and determined that some could justifiably be exterminated. Secondly, I will recount the course of the campaigns justified by his reasoning. Thirdly, I will outline the measures he implemented in the aftermath, with a view to achieving a better understanding of the relation between his political philosophy and ethics, civilizing discourse and measures, and the goals of the Ming state as he understood them. Finally, I will suggest that his two approaches to policy, legitimated as they were on strong philosophical grounds, tended to obscure in a doctrinal and formulaic manner the other factors that Wang Yangming recognized as responsible for this violence in Guangxi.

Why Employ the Military Instrument?

In his dealings with the rebellious native headmen of Sien and Tianzhou, Wang Yangming was opposed to the use of force, for intertwined strategic and philosophical reasons. For him, the state must distinguish between aggrieved subjects and savage bandits. In the end, he relegated the Yao of the Rattan Gorge and Eight Stockades to the latter category. The Rattan Gorge is a mountainous region located in southeast Guangxi, extending about forty miles along the Qian River 遷江 between Wuxuan County 武宣縣 and the prefectural seat of Xunzhou 潯州府. Traffic passing from Wuzhou 梧州 in the east to northwest Guangxi usually traversed this path. However, during the Ming, this route was considered dangerous, and officials frequently reported "bandits" emerging from inaccessible dwellings for the purpose of attacking merchant boats and plundering neighboring areas.[13] Equally problematic was the territory in and around Eight Stockades, another mountainous region located northwest of the Rattan Gorge. These stockades were fortresses located on steep cliffs in the vicinity of Hongshui 紅水 (Crimson Water) River where it passes through the bordering area of Qingyuan Prefecture's 慶遠府 Xincheng County 忻城縣 and Nanning Prefecture's 南寧府 Shanglin County 上林縣.[14] Just as is the case for the Rattan Gorge, Ming records are strewn with reports of disturbances originating from this area, and it was viewed as the source of much of the trouble plaguing the region, as well as the place to which Yao bandits would

---

13   Shin, "Tribalizing the Frontier," 117.

14   For a description, see Okada Takehiko 岡田武彦, Ō Yōmei kikō 王陽明紀行 [Journal of Wang Yangming's Travels] (Tokyo: Meitoku, 2007), 265–67.

flee and go into hiding whenever the Ming state sought to tame the area and suppress armed disturbances.[15]

Wang Yangming was well informed about the history of banditry in these two regions and the many campaigns and measures that the Ming state had engaged in to control it. "Since the beginning of the dynasty," he would state later in a victory memorial, "campaigns have been repeatedly undertaken but [the Yao] have never been brought to submission."[16] He recounted some of this background history in such a way as to suggest that the campaigns he led and the resulting successes were a normal response to necessity and even cosmic retribution eradicating a deep-rooted scourge upon the area. Wang reminded the court of several attempts by predecessors to quell the unrest, with one consistent theme running throughout: an endless cycle of military campaigns followed by appeasement, the result of which was invariably a temporary reprieve followed by increasingly "brazen" and "unscrupulous" outlawry.[17] Concerning the bandits living in Eight Stockades, he informed the court that they are "especially ferocious, tough, savage, and wicked. With their sharp spears and poisonous crossbows, none can withstand an attack by their vanguard. Furthermore, their walled stockades are located amidst natural obstacles, so there is no path by which troops can march."[18] Wang explained that ever since Commissioner-in-Chief Han Guan, early in the Ming, led tens of thousands of soldiers into the region and surrounded these bandits but was unable to exterminate them, officials had regrettably resorted to appeasement. Thereafter, officials attempted on many occasions to coordinate forces and attack but always failed to defeat the bandits, instead suffering extensive losses.[19]

---

15   A compilation of all incidents involving the military found in the *Veritable Records* can be found in the *Ming shi lu lei zuan: junshi shiliao juan* 明實錄類纂軍事史料卷 [Categorical Compilation of the Ming Veritable Records: Volume of Historical Records for Military Affairs], ed. Wu Bosen 吳柏森 et al. (Wuhan: Wuhan chubanshe, 1993), 388ff. Between 1380 and 1402, for example, we find in the *Ming Veritable Records* entries concerning approximately seventeen incidents of armed disturbances and banditry in and around the Rattan Gorge and Eight Stockades, as well as the campaigns led by the Ming state in response (388–410).

16   *WYMQJ*, vol. 1, 15:506.

17   For an account of Rattan Gorge events, see Frederick W. Mote, "The Ch'eng-hua and Hung-chih Reigns, 1465–1505," in *The Cambridge History of China*, vol. 7, eds. Frederick W. Mote and Dennis Twitchett (Cambridge: Cambridge University Press, 1986), 343–402.

18   *WYMQJ*, vol. 1, 15:506.

19   Ibid.

As for Han Guan 韓觀, it is unclear just how much Wang Yangming knew about this one-time Guilin guard assistant commander who was later promoted to regional military commissioner by the founding Ming emperor Zhu Yuanzhang. But Ming accounts certainly suggest that he was not one for dialogue under the guise of appeasement or benevolent paternalism. Han's solution was straightforward: slaughter in any way possible. His tactics were to encamp and cut off the bandits' connections to surrounding areas by killing off people, and then to attack strategically critical locations with concentrated force. Stories also had it that, when holding banquets, he would kill rebel-bandits until "blood filled the hall," slice up their skin for bedding, steam their heads for a fine delicacy, and in front of crowds use chopsticks to gouge out their eyes. Whatever the truth may have been, even the Yongle emperor (Ming Chengzu, r. 1402–1424) found it necessary to dispatch a sealed imperial letter admonishing him: "It is all too easy to incite the *man* to rebel, but difficult to bring them to submission, and the more they are killed, the more they become ungovernable. You proceeded there to quell them, and should make it your duty to placate and cherish them, not merely to slaughter."[20] Indeed, we have no evidence that the natives were for Han Guan ever considered human beings deserving of paternalistic largesse.

Wang also referred to massive campaigns led by Censor-in-Chief Han Yong 韓雍 (1422–1478), explaining that "during the reign of the Tianshun emperor, Han commanded two hundred thousand soldiers and came to pacify Guangdong and Guangxi, thereafter destroying their lairs and haunts. But not long after the soldiers withdrew, the bandits again attacked and made Xunzhou fall, occupied the city, and caused great turmoil. [Han] again assembled an army, simultaneously attacking and offering amnesty, after which they withdrew to their lairs and haunts."[21] Indeed, Han did lead two campaigns in the Rattan Gorge and surrounding territories he considered to be the "wings" of the Rattan Gorge bandits. However, these took place not during the reign of the Tianshun emperor Zhu Qichen, as Wang Yangming claimed, but rather during that of the Chenghua emperor Zhu Jianshen (1464–1487). In any case, after these campaigns, the commissioner implemented a series of measures to maintain

---

20   *MS*, 166:4479–80. For further discussion of Han Guan, see Han Zhaoming 韓肇明, "Mingdai Guangxi Da Tengxia yaomin qiyi 明代廣西大藤峽瑤民起義 [Uprisings by the Yao People of Guangxi's Great Rattan Gorge During the Ming Dynasty]," *Zhongyong minzu xueyuan xuebao*, vol. 4 (1981): 27; Gao Yanhong 高言弘 and Yao Shunan 姚舜安, *Mingdai Guangxi nongmin qiyi shi* 明代廣西農民起義史 [A History of Peasant Uprisings During the Ming Dynasty] (Nanning: Guangxi renmin chubanshe, 1984), 21.

21   *WYMQJ*, vol. 1, 15:506.

security in the region, but these too failed to control the violence in the region. According to Wang's assessment:

> From this time on, officials bent over backwards in every possible way to appease and settle them [the bandits], sometimes achieving several months of temporary peace. But when they felt the slightest bit of dissatisfaction, they again became violent, killing and plundering even more poisonously. Since the days of their ancestors, ruthlessness has passed down from generation to generation, and it has become their nature (*xing* 性) to be savage. They can't be changed into civilized subjects. In recent years, as officials' strategies for subjugation and appeasement have become increasingly exhausted, the bandits' venomous cruelty has worsened daily, to the point that it is no longer manageable.[22]

This conclusion is similar to that reached by nearly every official who had attempted to deal with the problem of Yao banditry. In the final analysis, the origins of the problem boiled down to a savage nature beyond hope of reform. In general, we find in Ming accounts the more frequent but brief characterization according to which the Yao bandits—as Han Yong stated in his "Chopped Rattan Gorge Memorial"—"by nature prefer to do as they please and hate being constrained by the law." This judgment led automatically to the conclusion that force was necessary.[23] When Han Yong was preparing to attack the Yao, he had a debate with Grand Secretary Qiu Jun 邱濬 (1420–1495) over the best strategy to employ. Whereas Han advocated penetrating the treacherous mountainous area and exterminating the bandits by destroying their "lairs and haunts," Qiu found this approach to be untenable. Nonetheless, his starting point was the same: "The rampant violence perpetrated by these bandits has continued for some ten years or longer up to today, and [they] have become increasingly arrogant and wanton (*jiao zi* 驕恣)."[24] Qiu believed the savages of the south were by nature feminine (*yin* 陰) and compared them to flies and

---

22   Ibid.

23   Han Yong 韓雍, "Duan Tengxia shu 斷藤峽疏 [Memorial Concerning Duan Tengxia]," in *Han Xiangyi ji* 韓襄毅集 [Collected Works of Han Xiangyi], in *Huang Ming jing shi wen bian* 皇明經世文編, ed. Chen Zilong 陳子龍, vol. 5 (Taipei: Guo lian tushu chuban youxian gongsi, 1964), 139.

24   Qiu Jun 邱濬, "Liangguang shi yi shu 兩廣事宜疏 [Memorials Concerning Matters in Guangdong and Guangxi]," in *Yue xi wen zai* 粵西文載 [Anthology of Literature in Guangxi], ed. Wang Sen, *Si ku quan shu* 四庫全書 ed., 1466:670–72. For a study of this policy debate, see Chu Hung-lam, "Qiu Jun yu Chenghua yuannian Da Tengxia zhi yi de guanxi 邱濬與成化元年 (1465) 大藤峽之役的關係 [The Relationship between Qiu

gnats. They relied on mountains, fleeing when soldiers arrive while returning to plunder when they leave. That is why they are hard to conquer.[25]

At least one predecessor, however, had urged some restraint on the part of the state, emphasizing largesse over might. In the 1450's, Grand Secretary Yu Qian 于謙 (1398–1457) received a memorial from the Provincial Surveillance Commission in Guangxi, in which it was stated that the bandits were growing in power and becoming increasingly savage, brazen, and "unbridled in their willfulness." The commission attributed this to excessive appeasement and failure sufficiently to apply the military instrument. On the contrary, Yu favored negotiation, and he clearly stated the best framework for handling unrest: "Because the Chinese (*huaxia* 華夏) and non-Chinese (*man mo* 蠻貊) are all children of the court, it is only as a matter of last resort that the military instrument and punishment are applied—what is to be treasured is the simultaneous implementation of both largesse and might, for afterwards none will not submit."[26]

This is precisely what, years later, Wang Yangming was formulating to eradicate the ongoing banditry: a policy of largesse and might, albeit with an emphasis first on might. Just like his predecessors, he believed that some among the Yao bandits, including whole settlements, were beyond the pale, and therefore could not be changed through "appeasing, settling, soothing, and subduing." Even before bringing peace to Tianzhou, when Wang had first arrived in Nanning—the provincial seat for Guangxi—he addressed the problem of Yao banditry in areas neighboring the Rattan Gorge. In a response to officials who reported ongoing disturbances in these areas, he asserted that the reason they had failed to bring this banditry under control was empty threats, which only encouraged even more brazen behavior: "This is all a result of the fact that in recent years [the threat] of raising a large force for a campaign has been nothing but empty words, and the eagle strike is no longer heard of. They have taken note of this, and act even more wantonly and unscrupulously."[27] His orders were that officials should gather accurate information about these "incorrigibly wicked bandit lairs," and make it their goal only to "kill those whose crimes are great and measure of evil extreme." He explained, however, that "as for the

---

Jun and the Campaigns in Great Rattan Gorge During the First Year (1465) of the Reign of the Chenghua Emperor]," 115–33.

25   Qiu, "Liangguang shi yi shu," 1466:674.

26   Yu Qian 于謙, "Lun yi shan zei shu 論山賊疏," in *Yue xi wen zai* 粵西文載 [Anthology of Literature in Guangxi], ed. Wang Sen, *Si ku quan shu* 四庫全書 ed., 1465:493.

27   *WYMQJ*, vol. 1, 18:627. The "eagle strike" refers to responding to changing strategic conditions by rapidly initiating surprise attacks.

rest, [you] may fully carry out generous appeasement, allowing them to mend their wicked ways and follow the good (*cong shan* 從善), making it your duty to extirpate the treacherous and remove the cruel, warning a hundred by punishing one, for there is no need to capture and kill in large numbers, such that jade and stone fail to be distinguished, near and far become alarmed and suspicious, and it becomes difficult to act at a later time."[28] Later, in his first memorial to the Ming court explaining why he was in the process of attacking the Yao bandits, Wang cited reports from subordinate military and civilian officials, exemplifying just how he had come to view the Rattan Gorge and showing how he had come to accept attitudes widely shared by local officials:

The Yao bandits of the Chopped Rattan Gorge, Niuchang, Liusi, Modao and other areas link up above with the Eight Stockades' savages and below with the bandit settlements at Baizhu, Gutao, Luofeng, Huaxiang, Fengmen, Fozi and other places. For years [they] have attacked and plundered prefectures, counties, and villages, killing people and setting [their homes] ablaze, kidnapping women and children and stealing property and livestock. The people have been afflicted with terrible suffering, fleeing for their lives, and abandoning their fields. Registered residents daily decrease in number, and each day the villages appear increasingly deserted. [The problem has] spread over thousands of *li*, which have already all changed into bandit territory. Although the civilians and soldiers who have suffered harm in each of these areas have repeatedly petitioned for a campaign of extermination, because officials are preoccupied with so many other affairs and lacking in sufficient force, they have quietly tolerated and accommodated, hoping for temporary calm. But the bandits have only become further emboldened and violent.... Recently, by good fortune, the native peoples of Sien and Tianzhou were touched by the transformative power of the emperor, bound themselves and came forward to surrender and offer their allegiance. Peoples near and far have turned to us and submitted.... It is only the rebellious bandits of the lairs of Chopped Rattan, knowing full well their crimes cannot be pardoned, that as before continue to rely on strategically inaccessible places, obstructing roads and plundering villages, without the slightest scruples.[29]

28   Ibid.
29   Ibid., 15:493.

As for Eight Stockades, in his memorial to the court outlining his plans for maintaining security, Wang explained why this region was at the heart of banditry and key to controlling it:

> It is only the bandits of Eight Stockades whose stockades each number over a thousand [people]. Encircled by mountains on four sides, they together occupy one strategic location difficult of access. When they have nothing better to do, they divide up along paths and come out to plunder, and when there is an emergency, they quickly flee to their lairs. This mob of thousands all bands together without even being rallied, with no advanced planning takes identical action, without prior strategizing coordinates. Therefore, although referred to as "Eight," in reality it is only one stockade. This is why these bandits have the power of numbers and great strength, and why for some time those who have attacked them have been unable to defeat them. The bandits of other lairs rely on Eight Stockades to harbor them, every time there is an emergency taking refuge there, so that there is no way to reach them for thorough questioning. Eight Stockades has only to call out to them and the mass of bandits responds and gathers. Thus, the mass of bandits is to Eight Stockades as spokes are to a hub and roots to trees.[30]

The conclusion for Wang Yangming was obvious: "If Eight Stockades is not removed, there is no hope the mass of bandits will dissipate."[31]

On the whole, Wang's justification for carrying out the ensuing campaigns of extermination in the spring of 1528 was, as he put it, "to remove the scourge and bring peace to the people."[32] After all, he chose to do this on his own initiative, for he had come to believe that he must act for the sake of the people and even as an agent of cosmic retribution. Indeed, the supreme commander would repeatedly urge officials to mirror the court's pity for those pressed by hardship, bearing in mind the havoc wrought by banditry. "If you do not capitalize on this opportunity," he urged them, "following my orders to carry out the punitive power of Heaven, in order to do justice to the grievances of the people, vent the anger of the spirits, and cleanse this scourge upon the region, [and if you instead] allow the remnant evildoers to remain, leaving behind the roots and sprouts—how can this be the mind and heart of one who serves as

---

30   Ibid., 15:511.
31   Ibid.
32   Ibid., 18:646.

mother and father to the people?"[33] Thus it was that at the outset, as part of his two-prong strategy, Wang Yangming first chose to display might and deploy the military instrument.

Using Military Force

As was the case with his plan for suppressing the princely rebellion in Jiangxi and his tactics for bringing peace to Tianzhou and Sien, Wang Yangming did not seek prior approval from the Ming court for his strategy to quell banditry in Rattan Gorge and Eight Stockades. As he would later explain in his victory memorial, key to success was preserving the element of surprise and "capitalizing on the opportune moment." Had those living in the "bandit lairs and haunts" caught wind of an impending campaign, word would have spread fast and they would surely have immediately banded together, withdrawn deep into the mountains, and barricaded themselves in virtually impregnable locations. But by availing himself of his discretionary powers as supreme commander, Wang was able to move his forces so rapidly that "mighty as a thunderbolt, pressing as wind and rain, the campaign occurred and yet near and far no one was aware that troops had waged war."[34] According to his estimate, no more than eight thousand soldiers carried out a campaign that lasted less than three months and resulted in only three thousand enemy dead. Expenses, moreover, were minimal, which explains why the "grievances of the people were cleansed away," and the "scourge of a century was extirpated."[35]

In fact, it does appear that in early 1528 a number of strategically favorable conditions were ripening at the very moment the supreme commander was receiving so many eye-opening reports about the bandits, something that may have indeed influenced his decision to march into these internal frontiers. Firstly, the native armies mobilized by former Supreme Commander Yao Mo to quell the Tianzhou uprising had yet to return home. At this point, Wang Yangming was just in the process of ordering officials in Guangxi to prepare the provisions necessary to ensure that these troops from two Pacification Commissions in the neighboring province of Huguang could depart the front without causing turmoil as they passed through villages and towns along the way. Conveniently enough, their route home would bring them very near to the Rattan Gorge. As Tang Kwok-leung has aptly noted, to demobilize and send home

---

33   Ibid.
34   Ibid., 15:507.
35   Ibid., 15:509.

these native troops without giving them the opportunity to achieve recognition and rewards for a victory could have caused much discontent. By moving quickly to campaign in the region, Wang was killing two birds with one stone.[36] Thus, in April he ordered officials of the Left River Circuit of Guangxi to oversee the pacification commissioners and their native troops in what would amount to a series of attacks on various stockades in the Rattan Gorge region. Wang explained to the court that although the bandit leaders had at first made defensive preparations and moved their families and livestock further up into the mountains, later they relaxed their guard because all appeared quiet in Nanning, where he was stationed. They had no intelligence indicating mobilization, and likely surmised that the native troops were preparing to depart.[37]

Furthermore, when the headmen of Tianzhou and Sien had come to Wang Yangming's military headquarters and surrendered in February, they also, as he explained to the court, "out of a sense of indebtedness to the emperor for his largesse in bestowing upon them the chance to continue in their livelihood, vowed to requite through the service of killing bandits."[38] Thus, in April he also ordered Lin Fu and Zhang You (who were sent to oversee the implementation of his policies for reconstruction in Tianzhou and Sien) to take command of government troops. In cooperation with the native armies of these headmen, they were to depart from those prefectures at their discretion, march to Eight Stockades, destroy the lairs, and build stockades for control and defense. At the same time, they were to "proclaim to each bandit that for the crimes of year after year killing and harming law-abiding subjects, attacking and plun-

---

36   Tang, "Tianzhou shi fei wo ben xin," 283–84. He further argues that Wang Yangming carried out this campaign for a variety of reasons: to satisfy native officials' desire for meritorious achievement; to resolve disputes between regional commanders unhappy with how the credit for the campaign against Cen Meng had been doled out; to test the loyalty of the recently surrendered Tianzhou headmen; and to satisfy supporters at court. But it is one thing to say that Wang Yangming carried out these campaigns because he could and that his choice of strategy was impacted by these factors, and it is altogether another thing to claim that he used the military solely for political reasons and to satisfy the desires of various parties. In fact, all the arguments in Wang's official communications and other evidence such as statements in letters suggest that he was principally concerned with outlawry in poorly controlled border zones. In addition, such behavior would certainly go against important precedents he had set throughout his life, including his willingness to repeatedly defy the emperor, even at risk of his and his family's life. I am thinking, for example, of his refusal to release the Prince of Ning to the emperor so that he and his commanders could earn meritorious recognition. As for this campaign, perhaps his principles just happened to align well with political expediency.

37   *WYMQJ*, vol. 1, 15:500.

38   Ibid., 15:509.

dering subprefectures, counties, and villages, the principal ringleaders shall all be destroyed, as well as evildoers who followed them, in order to manifest the punitive power of Heaven and permanently remove the roots of this calamity."[39]

So it was that while stationed in Nanning, Wang Yangming planned two different campaigns: one for Chopped Rattan Gorge and one for Eight Stockades. These commenced in late April and early May of 1528. For the most part, accounts in his victory memorial amount to routine lists stating which regular and native civilian and military officials led how many troops into what areas and settlements, took how many heads, and recovered how many kidnapped women, children, and other miscellaneous stolen property. Still, on occasion we find some vivid description of the battle scenes. On the April 20, some six thousand chiefly native officers and soldiers under the command of Left River Circuit civil and military officials went ashore at a trading port located along the Qian River. With the element of surprise on their side, these forces first attacked Niuchang and Liusi, catching the Yao bandits off guard. But although the enemy was "caught by surprise and at a loss as to how to respond," they nevertheless "relied on their courage and ferocity," swarmed into a mob, and staged a defense.[40] In response, the pacification commissioners and their troops, "without regard for their lives, gave their all, charging arrows and stones, repeatedly clashing and killing them, dealing a setback to the bandits' front line, and defeating them."[41]

These initial assaults were followed by a series of military operations aimed at bandit fortresses located in nearby mountains. After searching through settlements and pursuing the bandits in very difficult terrain that required "attacking higher positions from lower positions," climbing trees and ascending cliffs, the troops were ordered to withdraw and regroup in the prefectural seat of Xunzhou in preparation for a second assault on more bandit lairs located in the gorge.[42] Once again, soldiers were to proceed along rivers and go ashore at nearby ports. But this time the bandit leaders, now better informed, withdrew into mountain fortresses, planned ambushes, and "unified their strategic power, coming out to repel [our forces]."[43] Wang explained to the court that government troops and native soldiers charged "suddenly like wind and rain," and although the bandits' "fighting spirit was deflated," they nevertheless dropped all concern for their lives and fought more ferociously than the bandits of

---

39   Ibid., 18:644.
40   Ibid., 15:500.
41   Ibid.
42   Ibid., 15:501.
43   Ibid.

Niuchang. In the end, though, their ranks were broken and the leaders were all killed or captured.[44]

The campaign in Eight Stockades began in earnest on May 11, when a force of approximately six thousand soldiers reached the bandit stockades. During the night these soldiers, under the command of "headmen requiting the court through service" and regular civil and military officials, had advanced so silently to the enemy lairs that "whichever village stockade they passed remained so quiet that no one was aware there were soldiers."[45] Thus, when they attacked the next morning at dawn, "the bandit outlaws were only then awakened and alarmed, believing the soldiers had descended from the skies."[46] What followed was a series of victories and setbacks. After an initial rout, Wang explained, "the brave and fierce from stockades in all directions assembled a mob of some two thousand, each with long spears and poison crossbows, and united their strategic power, yelling, swarming, and advancing to repel us."[47] What followed was yet another rout, after which the remnant bandits fled to the mountains and barricaded themselves.

Over the ensuing three weeks, the supreme commander's forces would eventually attack and occupy remaining stockades, but they continued to face difficulties caused by bandits taking flight throughout a daunting terrain of meandering rivers and steep, densely forested mountains. Wang vividly described for the court how his troops hunted down the bandits:

> Although the bandits were at first routed, nevertheless some dispersed and some reassembled, but seeing that all their rebel leaders and their most valiant and fierce had by this time been captured and killed, they all fled deep into the mountains and far away.... Our forces pressed and pursued them from all directions, catching up with them at Hongshui River, but because the bandits had already boarded vessels and left shore, the soldiers could not reach them. Nevertheless, since there were many bandits and the vessels were small, they filled these up by piling up on top of each other, and the vessels could not transport them. Furthermore, because they were all fighting to cross over, and came to blows with one another at the very moment they were encountering a fierce gust of wind, all the boats capsized. [Those who] swam, climbed ashore, and escaped with their lives only numbered twenty or so.... After the weather cleared,

---

44 Ibid.
45 Ibid., 15:502.
46 Ibid.
47 Ibid.

our troops divided up along different paths, entering the mountains to hunt down and exterminate the bandits. There were no traces of the bandits, so [the troops] penetrated more deeply, and saw that between the cliffs and valleys those who had fallen to their deaths were innumerable. The stench was so suffocating they could not continue. In the grottoes located along cliffs near and far, sons, wives, young, and old piled up dead below the trees, numbering approximately four thousand. It was the case that these bandits, out of alarm, had taken flight amidst heavy rains without first provisioning themselves with grain or rice. They starved for weeks, and after the weather cleared the blazing sun scorched and roasted them. The poisonous miasma was suffocating and burning, and after another half a month or so, they all rotted away and died.[48]

Most campaigning had come to an end by late June, at which time Wang Yangming estimated that the majority of those principal culprits deemed irredeemable had been captured or killed. Although he continued to dispatch troops in order to round up remnants, he now turned his attention to implementing policies aimed at bringing about the willing submission of and civilizing those Yao bandits yet capable of "regretting their crimes and mending their ways (*hui zui gai guo* 悔罪改過)" and "complying with what is good." However, in the process of doing so, he would also advocate policies and acknowledge other possible reasons for unrest, which did not fit so well with his claim that it was largely a matter of the Yao bandits' character or nature, their willful wrongdoing. It is to these policies that we now turn.

Implementing the Path of Appeasing, Settling, Soothing, and Subduing

Although Wang Yangming found it necessary to remove "incorrigible Yao" from the scene in Guangxi by force, he had very different ideas about what would be required to achieve long-term stability in the region. At the very moment that forces were striking, pursuing, and exterminating recalcitrant elements in bandit settlements in and around Eight Stockades, he was already chastising officials for recommending more military operations in the Rattan Gorge, where major campaigning had already ceased. As summer approached in 1528, the supreme commander had already decided that a show of force through application of the military instrument was limited in what it could achieve.

---

48   Ibid., 15:503.

Officials thus had the duty to win over the minds and hearts of those yet capable of reform through implementation of the "path of appeasing, settling, soothing, and subduing," and it would be this approach that would dominate during his remaining time in Guangxi.

Wang Yangming understood that in order to have any chance of success in dealing with native peoples, capable officials with some knowledge of local customs and conditions should be appointed to serve and be allowed to remain for extended periods of time, something that rarely happened. Having used the military, Wang now reverted to his preference for nonviolent solutions achievable through an asymmetrically structured, hierarchical social setting. Negotiation was not to take place between equals seeking mutual understanding within the parameters of an egalitarian framework, nor between rational, self-interested individuals in a contractual setting, but rather between superiors and inferiors within the intersubjective framework provided by what I have called "benevolent paternalism."

At the most fundamental level, Wang believed that should the state fail to establish a sufficiently trusting relationship, peace would never be achieved in the region. However, from a contemporary perspective, the kind of relationship he envisioned would most definitely appear colonizing not only because the balance of power in paternalism is by its very nature asymmetrical, but also because Wang fully intended to impose an order upon these peoples, the goal of which was to enact a consciousness of the legitimate authority the Ming state. To his way of thinking, there could be no other meaningful grounds for resolving difference, and thus an element of forced acculturation was inevitably present in his policies.

In his official communications, Wang often spoke of the "way to govern the *yi*" and the "long-term policy of appeasing, settling, soothing, and subduing." The crux of this policy was to adopt strategies conducive to fostering communication with the natives in such a way that they would come to recognize their moral responsibility to representatives of the Ming state and therefore willingly submit to their authority. For example, when he dispatched a memorial declining his appointment as grand coordinator in Guangxi in early 1528, he proposed that the court should instead appoint Wu Wending, a former colleague who had served him during his campaign to suppress the Prince of Ning's rebellion. As with all such recommendations, uppermost in his mind were certain virtues conducive to winning the confidence of the people. "If subjects fail to be influenced by our kindliness," he wrote, "they will be without sincere, loving gratitude and sentimental attachment. If benevolent power fails to be spread afar, then the natives will not have implicit faith or the motivation to become subjects and adopt our ways."[49]

Similarly, in a communication to officials serving in neighboring Guangdong, Wang Yangming explained very precisely this long-term strategy when he stated, "Regarding the bandits in each area, this is all a matter of appropriately appeasing and settling them, causing them to fear power and yet remember with gratitude the kindness and beneficence of their superiors, thereby yearly civilizing and monthly transforming, such that they of their own accord will not dare to do evil—this is a good policy."[50] Clearly, he believed that no grounds for long-term peace would be established unless non-Chinese within the imperium could be brought into the moral community as he envisioned it. It did not enter his thinking that other ethnic groups might be independent moral communities with aspirations that were potentially incommensurable with those of the state. Insofar as the Ming state and its representatives were the bearers of moral community—and, ultimately, its foundational transcendent realities (human nature)—subjects were responsible to them at the level of conscience and to find their identity defined by their relation to the Ming.

With regard to his political practice, Wang Yangming's unifying ethical discourse often drew a curtain over complex social scenes so that they fit into a hierarchy that served the ends of the state. This tendency is evident from the following passage:

> On the whole, although customs and practices might perhaps differ, nevertheless Heavenly principles (*tianli* 天理) and ethics (*min yi* 民懿) are universal. If those who serve as county officials are truly able to put forth a whole-hearted effort, exhaust their intelligence, extend their genuine compassion and love for the people (*ce da ai min zhi cheng* 惻怛愛民之誠), and fully implement the path of appeasing, settling, educating, and nurturing, then even should [the people] be natives (*man mo* 蠻貊), there are none that won't become civilized. How much more so has that not been the case for those recently surrendered, newly resettled, outlaws of the prefectures and counties of the central territories? Prior [to becoming outlaws], they were also among those that could be classified as good people. If I am able to love them as if they are my own children, then afterwards could there be those that don't love me as a father?[51]

49 Ibid., 14:466.
50 Ibid., 18:629.
51 Ibid., 17:615.

That Ming officials had the authority to act based on principles they believed to be applicable to all is evident from this passage, and not surprisingly the approach that Wang Yangming adopted for non-Chinese ethnic groups also followed the same logic as his approach to teaching youth and governing subjects in general. "You must be genuine in your love and compassion, and truly in your heart look upon the people as you do your children," he declared, "and only then can you cultivate and nurture, subtly guiding, causing the people to be inspired and motivated . . . otherwise there will be no trust and you will only burden the people."[52]

Notably, when Wang spoke of genuine love and compassion (*cheng ai ce da* 誠愛惻怛) as the foundation for the kind of transformational and civilizing relationships he envisioned developing between officials and subjects, as well as between teachers and students, he was drawing upon language that had become critical to his philosophical teaching. In a letter of advice dispatched to his sons late in 1527 while en route to Guangxi, Wang explained that "what I have taught all my life when discussing learning is only the three characters *zhi liang zhi* 致良知 (extending the innate knowledge of the good). Humanity is the human heart. The dimension of innate knowledge of the good that is genuine love and compassion is humanity; without a truly loving and compassionate heart, there is also no innate knowledge of the good that can be extended."[53] That he was here stating concisely the crux of his teaching late in life would later be confirmed by one of his students, in a postface to this letter. According to his student Chen Jiuchuan:

> This is nothing but exhortation to diligently preserve long-standing precepts. As for the three characters *zhi liang zhi,* this is what our teacher always unflaggingly taught others. As for his speaking of "truly loving and compassionate self being the extension of the innate knowledge of the good," this was how he taught his followers late in life. . . . Therefore, from the fact that his family correspondence touches upon this, one can see that the way in which our late teacher cautioned and exhorted is no different from how his disciples benefited from him.[54]

Likewise, as idealistic as it might seem for the rough-and-tumble province of Guangxi, Wang Yangming provided the same guidance. This was how he justified this civilizing project, confident as he was in the universality of transcen-

---

52   Ibid., 17:626.
53   Ibid., 26:990.
54   Ibid., 26:993.

dent (Heavenly) moral principles (*tianli* 天理) and a shared ethic. Such a mission was further legitimated by the presence of the Ming state, the physical embodiment of those very principles he was preaching. As such, the state had the authority to impose its will—by force if necessary—on recalcitrant peoples residing in internal frontiers, as well as to expect them to conform to the kind of hierarchy that entailed.

Shortly after the conclusion to the campaign in the Rattan Gorge, Wang Yangming received reports from officials stating that bandits from the very lairs that had just been annihilated were still roaming into areas east of the gorge region and causing turmoil. These officials recommended stationing native troops under the command of native officials at the county seats of Pingnan 平南 and Guiping 桂平, close to the gorge. In response, the supreme commander composed a communication entitled "Placate and Comfort Roving Bandits." Here he laid out his vision for governing wayward non-Chinese ethnic groups in such a way that they would on their own initiative begin to participate peacefully in the universal empire. He called this "the way to govern the *yi* (*chu yi zhi dao* 處夷之道)."

Uppermost in Wang Yangming's mind was no longer the character of the savages themselves, but rather creating those conditions that would bring about their willing submission in the wake of campaigns aimed at the most unruly elements. As was the case with his proposals for bringing stability to Tianzhou, Wang turned his attention to external factors inciting people to banditry. He believed that at this stage—as he informed these provincial officials—continued deployment of the military would only place obstacles in the way of the strategy he wished to pursue: "As for the method for employing the military, the most important strategy is to attack enemy territory; but as for the approach towards managing the savages (*yi*), the highest [principle] is to attack their minds."[55]

Unpacking this further, the supreme commander explained, "Now that a campaign of extermination has been carried out against the Yao, officials should make a sincere effort to appease and comfort, in order to bring peace to [the savages'] minds. For if they are not made to submit in their hearts, even should we choose to retain Hu[guang Pacification Commission] forces for an extended period of time, as well as continue to deploy native wolf troops, relying on military force in order to maintain control and awe them into submission, this cannot in principle be called a long-term strategy."[56] He also elaborated upon the kinds of problems that stationing troops would likely

---

55   Ibid., 18:650.
56   Ibid.

cause. Soldiers from other provinces, resentful over being forced to live far from home and in need of provisions, harass and prey on the local population, which therefore invariably feels victimized and seeks revenge over accumulating grudges. In the end, the local population will be thrown into a state of turmoil and many would be compelled to turn to banditry.

In place of force, Wang advocated a policy aimed at building confidence from the ground up:

> If rewards and punishments are suitably applied, then good behavior can be encouraged, and bad behavior discouraged. If the path of exhortation and admonishment is clearly demonstrated, then governance will become stable. Today, as for the incorrigible Yao, troops have been raised to campaign against and destroy them and punishment has been applied to those who have committed crimes. But as for the others who have been attacked and defeated and have fled, even should you desire to appease them and seek their surrender, it is doubtful they will trust you. Thus, you must begin with nearby law-abiding lairs and offer generous appeasement and comfort, causing those who do good to be further encouraged, and therefore to become unwilling to continue relations with [the bandits]. By so doing, the gang of evildoers will be isolated and their power diminished. The law-abiding lairs can then spread the message, guide, and instruct the bandits, causing each bandit to have a change of heart and turn towards civilization. Thereafter, our [goal of] seeking surrender through appeasement can be achieved, and the path of governing through placation and cherishing implemented. As for cherishing men from afar, and appeasing the barbarians, how can one rely solely upon heavy militarization or might? The ancients were able to take Heaven, Earth, and the ten thousand things as one, and they were therefore able to comprehend the will of all under Heaven.

To now act in this way, Wang concluded, is to understand that "for any great matter, one must govern it according to circumstances, guide it according to its momentum, and move it along by taking advantage of the right moment."[57]

When Wang Yangming ordered officials to employ various methods for attacking Yao minds, he likely meant their will or intentions. He sought to redirect the will of these peoples by, on the one hand, fostering their desire to do what is good and right as well as to regret and correct their errors. In a sense, the state was here playing the morally corrective role of nourishing the innate

---

57   Ibid., 18:650–51.

knowledge of the good.[58] On the other hand, he wanted officials to implement concrete measures to appease and placate the people. Just what the latter meant—aside from ceasing hostilities—I will return to in a moment. But in terms of measures aimed at convincing resistant populations to settle down, the supreme commander ordered officials to send out proclamations. These were rich in moral rhetoric and hardly subtle, with their threats and insistence that officials had gone out of their way to give the Yao every chance for reformation:

> In recent years Niuchang and other stockades have become accustomed to evildoing, and troops were assembled for a campaign. As for those of your villages with good people, our prefectural officials have offered appeasement and comfort, and have absolutely not harassed you, for it is important for each of you to solidify your intention to do what is right, so that you can also together partake of the happiness of the great peace. For although there are those among you who have committed crimes, from this time on should you choose from deep in your hearts to mend your ways, officials will not pursue prosecution for your past crimes, so do not bring suspicion upon yourselves. But should others be incited by you, then you will bring destruction upon yourselves, and it will be too late for regrets. As for those remnant diehards who have escaped extermination, should you truly regret your crimes and begin anew, then officials will also treat you as they do the law-abiding and appease and comfort you. As for those who have long persisted in evildoing without regretting and mending their ways, one attack, ten attacks, one hundred attacks will assuredly lead to your destruction, and this is not an empty threat. Therefore, for each of your stockades, whether you choose what is right or choose what is wrong shall be seen in the days to come, and it is only right for you to be fully aware [of the consequences].[59]

The emphasis in the proclamation is on the moral reformation of resistant ethnic groups in Guangxi as the key to long-term stability. Such moral discourse runs throughout his official communications, just as it does in his approach to teaching more generally. In all cases, his didactic discourse is quite consistent: the focus is on fostering "the determination to mend errors and follow the good," for he believed "there are no instances where someone makes a mistake

---

58 For my explanation of the relationship between willing and innate knowledge of the good, see the opening to Chapter Four.

59 *WYMQJ*, vol. 1, 18:653.

and does not personally realize it; therefore, he should only worry that he is unable to correct it."[60] The language used in the following moral injunction closely parallels that used in his official communications:

> Regret is the beginning of goodness, and the recovery of sincerity. When the mean person regrets something, he doesn't dare to give free reign to his wickedness.... If the mean person regrets his wickedness and yet becomes even more disrespectful and clever, more resentful and swindling, then the wickedness becomes extreme and can't be dissipated. Therefore, regret is the source of the distinction between good and evil, the crux [of the distinction between] sincerity and falsity.[61]

When applied to resistant "others" living within the imperium, the implication of these moral injunctions becomes obvious: they knew they were in the wrong, and therefore had to be made to see this with their own eyes and conceive a desire to change their ways. This is the logic behind his moral discourse as applied to errant people.

Nevertheless, Wang's official communications concerning affairs in this region repeatedly point to the social, economic, and political troubles in Guangxi, evidence that he was all too aware of the complexity of issues underlying the social tensions. This would seem to belie the formulaic distinction between incorrigible and redeemable that was so critical to his portrayal of the social scene and to his decisions regarding where to employ the military and where to implement stabilizing measures. Indeed, describing the nature of the social tensions rather bluntly even prior to the first campaigns, the supreme commander had cited a report for the court stating that "because relations between Yao and registered subjects are irreconcilable, should they not be exterminated, then the registered subjects will have no way to pursue their livelihoods in peace."[62] Yet, in the aftermath of the campaign, he placed the blame for some of the conflict in the area on just such villages with resident commoners. These villagers, according to his reading, were domineering over recently resettled Yao and Zhuang peoples, encroaching on their land, and seeking vengeance for past grievances. But more importantly, they levied false accusations before local officials, bringing these officials over to their side, getting them caught up in cycles of revenge, and leading them to arrest some of these natives. Thus,

---

60   Ibid., 4:172.
61   Ibid., 24:909.
62   Ibid., 15:492.

villages that might conceivably be "turned towards civilization" through their "intention to turn towards the good" (and, hence, become law-abiding) were instead becoming alarmed and suspicious and therefore more inclined to rebel.[63] Indeed, there is a disconnect here between Wang Yangming's moral discourse and what is clearly an interpretation of political resistance as being rooted in social and ethnic tensions.

But even with the most incorrigible savages, as Wang had identified them, the picture remained throughout far messier than he may have wished it to be. He found it necessary to chastise even the native commanders of Sien and Tianzhou. He had reason to believe that, far from finishing off the Eight Stockades' bandits, these commanders were actually colluding with them and allowing them to go free. It appeared originally that these bandits, instead of repaying the court for choosing not to exterminate them, were simply taking advantage of an opportunity to plunder. Wang also frequently alerted officials to bandits who had fled and were hiding out in what he called "Yi Zhuang" villages in neighboring territory, while also bemoaning the fact that those responsible for patrolling these areas were simply cooperating with the bandits.

We find further evidence for the economic origins of resistance in a communication to officials governing a prefecture that included Chopped Rattan Gorge. Having called upon them to provide relief for resettled bandits, Wang pointed out that, although the incorrigible Yao bandits had been subjugated and remnant gangs had been resettled, the atmosphere in the region remained tense. Wang therefore claimed there was a need to implement further measures to calm alarmed villagers: "In the midst of such alarm and fear, they cannot suddenly trust, and thus we must first offer generous appeasement and relief to nearby law-abiding peoples, thereby encouraging and exhorting those who have the potential to become law-abiding. By so doing, the bandits will come to know that there is a place to which they can turn, and then you can gradually summon and appease."[64] The way to achieve this was fairly straightforward. Responsible civil and military officials in the area were to go to the law-abiding stockades and distribute fish and salt, as well as to issue official proclamations. It was now these officials' responsibility, he stated, to "cause those who intend to turn towards the good to become more firmly determined, so that they won't be incited and lured in by remnant bandit outlaws. As the good people daily grow in number, the evil gangs will be daily dissipated. Furthermore, they will be motivated to encourage and exhort the bandits one by one, allowing them to change mistaken ways and renew themselves. Should

63   Ibid., 18:654.
64   *WYMQJ*, vol. 2, 30:1105.

there be those who come forward to surrender with sincere intentions, then offer appeasement."[65] In addition, he ordered these officials to survey occupied lands to prevent later conflicts, select individuals who had the confidence of the local population, and appoint them as headmen.

This official communication indeed hints at a number of problems that were likely far more fundamental than character in producing individuals beyond the pale. Wang Yangming's calls for distributing fish and salt, surveying lands, and appointing competent and just officials familiar with local conditions for extended periods, all point to systemic problems within this border province that incited chronic disorder. It is at least clear that the ethnic groups living in the Rattan Gorge and Eight Stockades repeatedly faced scarcity, encroachment, and unjust treatment by officials who had little or no understanding of their language and customs or who always sided with registered Chinese migrants or cooperative native officials. As Wang pointed out in one memorial, many serving in the area were of such an inferior and vulgar nature that they did not belong in the ranks of the literati, and without correcting this problem, there was simply no way to cure violence on the frontier.[66] Indeed, if Wang Yangming's "path of appeasing, settling, soothing, and subduing" was to function as intended, this matter had to be addressed.

Towards Long-term Peace

The measures that Wang Yangming proposed for establishing long-term stability in the territory encompassing Eight Stockades and the Rattan Gorge illustrate clearly how he intended to bring the troublesome populations securely under the control of the Ming state. The first issue he faced was one encountered by every official assigned to the region. Give the configuration of power held by native chieftaincies and regular administrations in the region, the issue was how civilian and military institutions could be reorganized so that government would be effective in both maintaining security and winning the confidence of both registered and unregistered subjects, Chinese and non-Chinese alike.[67] To this end, Wang proposed relocating a guard and battalion, moving prefectural and county seats, founding a county, and reconfiguring jurisdictional boundaries. With the guards and battalions, his idea was

---

65   Ibid.
66   *WYMQJ*, vol. 1, 15:498.
67   For a study of political and military institutions in Guangxi, see Shin, *Making of the Chinese State*, 29–40.

to establish military garrisons in strategically critical locations and make the necessary adjustments to ensure they operated effectively. With the changes in civil administrative units, the idea was to bring the Ming state closer to non-Chinese ethnic groups so as to foster confidence and assert control. But in addition, he was also concerned with the best means to spread civilization throughout these unstable regions, so as eventually to tame and assimilate it, and to that end he promoted education.

In a memorial to the court entitled "Administering Eight Stockades and the Rattan Gorge So As To Achieve Enduring Peace," Wang divided the territory of Guangxi into two very different halves. He explained that those administrative divisions extending from the provincial capital in the south to the east were largely governed by centrally appointed officials. But in the west and northwest, from Nanning to Tianzhou, native villages were the norm. It was this territory that frequently posed serious problems for the court. But having now established administrative seats overseen by regular officials in Tianzhou and Sien, in coordination with the provincial seat at Nanning, these three could form a tripartite defensive configuration, thus promoting the goal of "bringing peace to the people and governing the country effectively."[68]

In this memorial Wang also presented to the court the rationale behind his proposals for bringing about order in the region:

> As for the strategy for now, it is surely appropriate to concurrently implement a policy of subjugation and accommodation. Destroying the thoroughly savage bandits is the way to warn against evil, and appeasing and providing relief to those Yao that have turned towards civilization (*xiang hua* 向化) is the way to encourage the good (*quan shan* 勸善). Now that evil has been punished, it is incumbent at once to govern through encouraging the good, by having respective officials travel the regions of those villages and stockades that have submitted and bring gifts for services rendered, express sympathy and provide relief, bring proclamations, provide fish and salt, and appoint and install tribal leaders. [They shall be] instructed that the reason the court attacked lairs was that they were accustomed to evildoing but that [the reason officials now appease] owes to the fact that obedient villages and stockades are now at ease and pursuing their work in peace. By so doing, [their] wish to be law-abiding shall be further solidified. [They will also instruct them that] should there be those who would yet resist, you should capture them and send them to the yamen and receive a hefty reward for your service; as for those

bandits that have escaped destruction, should they truly in their hearts regret their evildoing, they may be permitted to surrender and treated as good subjects. By so encouraging those inclined to turn towards civilization and day after day to come in person to offer allegiance, the remnant gang of evildoers will be isolated, and the power of the bandits will disperse naturally.[69]

Wang's moral rhetoric as expressed to the Ming court merely repeated in capsule form the very logic for pacifying the region that he had been presenting to his subordinate officials. He accepted the legitimacy of the native chieftain system so long as it could be shored up and remain tightly under the control of the paternalistic state. But it is principally in this memorial that we find just how this process was to be backed up with concrete measures aimed at addressing what amounts to a rather foggy picture of conflict between *man yi* ethnic groups, resettled outlaw populations, registered subjects, middlemen operating between the state and *man yi*, and the state itself.

Because he believed Eight Stockades served as the gathering point for normally disconnected bandit settlements spread out among surrounding prefectures, during the campaigns Wang Yangming traveled and studied the topography of the region, noting strategically critical locations. He emphatically claimed to the court that "the mass of bandits is to Eight Stockades like spokes to a hub or roots to trees,"[70] which is why he proposed cutting off and destroying those spokes and roots. In fact, by then he believed he had already achieved this goal because his campaigns had exterminated the most incorrigible elements in this region. His new objective was to put in place a civilian and military presence that would stay on top of the problem by "cutting of [the bandits'] vessels and clutching their throats."[71] To achieve this, he first proposed moving a military guard from the town of Binzhou 賓州 to the middle of Eight Stockades and building a walled town to house it.[72] This stockade was Zhou'an 周安, which his troops had recently cleared out and which he considered to be ideal because it was the place where roads traversed from all directions. To support this guard's approximately five hundred soldiers and their families, he advocated allocating nearby bandit fields to them so they could form a self-sustaining military farming colony.

69   Ibid., 15:517.
70   Ibid., 15:511.
71   Ibid., 15:510.
72   Ibid., 15:511.

In addition, Wang Yangming also recommended relocating several of the battalions stationed in Qianjiang Prefecture to barracks that were to be constructed just outside the walled town. These battalions were, however, commanded by native military officers appointed by the state, according to the Ming policy of "controlling the *yi* with other *yi*."[73] This policy was aimed at keeping a lid on violence, in this case originating from Eight Stockades, but Wang perceived that it was problematic, and indeed it commonly stirred up trouble during the Ming. These native commanders and their battalions were originally established to control Eight Stockades; however, as the power of the Eight Stockades' bandits grew, the native officials no longer dared to enter their territory. Instead, they formed agreements with the bandits and even colluded with them in exchange for a share of the plunder. Wang even believed these native officials used the power they gained through such contacts to manipulate regular officials.[74]

To contain this situation, Wang stated to the Ming court that he had the leaders of these battalions bound and brought before him in his headquarters, at which time he threatened to behead them as a lesson to others should they fail to change their ways. He claimed they pled for their lives and offered to atone for their crimes by rendering the service of killing bandits. He then ordered them to take their native troops to Eight Stockades and form, together with the guard, a military farming colony in and around the town.[75]

By instituting these two measures alone, Wang Yangming assured the court, in less than ten years campaigns would no longer be necessary at all, for the native peoples would all "become respectfully submissive and transform into obedient subjects."[76] Nonetheless, he also saw the need to establish a more effective civilian government. His third proposal was to relocate the prefectural seat of Sien from its then location of Qiaoli 喬利 to a courier station about 60 *li* to the southeast (Huangtian 荒田). He believed Qiaoli was altogether too inaccessible, located as it was in mountainous terrain. This new location was better suited for communication, commerce, and administration because it was level, surrounded by fertile land, and served by the Wuyuan River 武緣江, which linked it up with the provincial capital at Nanning. In addition, having little access to local officials in distant yamens, it was easy for the *yi* to become estranged and suspicious, but because this new location was far more accessible, he stated, "the *yi* will be able to meet their needs in this

---

73   Cf. Shin, *Making of the Chinese State*, 90–99; Wade, "Ming Shi-lu," 198–204.

74   *WYMQJ*, vol. 1, 15:512.

75   Ibid.

76   Ibid.

prefecture; coming and going day and night, they will submit to our authority and become allegiant subjects."[77] After a time, he proposed, "relying on governing through the headmen and local police offices, officials of the prefecture will be able to follow local customs in order to accommodate the feelings of the *yi*. But they will also be able to establish subcounty administrative divisions and implement our laws to govern the people of Wuyuan 武緣. The *yi* and the *xia* (non-Chinese and Chinese) will be on good terms, and public and private needs met. Therefore, moving and rebuilding the prefectural seat of Sien in Huangtian is also for the purpose of preserving peace and governing the people."[78]

This change was to be accompanied by relocation of a county seat, reorganization of the boundaries of this troublesome prefecture, and the creation of a new county. Wang Yangming believed that by so doing, prefectural authorities would be better financed and empowered, more areas could be settled with taxpaying registered subjects, and the native populations would have closer and more peaceful relations with the state and with registered Chinese populations. The last point was particularly important because, as he hinted throughout his communications, the natives were often short of foodstuffs, suffered the predation of middlemen mediating their conflicts and obligations to the state, and had no way to redress their grievances when their land was encroached upon.[79]

For the Rattan Gorge, he also proposed selecting a strategically critical location for garrisoning, specifically the former location of a defunct battalion at Wutun 五屯所. Positioned as it was at the juncture of routes leading to many of the lairs, he believed that should it be replenished with soldiers and placed under the command of a commandant, the end result would be "what is called completing a strategy and the enemy is defeated of itself."[80]

Nevertheless, he was less specific about how the regular civil administration was to maintain peace than he was in the case of Eight Stockades. For the most part, he stated that officials were to maintain closer contacts with villages. We have already seen how, in his communications with subordinates, he had envisioned winning over resistant *man yi* stockades and villages.[81] Overall, in both regions, and especially Eight Stockades, he was confident that with increased state presence "the transformative governance of prefectures and counties will

77   Ibid.
78   Ibid.
79   Ibid., 15:513–15.
80   Ibid., 15:519.
81   See pp. 298-300.

be renewed daily."[82] Therefore, the *man yi* could be more effectively controlled and influenced.

One of the methods Wang Yangming believed would be effective for furthering this assimilative process was one that officials had been resorting to since the early Ming: education. In his study of Guangxi during the Ming, Leo Shin points out that "efforts to educate the children of native domains evidently began soon after the founding of the dynasty." This included sending them to the imperial academy, having them attend Confucian schools established in the domains, promoting those who excelled, and requiring those who were designated heirs to attend these schools.[83] Similarly, Wang dispatched a number of communications ordering the construction of government schools in Sien, Tianzhou, the provincial capital at Nanning, and other areas populated by non-Chinese, as well as an academy at the provincial capital. The two characters composing the name of this academy—Fuwen 敷文—adequately sum up his goal: from the phrase "*fu wen lai yuan* 敷文來遠," these literally mean "spreading culture [to those who come from afar]."[84]

In an official communication to officials of Nanning Prefecture ordering them to appoint a scholar to a local Confucian school, Wang spelled out just how civilization was to be spread:

> For bringing stability to the country and governing the people there is nothing superior to ritual. Ideally, all families and homes would understand the ceremonies of capping, marriage, mourning, and sacrifices, but now these have all been discarded and are no longer discussed. Should one desire to seek what is good among customs, how can one find it? What is more, here in distant prefectures along the border, where natives are mixed up among the population, obstructive obstinacy has become the trend. Officials only apply physical punishment to their bodies and press them with their power, what is called "adding fuel to the fire." What benefit does that have for governing? Should you teach them ritual, then the result might perhaps be what is called "when the mean person studies the Way, he becomes easy to control." Recently the scholar Chen Dazhang of Putian in Fujian came to Nanning to seek learning, and when he called on me, everything we spoke of touched upon ritual.... These

82 Ibid., 15:515.
83 Shin, *Making of the Chinese State*, 71–72. For similar efforts in Yunnan, see Bin, *Between Winds and Clouds*, 5:49–73. Shin believes that these policies were limited in their impact (72).
84 *WYMQJ*, vol. 1, 18:634.

days, students from each school typically close their books and leave them on high shelves, satiate themselves with food and seek amusement through the pleasures of travel, frivolously passing away the days, but what could be better than requiring them to lecture and practice with this licentiate, amidst ceremony and supervision? . . . After these students have sprung to action because of what they have learned through observation [of Chen Dazhang], encouragement, and exchanging views, they can cultivate this in their home. From there [this learning] will spread to the lanes and alleys [i.e., neighborhoods], and from the neighborhoods reach the countryside. For this reason, afterwards the lands of the border regions will be transformed into the villages of Zou and Lu.[85]

Spreading the culture of the Central Kingdom to the periphery, which would then be transformed into a place akin to the homelands of Confucius and Mencius (Zou 鄒 and Lu 魯): ultimately, this was what Wang Yangming hoped to achieve with his method of exhortation and punishment and, thereafter, with his method of appeasing, settling, soothing, and subduing. As was the case with the native headmen and peoples of Tianzhou and Sien, he believed that, ultimately, they would all be brought into the moral community—one, however, that he could not envision as apart from the culture with which he was so familiar and the imperium of which he was a part.

Conclusion

On September 10, 1528, after having spent over nine months in Guangxi, Wang Yangming departed Nanning, the provincial capital. This was a risky move, because he did so without prior authorization. Even before arriving in Guangxi, he was already quite ill, and his condition only worsened throughout this period of service, to the point that he believed he had little chance of recovery should he not depart immediately and return home. It was only after nearly a month in Guangzhou, which he had reached on September 20, that he finally submitted a memorial requesting leave to recuperate in his hometown in Zhejiang Province.

In this memorial Wang explained to the emperor that, while he was preparing his memorial requesting to relocate or establish new military installations and counties, he had personally traveled the region to assess conditions. This entailed braving the torrid heat and damp conditions of a jungle filled with

---

85   Ibid., 18:638–39.

cliffs and ravines. Thus it was that his cough worsened, his feet swelled, and he suffered from vomiting and diarrhea. He also informed the emperor that although "exerting to the fullest his loyalty by serving the country has always been [this official's] aspiration," and that having experienced the profound magnanimity of the emperor, he "thought only of reducing his body to powder and crushing his bones in service," he realized there was no way he could do so given his deteriorating condition.[86]

This is why he had departed on his own authority, something that would later provide his detractors at court a convenient pretext for attacking him, even after he had passed away. But at this point, he assured the emperor that conditions in Guangxi were stabilized, in part because he saw to it that competent officials who would prevent excessive extortion and taxation and bring peace to the people were now in place, even while awaiting a replacement for the office of grand coordinator.

When Wang was in Guangzhou, a messenger arrived from the Ming court with a patent from the emperor and a reward for his meritorious achievement of securing the surrender of the headmen in Tianzhou and Sien, which, even from Wang Yangming's perspective, fit well with his ideal for handling relations with non-Chinese on the margins. In response, Wang dispatched a memorial thanking his ruler, and celebrating this event:

> At the time, your servitor had already been laid up in bed for over a month, in spite of illness standing up bent over, thankful but afraid, in a terrible way with fainting spells, having no idea how to proceed. But a moment later, having gradually come to, I thought to myself that Sien and Tianzhou's tens of thousands of innocents, fearing death and fleeing for their lives, had in the beginning not committed crimes for which they should suffer execution. Yet, prior to this, those in power proposed their desire to exterminate them, and thus they were in a state of turmoil and considered revolting. Therefore, they had been pushed into a situation whereby they believed death was inevitable, and were without any hope that they might survive. Yet, relying on the emperor's benevolent love for life and his unique consideration for the distant barbarians, out of fear that even just one thing might not find its due place, this official was specifically commissioned to proceed to, investigate, and bring stability to this area. But how could this official put into effect even one good policy? It was nothing more than spreading the news of [the emperor's] profound benevolence, effecting and manifesting sagely martialness, so that

---

86   Ibid., 15:523.

within a month, all had a change of heart and leaned towards civilization, leaving behind the path of death and leaping towards life, binding themselves and coming forth to surrender. This is all to be attributed to the sagely virtue of the emperor, who, sensing the will of Heaven, was touched by the highest sincerity, unrushed and yet so swift. Thus, placate them and they will come, move them and there will be peace.[87]

That this was not mere rhetoric is proven by a letter to his son, where Wang explained that the peaceful conclusion was "all a result of the court's virtuous love for the living touching them and causing them to come forward, the awesomeness of a god-like mightiness that without killing subconsciously wins trust and subtly moves people to submit to its will (*qian fu mo yun* 潛乎默運)."[88] That is just one example of how the Ming state might go about the process of influencing subjects' innate knowledge of the good.

As for the second stage—confronting the violence in Chopped Rattan Gorge and Eight Stockades—Wang Yangming also cited these very same factors as responsible for bringing about such excellent results: "Although there were several areas with powerful and large bandit lairs that had long served as the gathering point, the roots, and the trunk of the mob of bandits in Guangxi, and which even after several punitive campaigns had failed to be overcome, here also, by taking advantage of armies from Huguang that had been demobilized and were returning home, and employing newly resettled subjects whose courage to requite with service had been energized, without great expenditure and exhausting the people, the bandit bosses were subsequently exterminated, lairs and haunts cleaned out, and thus [villages] near and far began to see a measure of peace."[89]

Wang did on occasion state that "the ancients only employed the military instrument when they had no other choice; the former kings could not bear to see even just one person not attain his due place."[90] He understood that warfare filled gullies with the bodies of innocent people, and not solely because of fighting at the front, but also because wherever it transpires the land is laid waste. That is perhaps why, even in this case where he felt he had no choice but to act, he was also pleased with what he thought was a minimal use of force given the conditions, something he expressed in his poem "Pacification of Bazhai":

---

87   Ibid., 15:521.
88   *WYMQJ*, vol. 2, 26:992.
89   *WYMQJ*, vol. 1, 15:522.
90   Ibid., 25:964.

It is said that when Sir Han [Yong] attacked these savages, a hundred
thousand crack troops drove into these mountains;
Yet today by deploying only three thousand soldiers, this victory was won
in less than a month.
How could this be the result of human planning and wondrous calcula-
tions? [I] chanced upon the assistance of Heaven and demobilizing
troops.
Exhaustive pursuit and relentless attacks do not count as a long-term
plan; the obstinate shall be civilized with both beneficence and
authority.[91]

Having established control, Wang Yangming then put in place measures to
change recalcitrant peoples into law-abiding subjects. He could now leave the
region feeling confident that his goals had been achieved.

It was also in Guangzhou that Wang Yangming would compose some of his
last letters before heading north to Nan'an Jiangxi, where he would pass away
on January 1, 1529. In one of these, written to his disciple Nie Bao 聶豹 (1487–
1563), he touches on many aspects of his philosophy late in life, while criticiz-
ing scholars who do not apply their knowledge, preferring instead to pursue
tranquility. It is people like this, he noted, that lose control as soon as they
come across something even mildly disquieting. Rather, quoting from the philosophy of Mencius, Wang insisted that "one must always be engaged with
something (必有事焉)," adding that this is "only a matter of accumulating
righteousness" and "accumulating righteousness is only extending the innate
knowledge of the good." Summarizing what this entailed, he drew upon ideas
that he had been speaking about ever since his successful suppression of the
Prince of Ning's rebellion. "If one accumulates righteousness in and though his
own mind every hour and every minute," he explained, "the substance of his
innate knowledge will be absolutely clear and it will spontaneously see right as
right and wrong as wrong, neither of which can escape [being so] in the least.[92]

Would this have applied to Wang Yangming while he was in Guangxi? Was
he, in his own estimate, following just such dictates? This seems like a reasonable conclusion, given that he repeatedly legitimized his policies as being in
accord with the sentiments of the people, the spirit of the laws of the country,
and moral principle—especially the requirements of humanity and righteousness; given that he designed his policies to ensure that "not one thing does not
find its proper place"; and, more simply, given the integrity with which he car-

---

91   Ibid., 20:798.
92   Wang, *Instructions for Practical Living*, 174–75.

ried out what he certainly believed to be right. It is also worth pointing out that he uses the same analogy to describe innate knowledge of the good as he does the "long-term strategy for appeasing, settling, placating, and subduing." Both are akin to the oar with which one guides a vessel.

Nevertheless, Wang's efforts to bring long-term stability to central Guangxi did not achieve its intended result. As was the case throughout the fifteenth century, the Rattan Gorge and the Eight Stockades would remain troublesome places for the Ming state. In 1538, for example, following a rebellion led by Rattan Gorge bandit leaders, who apparently felt wronged by the encroachment of native headmen appointed to control the region, over fifty thousand soldiers had to be mobilized to restore order. Further incidents of violence arose throughout the sixteenth century.[93] We find a similar story in the Eight Stockades, for in 1554 rebels marched from there to Nanning and attacked this provincial capital. Other incidents followed between this time and 1579, when officials mobilized approximately sixty thousand soldiers to suppress an uprising by what officials said amounted to over ten thousand rebel soldiers. Some thirty thousand rebels were reported killed.[94]

Wang Yangming might very well have predicted some of this later violence. Whether or not his belief held true—that order could be instilled in the region through the civilizing power of benevolent officials familiar with and sympathetic to the peoples of the region, assigned for longer periods, and backed up by shored up institutions—the reality was that over-reliance on often feuding native chieftains, thinly spread or defunct military institutions, official corruption, and tensions between registered subjects and *man yi* were issues that remained throughout the Ming and prevented Wang's plan from working.[95]

---

93 For accounts of the record of violence in the Rattan Gorge and Eight Stockades, see Gao and Yao, *Mingdai Guangxi nongmin qiyi shi*, 19–94; Shin, *The Making of the Chinese State*, 117–25.

94 Gao and Yao, *Mingdai Guangxi nongmin qiyi shi*, 93–4.

95 Cf. Shin, *Making of the Chinese State*, 56–105.

Conclusion

The principal goal of this book has been to address a gap in the scholarship on Wang Yangming by providing a detailed account of his political career—that is, aspects of his political life specifically related to the series of appointments he received from the Ming court. While carrying out this study, I found not only that the preponderance of the impressive amount of writing on him concerned his influential philosophy and intellectual development, but also that scholars who write about him tend to assume that there is a strict relationship between his philosophical discourse and what he did as an official. As I have explained in the introduction, depending on the perspective brought to a particular study, those connections are usually spelled out in either positive or negative terms. Xu Fuguan, for instance, states that "Wang Yangming's political actions and meritorious achievements all derived from his self-cultivated humanity, which is also to say from his giving full scope to innate knowledge of the good."[1] Cai Renhou claimed that Wang's memorials show his profound empathy and concern for the welfare of the people,[2] while Bao Shibin goes so far as to state that Wang Yangming "successfully realized the unification of sageliness within and kingliness without."[3] Finally, Julia Ching simply notes that Wang's doctrine of the extension of innate knowledge of the good is "the great principal, to do always in one's life what one's mind-and-heart says is right and good."[4]

On the other extreme, some scholars see his thought primarily as an ideology that legitimated or served in some way a system of power relations, such as a patriarchal social order or autocratic political order. Because Wang Yangming insisted that those moral norms cementing together social relations in such an order originate from human nature and are first constituted in the subject as naturally and innately given moral knowing, his philosophy legitimized deeper intervention in an individual's moral life. Any knowledge or sentiments not in accord with those norms should be suppressed at the root, expressing as they do self-centered propensities for wrongdoing and even evil. Needless to say, given his involvement in military campaigns and the many measures he implemented in southern China, it is not surprising that the actions and policies

---

1   Xu, "Wang Yangming sixiang bu lun," 506–507.
2   Cai, *Wang Yangming zhexue,* 146.
3   Bao, *Mingdai Wang xue yanjiu,* 16.
4   Ching, *To Acquire Wisdom,* 115.

© KONINKLIJKE BRILL NV, LEIDEN, 2014 | DOI 10.1163/9789004280106_009

comprising Wang's official career have become fodder for driving home this point of view.[5]

Undeniably, Wang Yangming's doctrines and many statements that he made throughout his life seem to fully support the assumption that his philosophy deeply informed his personal, social, and political life. From his articulation of his theory of the "unity of knowledge and action" in 1508 to his unveiling of his doctrine of "the extension of the innate knowledge of the good" in 1520— at what was perhaps the height of his official career—Wang consistently maintained that practical action in any aspect of an individual's life ought to be the necessary and even spontaneous fruition of moral knowledge. He referred to this knowledge as principle, Heavenly principle, and innate knowledge of the good. Furthermore, he often stated that his confidence in the truth of these doctrines was based wholly on personal experiences, especially ones tied to his political career. That was certainly the case after he had weathered the political storm following his capture of the prince. He claimed that "ever since employing the military instrument, [I] have come increasingly to feel that this effort of extending the innate knowledge of the good and investigating matters is even more refined and penetrating."[6] But more generally, I find it fully valid to claim that from the time he received his first minor assignment in 1499 to his last campaign in Guangxi in 1528, Wang Yangming acted with integrity by attempting to embody his principles in practice, even if the conditions he faced and the measures he employed in response were at times morally ambiguous for him or something he viewed as the unfortunate but best possible solution within a political and institutional order to which he generally subscribed.

The philosophical implications of Wang Yangming's notion of the unity of knowledge and action can be reviewed in brief. For him, because moral principles are innately given and derive from human nature, they naturally manifest in any particular situation as moral knowledge-cum-sentiment of right and wrong. This knowledge is what Philip Ivanhoe refers to as "nascent moral sense"[7] and A.S. Cua calls "moral consciousness" and "moral discrimination" with an "implicit volitional character" and "the will to its actualization."[8] Sometimes Wang spoke of such moral knowledge as Heavenly principle and sometimes as innate knowledge of the good. Following Mencius, Wang believed that such knowledge was the expression of a universal moral mind, and that to know this mind is to know human nature and Heaven. Hence, to actual-

---

5   These views are fully discussed in the Introduction to the present work.

6   Wang Ji, "Du xian shi zai bao Hai Riweng Ji'an qi bing shu xu," in *WYMQJ*, 41:1600.

7   Ivanhoe, *Ethics in the Confucian Tradition*, 19.

8   Cua, "Between Commitment and Realization," 631.

ize such knowledge in one's political practice is to actualize a higher moral order and, therefore, to act with a view to bringing the political order in line with
the natural order. For Wang, the innate knowledge of the good was "what is
referred to as the 'great foundation of all under Heaven'," and to act in accord
with this was "what is referred to as "all under Heaven attaining the Way.""[9] In
other words, the ideal social and political order is one fully in accord with human nature and, consequently, with innate knowledge of the good. To follow
such knowledge is to return the world to the Way, and a person able to achieve
that is one who exemplifies the ideal combination of personal virtue and righteous political and social action. Such individuals are indeed the natural leaders of society, and their fundamental purpose in that capacity is to foster the
conditions necessary for the actualization of an order of virtue implicit in the
attributes of that innate knowledge of the good that all people possess.

   Nonetheless, it would be a stretch to say that Wang always bore his most
important ideas in mind while serving as an official, and that they informed his
actions to the degree that his statements in the aftermath of the princely rebellion and on other occasions might seem to imply, or to the degree that scholarship—both critical and laudatory—might suggest. That is, he may not have
been able to translate his philosophy into practical life as much as he would
have liked. In fact, Julia Ching is correct in saying that although Wang spoke
much about innate knowledge of the good, "he says remarkably little about
how it is to be extended and realized,"[10] and the same could be said about
preserving Heavenly principle. More generally, in his philosophical discourse,
when Wang states that "mind is principle," or speaks of according with Heavenly principle or extending the innate knowledge of the good, such principles
and knowledge are indeed spoken of largely in the abstract or in a general way
as self-evident Confucian norms, although at times definition is far more elu-
sive and reaches the heights of the mystical, suggesting a kind of prophetic
pure moral knowing unveiling itself as required by ever-changing circumstances in a perfectly timely way. But in terms of norms, the The "Inquiry on the
Great Learning," for instance, explains that innate knowledge of the good is
"the sense of right and wrong common to all men."[11] Those who sincerely
wish to do so and who do not delude themselves can become aware of this
sense and further it, over time becoming increasingly capable of willing the
good through their actions as well as of ridding themselves of any nascent immoral propensities. However, aside from referring to Confucian virtues for in-

---

9   *WYMQJ*, vol. 1, 8:279.
10   Wang, *Instructions for Practical Living*, 115.
11   Wang, "Inquiry on the *Great Learning*," 278.

terpersonal relationships, Wang Yangming leaves largely undefined just what that common sense is and what counts as good and evil in practical terms, no doubt because he assumed that this would and should be self-evident to those whom he was addressing.

In any case, because the majority of scholarship on Wang Yangming views his political career tangentially from the perspective of philosophy and intellectual history, while legitimately assuming that his ideas informed his practical life, and because Wang tended to speak about moral knowledge in only general terms, my method in this study has been to look at things in reverse—to give a full account of his political career and to view moral knowledge in that light, leaving aside systematic philosophical inquiry. Only then might it become clear what good and evil, and right and wrong, meant for him in practice. Thus, I have attempted to focus on the historical context, specifically by constructing dense descriptions of his political actions, in order to flesh out just what Wang Yangming meant by "the sense of right and wrong common to all men."

At times, it has been possible to explain just how Wang Yangming's philosophy informed his actions or policies, or at least how he claimed that it did. Where those connections are less clear, or less obviously relevant to the complex matters he was managing over time on the ground, I have found Charles Taylor's notion of the "social imaginary" to be helpful, because it provides a way to bring in rich historical and cultural contexts that fill in the gap between Wang's moral philosophy (and notions of moral order) and his political actions. Again, according to Taylor, social imaginary is "the way people imagine their social existence, how they fit together, how things go on between them and their fellows, the expectations that are normally met, and the deeper normative notions and images that underlie these expectations."[12] No doubt, cultural historians will see this as a term that sounds like a variation on *mentalités*, worldviews, and systems of representations, or those matters of concern to historians that often bring the seemingly natural, necessary, and universal down to the realm of the contingent and historical.[13]

I do find much merit in the argument that Wang Yangming did at times rise above the challenges he faced and address them in new ways, and that his solutions can't be fully understood apart from his moral philosophy. Indeed, it remains a compelling enigma that he navigated through harrowing trials by simply pointing to a natural and effortlessly ethical way of according with circumstances as they unfold. It is also the case that his belief in the individual as

---

12 Taylor, *Modern Social Imaginaries*, 23.
13 Cf. Chartier, *Cultural History*," 22–27.

the independent source of moral judgment provided a powerful counterweight to power plays and gross injustice, leading him at times (in his own view) to defy state authority. Moreover, Wang Yangming's insistence that genuine love and compassion are the foundation of humane governance brought with it a passionate desire for justice and empathy for those he governed. Therefore, he demonstrated a willingness to hear the claims of troublesome populations even when other officials were poised to attack. His resolution of the conflict with the headmen and followers of Cen Meng in Guangxi is a case in point. Also, the ultimate goal of the county- and subcounty-level policies he implemented was to produce a kind of stability that, he believed, would draw its strength from the people coming to see that it was morally right.

On the other hand, his policies did privilege the views of some groups over others, and often advanced the interests of particular groups in local societies he was assigned to govern at the expense of others he deemed immoral. Hierarchy was implicit in his conception of morality, and that impacted his social perceptions and policies as well. At a theoretical level, the voice of innate knowledge of the good was to an important degree enmeshed with, if not shaped by, a particular ethics—the assumptions about the nature of the political and social held by an elite of which he was a part, and the monarchical and meritocratic political-institutional order he served. Wang Yangming thus naturalized a particular set of norms as an expression of human nature shared by all, proposed that society be structured according to an order of virtue, and assumed that good institutions of an ideally functioning monarchy (sagely rule) and meritocracy (by men of virtue) were the natural venue for assisting subjects in the ultimately soteriological goal of recovering their natural moral goodness. He could not help but bring to his assignments a horizon of powerful assumptions which shaped how he saw the social disorder before him and how he chose to rectify it. In some cases, his measures were more obviously directly related to his belief in the goodness of people and ideas as to what kinds of institutions were most helpful in fostering that reality. More renowned examples include his programs for community covenants, community schools, and academies. As Frederick Mote has pointed out, by emphasizing the importance of these institutions, Wang "turned away from the traditional leadership role of the high elite in central government offices to the local context of social life in which elite and commoners shared in the responsibility for themselves and to one another. He had come to see this as the most hopeful arena of Confucian social action."[14] However, it is also important to recognize that such subcounty institutions, like the community covenant, were also intentionally

---

14   Mote, *Imperial China: 900–1800*, 682.

designed to make the dynamics of local society even more visible and respon-sive to county-level governments (covenant leaders, it will be recalled, were to report to them). Also, Wang gave equal weight to extending the reach of the state into poorly governed regions and unruly frontiers in more obviously forceful ways. Those measures included establishing county seats, implement-ing registration systems for the purpose of mutual surveillance, and reconfig-uring regional military installations and methods for policing populations. In all cases, it is clear that he believed that both the state and local communities had a critical role to play in helping people not only to recognize right and wrong, but also in encouraging people to do good and eliminate evil. Wang Yangming's moral philosophy might emphasize the moral autonomy of the in-dividual, but the morality that he believed individuals could access was strong-ly communal, and that communal dimension was not something apart from his social imaginary.

Of course, more generally, the goals of these measures were to restore stabil-ity and civilize populations by changing troublesome ones into law-abiding subjects. Perhaps nothing better captures the social imaginary of Wang Yang-ming in his dealings with these people than his civilizing discourse and institu-tions. In the final analysis, Wang imagined a transition to a state of affairs whereby resistant or disorderly populations and individuals would be integrat-ed into the Ming state not only politically but also culturally, through their coming to recognize the essential correctness of certain norms and principles, and sharing in the forms of community requisite to them. Whenever he decided he could not achieve this transition through peaceful means by ex-tending—in a benevolently paternalistic framework—every conceivable op-portunity for reform to peoples accused of outlawry, Wang Yangming labelled them as hopeless and beyond the pale and therefore felt justified in taking military action. In those cases, he was usually following the advice of local of-ficials and local elites and had come to share their demonizing views of these populations. In addition, although he often recognized how failed political in-stitutions, economic factors, and social and ethnic tensions led up to such im-passes, he was caught in a situation where he was serving a state that had a limited capacity to mediate such complex social conflicts. Thus, I believe, his moral (and civilizing) discourse and rhetoric of good and evil provided catego-ries that allowed him to oversimplify the nature of the social tensions before him, as well as to override any claim to more lenient treatment that such popu-lations may have had, in such a way that he could legitimately resort to force in what amounted to a number of unquestionably violent campaigns, in which thousands died.

Not surprisingly, at times Wang expressed a great deal of regret over having to resort to campaigns of extermination. Such fatalistic reactions are by no means isolated glimpses into the tension between Wang's ideals and the harsh realities of his political life, offering valuable insight into just what moral knowledge, sentiments, and effort were for him in practice and the degree to which these were shaped by ambiguous circumstances and difficult times. Another such glimpse is his justice of merit and desert, and the extent to which the goals of reform, deterrence, and retribution justified varying degrees of authority when applying the law or implementing measures for the purpose of rewarding and punishing. Finally, Wang identified certain virtues as particularly suited to the political climate around him, including most notably the capacity for serene detachment, a humility born of prudence, and tactical compromise. All told, this was how moral knowledge, or knowledge of the good, was shaped by his time, and by his sometimes frustrating efforts to mobilize institutions to create his vision of a Confucian social and political order, in light of his overarching desire to foster those conditions necessary for cultivation of virtuous conduct in a moral-political order rendering its peoples capable of leading a good and just life.

Epilogue

From the time he traveled over Meiling 梅嶺 Mountain by palanquin, passing from Nanxiong Prefecture in northern Guangdong to Nan'an, Jiangxi, where he had once led military campaigns, to the moment he passed away on January 9, 1529, Wang Yangming could not foresee what would happen to his reputation. Back in Beijing, a political faction at the Ming court, with the approval of a displeased emperor, would soon strip him of the hereditary title of nobility he had received for suppressing the rebellion by the Prince of Ning Zhu Chenhao. They would also refuse him any solatia—honors bestowed upon the occasion of the death of a high official. To be sure, part of the reason for this appalling treatment even in the wake of his successes in Guangxi must be attributed to the substantial following he had accrued over the years among literati. To the court, this was troubling because he espoused doctrines which diverged from and constituted an attack on orthodox Cheng-Zhu Neo-Confucianism. Yet there was another important matter at play here. Owing to the prominent reputation he had also earned over the years from his notable military campaigns and policy successes, he became, at least for a period of time, a political football in shifting power struggles at the Ming court. These had emerged at the very time he was finishing up his campaigns in Guangxi and preparing to depart.

Assuming a letter dispatched to his son while en route home is the most reliable indicator, Wang Yangming departed Nanning (where he had remained during much of 1528 while carrying out his Rattan Gorge and Eight Stockades operations) on September 10 and arrived in Guangzhou City about ten days later.[1] Furthermore, he indicated that he had already, sometime prior, submitted a memorial requesting leave and soon expected a response from the Ming court. The significance of this, of course, is that Wang had indeed left office without authorization. In fact, according to the *Ming Veritable Records*, it was only on August 8—several months after the fact—that his request to carry out those campaigns was first approved, and on September 8 that his request for leave was received, along with his record of the Eight Stockades campaigns.[2] That request was rejected, and he was ordered to remain in Nanning and receive treatment there while yet overseeing what the court viewed as an

---

1 *WYMQJ*, vol. 2, 26:992.
2 *MSLSZSL*, Jiajing 1528/8/12 嘉靖七年八月辛亥 (August 26, 1528) and Jiajing 1528/9/5 嘉靖七年九月甲戌 (September 18, 1528) entries.

insufficiently stabilized region. But by that time, Wang was already in Guang-zhou and would soon depart for his hometown.

Undoubtedly, Wang Yangming foresaw that his unauthorized departure might cause controversy and even leave him liable for prosecution, which is why he made every effort in his petition to explain why affairs in Guangxi were in good enough order that the emperor could feel at ease. He also described how unbearably difficult it was for him, as a devoted and loyal official, to leave. If nothing else, he suggested, that demonstrates just how serious his condition had become, for should he not return home he would surely die and therefore be forever unable to requite the emperor for his gracious treatment.[3] Wang requested that a grand coordinator be appointed to replace him, and assumed he would arrive fairly soon. Hence, sometime towards the end of 1528 he traveled to northern Guangdong, indicating in a letter to his colleague and one-time student Huang Wan, who was then stationed at the capital, that even should the new grand coordinator fail to arrive, he would still risk the consequences and continue his journey home.[4] That is indeed what Wang did, but he passed away before his actions became fodder for Grand Secretary Gui E to curry favor with the Jiajing emperor and strengthen his position vis-à-vis a group of men who were students or admirers of Wang Yangming and had up to this time sought to bring him into the Ming court also as a grand secretary.

What Wang did not understand was just how precarious his standing had become in the eyes of the Jiajing emperor. The background to this, as so well explained by Carney Fisher and Timothy Brook, has to be traced back to the early years of the emperor's reign during what became known as the Great Rites controversy, and how the outcome of that struggle brought to power a number of mostly mid-level officials who happened to be followers of Wang Yangming.[5] From the time he ascended the throne, the emperor had struggled with a large contingent of civil officials led by Chief Grand Secretary Yang Tinghe over the proper titles to be granted to his own mother and father. He refused to accept that he had to play the role of adopted son to his deceased cousin's father, the Hongzhi emperor, as well as refer to his own parents as "imperial aunt and uncle." In the end, though, the emperor's will triumphed, and his father was recognized as "deceased imperial father" and mother as

---

3 *WYMQJ*, vol. 1, 15:522–23.

4 Ibid., 21:832–33.

5 See Timothy Brook, "What Happens when Wang Yangming Crosses the Border?," in *Chinese State at the Borders*, ed. Diana Lary, 76–90 (Vancouver: University of British Columbia Press, 2007), 76–78; and Carney Fisher, *Chosen One: Succession and Adoption in the Court of Ming Shizong* (Sydney: Allen and Unwin, 1990).

"empress dowager." Not surprisingly, those who supported him were elevated to influential positions at the capital, while many who did not were demoted. Yang Tinghe retired in 1524.[6]

Much of the controversy came to a head and was resolved in 1524, but in actual fact it began in 1522 and had repercussions that were felt until 1528, from the time the Jiajing emperor ascended the throne until the issuing of the *Great Compilation Clarifying Ethics*, a collection of documents legitimating the events surrounding and the outcome of the Great Rites controversy on historical grounds. Those happened to be roughly the years that Wang Yangming was in retirement in his home province of Zhejiang, traveling back and forth between Yuyao and Yue City, teaching in schools, academies, and informal settings to crowds that frequently numbered into the hundreds. Although we have no evidence that Wang ever involved himself in the raging debate, it is well known that some of his students who happened to be very directly involved felt that the emperor was fully justified in honoring his natural sentiments towards his parents and rejected the idea that he must adhere to the ritual prescriptions proposed by his chief grand secretary. Indeed, Wang's teaching of the innate knowledge of the good would have seemed to fully support that position.[7] To be sure, there was also a great deal of opportunism, for some of those students would then rise to positions of power as a result of siding with the Jiajing emperor, and so it was no surprise that they memorialized to the court calling for Wang Yangming to be brought out of retirement.

After Wang completed his period of mourning for his father's death in 1524, some of his friends, students, and colleagues—such as Xi Shu 席書 (1461–1527), Fang Xianfu 方獻夫 (1484–1544), Huang Wan 黃綰 (1477–1551), and Huo Tao 霍韜 (1487–1540) —recommended that he be appointed to such high offices as grand secretary, minister of war, or supreme commander of the three borders. This began at the very moment these men were being rapidly elevated to influential offices for standing behind the emperor during the controversy. But none of their recommendations received anything more than acknowledgment, and Wang Yangming never was summoned to the capital. The reason for this is clear enough: other powerful officials in the grand secretariat, such as Fei Hong 費宏 (1468–1535) and later Yang Yiqing 楊一清 (1454–1530), felt threatened by the idea of his presence at the Ming court.[8]

---

6 Brook, "What Happens when Wang Yangming Crosses the Border?," 78.

7 Dardess, *Ming China, 1368–1644*, 49–50; James Geiss, "The Chia-ching Reign, 1522–1566," in *The Cambridge History of China*, vol. 7: *The Ming Dynasty, 1368–1644*, ed. Frederick Mote and Dennis Twitchett (Cambridge: Cambridge University Press, 1988), 445–50.

8 For the *Chronological Biography* entry see NP, 35:1293; for the *Ming History*, see MS, 195:5166–68.

In 1527, as explained in Chapter Five, Wang Yangming was eventually appointed supreme commander and dispatched to Guangxi to manage uprisings by the native headmen in Tianzhou and Sien. The two key capital officials behind those appointments—Zhang Cong and Gui E—were also men who had received rapid promotions for arguing in support of the emperor during the Great Rites controversy, but although Zhang admired Wang Yangming, Gui did not, and apparently only supported this recommendation at the urging of his colleague and perhaps because he wanted to take some of the credit for any potential success and thereby strengthen his own position at the court.[9] However, it may have also been just another way to distance Wang from the Ming court: according to Huang Wan, the reason then Grand Secretary Yang Yiqing and Minister of Pesonnel Gui E gave him the concurrent assignment of grand coordinator late in 1527 was their concern that upon completing his assignment he would be ordered to appear before the emperor and possibly end up serving in the grand secretariat in Beijing. They may have simply wanted to keep him in faraway Guangxi.[10]

Huang recounts many other events at the capital that demonstrate how, while carrying out his last assignment in life, Wang Yangming became the unwitting pawn of an emerging power struggle for dominance at the Ming court among the very coterie of men who had risen to power on the tide of their support for the Jiajing emperor. Zhang Cong, for instance, attempted to use Wang's Tianzhou victory memorial not only as evidence of his own great foresight in appointing him but also to have him recommended to the grand secretariat. Gui E and Yang Yiqing responded by directing a guard in the imperial bodyguard to trump up allegations of improprieties on Wang Yangming's part, thereby implicating his supporters. This guard proceeded to instruct a certain retired official to submit a memorial claiming that Wang Yangming had bribed Xi Shu, Huang Wan, and Zhang Cong to recommend him [Wang] for the appointment. Despite the fact that Huang memorialized disputing the allegations and the matter was dropped (the guard was prosecuted and exiled to a military garrison), matters only worsened for Wang, for when his requests for leave arrived, Gui either concealed or simply denied them. At that point, about the time Wang Yangming left Guangxi and was residing in Guangdong await-

---

9   Tang Kwok-leung states that Gui's policy memorials concerning frontier defense appear to be deliberately formulated in opposition to the policies of retired Grand Secretary Fei Hong because Gui saw him as a threat and wished to discredit him. See Tang, "Tianzhou shi fei wo benxin," 274–75. For Gui E's biography, see *MS*, 196:5181–85.

10   Huang, "Shi de ji," in *WYMQJ*, vol. 2, 38:1425.

ing a response to his petition to appoint a replacement grand coordinator, Gui began accusing him of a number of serious crimes.[11]

The motives behind Gui's attacks on Wang Yangming need not concern us greatly. It may have simply been that he felt his position could be threatened by this formidable scholar-official and his followers, or possibly, as Huang Wan claims, that he was angered by Wang Yangming's refusal to respond to his suggestion that he take armies into northern Vietnam (Annam).[12] Regardless, on December 6, 1528, Minister of Rites Fang Xianfu and Head of the Household Administration of the Heir Apparent Huo Tao submitted a memorial defending Wang Yangming against several allegations: namely, that his campaigns in Eight Stockades and the Rattan Gorge were unauthorized; and that he conspired with the rebel Prince of Ning prior to subjugating him only to then in the aftermath steal property from his establishment.[13] Even more troubling was the fact that, just five days prior, Wang's victory memorial for these two regions had arrived at the Ming court, only to be met with suspicion by the emperor, who suggested that it was exaggerated and even deceitful and therefore ordered an investigation by a touring censor.[14]

But, of course, by this time Wang Yangming had already left his post and would pass away just one month later. His supporters in the capital fiercely defended him, spelling out the obvious facts that Wang had rapidly suppressed the rebellion of a prince who had been plotting and preparing for years, and that afterwards Wang had so deftly handled, at so little cost in terms of finding resources to mobilize and move large armies, large ungovernable regions in South China that had been major trouble spots since the founding of the Ming dynasty. But this was all to no avail. Although Huo and Fang pointed out that in the aftermath of both campaigns Wang had not been properly recognized or rewarded and had therefore been doubly wronged, the emperor brushed this off by stating simply that he had already ordered him to deliberate further on plans for Guangxi and report back.[15]

The last step leading up to the revocation of his title of nobility came only after Wang Yangming had passed away. When news that he had indeed left Guangxi without approval came to the attention of the court, his adversaries—led by then Grand Secretaries Gui E and Yang Yiqing—used this as grounds for taking strong action against him, thus undermining the influence

11   Ibid., 38:1428–29.
12   *MS*, 195:5167.
13   Huo Tao 霍韜, "Difang shu" 地方疏, in *WYMQJ*, 39:1463–67.
14   *MSLSZSL*, Jiajing 1528/run10/20 嘉靖七年閏十月戊子 (December 1, 1528) entry.
15   Ibid., Jiajing 1528/run10/25 嘉靖七年閏十月癸巳 (December 6, 1528) entry.

of Wang's supporters in the capital. Even during the funeral procession transporting Wang's coffin from southern Jiangxi to his hometown of Shaoxing, in Zhejiang, between January 12 and March 13, 1529, the emperor was already issuing edicts with serious indictments of Wang Yangming's doctrines and conduct.

The first entry in the *Veritable Records* for Shizong's reign that touches upon the memorial Wang had submitted months before explaining why he was departing Guangxi dates to early February of that same year. By this time his casket had been transported from the yamen in Nan'an north through Nanchang and then east to Guixi County (all in Jiangxi Province). The fact that at every stop along the way the funeral procession was met by officials who carried out ceremonial sacrifices and large crowds of literati and commoners alike that are said to have clogged the streets while crawling and wailing in mourning was of no significance to the emperor. His response was anger over an official who, though granted an assignment of such magnitude, would set such a bad precedent by choosing to arrogate to himself the authority to depart a post unauthorized.[16] On March 11, just two days before the coffin arrived at his home, where family and lineage members, students, and friends from throughout the region were arriving in droves to mourn and offer condolences, the Ming court was ordered to deliberate more fully on this matter. That is because the Jiajing emperor had expressed his opinion that Wang had not served his ruler with the Way and indicated that there were many question marks concerning both his doctrines and his service.[17]

The outcome of deliberations by the Minister of Personnel and other court officials came on March 17, 1529 in what amounted to a multi-faceted attack on nearly everything for which Wang Yangming had obtained renown. This time the principal targets were his doctrines and the growing size of the number of his students, the scale of their activities, and the fact that they were beginning to constitute a notable constituency among the scholar-official class, with adherents reaching up the highest levels of the bureaucracy. While the full story behind both the methods Wang Yangming employed to foster that movement and its development has been one left outside the scope of this book, that was an equally if not more important reason for the emperor to become so susceptible to the negative portrayals of and outright lies about Wang's service by men at the capital who viewed him as a threat. He therefore consented to have his titles revoked. It may very well be the case, as Deng Zhifeng has pointed out,

---

16   Ibid., Jiajing 1529/1/8 嘉靖八年一月乙巳 (February 6, 1529) entry. Events during the funeral procession are recounted in the *Chronological Biography*. See *NP*, 35:1324–27.

17   *MSLSZSL*, Jiajing 1529/2/2 嘉靖八年二月戊辰 (March 11, 1529) entry.

that the emperor saw Wang's doctrines and the influence they were having among literati as a challenge to his own authority.[18] Certainly, he should have realized that there was something in those teachings that allowed a number of Wang's followers to support him in his demand that his own sentiments regarding his parents be honored over and above ritual precedents.

Nevertheless, the same emperor who in 1521, just prior to his inauguration, had supported conferring Wang Yangming with a title of nobility and possibly high office at the Ming court had now turned against him. In an edict, the emperor stated that Wang had recklessly and deceptively dishonored former Confucians by putting forward doctrines harmful to the learning of the mind-heart (and, therefore, pedagogy). What's more, he noted, even though it was true that Wang's military campaigns were notable for what they had achieved, his armies were undisciplined and without clear lines of command, and his victory memorial exaggerated his achievements. All of this was to count as evidence that Wang was a man merely fishing for fame and those literati now following him were simply attaching themselves to an empty reputation for similar reasons.[19] That is why his title of earl was to be removed, no solatium was to be granted, and a public proclamation proscribing heterodox doctrines was to be released. As a result, when on December 9, 1529 Wang Yangming was finally laid to rest in Hongxi 洪溪, about fifteen kilometers from Yue City, although nearly one thousand family members, friends, and students were present, the Ming court was deafeningly silent about the event. And despite the fact that the proscription was only weakly enforced at first and eventually neglected, and that the remainder of the Jiajing emperor's reign will be characterized by a vigorous educational movement led largely by Wang Yangming's followers (which eventually won backing from high officials in Beijing), the issue of his proper recognition and rewards would not be redressed until the reign of the Longqing 隆慶 emperor (Zhu Zaihou 朱載垕, r. 1567–1572).[20]

In his first year after ascending the throne, the new emperor issued an edict calling upon his ministries and especially speaking officials to bring to the court's attention any deceased high officials who they believed did not receive the proper posthumous honors. Thus in 1567, thirty-eight years after Wang

---

18   Deng Zhifang 鄧志峰, *Wang xue yu wan ming de shidao fuxing yundong* 王學與晚明的 師道復興運動 [Wang's Learning and the Movement to Rejuvenate the Way of the Educator during the Late Ming] (Beijing: Shehui kexue wenxian chubanshe, 2004), 140.

19   *MSLSZSL*, 1529/2/2 嘉靖八年二月甲戌 (March 17, 1529) entry.

20   The political events surrounding the issue of Wang Yangming and his proper recognition at the Longqing court are covered by Hung-lam Chu in "The Debate over the Recognition of Wang Yang-ming," *Harvard Journal of Asiatic Studies*, vol. 48, no. 1 (1988): 47–70.

Yangming's death, several secretaries of scrutiny and censors signed onto a memorial calling for his case to be reconsidered. Pursuant to the recommendations of the Ministry or Rites and Personnel, an edict was issued by the emperor citing both his achievements as a scholar and official and bestowing the posthumous titles Wencheng 文成 and the Marquis of Xinjian 新建侯.[21] In addition, they submitted a memorial requesting that the noble title Earl of Xinjian be inherited by his descendants. At the same time, the grand coordinator in Jiangxi also carried out a full investigation of the events surrounding Wang's suppression of the rebellion by the Prince of Ning, clearing him of all the fallacious claims of complicity and incompetence that had been left unaddressed by the Ming court for nearly fifty years. The more favorable court of the Longqing emperor also granted this request, citing his meritorious achievement in coming to the aid of the emperor and capturing the rebel prince.[22] Thus it was that Wang Yangming was finally fully recognized and rewarded for his achievements as a high official, one who had repeatedly been appointed to high office from 1516 to 1528 for the purposing of quelling social disorder in Ming China and implementing measures to maintain peace over the long term.

---

21   *NP*, 36:1353.
22   *NP*, 36:1354.

Works Cited

Angle, Stephen. "Wang Yangming as a Virtue Ethicist." In *Dao Companion to Neo-Confucianism*, edited by John Makeham, 315–336. London: Springer, 2010.

Bao Shibin 鮑世斌. *Mingdai Wang xue yanjiu* 明代王學研究 [Research on Wang Learning during the Ming Dynasty]. Chengdu: Bashu shushe, 2004.

Barlow, Jeffrey. "The Zhuang Minority in the Ming Era." *Ming Studies* 28 (1989): 15–41.

Berns, Laurence. "Thomas Hobbes." In *History of Political Philosophy*, edited by Leo Strauss and Joseph Cropsey, 396–420. Chicago: University of Chicago Press, 1987.

Bin Yang. *Between Winds and Clouds: The Making of Yunnan (Second Century BCE to Twentieth Century CE)*. New York: Columbia University Press, 2009. www.gutenberg-e.org/yang/index.html

Bol, Peter. *Neo-Confucianism in History*. Cambridge, MA: Harvard University Asia Center, 2010.

Bourdieu, Pierre. *Distinction: A Social Critique of the Judgment of Taste*. Translated by Richard Nice. Cambridge, MA: Harvard University Press, 1984.

Brook, Timothy. *The Chinese State in Ming Society*. London and New York: Routledge-Curzon, 2005.

———. "What Happens When Wang Yangming Crosses the Border?" In *Chinese State at the Borders*, edited by Diana Lary, 76–90. Vancouver: University of British Columbia Press, 2007.

Cai Renhou 蔡仁厚. *Wang Yangming zhexue* 王陽明哲學 [The Philosophy of Wang Yangming]. Taipei: Sanmin shuju, 1974.

Chan, Wing-hoi. "Ethnic Labels in a Mountainous Region: the Case of the She Bandits." In *Empire at the Margins: Culture, Ethnicity, and Frontier in Early Modern China*, edited by Pamela Kyle Crossley, Helen Siu, and Donald S. Sutton, 255–84. Berkeley: University of California Press, 2006.

Chan, Wing-tsit. "How Buddhistic is Wang Yang-ming?" *Philosophy East and West* 4, no. 4 (January 1955): 203–15.

———, ed. *A Sourcebook in Chinese Philosophy*. Princeton: Princeton University Press, 1963.

Chang, Yu-chuan. *Wang Shou-jen as a Statesmen*. Beijing: Chinese Social and Political Science Association, 1940.

Char, Andrew. "Social Origins of Ethnicity: the Hakka in Central Kwangtung." *Stone Lion Review* 9 (Spring, 1982): 53–79.

Chartier, Roger. *Cultural History: Between Practices and Representations*. Translated by Lydia V. Cochrane. Ithaca, NY: Cornell University Press, 1988.

Chen Hanming 陳寒鳴. "Wang Yangming xin xue ji qi houxue de zhengzhi sixiang 王陽明心學即其後學的政治思想 [Wang Yangming's Learning of the Mind-heart and the Political Thought of His Students]." In *Zhongguo zhengzhi sixiangshi* 中國政治思想史 [A History of Chinese Political Thought], edited by Liu Zehua 劉澤華. Hangzhou: Zhejiang renmin chubanshe, 1996.

Chen Hongmo 陳洪謨. *Ji shi ji wen* 繼世紀聞 [A Record of Things Heard Concerning What Was Transmitted from the Ancestors]. Beijing: Zhonghua shuju, 1997.

Chen Hongmo 陳洪謨 and Zhou Ying 周瑛, eds. *Da Ming Zhangzhou fu zhi* 大明漳州府誌 [Prefectural Gazetteer for the Great Ming Zhangzhou Prefecture], 1513 ed. Beijing: Zhonghua shuju, 2012.

Chen Lai 陳來. *You wu zhi jing: Wang Yangming zhexue de jingshen* 有無之境:王陽明哲學的精神 [Amidst the Realm of Being and Nonbeing: the Spirit of Wang Yangming's Philosophy]. Beijing: Renmin chubanshe, 1991.

Chen Lisheng 陳立勝. *Wang Yangming wan wu yi ti lun: cong shen yiti de lichang kan* 王陽明萬物一體論:從身一體的立場看 [Wang Yangming's Discourse on the One Substance of the Ten Thousand Things Examined from the Standpoint of the One Body]. Taipei: Taida chuban zhongxin, 2005.

Chen Rongjie 陳榮捷, ed. *Wang Yangming chuan xi lu xiang zhu ji ping* 王陽明傳習錄詳注集評 [Wang Yangming's Instructions for Practical Living with Detailed Annotations and Compiled Commentary]. Taipei: Taiwan xuesheng shuju, 1983.

Cheng Yi 程頤 and Cheng Hao 程顥. *Er cheng ji* 二程集 [Collected works of Cheng Yi and Cheng Hao]. 3 vols. Beijing: Zhonghua shuju, 1981.

Chilton, Stephen. *Grounding Political Development*. Boulder: Lynne Rienner Publishers, 1991.

Ching, Julia. *To Acquire Wisdom: The Way of Wang Yang-ming*. New York: Columbia University Press, 1976.

Ching, Julia. *Mysticism and Kingship in China: The Heart of Chinese Wisdom*. Cambridge: Cambridge University Press, 1997.

———. *The Philosophical Letters of Wang Yang-ming*. Columbia, SC: University of South Carolina Press, 1973.

———. *The Religious Thought of Chu Hsi*. Oxford: Oxford University Press, 2000.

Chu, Hung Lam. "The Debate over the Recognition of Wang Yang-ming." *Harvard Journal of Asiatic Studies*, vol. 48, no. 1 (1988): 47–70.

Chu, Hung Lam. 朱鴻林. "Qiu Jun yu Chenghua yuannian (1465) Da Tengxia zhi yi de guanxi 丘邱浚濬與成化元年 (1465) 大藤峽之役的關係 [The Relationship between Qiu Jun and the Campaigns in Great Rattan Gorge During the First Year (1465) of the Reign of the Chenghua Emperor]." *Zhongguo wenhua yanjiusuo xuebao* 48 (2007): 115–133.

Clayton, Ted. "Political Philosophy of Alasdair MacIntyre." *Internet Encyclopedia of Philosophy*. Last modified December 21, 2005. Accessed January 30, 2014. http://www.iep.utm.edu/p-macint/.

Clunas, Craig. *Screen of Kings: Royal Art and Power in Ming China*. Honolulu: University of Hawaii Press, 2013.

Confucius. *The Analects*. Translated by D.C. Lau. London: Penguin, 1979.

Cua, Antonio S. "Between Commitment and Realization: Wang Yang-ming's Vision of the Universe as a Moral Community." *Philosophy East and West* 43, no. 4 (October 1993): 631.

――――. *The Unity of Knowledge and Action: A Study in Wang Yang-ming's Moral Psychology*. Honolulu: University of Hawaii Press, 1982.

Dardess, John. *Confucianism and Autocracy: Professional Elites in the Founding of the Ming Dynasty*. Berkeley: University of California Press, 1983.

――――.*Ming China, 1368–1644: A Concise History of a Resilient Empire*. Lanham: Rowman and Littlefield, 2012.

De Bary, William Theodore. *The Trouble with Confucianism*. Cambridge, MA: Harvard University Press, 1991.

Deng Aimin 鄧艾民. *Zhu Xi Wang Shouren zhexue yanjiu* 朱熹王守仁哲學研究 [Research on the Philosophy of Zhu Xi and Wang Shouren]. Shanghai: Huadong shifan daxue chubanshe, 1989.

Deng Zhifang 鄧志峰. *Wang xue yu wan ming de shidao fuxing yundong* 王學與晚明的師道復興運動 [Wang's Learning and the Movement to Rejuvenate the Way of the Educator during the Late Ming]. Beijing: Shehui kexue wenxian chubanshe, 2004.

Dong Ping 董平. *Wang Yangming de shenghuo shijie* 王陽明的生活世界 [The World in Which Wang Yangming Lived]. Beijing: Zhongguo renmin daxue, 2009.

Dreyer, Edward. Review of *Cultural Realism: Strategic Culture and Grand Strategy in Chinese History*, by Alastair Iain Johnston. *The American Historical Review*, vol. 104, no. 2 (April 1999): 525–26.

Duffield, John S. "Political Culture and State Behavior: Why Germany Confounds Neo-Realism." *International Organization* 73, no. 4 (September 1999): 765–803.

Dworkin, Gerald, "Paternalism." In *Paternalism*, edited by Ralph Sartorius, 19–34. Minneapolis: University of Minnesota Press, 1983.

Epstein, Maram. *Competing Discourses: Orthodoxy, Authenticity, and Engendered Meanings in Late Imperial China*. Cambridge, MA: Harvard University Press, 2001.

Fairbank, John K. "Varieties of Chinese Military Experience." In *Chinese Ways of Warfare*, edited by Edward L. Dreyer, John K. Fairbank, and Frank A. Klierman, 1–26. Cambridge, MA: Harvard University Press, 1974.

Fan Yuchun. "Mingdai dufu de zhiquan ji qi xingzhi 明代督府的治權即其性質 [The Administrative Authority and Character of the Office of the Supreme Commander during the Ming Dynasty]." *Guangxi shifan daxue xuebao* 4 (1989): 49–55.

Fang, Thomé H. "The Essence of Wang Yangming's Philosophy in a Historical Perspective." *Philosophy East and West* 23, no. 3 (July, 1973): 73–90.

Fang Tie 方鐵. *Xinan tongshi* 西南通史 [A Comprehensive History of the Southwest Borderland]. Zhengzhou: Zhengzhou guji chubanshe, 2003.

Farmer, Edward. "Social Order in Early Ming China: Some Norms Codified in the Hung-wu Period." In *Law and State in Traditional East Asia*, edited by Brian E. McKnight, 1–36. Honolulu: University of Hawaii Press, 1987.

Faure, David. "The Yao Wars of the Mid-Ming and Their Impact on Yao Ethnicity." In *Empire at the Margins: Culture, Ethnicity, and Frontier in Early Modern China*, edited by Pamela Kyle Crossley, Helen F. Siu, and Donald S. Sutton, 171–89. Berkeley: University of California Press, 2006.

Feng Menglong 馮夢龍. "Huang Ming da ru Wang Yangming xiansheng chu shen jing luan lu" 皇明大儒王陽明先生出身靖亂錄 [Record of the Pacification of Disorder by the Great Ming Great Confucian Wang Yangming]. In *Feng Menglong quan ji* 馮夢龍全集 [Complete Collected Works of Feng Menglong], vol. 30. Shanghai: Shanghai guji chubanshe, 1993.

———. *Huang ming da ru Wang Yangming* 皇明大儒王陽明 [The Great Ming Great Confucian Wang Yangming]. Edited by Zhang Zhaowei 張昭煒. Beijing: Jiuzhou Press, 2014.

Fisher, Carney T. *The Chosen One: Succession and Adoption in the Court of Ming Shizong*. Sydney: Allen and Unwin, 1990.

Fu Weilin 傅維麟. *Ming shu liezhuan* 明書列傳 [Book of Ming Biographies]. In *Mingdai zhuanji congkan* 明代傳記叢刊, edited by Zhou Junfu, vol. 7. Taipei: Ming wen shuju, 1991.

Gao Yanhong 高言弘 and Yao Shunan 姚舜安. *Mingdai Guangxi nongmin qiyi shi* 明代廣西農民起義史 [A History of Peasant Uprisings during the Ming Dynasty]. Nanning: Guangxi renmin chubanshe, 1984.

Geiss, James. "The Chia-ching Reign, 1522–1566." In *The Cambridge History of China*, vol. 7: *The Ming Dynasty 1368–1644*, edited by Frederick Mote and Dennis Twitchett, 440–510. Cambridge: Cambridge University Press, 1988.

———. "The Cheng-te Reign, 1506–1521." In *The Cambridge History of China*, vol. 7: *The Ming Dynasty 1368–1644*, edited by Frederick Mote and Dennis Twitchett, 403–439. Cambridge: Cambridge University Press, 1988.

———. "The Leopard Quarter during the Cheng-te Reign." *Ming Studies* 27 (1987): 1–38.

Gong Yin 龔蔭. *Zhongguo tusi zhidu* 中國土司制度 [The Institution of Native Offices in China]. Kunming: Yunnan minzu chubanshe, 1992.

Goodrich, L. Carrington and Fang Chaoying, eds. *Dictionary of Ming Biography*. 2 vols. New York: Columbia University Press, 1976.

Habermas, Jürgen. *Communication and the Evolution of Society*. Translated by Thomas McCarthy. Boston: Beacon Press, 1979.

Han Yong 韓雍. "Duan Tengxia shu 斷藤峽疏 [Memorial Concerning Duan Tengxia]." In *Han Xiangyi ji* 韓襄毅集 [Collected Works of Han Xiangyi]. In *Huang Ming jing shi wen bian* 皇明經世文編, edited by Chen Zilong 陳子龍, vol. 5. Reprint. Taipei: Guo lian tushu chuban youxian gongsi, 1964.

Han Zhaoming 韓肇明. "Mingdai Guangxi Da Tengxia Yao min qiyi 明代廣西大藤峽瑤民起義 [Uprisings by the Yao People of Guangxi's Great Rattan Gorge during the Ming Dynasty]." *Zhongyong minzu xueyuan xuebao* 4 (1981): 25–34.

Hanyu da cidian 漢語大詞典 [Comprehensive Chinese Dictionary]. Shanghai: Hanyu da cidian chubanshe, 1989.

Harrell, Steven, ed. *Cultural Encounters on China's Ethnic Frontiers*. Seattle: University of Washington Press, 1995.

Hauf, Kandice. "The Community Covenant in Sixteenth Century Ji'an Prefecture, Jiangxi." *Late Imperial China* 17, no. 2 (1996): 1–50.

He Yun 何雲, Wu Yan 伍晏, and Shao Youdao 邵有道, eds. *Jiajing Tingzhou fu zhi* 嘉靖汀州府誌 [Tingzhou Prefectural Gazetteer of the Jiajing Reign]. Shanghai: Shanghai shudian, 1990.

Herman, John. *Amid the Clouds and Mist: China's Colonization of Guizhou, 1200–1700*. Cambridge, MA: Harvard University Asia Center, 2007.

Hou Wailu 侯外蘆. *Zhongguo sixiang tongshi* 中國思想通史 [Comprehensive Intellectual History of China]. 6 vols. Beijing: Renmin chubanshe, 1957–1963.

Huang Wan 黃綰. "Shi de ji 世德記 [Record of Conduct]." In *WYMQJ*, vol. 2, 39: 1406–30.

Huang Zhifan 黃志繁. *"Zei" "min" zhi jian: 12–18 shiji Gan nan diyu shehui* " 賊 " " 民 " 之間: 12–18 世紀贛南地域社會 [Between "bandits" and "commoners": Southern Gan Regional Society from the 12th to the 18th Centuries]. Beijing: San lian shudian, 2006.

Huang Zuo 黃佐 and Lin Fu 林富, eds. *Guangxi tong zhi* 廣西通志 [Comprehensive Gazetteer of Guangxi]. 1531 ed. In *Beijing tushuguan guji zhenben congkan* 北京圖書館古籍真本叢刊, vol. 41. Reprint, Beijing: Shumu wenxian chubanshe, 1988.

Hucker, Charles. *A Dictionary of Official Titles in Imperial China*. Stanford: Stanford University Press, 1985.

Israel, Larry. "The Prince and the Sage: Concerning Wang Yangming's 'Effortless' Suppression of the Ning Princely Establishment Rebellion." *Late Imperial China*, vol. 29, no. 2 (December, 2008): 68–128.

Ivanhoe, Philip J. *Ethics in the Confucian Tradition: The Thought of Mengzi and Wang Yangming*. Indianapolis: Hackett Publishing Company, 2002.

Ji Ben 季本. *Ji Pengshan xiansheng wenji* 季彭山先生文集 [Collected Works of Sir Ji Pengshan]. In *Beijing tushuguan guji zhenben congkan* 北京圖書館古籍珍本叢刊, vol. 106. Beijing: Shumu wenxian chubanshe, 1988.

Jiao Hong 焦竑, ed. *Guo chao xian zheng lu* 國朝獻征錄 [Record of the Evidence for the Worthies of Our Reigning Dynasty]. In *Mingdai zhuanji congkan* 明代傳記叢刊, edited by Zhou Junfu, vol. 109–14. Ming wen shuju, 1991.

Jin Runcheng 靳潤成. *Mingdai zongdu xunfu xiaqu yanjiu* 明代總督巡撫轄區 [Research on the Territorial Jurisdiction of Supreme Commanders and Grand Coordinators during the Ming Dynasty]. Tianjin: Tianjin guji chubanshe, 1996.

Johnston, Alastair Iain. *Cultural Realism: Strategic Culture and Grand Strategy in Chinese History*. Princeton: Princeton University Press, 1995.

Ko, Dorothy. *Teachers of the Inner Chamber: Women and Culture in Seventeenth-Century China*. Stanford: Stanford University Press, 1994.

Lao-Tzu [pseud.]. *Tao Te Ching*. Translated by D.C. Lau. New York: Penguin, 1963.

Leong, Sow-Theung. *Migration and Ethnicity in Chinese History: Hakkas, Pengmin, and Their Neighbors*. Edited by Tim Wright. Stanford: Stanford University Press, 1997.

Li Mo 李默. "Lun kejia de xingcheng ji minzu ronghe 論客家的形成及民族融合 [Analysis of the Formation of Hakka and Ethnic Blending]." *Zhongguo shi yanjiu* 4 (1993): 117–130.

Li Zhi 李贄. *Xu cang shu* 續藏書 [Books Concealed Continued]. In *Mingdai zhuanji congkan* 明代傳記叢刊, edited by Zhou Junfu, vol. 106. Ming wen shuju, 1991.

Liang Qichao 梁啓超. *Rujia zhexue* 儒家哲學 [Confucian Philosophy]. Shanghai: Zhonghua shuju, 1941.

Lin Jiping 林繼平. *Wang xue tan wei shi jiang* 王學談微十講 [Discussing Subtle Dimensions of Wang Learning: Ten Lectures]. Taipei: Lantai chubanshe, 2002.

Liu Cong 劉聰. *Yangming xue yu fo dao guanxi yanjiu* 陽明學與佛道關係研究 [Research on the Relationship between Yangming Studies and Buddhism and Daoism]. Chengdu: Bashu shushe, 2009.

Liu Jie 劉節, ed. *Jiajing Nan'an fu zhi* 嘉靖南安府誌 [Jiajing Period Nan'an Prefectural Gazetteer]. Shanghai: Shanghai shudian, 1990.

Luo Qingxiao 羅青霄, ed. *Zhangzhou fu zhi* 漳州府誌 [Gazetteer of Zhangzhou Prefecture]. 1572 ed. Zhangzhou: Guan kan ben. Microfilm.

Lu Miaofen 呂妙芬. *Yangmingxue shi ren shequn: lishi, sixiang, yu shijian* 陽明學士人社群: 歷史, 思想, 與實踐 [Yangming Learning Literati Societies: History, Thought, and Practice). Taipei: Zhongyang yanyuan lidaishi yanjiusuo, 2003.

MacCormack, Geoffrey. *Traditional Chinese Penal Law*. Edinburgh: Edinburgh University Press, 1990.

———. *The Spirit of Traditional Chinese Law*. Athens, GA: University of Georgia Press, 1996.

MacIntyre, Alasdair. *After Virtue: A Study in Moral Theory*. 3rd ed. Notre Dame: University of Notre Dame Press, 2007.

———. *Whose Justice? Which Rationality?* London: Duckworth, 1988.

Makeham, John. *Dao Companion to Neo-Confucian Philosophy*. London: Springer, 2010.

Mengzi. *Mengzi yi zhu* 孟子譯註 [Mengzi, Translated and Annotated]. Translated and annotated by Jin Liangnian 金良年. Shanghai: Shanghai guji chubanshe, 2005.

Metzger, Thomas. *A Cloud across the Pacific: Essays on the Clash between Chinese and Western Political Theories Today*. Hong Kong: The Chinese University Press, 2005.

Ming shi lu lei zuan: junshi shiliao juan 明實錄類纂軍事史料卷 [Categorical Compilation of the Ming Veritable Records: Volume of Historical Records for Military Affairs], edited by Wu Bosen 吳柏森. Wuhan: Wuhan chubanshe, 1993.

Mote, Frederick W. "The Ch'eng-hua and Hung-chih Reigns, 1465–1505." In *The Cambridge History of China*, vol. 7, edited by Frederick W. Mote and Dennis Twitchett. Cambridge: Cambridge University Press, 1988.

———. "Confucian Eremitism in the Yuan Period." In *The Confucian Persuasion*, edited by Arthur F. Wright. Stanford: Stanford University Press, 1960.

———. *Imperial China: 900–1800*. Cambridge, MA: Harvard University Press, 1999.

Nagel, Thomas. *The View from Nowhere*. New York: Oxford University Press, 1986.

Nivison, David. "The Philosophy of Wang Yangming." In *The Ways of Confucianism: Investigations in Chinese Philosophy*, edited by Brian W. Van Norden. Chicago: Open Court, 1996.

Okada Takehiko 岡田武彦. *Ō Yōmei kikō* 王陽明紀行 [Journal of Wang Yangming's Travels]. Tokyo: Meitoku, 2007.

———. *Ō Yōmei taiden* 王陽明大伝 [Comprehensive Biography of Wang Yangming]. 5 vols. Tokyo: Meitoku, 2002–2005.

———. *Yomeigaku no sekai* 陽明學の世界 [The World of Wang Yangming]. Tokyo: Meitoku, 1986.

Qian Dehong 錢德洪. "Zheng Chenhao fan jian yi shi 征宸濠反間遺事 [Stories Concerning the Use of Stratagem While Waging War on Chenhao]." In *WYMQJ*, 39:1472.

Qian Ming 錢明. *Yangming xue de xingcheng yu fazhan* 陽明學的形成與發展 [The Formation and Development of Yangming Learning]. Nanjing: Jiangsu gu ji chubanshe, 2002.

Qin Jin 秦金. *An chu lu* 安楚錄 [Record of the Pacification of Chu]. In *Zhongguo yeshi jicheng xubian* 中國野史集成續編, vol. 16. Chengdu: Bashu shushe, 2000.

Robinson, David. *Bandits, Eunuchs, and the Son of Heaven: Rebellion and the Economy of Violence in Mid-Ming China*. Honolulu: University of Hawaii Press, 2001.

———. "Princes of the Polity: The Anhua Prince's Uprising of 1510." *Ming Studies* 65 (May 2012): 1–12.

Roetz, Heiner. *Confucian Ethics in the Axial Age: A Reconstruction under the Aspect of the Breakthrough toward Postconventional Thinking*. Albany, NY: State University of New York Press, 1993.

Rowe, William. *Saving the World: Chen Hongmou and Elite Consciousness in Eighteenth-Century China*. Stanford: Stanford University Press, 2001.

Ryor, Kathleen. "*Wen* and *wu* in Elite Cultural Practices during the Late Ming." In *Military Culture in Imperial China*, edited by Nicola Di Cosmo, 219–42. Cambridge, MA: Harvard University Press, 2009.

Sawyer, Ralph D. *The Seven Military Classics of Ancient China*. Translated by Ralph D. Sawyer and Mei-Chun Sawyer. Boulder, CO: Westview Press, 1993.

Shin, Leo. "The Last Campaigns of Wang Yangming." *T'oung Pao* 92:1–3 (2006): 101–28.

———. *The Making of the Chinese State: Ethnicity and Expansion on the Ming Borderlands*. Cambridge: Cambridge University Press, 2006.

———. "Tribalizing the Frontier: Barbarians, Settlers, and the State in Ming South China." Ph.D. diss., Princeton University, 1999.

Slingerland, Edward. *Effortless Action: Wu-wei as Conceptual Metaphor and Spiritual Ideal in Early China*. Oxford: Oxford University Press, 2003.

Snyder, Jack. *The Soviet Strategic Culture: Implications for Limited Nuclear Options*. Washington D.C.: Rand, 1977.

Strauss, Leo. *Natural Right and History*. Chicago: University of Chicago Press, 1965.

Sun Degao 孫德高. *Wang Yangming shigong yu xin xue yanjiu* 王陽明事功与心學研究 [Research on Wang Yangming's Worldly Achievements and Learning of the Mind-Heart]. Chengdu: Xinan jiaotong daxue chubanshe, 2008.

Swaine, Michael D. and Ashley J. Tellis. *Interpreting China's Grand Strategy: Past, Present, and Future*. Santa Monica: Rand, 2000.

Swartz, David. *Culture and Power: the Sociology of Pierre Bourdieu*. Chicago: Chicago University Press, 1997.

Tan Qi 談琪. "Cen Meng fanpan chaoting zhiyi 岑猛反叛朝廷質疑 [Questions Concerning Cen Meng's Rebellion against the Ming Dynasty]." In *Zhuangzu lungao* 壯族論搞, edited by Fang Honggui and Gu Youshi, 275–83. Nanning: Guangxi renmin chubanshe, 1989.

Tan Qian 談遷. *Guo Que* 國榷 [Deliberations on the Reigning Dynasty]. Beijing: Zhonghua guji chubanshe, 1958.

Tang Kwok-leong 鄧國亮. "Tianzhou shi fei wo ben xin—Wang Shouren de Guangxi zhi yi 田州事非我本新- 王守仁的廣西之役 [The Affair in Tianzhou Was Not What I Originally Intended—Wang Shouren's campaigns in Guangxi]." *Qinghua xuebao*, vol. 40, no. 2 (2009): 265–93.

Taylor, Charles. "Interpretation and the Sciences of Man." *Review of Metaphysics* 25, no. 1 (September 1971).

———. *Modern Social Imaginaries*. Durham: Duke University Press, 2004.

Taylor, Rodney. *The Religious Dimensions of Confucianism*. New York: State University of New York Press, 1990.

Tian Rucheng 田汝成. *Yan jiao ji wen* 炎徼紀聞 [Record of Things Heard on the Scorching Hot Frontier]. 1558. In *Si ku quan shu* 四庫全書, vol. 352. Shanghai: Shanghai guji chubanshe, 1987.

Tien, David W. "Metaphysics and the Basis of Morality in the Philosophy of Wang Yangming." In *Dao Companion to Neo-Confucian Philosophy*, edited by John Makeham, 295–314. London: Springer, 2010.

———. "Oneness and Self-Centeredness in the Moral Psychology of Wang Yangming." *Journal of Religious Ethics* vol. 40, no. 1 (2012): 52–71.

Tomlinson, John. *Cultural Imperialism: A Critical Introduction*. Baltimore: The John Hopkins University Press, 1991.

Tong, James W. *Disorder under Heaven: Collective Violence in the Ming Dynasty*. Stanford: Stanford University Press, 1991.

Tsai, Henry Shi-Shan. *The Eunuchs in the Ming Dynasty*. New York: State University of New York Press, 1996.

Tu, Weiming. *Neo-Confucian Thought in Action: Wang Yang-ming's Youth (1472–1509)*. Berkeley: University of California Press, 1976.

Van de Ven, Hans, ed. *Warfare in Chinese History*. Leiden: Brill, 2000.

Waldron, Arthur. *The Great Wall of China: From History to Myth*. Cambridge: Cambridge University Press, 1990.

Wang Chunyu 王春瑜. "'Qi wu' lun: tan Mingdai zongfan 齊物論:談明代宗藩 [Discourse on 'Leveling All Things': On Ming Dynasty Princely Establishments]." In *Ming Qing shi sanlun* 明清史散論 [Varied Articles Discussing Ming and Qing History]. Shanghai: Dongfang chuban zhongxin, 1996.

Wang Gung-wu. "Feng Tao: An Essay on Confucian Loyalty." In *Confucian Personalities*, edited by Arthur F. Wright and Denis Twitchett, 187–210. Stanford: Stanford University Press, 1962.

Wang Ji 王畿. "Du xian shi zai bao Hai Riweng Ji'an qi bing shu xu 讀先師再報海日翁吉安起兵書序 [Preface Composed upon Reading My Former Master's Second Letter Reporting Mobilizing Armies in Ji'an to Hairi Weng]." In *WYMQJ*, vol. 2, 41:1599.

Wang, Richard G. *The Ming Prince and Daoism: Institutional Patronage of an Elite*. Oxford: Oxford University Press, 2012.

Wang Sen 汪森. *Yue xi wen zai* 粵西文載 [Anthology of Literature in Guangxi]. *Siku quanshu* 四庫全書, vols. 1465–67. Shanghai: Shanghai guji chubanshe, 1987.

Wang Shizhen 王世貞. "Xinjian bo Wang Wencheng gong Shouren zhuan 新建伯王文成公守仁傳 [Biography of the Earl of Xinjian Sir Wang Wencheng Shouren]." In *Guo chao xian zheng lu* 國朝獻征錄, edited by Jiao Hong. In *Mingdai zhuanji cong-kan* 明代傳記叢刊, edited by Zhou Junfu, vol. 109. Taipei: Ming wen shuju, 1991.

Wang Yangming. *Instructions for Practical Living and Other Neo-Confucian Writings by Wang Yangming*. Translated and edited by Wing-tsit Chan. New York: Columbia University Press, 1963.

Wang Yangming 王陽明. *Wu jing qi shu ping* 武經七書評 [Commentary on the Seven Military Classics)]. Taipei: Taiwan chubanshe, 1978.

Wang Yuangang. "Power Politics in Confucian China." PhD diss., University of Chicago, 2001.

Weber, Max. *The Religion of China*. Translated by Hans H. Gerth. New York: Free Press, 1951.

Wei Jun 魏濬. *Xi shi er* 西事珥 [Miscellanea of Guangxi]. In *Si ku quan shu cun mu congshu* 四庫全書存目叢書, *shi bu* 史部, vol. 247. Jinan: Jilu shushe chubanshe, 1996.

Whelan, Frederick G. "Justice: Classical and Christian." *Political Theory*, vol. 10, no. 3 (August 1982): 435–60.

Whitmore, John K. "Chiao-chih and Ming Confucianism: the Ming Attempt to Transform Vietnam." *Ming Studies* 4 (1977): 51–92.

Wiens, Herold J. *Han Chinese Expansion in South China*. Hamden, CT: Shoe String Press Inc., 1967.

Wrightson, Keith. *English Society, 1580–1680*. New Brunswick, NJ: Rutgers University Press, 1982.

Wu Zhen 吳震. *Wang Yangming zhushu xuanping* 王陽明著書選評 [Selected Writings from the Works of Wang Yangming with Criticism]. Shanghai: Shanghai guji chubanshe, 2004.

Xie Fen 謝賁. "Ning fu zhao you 寧府招由 [Deposition of the Ning Princely Establishment]." In Deng Shilong 鄧士龍, *Guo chao dian gu* 國朝典故, edited by Xu Daling 許大齡 and Wang Tianyou 王天有. Beijing: Beijing daxue chubanshe, 1993.

Xie Xianghao 謝祥皓. *Zhongguo bingxue: Song Ming Qing juan* 中國兵學: 宋明清卷 [Chinese Military Studies: Song, Ming, and Qing Volume]. Jinan: Shandong renmin chubanshe, 1998.

Xu Fuguan 徐復觀. "Wang Yangming sixiang bu lun 王陽明思想補論 [Supplemental Discussion of Wang Yangming's Thought]." In *Zhongguo sixiangshi lunji xubian* 中國思想史論集續編. Taipei: Wenqun yinshua youxian gongsi, 1982.

Xu Wei 徐渭. *Xu Wei ji* 徐渭集 [Collected Works of Xu Wei]. 4 vols. Beijing: Zhonghua shuju, 1983.

Xu Xiaowang 徐曉望, ed. *Fujian tong shi* 福建通史 [Comprehensive History of Fujian]. 5 vols. Fuzhou: Fujian renmin chubanshe, 2006.

Yang, Xiaomei. "How to Make Sense of the Claim 'True Knowledge is What Constitutes Action': A New Interpretation of Wang Yangming's Doctrine of Unity of Knowledge and Action." *Dao* 8(2) (2009): 173–88.

Yang Yang 楊陽. *Wang quan de tutenghua: zheng jiao heyi yu Zhongguo shehui* 王權的圖騰化: 政教合一與中國社會 [The Totemization of Royal Authority: Chinese Society and the Unification of Politics and Education]. Hangzhou: Zhejiang renmin chubanshe, 2000.

Yao Mo 姚鏌. *Dongquan wenji* 東泉文集 [Collected Works of Yao Dongquan]. In *Si ku quan shu cun mu congshu* 四庫全書存目叢書, vol. 46. Jinan: Qi lu she chubanshe, 1997.

Yu Huaiyan 余懷彥. *Wang Yangming yu Guizhou wenhua* 王陽明與貴州文化 [Wang Yangming and the Culture of Guizhou]. Guiyang: Guizhou jiaoyu chubanshe, 1996.

Yu Yingshi 余英時. *Song Ming lixue yu zhengzhi wenhua* 宋明理學與政治文化 [The Learning of Principle and Political Culture during the Song and Ming Dynasties]. Taipei: Yunnong wenhua, 2004.

Zhan Ruoshui 湛若水. "Yangming xiansheng muzhiming 陽明先生墓誌銘 [Epitaph for Sir Yangming]." In *WYMQJ*, vol. 2, *juan* 38.

Zhang Dainian. *Key Concepts in Chinese Philosophy*. New Haven, CT: Yale University Press, 2002.

Zhang Fentian 張分田. *Zhongguo di wang guannian: shehui pubian yishi zhong de "zui jun-zun jun" wenhua fa shi* 中國帝王觀念: 社會普遍意識中的罪君尊軍文化法式 [The Concept of Emperor in China: the Cultural Norm of Praising and Blaming the Emperor as an Ideology Widely-Held throughout Society]. Beijing: Zhongguo renmin daxue chubanshe, 2004.

Zhang Zhelang 張哲郎. *Mingdai xunfu yanjiu* 明代巡撫研究 [Research on Ming Dynasty Grand Coordinators]. Taipei: Wen shi zhe chubanshe, 1995.

Zheng Xiao 鄭曉. *Jin yan* 今言 [Speaking of Our Times]. Beijing: Zhonghua shuju, 1997.

Zhongguo lidai renming da cidian 中國曆代人名大詞典 [Great Biographical Dictionary of China]. Shanghai: Shanghai guji chubanshe, 465.

Zhou Weiqiang 周維強. "Folangji chong yu Chenhao zhi pan 佛朗機銃與宸濠之叛 [The Folangji Gun and Chenhao's Rebellion]." *Dong Wu lishi xuebao* 8 (2002): 93–127.

Zhu Siwei 朱思維. *Wang Yangming xunfu Nan Gan he Jiangxi shi ji* 王陽明巡撫南贛和江西事輯 [Compilation of Events Transpiring during Wang Yangming's Period of Service as Grand Coordinator of Southern Gan and Jiangxi]. Nanchang: Jiangxi renmin chubanshe, 2010.

Zou Shouyi 鄒守益. *Wang Yangming xiansheng tu pu* 王陽明先生圖譜 [Illustrated Biography of Master Wang Yangming]. Beijing: Beijing chubanshe, 2000.

Zuo Dongling 左東嶺. *Wang xue yu zhong wan Ming shi ren xintai* 王學與中晚明士人心態 [The Relationship between Wang Learning and the State of Mind of Mid- and Late-Ming Scholars]. Beijing: Renmin wenxue chubanshe, 2000.

Index

RECEIVED

FEB 1 7 2015

GUELPH HUMBER LIBRARY
205 Humber College Blvd
Toronto, ON   M9W 5L7